Tarek Cherkaoui is a strategic communication expert. He holds a PhD in Media and Communications from the Auckland University of Technology.

'Tarek Cherkaoui here provides an excellent analysis of media coverage of the Iraq War focusing primarily on the coverage of CNNI and Al Jazeera. His book is strongly and clearly written, grounded in scholarly research, and provides a close reading of the ways in which the two networks present the 2003 Iraq War.'

**Douglas Kellner, George F. Kneller Chair
in the Philosophy of Education, UCLA**

'Tarek Cherkaoui's book is an original scholarly work that backs its arguments with sound research methods and good empirical evidence. This book is a very welcome contribution to Arab media studies and a must-read for scholars and students working on propaganda, war coverage and the sociology/politics of news.'

**Tarik Sabry, Reader in Media and Communication Theory,
University of Westminster**

TAREK CHERKAOUI

THE NEWS MEDIA AT WAR

THE CLASH OF WESTERN AND ARAB NETWORKS IN THE MIDDLE EAST

BLOOMSBURY ACADEMIC
LONDON • NEW YORK • OXFORD • NEW DELHI • SYDNEY

BLOOMSBURY ACADEMIC
Bloomsbury Publishing Plc
50 Bedford Square, London, WC1B 3DP, UK
1385 Broadway, New York, NY 10018, USA
29 Earlsfort Terrace, Dublin 2, Ireland

BLOOMSBURY, BLOOMSBURY ACADEMIC and the Diana logo
are trademarks of Bloomsbury Publishing Plc

First published by I. B. Tauris
This paperback edition published in 2021

Copyright © Tarek Cherkaoui

Tarek Cherkaoui has asserted their right under the Copyright,
Designs and Patents Act, 1988, to be identified as Author of this work.

All rights reserved. No part of this publication may be reproduced or
transmitted in any form or by any means, electronic or mechanical,
including photocopying, recording, or any information storage or retrieval
system, without prior permission in writing from the publishers.

Bloomsbury Publishing Plc does not have any control over, or responsibility for,
any third-party websites referred to or in this book. All internet addresses given
in this book were correct at the time of going to press. The author and publisher
regret any inconvenience caused if addresses have changed or sites have
ceased to exist, but can accept no responsibility for any such changes.

A catalogue record for this book is available from the British Library.

A catalog record for this book is available from the Library of Congress.

ISBN: HB: 978 1 78076 104 6
PB: 978 1 3502 4304 0
ePDF: 978 1 78673 143 2
eBook: 978 1 78672 143 3

Library of Modern Middle East Studies 125

To find out more about our authors and books visit
www.bloomsbury.com and sign up for our newsletters.

Contents

List of Illustrations vii

	Introduction	1
1	War, Propaganda, and the Mobilisation of Frames	13
2	Orientalism, Terrorism, and American Media Discourse	34
3	CNNI Framings of Middle East Conflict, 1991–2001	74
4	The Origins of Modern Arab Nationalism	93
5	The Prospect of War in Iraq: Frames, Propaganda, and Debate	120
6	Hostilities Begin: 'Decapitation Strike', 'Shock and Awe', and Contesting Realities	140
7	Journalists as Combatants: US Bombing of Al Jazeera's Office and the Palestine Hotel	182
8	Liberation vs. Occupation: The Toppling of Saddam's Statue	209
	Conclusion	230
	Postscript	238

Notes 245
Bibliography 265
Index 302

List of Illustrations

Figures

1.1	Information warfare and environment shaping (Dearth 2002: 8).	24
6.1	Real-time footage of CNN and Al Jazeera during 'Shock and Awe' (21 March 2003).	140
6.2	CNN headline during 'Shock and Awe' (21 March 2003).	177
7.1	Footage of CNN and Al Jazeera after the 8 April 2003 bombings in Baghdad (8 April 2003).	182
7.2	Al Jazeera broadcasting footage via Abu Dhabi TV showing its crew members carrying the late correspondent Tareq Ayyoob (8 April 2003).	197
7.3	Al Jazeera airing Tareq Ayyoob's last report to commemorate his memory (8 April 2003).	198
7.4	Al Jazeera's footage showing a wide shot of the tank which targeted the hotel (8 April 2003).	199
8.1	Footage of CNN and Al Jazeera showing the toppling of Saddam's statue (9 April 2003).	209
8.2	Al Jazeera footage showing the American flag on the top of the Saddam statue (9 April 2003 10:41 ET).	214

Table

6.1	Table comparing the terminologies used by CNN and Al Jazeera during 'Shock and Awe'.	180

Introduction

The eye sees only what the mind is prepared to comprehend.

Robertson Davies

In the opening months of 2011, a series of uprisings shook the Arab world and took observers by surprise. This wave of demonstrations, protests, and riots began on 18 December 2010 in Tunisia with the self-immolation of Mohamed Bouazizi,[1] and immediately spread throughout the Arab countries, resulting in civil uprisings in Egypt and Bahrain, large street demonstrations in Algeria, Iraq, Jordan, Kuwait, Morocco, Yemen, and Oman, and minor protests even in Saudi Arabia. These dynamics soon led to major insurgencies in Libya, Syria, and Yemen.

The 'Arab Spring', as it was subsequently coined, turned into a defining moment in the history of the region. For not only were these uprisings momentous, contagious and successive, but they were also deeply infused and instigated by media and communication to the extent that several researchers and pundits labelled these episodes 'Facebook uprisings' and 'Twitter revolutions'.[2] These were, however, no sudden occurrences that happened overnight. In fact, complex dynamics with deep-seated and multi-layered political, economic, social, and historic roots all came into play as a trigger to these events.

Among the key developments that have undeniably played a big role in this context is the evolution of Arabic news satellite broadcasting, most notably the Qatar-based news outlet Al Jazeera. Since its inception, the latter has contributed to energising the Arab public sphere, and constituted a nail in the coffin of the oppressive regimes in the Middle East and North Africa region (MENA) since the mid-1990s. In that era, it was virtually impossible for opposition figures to make their views known to a wide audience, but satellite news outlets allowed them to bypass the barren and restrictive state media, connect with their communities, challenge the official discourse, and expose the regimes' abuses and lack of legitimacy. The challenge to Arab dictators, such as Hosni Mubarak in Egypt and Zine al-Abedine Ben Ali in Tunisia, to name a few, started in fact from that period, and slowly but surely shook the foundations of these regimes and eroded their legitimacy.

In effect, the Arab Spring – at least initially – channelled energies for change within MENA, and was by large perceived as a historic moment, comparable in its magnitude to the events that took place in Eastern Europe at the end of the Cold War during the early 1990s. Several media outlets, both pan-Arab and international, generally helped convey the human dimension of these events, airing the emotions and expectations of Arab Spring participants to millions of their fellow Arab and international viewers in their living rooms. Such coverage overturned – initially at least – a host of stereotypes about the Arab region, particularly in the West, by revealing the commitment of Arab masses to a peaceful transition to power, civic rights, democratic accountability, checks on the power of leaders, and the establishment of a just and fair governance system.

However, as time passed and the internal crises worsened, Arab regimes built internal and external coalitions, who then fought back violently. These regimes managed to deteriorate the situation by using a mix of *coups d'état*, counter-revolutionary movements, false-flag terrorist groups, and extended repressive means, while also – in some cases, as in the Gulf Cooperation Council (GCC) region – providing economic handouts, patronage, and introducing limited political and economic reforms.[3] Such methods managed to turn peaceful demonstrations into militarised forms of struggle,[4] in effect triggering several civil wars in the region, such as in Libya, Syria, and Yemen. Hence, the image of the Middle East, which was

Introduction

constructed in the Western psyche for centuries as a beacon of violence, intolerance, and backwardness, gained further traction and reinforced the fundamental gap in worldview, perception, and communication between the West and the Arab world; a trend which has been undeniably exacerbated since the suicide attacks of September 11 2001 (9/11).

The re-alignment of the United States and several of its European key allies in their approach towards the MENA region was not initiated at this juncture. In reality, the transformation of their strategic posture was detected as early as the Gulf War in 1991. On the other hand, the 9/11 suicide attacks constituted the perfect justification for several power centres within the United States, and chiefly those influenced by neo-conservatives forces, to accelerate that process, while also reshaping the American state identity, and reinforcing a Western common identity. For this purpose, vitriolic rhetoric, emanating now and again from the top of the US administration (as during the George W. Bush presidency) and from key figures of US politics (e.g. Donald Trump), frequently uses Islam and Arabs as the quintessential 'other', or the touchstone against which the state identity is measured.

It is also apparent that officialdoms, prominent political parties, and high profile public personalities that are affiliated with the right and the far-right political spectrum, both in the United States and Europe, have frequently orchestrated mass-mediated demonisation campaigns, targeting not only those involved in reprehensible acts of indiscriminate violence, but Islam and Arabs as a whole. In this context, past imagined narratives were connected to present populations in the Middle East, and ancient myths were refashioned to identify Islam and Arabs as the major – if not the only – threat to the Western world. By focusing on the Arab/Muslim 'other', this renewed form of Orientalism has not only legitimised an ultra-expansionist US/NATO policy in the Middle East, but has also provided the framework for media coverage that has reinforced this dichotomy and inflamed the US opinion, and by extension the European opinion as well.

It is a matter of fact that myths and narratives combine over time to forge the psyche of social entities. Myths, in particular, are very relevant to media studies and the concept of framing, as myths are a particular kind of image-making, which affect perception and imagination. The combination of both myths and ideologies let individuals mistakenly believe that they are in control of their values and beliefs, whereas the reality is that individuals are subjects formed through social processes, which instil in them sets of values, beliefs and norms (Stevenson, 2002: 150). The media subsequently play to circulate the dominant values and beliefs, thus helping the elites to forge consensus around their political platforms and worldviews, at the same time as the media disregard or downplay other competing discourses. Media is thus a major player when it comes to shaping 'collective representations of society' using the words of Durkheim. They shape what can be termed as *Deep Frames*, which 'represent internalised power structure or deep-rooted belief systems or shared culture in a society' (Hyun, 2004). These frames involve and mix a multitude of ideological, political and cultural contexts, and their fusion produces a representation of images, from which individuals picture the world in their heads, and construct their conception of 'us' and 'them' (Kellner, 1995).

Since the 1960s, framing research has provided guidance to literature concerning media content, and to studies exploring the relationship between media and public opinion. As a result, psychologists, sociologists, political scientists, and communication and media scholars all deploy the framing concept, for the framing of a social situation forms expectations, establishes norms and influences behaviour. Subsequently, individuals constantly classify and interpret their life experiences to understand the world around them. In this context, cultural values, religious indoctrination, personal experiences, education, etc. are all factors that shape the human framing of social reality, and thus people use a set of stereotypes, social roles, and worldviews to organise current knowledge and provide a framework for future understanding.

In *The News Media at War*, the approach to framing is primarily concerned to explain how a given news story is presented, and the related process of inclusion, exclusion and emphasis, which is designed to make some portions of reality more salient than others. It is now established that media framing obscures some kinds of information about a particular issue and makes other information about that issue more significant and memorable to audiences.

Among the deep frames of particular relevance to this book is the Orientalist frame. While the origins and development of Orientalism will be detailed in Chapter 2, it is suffice here to note that Palestinian American

Introduction

scholar Edward Said analysed the Orientalist discourse in his seminal work *Orientalism* (1979), in which he demonstrated how Orientalism produced a false description of Arabs and Islamic culture. This book was essential in re-examining the foundations of the Orientalist discourse. Edward Said provoked a noticeable shift in academic perceptions vis-à-vis Orientalism.

Said affirmed that Orientalism was a discourse in the service of power that used the rhetoric of 'otherness' to justify political, economic and military imperialism. Western constructions of the Orient produced an underlying discourse, which positioned Eastern cultures and religions as inferior to the West. Such a discourse effectively paves the ground to a discourse of the West versus 'the rest' on the international level, thus justifying Western political, economic and military hegemony vis-à-vis the non-Western World.

Edward Said's works also demonstrated how the Orientalist worldview was carried on throughout centuries in a stunning continuity, depicting Islam, Arabs and Orientals in general as backward, despotic and irrational. In his subsequent work, *Culture and Imperialism* (1993), Said was also able to reveal how the centre of gravity of Orientalism moved from Europe to America (Said 1993: 7) in a geographic shift, which was accompanied by an extension of Orientalism beyond academia, namely to popular culture and mass media.

Such development has had deep repercussion on representations of Islam and Arabs, and consequently these Orientalist clichés regularly find their way to a worldwide audience through the various types of media, such as film, news, cartoons and television. In actual fact, research has revealed that Arabs/Muslims are essentially covered in media and cinema, either as oil suppliers, or as potential terrorists; very little about the human density is ever discussed or broadcasted (Hafez 2000; Suleiman 1988; Kamalipour 1995; Wolfsfeld 1997). In this context, Jack Shaheen (2003) analysed more than 900 films produced by Hollywood. He concludes that 95 per cent of the movies project negative imagery of the Middle East, portraying its people as heartless, brutal, and uncivilised.

In the post-9/11 context, for instance, the Orientalist frame was immediately used to interpret the September 11 attacks as an expression of the clash between Western and Islamic civilisation; a self-fulfilling prophecy reminiscent of Samuel Huntington's *Clash of Civilizations* (1996), according to which no peace will happen in this world until one civilisation defeats and dominates the other politically, economically, militarily, and culturally. Like other mythologies, the Orientalist worldview is very reductionist and simplistic. For instance, Orientalist experts, suddenly metamorphosed into counter-terrorist experts, offered very naïve explanations towards the motives of the 9/11 hijackers: to wit, they perpetrated these attacks in order to get dozens of virgins in paradise. These analyses conveniently chose to disregard the entrenched economic, social and political problems ravaging the Middle East, and which constitute the root cause of terrorism.

An additional example illustrating the working of this deep frame is that acts of violence perpetrated by Arab or Muslim culprits will be interpreted from the Orientalist prism, regardless of any social, political or economic analysis, as Islam versus Christendom. In fact, the Orientalist frame was so powerful that no matter how frequently Muslims affirm that violent indiscriminate acts are not Islamic at all because they have no relation whatsoever with the essential metaphysical, religious or spiritual dimension of the Islamic faith, these acts are still considered in the media as 'Islamic terrorism'. On the other hand, double standards are striking: Timothy James McVeigh and his associates perpetrated the Oklahoma City bombings in 1995 but were never referred to as 'Christian terrorists' despite his belonging to extremist Christian militias. Ultra-conservative Baruch Kappel Goldstein perpetrated the 1994 Cave of the Patriarchs massacre in the city of Hebron, murdering 29 Muslims at prayer in the Ibrahimi Mosque and wounding another 150 in a shooting attack. However, he was never called 'Jewish terrorist' in the Western media.

Other politically motivated armed attacks took place recently all over the Western hemisphere. Yet, when the perpetrators were Caucasian, they were rarely – if ever – framed as terrorists. The mainstream media considered them as mere people with psychological issues without dwelling further on their political agendas. For example, during the political campaign pertaining to the United Kingdom European Union membership referendum (23 June 2016), British Labour MP Jo Cox was brutally murdered (16 June 2016). The culprit, Thomas Mair, a 52-year-old white male was motivated by political ideology, had years of affiliation with neo-Nazi groups, carried out the attack while yelling 'Britain First', the name of a right-wing anti-immigrant party. Journalist Glen Greenwald comments that 'despite all of this, it's virtually impossible to find any media outlet calling the attacker a "terrorist" or even suggesting that it might be "terrorism." To the contrary, the suspected killer – overnight – has been alternatively described as a gentle soul or a mentally ill "loner"' (Greenwald 2016).

Greenwald also contrasts such labelling with another comparable incident that took place in Britain in 2010, when a British MP, Stephen Timms, was viciously stabbed and almost killed by a woman angry over his vote in support of the Iraq War. In that instance, British media outlets almost uniformly called the attack 'terrorism'. For him, 'the difference is obvious: Timms' attacker was a Muslim of Bangladeshi descent, while Cox's alleged killer … is not' (Greenwald 2016). Such examples and many more underline the inherent double standards of the Orientalist frame.

The *Terrorist Frame* is yet another deep frame that heavily influenced mass media post-9/11 and which will be discussed at length in this book (Chapter 2). Terrorism is such a complex topic that even international jurists could not succeed to limit its contours, or to reach a comprehensive definition to this phenomenon. However, some US and European media tend to handle this issue in very simplistic terms. As is usually the case with myths, no meaningful analysis, context or historical background is generally offered to viewers. Through this ploy, and by representing terrorism as illegitimate political violence contrasting with the legitimate force exercised by the US/Western state(s), ruling elites are able to use the media discourse on this matter to reaffirm the legitimacy of the state both internally and externally.

The terrorist frame has all the ingredients of a powerfully deep frame. It defines the problem, offers a diagnosis of its causes, judges the culprits, and suggests the solution. This frame defined the attacks of 9/11 as an act of war, avoiding its categorisation as a criminal act, although similar attacks were framed in the past as 'criminal investigations' (examples include the bombings of the World Trade Center in 1993, Pan Am 103 in 1988, the US embassies in Kenya and Tanzania in 1998, and the Alfred P. Murrah building in 1995). This was an important development: by shunning the legal framework, and choosing the path of war against group(s) with no positive legal status, the US administration chose to operate outside the international law framework.

The terrorist frame diagnosed the 9/11 attacks and subsequent armed incidents as stemming from the hatred of the benevolent and democratic USA for its freedoms and affluent way of life. This simplistic diagnosis followed the logic of mythologies, which selects and highlights certain aspects, while intentionally dismissing or minimising meaningful details. In this respect, the 'terrorist' frame omitted any reference to Washington's long list of covert and overt actions in the Middle East as a major cause for the prevalent anti-Americanism there. Only rare references were made in the media to the fact that the CIA might have actively contributed in producing the groups implicated in the terrorist attacks, when it routinely supported, funded, trained, and armed militant groups (including but not limited to the Afghan Mujahedeen) around the world to implement armed operations. These were of course never officially acknowledged or fully disclosed by US officials.

Furthermore, the terrorist frame includes a moral judgement. It asserts that the terrorist is evil. By linking terrorism with evilness, and by using expressions such as honour, trust, and faith, this frame creates another myth, aligning God with the nation-state, and therefore touching a sensible nerve with conservative Americans and likeminded parties in Europe and elsewhere. This deep frame dehumanises the 'evildoers', the racial/religious 'others', whose grievances, the root causes for political violence, became redundant. In this myth, the terrorists are just monsters controlled by a malevolent force. Last but not least, the terrorist frame also suggests the remedy, namely that the United States needs to immediately increase its military and covert forces, and engage in a long-term crusade against terrorism.

Dovetailing with the previously mentioned suggested cure to terrorism, the US military institution has understood since the Vietnam War that the use of the media is a quintessential factor to win wars. While this is analysed in-depth in Chapter 1, it should be mentioned that the weaponisation of media in the post-9/11 world has reached a point where military and media networks have converged to become virtually indistinguishable (Thussu and Freedman 2003). Since the creation of the 24-hour news cycle, the US military have become extremely media savvy, and have transformed the media into a battlefield on its own. Thus, more than ever before, the Pentagon is giving the utmost consideration to media strategies, planning them as carefully as the military campaigns.

Such perspective is best conveyed by Colonel (ret.) Alan Campen, who states that 'television reporters have become a critical instrument in a totally new kind of warfare. Satellite technology [...] can transform reporters from dispassionate observers to unwitting, even unwilling, but nonetheless direct participants' (Crumm 1996: 2). The institution of 'embedded journalism' practices during the 2003 war in Iraq is a renewed manifestation of the relationship between military commanders and media practitioners seeking to cover military conflicts. Consequently, during the Iraq War, two wars were waged in parallel: the actual war in Iraq, and the battle to persuade the Western public opinion of the necessity of the war, employing highly persuasive techniques directly inspired from commercial/entertainment television.

A second framing level, which is discussed in this book, can be described as *Meso-Frames*. This kind of framing is used by media extensively and is meant to capture audience interest. Meso-frames put greater emphasis on conflict between individuals, groups, or institutions, and works in binaries making use of myth and metaphor. Examples of meso-frames include the conflict frame, human-interest frame, economic consequence frame, and the morality frame. The conflict frame is predominant during times of war and conflict, and can take numerous shapes, such as the military frame, which focuses on military prowess in times of war, praises the power of military technology and the courage of the troops. The human-interest frame, on the other hand, brings a human face or an emotional angle to the presentation of an event, and may focus upon the plight of victims, especially those deemed newsworthy.

Last but not least, a third framing level, also scrutinised in this book, are known as *Story Frames*. The latter are centred on sets of storytelling techniques that organise the story into a set of shorter stories, and select key themes or ideas that are the message's focus. While these storytelling methods are traditionally determined by news values, such as impact, timeliness, prominence, proximity, conflict etc., their principal aim is to attract the attention of the audience by giving meaning to events, and to translate particular occurrences into public events, so that they become socially and situationally established. This process also includes a temporal element, which is built into the sequential ordering of events, as well as the mentioning of characters.

The essence of *The News Media at War*

This book examines the complexities of the news coverage of the 2003 Iraq War[5] against a backdrop of clashing Orientalist and pan-Arab paradigms. The importance of this war cannot be understated given that highly influential right-wing strategists and think tanks positioned this war within an agenda of complete US dominance and total subjugation of the Middle East's economy to US interests and control. This perspective considers that 'global dominance is impossible without Middle East dominance' (Everest 2004: 235). American author Daniel Pipes, whose writings are closely examined in ensuing chapters, clearly echoed the aforementioned stance, when he openly spelled out the reason behind the 2003 invasion of Iraq:

> The Weapons of Mass Destruction (WMD) were never the basic reason for war. Nor was it the horrid repression in Iraq. Or the danger Saddam posed to his neighbors. [...] The campaign in Iraq is about keeping promises to the United Sates or paying the consequences. [...] Keep your promises or you are gone. It is a powerful precedent that US leaders should make the most of (Pipes 2003).

The so-called 'promises' in this context are about the acceptance of the permanent status of client-state without any questions asked. It is in under this light that leftist intellectuals, such as Tariq Ali, argued that the War on Iraq was not motivated by oil only, 'but was essentially a war to assert imperial hegemony' (Ali 2003: 143).

The fact that corporate media played an integral part in advocating the war agenda warrants a serious study. While many could assume that one of the basic functions of the press in a liberal democratic society is 'the right and duty of the press to serve as an extralegal check on government' (Siebert 1956: 56), and therefore to act as a watchdog and expose any arbitrary or authoritarian practice, it is now widely acknowledged that the US administration used faulty and false information to justify the 2003 war on Iraq. Yet again, the mainstream media did not effectively investigate the case for war, and could be considered as accomplice with the project, even if such substandard performance – to say the least – was acknowledged by a few outlets after the war was over. A notable example was *The New York Times'* editorial on 25 May 2004, which stated that in several instances, their coverage of the Iraq War was not as rigorous as it should have been and that 'information that was controversial then, and seems questionable now, was insufficiently qualified or allowed to stand unchallenged' (*New York Times* 2004).

One of the aims of this book is indeed to explain why the media fail to meet the democratic needs of societies. *The News Media at War* analyses media coverage of the 2003 War on Iraq to examine the contours of media and government strategies that ensured a prevalence of pro-war arguments. Information control was successful, I argue, due to several overlapping factors: the development of military information control strategies since the Vietnam War, the emergence of a giant corporate for-profit conglomerate media apparatus that allows itself to spread biased information since profits often supersede the following of proper journalistic best practices, and last but not least, the existence of a collective mindset prone to consuming media biases.

The book focuses on two perspectives represented by leading global and transnational news networks, namely CNN International (CNNI) and Al Jazeera. CNNI was selected because it is the perfect example of a global news organisation. During the War on Iraq, CNNI reached more than 150 million television households throughout 212 countries. It is also a reference in terms of global news and is often referred to as 'the war channel'. On the other hand, Al Jazeera was selected because it was the leading transnational satellite channel in the Middle East at the time of the war with an estimated viewership of 70 million. Al Jazeera became known on the world stage following its leading role in the coverage of the 2001 War in Afghanistan, in which it emphasised civilian casualties and anti-war reactions. Al Jazeera's constituency has grown steadily steadily since then. Its success has been linked to the fact that its news frames and news values differ from its Western counterparts.

Using a triangulated analytical approach, which includes keywords, rhetoric, frame, textual and visual analysis, four key events of the war are thoroughly dissected. These events were selected according to their newsworthiness and the fact they were covered not only extensively, but also in real time, by both television networks, CNNI and Al Jazeera.

The originality of *The News Media at War*

The originality of this book is three-fold. Firstly, it captures, in real time, a defining event of the twenty-first century, namely the 2003 Iraq War and the mediated representation of this war via contrasting global networks. Secondly, this book provides a very useful background on the geo-political and ideological legacies of Western-Middle Eastern conflicts. This allows the readers to fully grasp the larger picture when the contesting framing of the coverage is scrutinised in the latter chapters. Thirdly, the accompanying explanations of the contesting televisual frames at the height of the conflict highlight the social and political realities making the visual and textual representations.

Given that there are relatively few studies comparing Western and Arab media coverage of the Iraqi War, this book aims to provide a better understanding of the media dynamics surrounding international conflicts in this region. Coverage will be examined on several dimensions, including the underlying ideologies used during the war to promote or to oppose the war, as well as the way protagonists were depicted. Accordingly, the news framing of key newsworthy events of the war will be closely analysed. It is expected that the collected data and subsequent analysis will provide a better understanding of the media dynamics surrounding international conflicts in the Middle East, and the ideological load carried by media belonging to different cultures.

1

War, Propaganda, and the Mobilisation of Frames

Military propaganda and psychological warfare

Two thousand years ago, Sun Tzu's[1] *Art of War* emphasised the need to subdue the enemy without fighting. He thus revealed the centrality of propaganda within military thought, since ultimately, victory or defeat resides in the mind. This view was shared by a third-century Chinese military theoretician, who stated that 'in military actions, attacking minds – that is the primary mission; attacking fortifications, that is a secondary mission. Psychological war is the main thing, combat is secondary' (Thomas 1999: 23). Reliance on deception was common in ancient history. Alexander the Great would try to weaken the leadership and morale of his foes by killing or capturing the enemy king as soon as possible. Likewise, Genghis Khan gave priority to disinformation, by emphasising local agents as a fifth column ahead of his advancing troops. They would spread rumours amongst the local people, convincing them of the invincibility of Khan's army. They also convinced the locals that Khan and his troops would give lenient treatment to those who surrendered. The tactics were successful, as Khan's Armies' conquered large areas of the world (Owen 1978: x, xi).

In the modern age, during World War I, the Axis powers employed propaganda strategies with some success. For instance, Austrian leaflets and agent provocateurs undermined Italian morale immediately preceding their disastrous defeat at Caporetto in 1917. On the Allied side, Britain's first Ministry of Information (MOI) was established, and concerted propaganda activities were led by Lord Northcliffe, the founder of modern popular journalism, and the owner of the *Daily Mail* and *The Times*. The Allies' psychological warfare was especially effective against the polyglot Austrian army. Their cohesiveness was shaken by the dissemination of anti-Austrian national feeling among Magyars, Czechs, Poles, and other peoples serving as soldiers. At the close of World War I, many Germans concluded that British military propaganda had significantly contributed to their defeat.[2]

During World War II, military propaganda became more sophisticated. The term 'psychological warfare' itself entered the modern military lexicon as a 1941 translation of the German term *Weltanschauungskrieg* (literally worldview warfare). The activation of this concept has been described as 'the scientific application of propaganda, terror and state pressure as a means of securing an ideological victory over one's enemies' (Daugherty and Janowitz 1958: 12). For both the Axis and Allied powers, the development of mass radio communications provided exceptional tools to target both the troops and the civilian populations, alongside leaflets. Strategically, psychological warfare was employed to 'increase the fighting spirit of friendly populations, weaken domestic and international support for the enemy's war effort, and persuade the government of the enemy side to cease hostilities on terms acceptable to the friendly side' (Hosmer 1999: 218). To achieve such an effect, Psyops (psychological operations) require professionals from different backgrounds with linguistic and cross-cultural skills, some military experience and area knowledge (often in the form of educational, journalistic or business experience in the target nation). Psyops teams also include researchers with backgrounds in psychology, sociology and political science in addition to creative personnel such as writers, artists, photographers, and cameramen, who actually create the messages (Macdonald 2007: 39).

It is well established that the American war effort during World War II – like all other protagonists – entailed the use of Psyops. Such tasks were primarily undertaken by the Office of War Information's (OWI), which sought to play an active role in winning the war by affirming 'the value of democracy of any totalitarian threat.' The leadership of OWI 'were sure that if they could simply repeat it loudly enough and often enough, it would win the hearts and minds of all who heard' (Winkler 1978: 150). However, disagreements among powerful internal political forces, including a sceptical Congress and a suspicious State Department, did not allow the OWI to play the wider role it aspired, namely to define American policy by determining 'what kind of propaganda should be served and who should do the serving' (Melosi 1978:157). It is believed that the disagreements on the OWI's role were in fact inherited from the 'distrustful memories of George Creel's Committee on Public Information in the First World War' (Sharp 1980:152). Ultimately, OWI's greatest contribution was in the field of military Psyops, supporting the operational theatres of the war. Accordingly, as soon as the war ended and its role becoming effectively superfluous, OWI was abolished by President Truman on 31 August 1945, merely three years after its inception (Fisher 1978: 408).

But the influence of Psyops did not end with the burial of OWI, far from it. In fact another agency, the Office of Strategic Services (OSS), was very active during World War II, and became renowned for its use of a variety of covert political, psychological, paramilitary and economic actions. Therefore, it was not surprising that shortly before the major operations of World War II ended, William Joseph Donovan (aka Wild Bill Donovan), the wartime head of the OSS, put forward a proposal in November 1944 for a post-war central intelligence organisation in charge for covert action, defined as 'subversive operations abroad,' to play a unique, yet defining, aspect of America's international engagement during the Cold War (Rudgers 2000: 249).

Essentially, the aforementioned proposal, as well as other consultations among different military and civilian governmental entities, came to reorganise the entire national security apparatus in 1947 with several goals, among which the need to counter Soviet-inspired Communist propaganda. This reorganisation assigned 'the conduct of covert activities to the Central Intelligence Agency.' The latter was tasked to 'undermine the strength of foreign instrumentalities, whether governments, organizations or individuals, which are engaged in activities inimical to the United States' and to support US foreign policy 'by influencing foreign public opinion in a direction favourable to the attainment of US objectives' (Rutgers 2000: 252–253). The CIA, through its

Special Procedures Group (SPG), began its covert operations almost immediately. Historians, such as Thomas Powers, tend to believe that the Italian election crisis of early 1948 provided the first opportunity to apply its undercover actions to stop a widely anticipated communist victory. The aforementioned actions ranged from lobbying by Italian-American community leaders to the financing of non-communist political parties (Powers 1981: 36–37). These acts managed to influence the 1948 Italian elections in favour of the Christian Democrats. Other subsequent CIA covert actions in that period included the staging of the 1953 Iranian and 1954 Guatemalan *coups d'état*.

In the meantime, numerous wars of decolonisation and liberation took place by the end of World War II. The psychological aspect of these wars was crucial. For instance, the Chinese leader Mao Tse Tung frequently asserted that 'the mind of the enemy and the will of his leaders is a target of far more importance than the bodies of his troops' (Blaufarb and Tanham 1989: 6–16). The use of psychological warfare was also the main component of counter-insurgency efforts. For instance, the British successfully waged psychological warfare against communist insurgents in Malaya (now Malaysia), and it was there where General Gerald Templer said: 'the shooting side of the business is only 25 per cent of the trouble, and the other 75 per cent lies in getting the people of this country behind us.' Through the Department of Information Services, new tools were used to carry an all-out psychological war. Using printed publications, radio programmes, and newsreels, the government managed to reach people in rural areas where communist insurgents were the most active, thus denying them crucially needed public support (Quoted in Stubbs 1989: 183). The French experience is vividly highlighted by Gillo Pontecorvo's film *The Battle of Algiers* (1965), which realistically portrays the urban struggle between French troops and Algerian nationalists.[3] The latter mounted a campaign of terror against French settlers in order to force their departure. On the other hand, the French colonial forces relied upon state terrorism via torture, intimidation, and mass indiscriminate punishment against the population. The battle for the city eventually ended in 1957 in apparent triumph for French troops when they killed the insurgents' leader and destroyed his network. However, the insurrection continued throughout Algeria, and the French ultimately lost the war in Algeria because they had lost the battle for hearts and minds.[4]

Military–media relationship: The US experience

Before the 1960s, the US military-media relationship only faced a few major hiccups.[5] In Vietnam, however, the relationship broke down particularly during the 1968 Têt offensive. Although the Viet Cong failed to achieve their immediate military and political objectives in this offensive (namely fomenting popular uprisings and assuming control within South Vietnamese towns and cities), the associated television coverage within America undermined public confidence in the war. Prospects for the US military appeared to diminish (Hosmer 1999: 218). However, Daniel C. Hallin rejects this simplistic explanation. His extensive research into a major random sample of 779 television broadcasts from August 1965 to January 1973 revealed a different pattern. For Hallin, the media kept an 'intimate institutional connection' with the government in the early period of the Vietnam War, and thus heavily favoured the official perspective. The tone of coverage only changed when opposition to the Vietnam War moved from the fringes of society into the social mainstream including factions within the political elite (Hallin 1984: 19–23). From the military perspective, the presence of war correspondents had advantages and disadvantages. They could persuade the public to support the war effort but negative reportage sapped the will of Washington's political elites and the morale of troops on the ground. Therefore, the Pentagon decided to change its way of handling the media. In the 1983 Grenada Campaign, media were simply excluded from covering the initial operations, provoking outrage among American news outlets. Consequently, a panel investigating the military-media relationship was established in 1984; they subsequently recommended the creation of a media pool system (Hill 1997: 10). This was designed to give a select group of journalists' early access to military operations. In the 1982 Falklands conflict for example, only twenty-nine journalists accompanied the British Task Force amidst heavy censorship measures (Taylor 1992: 116–117). This impressed the US high military command. So when on 20 December 1989 President Bush Sr sent American troops into Panama to oust General Manuel Noriega, a media pool system was employed. The Pentagon restricted the movement of the media pool by confining them to a US base in Panama during the first hours of fighting. When they were released, the heaviest combat phase was already over (Soderlund et al. 1994: 597). This situation obliged the correspondents to rely on the Pentagon's pictures and information (Johns and Johnson 1994: 63–64).

During the First Gulf War in 1991, the US military dealt with the media through a system of pools and formal briefings, whereby information was submitted to the public only from the Pentagon. Almost everything went according to plan. The press pool, which included about 1,600 journalists in Saudi Arabia, ran smoothly. There was however a major technological innovation, namely the introduction of live war television coverage. The Pentagon was well prepared to make war a 'staged event'. Thus, the start of the air campaign was scheduled for US prime-time television. American audiences knew through CNN that 'Desert Storm' had begun; half an hour before the formal announcement by the Pentagon (Van Tuyll 2002: 234). President Bush Sr was reported to be delighted, 'when the raid on Baghdad came through live on television at the time he had ordered it' (Taylor 1992: 32). The military arranged, months in advance, the types of stories the press would cover during the different phases of the campaign. The focus in the build-up phase was to be on personal interest stories concerning the deployed troops. Later, coverage of the air campaign emphasised the success and spectacle of hi-tech weapons deployment (Wolfsfeld 1997: 133). There were a few false notes in the Pentagon's symphony. Peter Arnett on CNN undermined US military propaganda, by referring to images of Iraqi civilians hit by American bombs and missiles. There was also exasperation from journalists, who expected to cover the war alongside fighting units, but ended up attending boring press conferences in which very little information was given. In the pools, military escorts accompanied journalists at all times, and often interfered during interviews with servicemen. Reporters critical of the military were blacklisted. For example, John Laurence, from the US television network ABC, was refused access to troops after he reported equipment problems and ammunition shortages. One can speculate that if 'Desert Storm' had not ended in such a record time (100 hours), the discontent of the participants in the press pools could have damaged media-military relationships.

Operation 'Restore Hope' in Somalia was supposed to introduce new arrangements with the media, however difficulties arose from the outset. For many military commanders, the whole American intervention was implemented as a result of media pressure. However, a series of content analysis investigations (Livingston and Eachus 1995; Mermin 1997) subsequently criticised this view. These studies showed that both television and print media paid little attention to Somalia until the Bush Sr administration took the decision to intervene there. During operations in Haiti (1994) and Bosnia (1995), the military–media relationship was more harmonious. The press willingly complied with most of the military's operational security concerns, and adhered to the concept of 'embedded media'; an arrangement that has a long history. An embedded reporter lives with a unit throughout the period of operations; in return he must not only respect soldiers' privacy, but also avoid reporting on anything that has to do with intelligence collection, special operations, or casualties (Porch 2002).

The Kosovo War differed from other 1990s conflicts, such as Somalia, Bosnia, Rwanda; these were described as intra-state crises involving the collapse of civil society. By contrast, the intervention of NATO in Kosovo, much like the 1991 Gulf War, was portrayed in the media as the action of 'a "benevolent" West, led by the USA, liberating citizens from a dictatorship' (Thussu 2000: 345). Nonetheless, NATO still found difficulties getting this message across as it was constantly challenged by Serbian regime declarations, disseminated through the internet by Serbian citizens. They successfully put forward their version and interpretation of events in European and American chat-rooms and other discussion forums (Badsey 2000). Independent non-embedded journalists were also a source of concern for NATO. For example, Paul Watson (*Los Angeles Times*) and John Simpson (BBC) reported regularly on the effects of bombing on Serbian civilians.

From Psyops to information dominance

At the end of World War II, the Supreme Commander of Allied Expeditionary Forces, General Eisenhower, expressed his admiration for the effectiveness of psychological warfare in winning the war (Gough 2003: 9). Classified US governmental records revealed the scope of psychological warfare. It included measures ranging from counterinsurgency to assassinations and covert operations. In short, it was all about merging violence and propaganda. In a memo written on 24 October 1953 by US President

Dwight D. Eisenhower to his Secretary of State John Foster Dulles, psychological warfare is said to range 'from the singing of a beautiful anthem, up to the most extraordinary kind of physical sabotage' (Emorys 1997).

In US military manuals, the tactical and operational side of psychological warfare 'Psyops' emerged as a distinct sub-discipline. This entails the formulation, conceptualisation, implementation, and evaluation of government-to-government and government-to-people persuasion. The purpose is to influence the opinions, emotions, attitudes, and behaviours of a target audience. Joint Publication 1-02 of the US Department of Defense defines Psyops as 'planned operations to convey selected information and indicators to foreign audiences to influence their emotions, motives, objective reasoning and, ultimately, the behaviour of foreign governments, organisations, groups or individuals'.[6] During the 1960s and 1970s, the United States military employed Psyops against Viet Cong controlled areas in South Vietnam. Messages in the native tongue were broadcast over loudspeakers, on the ground and from aircraft circling overhead. Millions of leaflets were dropped from airplanes, and posters were passed out to villagers in regions infiltrated by the Viet Cong. They were encouraged to give up their guerrilla ways, return to their villages, and give support to the (non-Communist) South Vietnamese government. Although there were defections, success was limited. This has been attributed to tensions between Psyops practitioners and conventional commanders, who were sceptical of such practices (Jeffery 1996). Another plausible explanation was that the US forces were 'out-Psyoped', since the American public's will to fight was successfully weakened by North Vietnam and its allies (Valley and Aquino 1980). After the Vietnam debacle, US military commanders decided to widen their Psyops capabilities and objectives. Psyops was designed to reduce moral and combat efficiency within the enemy's ranks; to promote mass dissension within and defections from enemy combat units and/or revolutionary cadre; to support cover and deception operations undertaken by US forces and their allies; and to promote cooperation, unity and morale within US forces and allied units (as well as within resistance forces behind enemy lines). The results were striking twenty years later[7] (Goldstein and Findley 1996).

In US military circles, news organisations and television reporters were blamed for the Vietnam defeat.[8] During and after the Têt offensive in 1968, most correspondents portrayed Vietnam as a quagmire for the US army (such that public support for the war was undermined). This latent impression shaped the US military attitudes toward the news media for decades. The US military media relationship was substantially reorganised in the lead up to the 1991 Gulf War. French cultural theorist Paul Virilio in *Desert Screen* (2002) analysed this process:

> [The 1991 Gulf War] was prepared by a total control of the electromagnetic environment above Iraq, and by a complete jamming of telecommunications that must have made Radio Baghdad inaudible. It was necessary that the Gulf War begin, on the night of 16 January, with the destruction of the army's communications centre, situated in the Iraqi Capital, the laser-guided bomb launched towards its objective in total impunity by a 'stealth' airplane.
>
> In this conflict where, for the first time in history, the various satellites played a major role, the control of communications outweighing the control of the geographical territory of the enemy, the five weeks of aerial bombardment demonstrated less the will to raze towns (as was once the case) than the will to eliminate the entire Iraqi communication and telecommunication infrastructure – the ground offensive itself becoming a simple formality, a sort of postscript to a 'total electronic war' that was bound to influence all of public opinion, thanks to the control of the media by the Pentagon. (Virilio 2002: 95–96)

In this war, US military commanders saw the capacity of the news media to be a 24/7 wartime player. More importantly, the media as such formed part of the battlefield. As a consequence, military planners sought to make media spin a central component of wartime operations (Felman 1992; Aukofer and Lawrence 1995: 45).

The contemporary information warfare paradigm was pioneered during the 1991 'Desert Storm' campaign. To this end, sanitisation was a major objective and outcome. Instead of allowing a realistic representation of war, the Pentagon provided infrared images of Baghdad with assorted flashes and lights. This positioned the war as an arcade videogame. As Steve Best and Douglas Kellner observed, 'the Gulf spectacle was "post-modern" because it managed to blur the distinction between truth and reality in a triumph of the orchestrated image and spectacle ...[and]... exhibited a heightened merging of individuals and technology, previewing a new type of cyber war that featured information technology and "smart" weapons' (Best and Kellner 2001: 73).

In the United States and the Western countries, information warfare was premised on the fact that citizens were spectators of war rather than mass participants. Thus, wars are no longer experienced directly in the West; rather they are viewed from afar. Western populations tend to 'spectate from a safe distance, empathizing but not experiencing, sympathizing but not suffering' (McInnes 2002: 55, 62). So, while the theatre of operations is situated everywhere, operational outcomes are partly decided in living rooms. From a military perspective, this 'theatrification' requires the news spectacle to fit military plans and strategies. In fact, military organisations themselves seek to produce the spectacle by making it an integral part of strategic planning (Weber 2002). The military-devised strategies involve total control over information, or information dominance, in all theatres of war.[9] By the late 1990s, this concept had become part of the 'Revolution in Military Affairs' (RMA).

The purpose was to boost the capabilities of the United States armed forces by creating smaller networked units equipped with information age technologies (Czege 2006: 16). In simple terms, the digital and communications revolution triggered a shift in military consciousness. Alvin and Heidi Toffler prefigured this change. In *The Third Wave*, they argued that the first wave of warfare was about control of lands, the second wave was about the control of productive capacity, whereas the third wave of wars is about the control of knowledge (Toffler and Toffler 1993: 141). Information dominance entered the military lexicon under different appellations. These included: Media Warfare,[10] the use of media outlets including the internet to disseminate propaganda or support deception operations; Mind War,[11] the deliberate, aggressive convincing of all participants in a war that victory is inevitable; Soft War,[12] the use of global television to shape another nation's view of reality; Neocortical Warfare,[13] the influence over, and the regulation of, the consciousness, perceptions, and will of the adversary's leadership; Perception Management,[14] the manipulation of information that shapes perceptions of reality; and Orientation Management,[15] the manipulation of the information as both a target and a weapon. These multiple terms, often indicating the same practices, were confusing. Academics added to the problem by coining their own appellations such as, Virtual War (Ignatieff 2000) and MIME Net[16] (Der Derian 2001). A central point of confusion was the blurred distinction between information warfare and information *in* warfare. The latter simply involves the use of information technology to instil combat operations with unprecedented economies of time and force. There was also confusion between information dominance and information superiority. According to Jim Winters and John Giffin, of the US Space and Information Operations Directorate, 'Dominance implies "a mastery of the situation," superiority "only an edge." For Winters and Giffin, 'when dominance occurs, *nothing done makes any difference*' which meant that 'we have sufficient knowledge to *stop anything we do not want to occur, or do anything we want to do.*' (Miller 2004b: 8) (Miller's emphasis). Information dominance is a comprehensive concept. It includes operations, such as 'the employment of the core capabilities of electronic warfare, computer network operations, psychological operations, military deception, and operations security, in concert with specified supporting and related capabilities, to affect or defend information and information systems, and to influence decision making' (Sieting 2003:56). In the 'immaterial battlefield of perception,' as Paul Virilio terms it, information itself becomes 'a separate realm, potent weapon, and lucrative target' (Whitehead 1997).

Undeniably, the information dominance paradigm surpasses earlier manifestations of propaganda. While traditional propaganda practices involve crafting the message and distributing it to government or independent media, information dominance requires 'the gathering, processing, and deployment of information'. This incorporates all other propagandistic activities conducted by the state, such as public and civil affairs, media relations and public diplomacy. This entails the integration of traditional propaganda and psychological operations into a much wider conception of information war. And information war becomes integrated into the core of military strategy (Miller 2004b: 8-9). In this regard, Bruce Berkowitz wrote that 'today the ability to collect, communicate, process

Environment Shaping

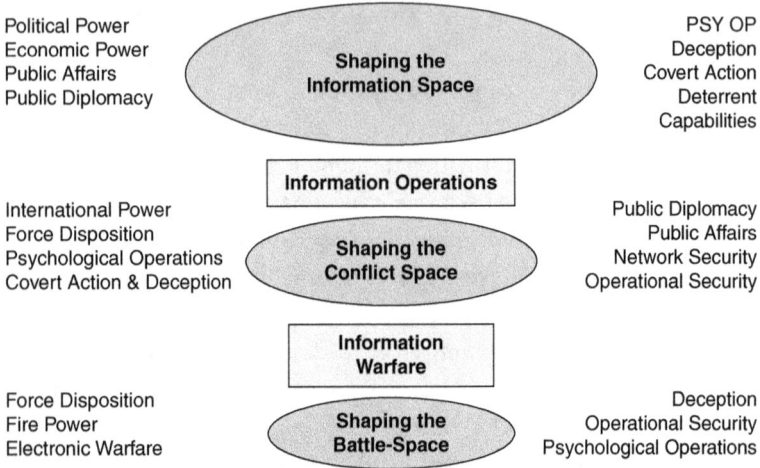

Figure 1.1: Information warfare and environment shaping (Dearth 2002: 8).

and protect information is the most important factor defining military power'. Having the edge in this feature is more important than armour, firepower, or mobility (quoted in Hiebert 2003: 244). This state of affairs undeniably blurs the boundaries between news and psychological warfare (Arkin 2002).

Information dominance after September 11

Research has shown that the post-9/11 information environment was shaped by the information dominance paradigm (Hiebert 2003; Brown 2002; Taylor 2003). To understand this development, it is necessary to subdivide the paradigm as follows; Perception Management (information is 'our' message); Information Exploitation (information is an opponent's resource to be contained); and System Destruction (information is the medium of the 'enemy' to be destroyed) (Bellamy 2001).

Perception management

Perception management is about shaping the information space in both politics and conflict. It involves practices which are truth-telling and truth-corrupting in the areas of operational security, cover and deception and psychological operations. This means that lethal and soft power mechanisms operate hand in hand. However, the overriding objective is to ensure the dominance of a certain interpretation of reality (Dearth 2002).

Following the events of September 11 2001, perception management was contracted to the Rendon Group, a private public relations firm, which had promoted the 1991 'Desert Storm' campaign. They immediately focused on the 24/7 updating news cycle as a vehicle for shaping opinions. Rendon helped create Coalition Information Centers (CIC) based in Washington, London and Islamabad, in order to monitor news flows from different geographic localities and time zones. The CIC also prepared daily press releases and responses, and commissioned opinion polling in the Muslim world. In addition, they sought to give key members of the US administration a profile on major Arab Networks (Foer 2002). At the same time, the Pentagon authorised certain operations for their visual Psyops-effect. For example, in late October 2001 images of the US Army Rangers parachuted into a Taliban airbase near Kandahar were broadcast around the globe. This operation was described by some senior military officials as a television show, designed to persuade domestic audiences and world opinion that the United States was winning the war (Campbell 2003).

The Rendon Group was also instrumental in setting up the Pentagon's Office of Strategic Influence (OSI).[17] This office coordinated the distribution of news releases and devised foreign advertising campaigns (as well as covert disinformation programmes designed to plant pro-American stories throughout the international media, even if they were false) (Campbell 2003). In February 2002, this plan was uncovered by the *New York Times*. Worldwide indignation and domestic political fallout was sparked by the revelation that journalists were involved in a large scale disinformation campaign. Because of this, Secretary of Defense Donald Rumsfeld was forced to abolish the OSI less than five months after its establishment. Yet the same programmes and practices intended for OSI continued under other names, as the Pentagon was committed to the policy of co-ordinating perception management on a high-level (Fair 2002).

But this was not all; Middle Eastern audiences were targeted through the United States Broadcasting Board of Governors (BBG). This new broadcasting authority launched Radio *Sawa*, an Arabic entertainment and news station in March 2002. Its mix of Western pop music, sports, weather, and short newscasts, was designed to influence the perceptions of younger Arabs concerning the 'American way of life'.

Information exploitation

Information exploitation covers a wide range of actions, such as withholding information, omission, and censorship. These measures intensify during battlefield situations. For example, during the Afghanistan campaign, when reports emerged that US military actions had caused civilian fatalities, the Pentagon immediately bought exclusive rights to high resolution satellite photos. This prevented the circulation of embarrassing photographic evidence (Campbell 2001).

The US administration stepped up its censorship measures, to the point where Condoleezza Rice requested American news outlets to be 'very careful about what they say' (Schechter 2002). The mainstream media zealously complied with those directives, and became in many instances mere transcribers of official utterances. Journalists did not challenge the official pro-war line, or even demand hard evidence for statements concerning the Afghanistan campaign. Most journalists did not question the administration's failure in preventing the 9/11 attacks. Instead, corporate media organisations adhered to the militarisation of foreign policy. Opposing opinions and viewpoints were curtailed. Voice of America (VOA) was prevented by the State Department from broadcasting an interview with the Taliban leader Mullah Omar (the interview took place on 21 September 2001). The Bush presidency also tried to stop Al Jazeera from broadcasting taped interviews with Bin Laden. During the 2003 War in Iraq, CBS News anchor Dan Rather was strongly criticised for granting an interview to Saddam Hussein (Rich 2003) and war correspondent Peter Arnett was fired from NBC after stating on Iraqi national television that the American military plans had failed (Jensen 2003). Along with media, American universities were pressured to restrict debate concerning America's new imperial ventures (Bello 2001).

System destruction

Information warfare literature specifies that the primary objective is to undermine the adversary's will and capacity to fight. Thus, neutralising the enemy's communications and control facilities becomes a priority. Because media outlets relaying the enemy's perceptions effectively boost the enemy's morale, they are considered as primary targets from an information warfare perspective. In this context, during the 1991 Gulf War, American aircraft silenced Iraqi radio broadcasts by targeting stations, transmission towers, and power plants in Baghdad. Similarly, during the Kosovo War (1999), NATO aircraft attacked the Serbian Radio and Television headquarters in Belgrade (22 April 1999).[18] Likewise, during the 2001 Afghanistan War, US cruise missiles destroyed the Taliban's main radio station in Kabul (8 October 2001). Al Jazeera's office in Kabul was also destroyed in December 2001 by an air attack. Regarding the latter incident, Major Samuel Morthland emphasised the need to prevent Al Qaeda from getting its message out (Morthland 2002: 40). Likewise, for military propaganda specialist Robin Brown, the attack on Al Jazeera made perfect sense from an Information Warfare perspective. Its main advantage is that 'it removes an enemy outlet', although he acknowledges that its side-effect damages 'the broader US brand' with its claims of democracy and freedom of speech (Brown 2002: 46).

Counter mobilisation: Propaganda, war and the public sphere

In the quest to critique propaganda and communication campaigns, many perspectives have been developed. The 'watchdog' or 'fourth estate' model assumes that the media is an independent monitor of military behaviour during war. American news media organisations have often depicted themselves as the defenders of citizens' rights and the public interest against the hidden agendas of elites. However, Philip Knightley's historical review of the military-media relationship suggests that 'fourth estate' principles have been marginalised. Field reporters generally served the designs of the military establishment. This was evident during the Vietnam War, even though the media is perceived to have played some role in pressuring the Presidency to withdraw troops. The propaganda model of Noam Chomsky and Edward Herman suggests that media organisations serve ruling power structures; rather than the public interest. Studies of numerous military conflicts confirm that American television overwhelmingly relays the perspectives of the Pentagon (O'Heffernan 1993; Paletz 1994). However, this line of argument predates the information dominance paradigm (whereby information becomes an element of combat power). Thus, a third model of communicating conflict has been proposed suggesting that military and media networks have converged to the point where they become virtually indistinguishable (Thussu 2003; Miller 2004b).

Both the propaganda model and the information dominance paradigm represent a serious threat to fourth estate principles. More broadly, by circumventing the informed, rational, and reflective judgement of the citizens, propaganda and information dominance undeniably erodes the democratic process. In this context, Jürgen Habermas outlines and argues on behalf of a public sphere created through dialogic critical-rational discourse (Habermas 1989). Oliver Hahn identifies three conceptions of the public sphere: the traditional sceptical model, which discounts the existence of a public sphere; the liberal-representative model, in which the media is understood to serve as intermediary institution between politics and citizens; and the deliberative-discursive model, which regards the public sphere as being shaped by relations of power involving national media domains (Rosenwerth et al. 2005: 13–14). The public sphere is expressive of deliberation mechanisms which give legitimacy to democratic politics. For Habermas, 'a legitimate decision does not represent the will of all, but is one that results from the deliberation of all. It is the process by which everyone's will is formed that confers it legitimacy on the outcome, rather than the sum of already formed wills' (Habermas 1989: 446). Democracy thus entails collective decision-making processes, in which individuals have the opportunity and the necessary information to form reasoned judgments. These will be taken in account by ruling institutions before making decisions (Thompson 1995: 255). The concept of the public sphere contrasts with the view that democracy is primarily a voting exercise, in which fixed preferences and interests compete via fair mechanisms of aggregation.

War, Propaganda, and the Mobilisation of Frames

In this regard, media institutions contribute to the development of a public sphere not only as a means of information but also as a means of expression. Media organisations ought to act as an agency of representation by allowing diverse social groups to express their views. They should promote open debate on given issues and outline various alternative arguments and actions (Thompson 1995: 257). These principles constitute a serious challenge to propaganda and opinion management, since everyone, including marginalised groups, is allowed the opportunity to participate in decision-making processes.

One central attribute of propaganda (in contrast to the public sphere) is that of untruthfulness. In a working democracy those who hold public office are supposed to persuade the citizens of the rightness of their views, and they are supposed to do so without misleading. They can decently appeal to their superior knowledge in some matters, but in general they are obliged to gain citizens' assent by telling the truth. By truth, I mean the correspondence between what is thought, believed, judged, or said and what is the real state of affairs in the world. The imparting of truth and truthfulness is an esteemed value which, of itself, transcends mere utility. Since ancient classical times, truth and truthfulness have been the necessary ingredients of knowledge and understanding (Allen 1993: 18–26). By contrast, propaganda systematically disregards this superior epistemic value. If there is a connection between truth and propaganda, it is a twisted one: it achieves 'the advantage of a lie without telling a literal untruth' (Gaffney quoted in Baker and Martinson 2001: 150). Stanley Cunningham emphasises this point when he notes that 'propaganda uses facts and poses as truthful information; it instrumentalizes truth; it does falsify, but in ways that involve the use of truths and facts as much as possible' (Cunningham 2002: 98). So truth – from the perspective of a propagandist – is reduced to the status of a means. Propaganda does not burden itself with the various theories of truth; it stays outside any framework of truth, and remains eminently practical. Propaganda also involves the construction of falsities on a large scale, and is often synonymous with terms such as distortion, exaggeration, disinformation, and deception. On the other hand, truth telling is among the principal features of journalistic ethics. In fact, 'all the ethical codes begin with the newspaperman's duty to tell the truth under all conditions' (Christians et al. 1987: 49). As such, journalists work to create an informed and active citizenry. They have to seek the truth and to report it accurately. They should not be deliberate carriers of propaganda and fraud.

In light of the discussion so far, the problem with the information dominance paradigm is that it is not limited to the enemy; rather it extends to friendly and neutral audiences (i.e. local public spheres). Consider NATO's definition of Psyops; it includes activities 'conducted in peace, crisis and war and directed toward friendly, hostile, potentially hostile or neutral audiences. Normally, the objectives of strategic psychological activities are long-term and political in nature, they aim to undermine the adversary's, or a potential adversary's readiness for conflict and will to fight. Reducing the opponent's war-making capability is also advanced by gaining the support and cooperation of neutral and friendly populations' (Collins 2002: 44). The spreading of falsehood within the public sphere seems to be widely accepted within military ranks. In 1995, the Freedom Forum First Amendment Centre found that 60 per cent of 1,000 US officers surveyed agreed that 'military leaders should be allowed to use the news media to deceive the enemy, thereby deceiving the American public' (Macdonald 2007: 156). The distorted communication and deception that results from such endeavours represents an assault on the trust invested by the public in the media. This trust is itself a social good to be protected; all societies have injunctions against fraud (Bok 1989). Therefore, even in times of war and insecurity, responsible journalism should be aware that information warfare undermines democratic politics. Consequently, the commitment to truth telling must be very high in the journalists' agenda. Robert McChesney reminds us of the fact that 'war is the most serious use of state power: organized, sanctioned violence'. Therefore, according to him, it is important to evaluate 'how well [war] is under citizen review and control' which 'is not only a litmus test for the media but for society as a whole' (Nichols and McChesney 2005: 37).

To counteract the devastating effects of untruthfulness in communication, Sherry Baker and David Martinson have proposed an ethical test named TARES; an acronym consisting of five principles: Truthfulness (of the message), Authenticity (of the persuader), Respect (for the persuadee), Equity (of the persuasive appeal) and Social Responsibility. This test can be seen as a valid attempt to protect the public sphere from the taint of military propaganda. Here, the principle of truthfulness not only requires the persuader's intention not to deceive, it also requires that people receive the truthful information they legitimately need to make informed decisions about the destiny of their countries. As for source authenticity, this requires every communicator to take responsibility for their own actions (rather than concealing the origin of communication as is often the case with black and grey propaganda).[19] In these cases, biased communication becomes the norm since governmental organisations assume no responsibility over it. Respect for the persuadee contrasts with the propagandists view that that ordinary people are objects of manipulation. Respect also implies that the content and execution of persuasive appeals should be equitable (rather than targeted against a given population). Finally, the social responsibility part of this test requires the communicator to consider the wider public interest. Responsibility to community should overrule self-interest and profit. It is also a reminder to governmental agencies – including military institutions – that they should promote understanding, dialogue and cooperation among constituent groups (instead of stereotyping them for the purpose of propaganda) (Baker and Martinson 2001: 148–175).

In every society there are beliefs related to societal goals, aspirations, conditions, norms, and values which reflect the outlook of dominant groups. These beliefs are publicly prominent and play a defining role in the process of 'othering'. They tend to be reflected in language, stereotypes, images, myths and collective memories (Bar-Tal 2005: 13–15). The process of 'othering' defines and secures one's own identity by distancing and stigmatising those who are different. Its purpose is to reinforce the 'normality' of dominant groups, and to externalise the difference of others. The mainstream media contribute to this process; news journalists often construct normalcy and difference through stories of villains, victims, and heroes. Implicitly, 'people like us' are positioned in opposition to the 'others' (Hallin 1986a). In periods of conflict, societal beliefs are highlighted to ensure dominance and victory. Ones' own deeds are portrayed in a positive light, whereas the other side's are linked to atrocity, cruelty, and viciousness. Furthermore, one's own group is often portrayed as the victim of the opponent. One's own goals are just while those goals of one's opponent are illegitimate and/or evil (Bar-Tal 2005: 17).

During the Cold War, Western audiences constantly received images of an implacable Soviet enemy who was bent on conquering the world and whose basic values conflicted with the principles of democratic countries. At that time, especially in the United States, labelling someone a 'communist' was to deprive him or her of his fundamental rights, as reflected in the slogan 'better dead than red' (Porras 1995: 301). The phobic fear of the communist 'other' prompted Western states to equate belief in communism with treason, thus institutionalising the invasion of privacy of citizens. McCarthyism in America illustrated such paranoia, as it divided Americans along Manichean lines: they were either suspects or surveillance eyes for the state. Perpetuating the 'otherness' of counter-hegemonic discourses facilitates the official task of delineating the limits of the political space, and of writing 'the script for historical interpretations of national identity and political sovereignty' (Oliverio 1997: 6). To this end, the prevalence of anti-communist imagery did not just perpetuate animosity during the Cold War period, it contributed to the maintenance of Russian and Eastern European stereotypes for years to come (Ibroscheva 2002). After the fall of the Soviet Union and the disappearance of the communist menace, American elites felt the loss of an 'other' to compete against. This anxiety was clearly expressed by Chairman of the Joint Chiefs of Staff Colin Powell; in a 1991 interview; 'Think hard about it. I'm running out of demons. I am running out of villains. I am down to Castro and Kim Il Sung' (Quoted in Gibbs 2004: 315). Saddam Hussein's invasion of Kuwait and the prosecution of 'Desert Storm' created new opportunities; the 'othering' of Iraqis, Arabs, and Islam skyrocketed. During that war, Iraqis were dehumanised as a pestilence to be removed; an impression conveyed by an American pilot, who boasted of killing the 'cockroaches' (Muscati 2002: 132).

After the 1991 Gulf War, Western official discourse started brandishing the menace of Islamic fundamentalism. This rhetorical strategy met little resistance as prejudices already existed in the European and American psyche. Indeed, Islam was perceived to represent an obstacle to Western hegemony with its non-Christian philosophy (Butko 2006: 149). In addition, Islamism replaced Marxism as the ideology of the dispossessed in the Muslim countries (Ali 2000: 25), while Islamist movements adopted an uncompromising stance against pro-Western regimes in the region (Hippler and Lueg 1995: 131). Western decision makers were also anxious about the Muslim world's perceived demographic advantage. During the

1990s, approximately one billion Muslims contributed to a majority in more than 48 countries, and were a rapidly growing minority in Europe and America (Esposito 1994: 19). As the new 'other', Islam was perceived as the main enemy within the West (embodied by the Muslim minorities) and outside the West (embodied by the Muslim world). As a result, many Western politicians denounced Islam as a threat to Western civilisation. For instance, French Defence Minister Francois Leotard declared in 1994: 'Islamic fundamentalism is as dangerous today as Nazism once was' (Hashemi, 2002). Also, Willy Claes, the then Secretary General of NATO, stated in 1995 that 'Islamic fundamentalism is at least as dangerous as communism was. Please do not underestimate this risk' (Hashemi, 2002). Similar remarks were made by the German Chancellor Helmut Kohl, who claimed that 'the danger of fundamentalism … is one of the greatest dangers we are facing today'.[20] Therefore, Islam was the implied target of Psyops and information campaigns, cultivated by military elites.

On the one hand, it must be stated that military propaganda – no matter how potent it is – might be conceivably counteracted in a warfare situation. The existence of a lively public sphere is a prerequisite to such a development. As originally envisioned by Jürgen Habermas, the concept of the public sphere allows citizens to foster political debate and political action. In this context, critical journalism – based on speaking the truth to power – can serve as an anti-propaganda resource. And because propaganda is necessarily linked to processes of othering (as with the Orientalist frame, or its mirror image the Occidentalist[21] frame), critical journalism and oppositional public spheres give voice to marginalised 'others'. On the other hand, military propaganda has ways to circumvent public scrutiny and plays in contrast upon the fear of the 'other' and exploits its resonance among the public. Attention in the following chapter is devoted to the Orientalist and counter terrorist worldviews since they represent the platform upon which the process of othering is constructed.

2

Orientalism, Terrorism, and American Media Discourse

On Orientalism

During the seventh century, Muslim conquests sharpened geopolitical tensions within the Christian Byzantine Empire.[1] Disputed control of the Mediterranean Sea was a constant mutual concern. The European position was exemplified by a series of crusades from the eleventh to the thirteenth century.[2] As their lands were invaded, Muslims incurred deep seated feelings of humiliation (Malouf 1984: xiv). Early Muslim historians were shocked by crusader atrocities[3] and by their untrustworthiness vis-à-vis treaties.[4] Having coexisted with Christians from the East for centuries (in the Levant and Egypt), the Muslim side refused to equate the crusades with Christianity as such. Instead, they regarded specific European nationalities, namely the Franks, as perpetrators of war because they constituted the majority within the crusaders' ranks. The crusades were termed 'Frankish Wars' by Muslim historians (Malouf 1994; Hillenbrand 1999). Meanwhile, the crusades were seen by papal clerics as an opportunity to forge a Pan-European Christian identity against a threatening Islam (Djait 1986: 109). This worldview underpinned the emergence of Orientalist discourse, which came to shape the Western psyche long after religious fervour declined.

The root word 'Orient' derives from a Latin word *Oriens,* meaning the rising of the sun; 'the East' is invoked only in the most general sense. Figuratively, according to the online version of the Oxford English Dictionary, the term 'Orientalism' meant in the past: (1) 'Oriental style or quality; the character, customs, etc., of oriental nations; an oriental trait, feature, or idiom' and (2) the 'Knowledge of the languages, cultures, etc., of the Orient.' (Oxford English Dictionary [online]). Broad neutral definitions like these referring to academic traditions were the most readily accepted for a long time, yet according to Edward Said, Orientalism includes at least three categories: academic, general and corporate (Said 1979: 2–3). Said regards the latter category as instrumental in forging Orientalism as an ideological discourse rather than an intellectual endeavour. Corporate Orientalism defines for Europeans what the Orient is about, and how it should be institutionally and educationally explained. For Said, this discourse exemplifies the 'Western style for dominating, restructuring, and having authority over the Orient' (Said 1979: 3). Such is confirmed by historical evidence. Within the British Empire for example, scores of academics worked to spread and stabilise British colonial rule overseas. The architect of Britain's Educational Policy in India, Thomas Macaulay, concisely articulated the methods of British imperialism: 'We must do our best to form a class who may be interpreters between us and the millions whom we govern, a class of persons Indian in blood and colour, but English in taste, in opinions, words and intellect' (Macaulay 1835).[5] Some contemporary authors such as Gauri Viswanathan argue that British colonial hegemony in India rested ultimately on the teaching of English literature, and not on the exercise of direct force (Eaton 2000: 63).

Because of this linkage with colonialism, Orientalism as a discipline started to carry a negative connotation especially after the wave of decolonisation in Asia and Africa, and the proliferation of nationalisms. Anouar Abdel-Malek, an Egyptian Marxist philosopher, wrote an article entitled *Orientalism in Crisis* (1962), in which he argued that Asian anticolonial movements after World War II had exposed the intimate relationship between Orientalist scholars and the colonial powers. Previously, this close association had legitimised the Western appropriation of Asia's treasures (texts, manuscripts, and artefacts) for Western libraries, museums and archives. At the same time, Orientalists depicted Asians as obstacles to, or supporters of, development and civilisation. Abdel-Malek points to the crisis of Orientalism during the post-colonialist era. The collapse of colonialism had uncovered the metaphysical and essentialist mythologies of Orientalism contained within religious and historical texts. Orientalists had positioned the Orient as an object of knowledge and domination. In his later writings, Abdel-Malek echoes Foucault by stressing 'the organic interrelation between *power* and *culture*', observing that 'never in history have we witnessed power without culture' (Abdel-Malek 1977: 60; original emphasis). As a solution, Abdel-Malek advocated more specialised disciplinary inquiry that could address both the Orient and Occident from a universalistic perspective.

Another pioneering critique of Orientalism was developed by the Palestinian Islamic academic A.L. Tibawi. His two important articles on this subject, namely *English-speaking Orientalists* (1964) and *A second critique of English-speaking Orientalists* (1979), clearly demonstrated the Orientalists' misunderstanding of the Orient in general and Islam in particular. Tibawi analyses the historical background of mutual hostility between the Islamic and the Christian world. He argues that Christian missionaries formed an alliance with the classical Orientalists in order to represent Islam and Muslims in offensive terms. Thus, according to Tibawi, the Orientalists misunderstand Islam completely; because of this, it is impossible for a Western scholar to adopt a fresh point of view on Islam (Tibawi 1979: II-V).

Bryan Turner, the English scholar, also objected to Orientalism. In *Marx and the End of Orientalism* (1978), Turner argued that Marxism can demolish Orientalism and transform the existing theoretical models about the 'Orient' into 'proper objects of theoretical work', with the provision that Marxism purges itself of Orientalist bias (Turner 1978: 82). Some remarks made by Marx and Engels were interpreted as justifying colonialism. For example, in *Capital*, Marx made reference to British colonial officers who regarded the use of violent exogenous force as means of bringing 'progress' to 'stagnant' Asia. Marx shared the view that Asia was trapped in a state of despotism and civilisational decline. He relied on these colonial sources to develop his theory of the Asiatic mode of production. The revisions proposed by Turner include the elimination of 'teleological versions of Marxism which, for example, treat history as a series of necessary stages and thereby relegate the Middle East to a stage prior to "real history"' (Turner 1978: 8).

It is important to note that these scholars approached Orientalism from particular points of view; Abdel-Malek Egyptian-Marxist, Tibawi Palestinian-Islamic, and Bryan Turner English-Marxist. However, they all reached the same conclusion: Orientalism as an academic discipline was deeply flawed, in crisis, and in need of radical reform. This conclusion was also shared by Professor Edward Said, a primary contributor to the debate surrounding Orientalism. His major work *Orientalism* (1979) critically examined Orientalism via Foucault's notion of discourse.[6] Said delineated the European constructions of the 'Oriental', and the ways in which Orientalist discourse became, in Foucault's terminology, a regime of truth,[7] which remoulded the complexities of the Orient into a manageable entity. In his view, 'without examining Orientalism as a discourse one cannot possibly understand the enormously systematic discipline by which European culture was able to manage – and even produce – the Orient politically, sociologically, militarily, ideologically, scientifically, and imaginatively during the post-Enlightenment period' (Said 1979: 3).

Orientalist discourse thereby constructed narratives and images that served to reinforce feelings of unity among one's own imagined community, while assuming superiority over the other. Said considered Orientalism as a generic descriptor for Western conceptions of the Orient. It was, he stated, 'a political vision of reality whose structure promoted the difference between the familiar (Europe, the West, "us") and the strange (the orient, the East, "them")' (Said 1979: 43). Charles Paul Freund goes further by saying that 'Orientalism transforms the East and its people into an alien "other"'. In his view, that other, usually a dark other, was in every way the inferior of the West: unenlightened, barbarous, cruel, craven, enslaved to its senses, given to despotism, and, in general, contemptible' (Freund 2001: 3).

This deep seated binary opposition between Orientalism and its other constitutes hegemony in its purest form. Drawing from Antonio Gramsci, Stuart Hall points out that hegemony as an ideological force involves 'the power to represent someone or something in a certain way within a certain regime of representation' (Hall 1997: 259). Said's notion of hegemony is also drawn from the writings of Antonio Gramsci. In his view, hegemony is a form of cultural control, wherein ideas are not enforced through coercion but through consent. Gramsci considers that the political society (the police, the army, legal system, etc.) takes the leadership of civil society (the family, the education system, trade unions, etc.) within a capitalist mode of production. Gramsci suggests that capitalist relations of power are maintained not just through political and economic coercion, but also ideologically, through a hegemonic culture in which the values of the bourgeoisie became the 'common sense' values of all. Gramsci's ideas seem to have deeply influenced Hall and Said's critique of Orientalism. For Hall, Orientalist 'truth' resided in the power of writers and academics to tell stories of the Orient, claiming that they successfully represented it (Hall 2004: 236). Similarly Said observed that: 'In any society not totalitarian, certain cultural forms predominate over others, just as certain ideas are more influential than others' (Said 1979: 7). In this regard, European hegemony has affected Orientalist ideas about the Orient by constantly 'reiterating European superiority over Oriental backwardness'. This superiority has been achieved through the constant repetition of entrenched presuppositions and idioms by European scientists, scholars, missionaries, traders and soldiers (Said 1979: 7); these idioms underpinned Orientalist myths and doctrines, which in turn imprinted the so-called Oriental character (despotic, irrational etc.) in the Western mind.[8]

Overall, Edward Said made three important claims in *Orientalism*. Firstly, in spite of claiming to be an academically oriented discipline, Orientalism has in fact functioned to serve political ends, and more especially imperialist endeavours. Secondly, Orientalism helped define Europe's self-image. Thirdly, Orientalism has produced a false description of Arabs and Islamic culture. The resulting Western imagery of the Orient has produced a discourse that has evolved into a kind of imagined binary ontology; an ontology that has remained strong despite contemporary manifestations of globalisation.

Orientalism and the representation of Islam and Arabs

Orientalists' writings provide a distorted picture of Islam as religion. The distortion began with Christian missionaries, who sought to devalue Islam relative to Christianity. For centuries, conflict in the Mediterranean was mainly interpreted through religious rhetoric, and Islam was portrayed as the anti-Christ, in spite of the existence of numerous commonalities between the two religions (Hurd 2003: 25–41). Echoes of this discourse continue to resonate. This occurs when Muslim culture is positioned as a threat to national identity and to local ways of life. For example, the building of a mosque in Lodi (Italy) in 2000 triggered a hostile response from Cardinal Biffi. He stated on the primetime television news of RAI (the Italian public service broadcaster) that Muslims are not 'part of our humanity' (Cere 2002: 133).

Christian missionary writings of the early nineteenth century pictured Islam as a Christian heresy and Muhammad as a fraud and charlatan. For example Pierre Bayle's *Dictionnaire historique et critique* argues that the prophet of Islam was deluded by the devil into the belief that he was a prophet. For Bayle, Muhammad was quite simply an impostor, while Herbelot, the writer of *Bibliothèque Orientale*, declared 'this is the famous impostor Mahomet, Author and Founder of a heresy, which has taken on the name of a religion that we call Mahometan' (Almond 2003: 412–413). Such judgements had a major impact on Orientalism and contributed to a long-lasting Western antipathy toward Islam. Other 'oriental' faiths such as Buddhism and Hinduism have generated a fair amount of sympathy and interest in the West. Islam on the other hand, despite being closer to Judaism and Christianity, and claiming the same Abrahamic source, was misjudged and misrepresented by most of the Orientalists. Although centuries of wars have produced a legacy of animosity between the world of Islam and the Christian West, there was much common ground. They both claim a universal message and share much of the same Judeo-Christian and Greco-Roman heritage (Gerges 2003: 588). Furthermore, there was considerable cultural exchange between Muslim and Christians from the eighth century onwards. It is a matter of fact that the Christian civilisation received significant technological and scientific contributions from Islam (Turner 2003: 17). Robert W. Cox notes that 'it was through contact with the higher culture of Islam that the Christian West recovered knowledge of Greek philosophy' (Cox 1992: 151). In this regard, Arab Institutes in Cordoba, Seville, Granada, Valencia and Toledo attracted the great Christian thinkers of that time, including Albertus Magnus, Roger Bacon, Thomas Aquinas, William of Ockham, and Gerbert of Aurillac (later to become Pope Sylvester II). This side of history is rarely explored by Orientalists, most probably because the animosity helped to forge Christian self-identity (Almond 2003: 416).

Said provides case studies of how Orientalists have handled Islam. He analysed for example the works of Renan, who claimed that 'the sword of Muhammad and the Koran are the most stubborn enemies of Civilization, Liberty and the Truth which the world has yet known' (Said 1979: 151). The idea that the spread of Islam is inherently forceful is quite common among Orientalists. Isaac Barrow (1630–1677) declared that Islam 'diffused itself by rage and terror of arms; convincing men's minds only by the sword, and using no arguments but blows' (Almond 2003: 417). A contemporary version of this viewpoint was articulated by Pope Benedict XVI at an address at German University (12 September 2006). Pope Benedict quoted criticism of Islam and Prophet Muhammad by the fourteenth century Byzantine Emperor Manuel II Palaeologus.[9]

The assumption that Islam was spread by the sword implies that Christianity was spread through divine help. This Orientalist reductionism overlooked evidence that the sacred texts of Islam forbade coercion in areas of religion. The Koran clearly states: 'Let there be no compulsion in religion' (Koran 2: 256) and also states: 'Say: "The Truth is from your Lord." Let him who will believe, and let him who will, reject [it]' (Koran 18: 29). This is why Muslim administrators did not forcibly convert people from other religions. Christians and Jews lived without persecution in Islamic lands for centuries. When the Muslim armies captured Jerusalem in 638, Caliph Omar assured the Patriarch that Christian lives and property would be respected. When Jerusalem fell to the crusaders in 1099, the majority of the population was still Christian (Jones and Ereira 1996: 54). Muslim tolerance explains the existence of sizeable Eastern Christian communities, such as the Coptic Christians in Egypt and the Maronite Christians in Lebanon.[10] The Christians lived in peace and harmony with their neighbours for centuries. In *Muhammad, a Western Attempt to Understand Islam*, Karen Armstrong argues that 'in the Islamic empire Jews like Christians had full religious liberty; the Jews lived there in peace until the creation of the State of Israel in our own century. The Jews of Islam never suffered like the Jews of Christendom ... [There is] a history of 1,200 years of good relations between Jews and Muslims' (Armstrong 1992: 209).

As with Islam, the Orientalists heavily distorted the Arab image. They have long described the experiences of the Arabs, in ways which deprive the Oriental Arab of any individuality. Through their monopoly of knowledge,

Orientalists perpetuated the myth that the Arabs did not provide any meaningful contribution to history. The history of the Arabs was subsequently depicted as a timeline containing no creative intelligence. This erroneous portrayal of Arabs happened because of Orientalism's essentialist assumption that it was possible to define the qualities of Arab peoples. In fact, there has never been any such thing as a monolithic Arab world. As Nadine Naber has pointed out, there are twenty four countries and a configuration of religions, including 'Maronites, Catholics, Protestants, Greek Orthodox, Jews, Sunnis, Shi'a, Druze, Alawites, Nestorians, Assyrians, Copts, Chaldeans, and Baha'is. Naber also identifies different ethnic groups such as the Berbers, Kurds, Armenians, Bedu, gypsies and many others with different languages, religions, ethnic and national identifications and cultures. All of these are 'congealed as Arab in popular Western representations, whether or not those people identify as Arab' (Naber 2000: 43).

American Orientalism

In *Orientalism*, Edward Said concentrates mainly on the French and British varieties of the nineteenth and early twentieth centuries. He only partly addresses American Orientalism on the grounds that it only emerged in the post-World War II period, when the United States became the pivotal Western superpower (at the expense of Britain, France and Germany) (Said 1979: 290). This argument holds some substance insofar as the academic institutionalisation of Orientalism is concerned. Yet, if one regards Orientalism as a discourse in the service of imperial power over the Orient, and if one considers Orientalism as central to the Western self-image, then the omission of an earlier American Orientalism is surprising.

Subsequently, Said duly addressed American Orientalism in *Culture and Imperialism*. He carefully distinguishes imperialism from colonialism, while at the same time linking the two terms. He defines imperialism as 'thinking about, settling on, controlling land that you do not possess, that is distant, that is lived on and owned by others' (Said 1993: 7). This definition allowed him to argue firstly, that imperialism had survived the dismantlement of the colonial empires, and secondly, that the repetition of the old imperialist attitudes underpinned America's interventions in the developing world (Said 1993: xxiii, 63, 241–242). Said depicts America 'as an immigrant settler society superimposed on the ruins of a considerable native presence' (Said 1993: xxv). Contrary to American self-perceptions of their nation as an anti-imperial opponent of the British Empire, Said points out that the United States was founded upon a successful imperial conquest. For him, the American Revolution was not anti-colonial but an effort from local American colonists to get their share of the colonial pie. Thus, the American move to become an empire was hardly surprising. *Culture and Imperialism* demonstrates how European colonial empires and their American offshoot combined culture and politics, knowingly or otherwise, to produce a system of domination that complements military power.

Adhering to Said's paradigm, John Kuo Wei Tchen has provided a more detailed historical evolution of American Orientalism in his examination of Chinese migrants in American literature. In *New York Before Chinatown: Orientalism and the Shaping of American Culture, 1776–1882*, Tchen points out that Orientalism has played a significant role in the formation of American cultural identity and American racial attitudes. Specifically, Tchen distinguishes between three overlapping and successive cultural formations. First of all, 'patrician Orientalism' refers to the fact that the American founding fathers liked to possess oriental things (porcelains, tea sets, silk) because it conferred a 'distinguished' social status (Tchen 1999: 13). A 'commercial Orientalism' then emerged during the period of 1825–65. The Oriental 'other' was routinely represented in the penny press, theatre, and museums. The aim was to satisfy consumer curiosity about Oriental 'exoticism'. Finally, by the 1870s, 'political Orientalism' changed the framing of Orientals in relation to white people away from 'desire-imbued and ambiguous representation' to that of 'an exclusionary and segregationist discourse' (p. xx).

Fuad Sha'ban has investigated American 'political Orientalism' in his book *Islam and Arabs in Early American Thought: the Roots of Orientalism in America* (1991). He defines American Orientalism as a descendant of European heritage and influence, yet with uniquely American characteristics. For Sha'ban this form of Orientalism projects a dual image, namely 'the vision of Zion' and 'the dream of Baghdad' (Sha'ban 1991: xi, 23–26). The vision of Zion refers to the popular American self-image derived from the Old Testament, as God's chosen people. They had fled tyranny and established a new city on a hill (Sha'ban 1991: 141–143).

The metaphor of 'a city upon the hill' used by John Winthrop in his famous 1630 sermon *A Model of Christian Charity*, captures the Puritans' sense of exceptionalism. They believed their undertaking to be divinely ordained. Winthrop also identified the exemplary lessons of this special experience for the rest of humanity. The city, after all, was on high ground with the 'eyes of all people' upon it. In this regard, it is common to find the comparison between the Pilgrim Fathers' trip to the New World and the Biblical Tribes of Israel's flight to the land of Canaan. The settlements of the Pilgrims and Puritans were generally thought of as a 'new Israel'. Many writers embraced this discourse. Consider for example Herman Melville's mid-nineteenth century statement that 'we Americans are the peculiar chosen people – the Israel of our time; we bear the ark of the liberties of the world. God has predestined, mankind expects, great things from our race. Indeed, the political Messiah has come. But he has come in us' (quoted in Sha'ban 2003: 24). The sense that Americans were God's own people in God's own country is the hallmark of a religious conviction that classifies America as the exemplary modern nation.

The editor and essayist John L. O'Sullivan (1813–1895) exemplified this outlook. He declared that America's divinely sanctioned project was to overrun the continent and then to establish 'on earth the moral dignity and salvation of man' (Davidson 2005: 159). O'Sullivan coined the expression 'manifest destiny' to justify the annexation of Texas and the claim to Oregon territory in 1845. During the twentieth century, his famous phrase was frequently invoked to conjoin the will of God with the national objectives of the United States. This constituted one of the founding myths of American politics. Said noted the 'correspondence … between the nineteenth-century doctrine of Manifest Destiny … the territorial expansion of the United States … and the ceaselessly repeated formulae about the need for an American intervention against this or that aggression since World War Two' (Said 1993: 288).[11]

Manifest destiny undeniably encapsulated feelings of American exceptionalism and fostered public belief in the essential union of American virtue and power. Political-religious statements abound in US national rhetoric to the extent that Robert Bellah labelled this language the 'American civil religion' (Bellah 1974: 75). American presidents often invoked manifest destiny in their speeches when mobilising their people for war. Richard Nixon did so explicitly, whereas Presidents George Bush Sr and Bill Clinton inferred their commitment to manifest destiny when they, respectively, prepared for the 1991 Persian Gulf War and the 1999 military campaign in Kosovo (Coles 2002). For example, Bush Sr states several times 'You know … America is a nation founded under God. And from our very beginnings we have relied upon his strength and guidance in war and in peace. And this is something we must never forget' (Coles 2002: 412). Likewise, Clinton referred to the 'chosen nation' as an analogy for America shortly after the bombing of Kosovo had begun. On the observance of Passover, Clinton made an analogy between America and God's Promised Land. In that speech, Clinton stated: 'all Americans can draw inspiration from the story of Passover. It reminds us of our ongoing journey to build our own Promised Land, where all people are free to worship according to their conscience and where our children can grow up safe from the shadows of intolerance and oppression' (Coles 2002: 414). Therefore, it was no surprise when President Bush invoked America's divine destiny in his State of the Union Address subsequent to the 9/11 attacks (29 January 2002):

> Americans will lead by defending liberty and justice because they are right, true and unchanging for all people everywhere … In a single instant, we realized that this will be a decisive decade in the history of liberty – that *we have been called* to a unique role in human events (emphasis added).

The other American Orientalist dimension considered by Sha'ban is the 'dream of Baghdad'. This represents the combination of romance and exoticism deriving from 'a long, cumulative tradition of the imaginary world of The Arabian Nights' (Sha'ban 1991: 177). In this clichéd fantasy, Muslim women are represented as sensual and submissive. Said had already noted the nineteenth-century Orientalist portrayal of Muslim women as 'the creatures of a male power-fantasy,' in which 'they express unlimited sensuality, they are more or less stupid, and above all they are willing' (Said 1979: 207). Sha'ban points out that a commonly printed book in the United States during the nineteenth century was a translation of the Arabian Nights. That collection of fables and fairy tales, often coloured by the sexual desires of the translator, was taken as an accurate portrayal of a timeless, exotic, and mystical East. Tales of harems, genies, and magic carpets found their way into most American homes and libraries.

The works of Bayard Taylor (1825–1878) also exemplify this trend. Taylor travelled throughout Europe, Mexico, Palestine, India, China and Japan. He published twelve best-sellers about his travels, including *A Journey to Central Africa; Life and Landscapes from Egypt to the Negro Kingdoms of the White Nile* (New York, 1854); *The Lands of the Saracen; Pictures of Palestine, Asia Minor, Sicily and Spain* (1854); and *A Visit to India, China and Japan in the Year 1853* (1855). Taylor was very forthcoming about his experiences, gave countless speeches and seminars all over the United States, and wrote many columns in newspapers and literary magazines. Most importantly, Taylor is considered one of the first American Orientalists. *Journey to Central Africa* was the first of Taylor's Oriental books, from which he drew extensively in a series of lectures, entitled *The Arabs*. Taylor's encounters with the Arab Islamic world were framed, categorised and then represented for his audience through historical generalisations.

Taylor's representations evoke the Orient firstly, as the dream location for sensuality, secondly, as an escape from American society, and thirdly, as a realm of fixedness, constancy, and immutability (Moran 2005: 181). Those representations with the strongest legacy derive from the Middle East's supposed pseudo-libertarian depravity in the Middle East. Here, Taylor's Orient embodied the traditional Christian criticism of Islam. The European clergy tended to consider the prophet of Islam as perverse. For example, Dominican Friar Humbert of Lyons (c. 1300) stated that 'Nor did Mahomet teach anything of great austerity … indeed he even allowed many pleasurable things, to do with a multitude of women, abuse of them, and suchlike' (Daniel 1984: 70). Papal propaganda during the crusades contained similar sentiments. Muslim women were depicted 'as defiled and wanton whores and seductresses,' whereas Muslim ease with sexuality was seen as 'offensively non-ascetic behaviour' (Stannard 1992: 179).

But beyond these medieval echoes, the sensual imagery also mirrors Taylor's own desire and that of his readership. As Holly Edwards suggests, 'he presented himself as a charismatic adventurer, causing Victorian women to swoon, and becoming, in a straight-laced nineteenth-century way, a sort of sex symbol, anticipating the stardom of Rudolph Valentino, who also rose to fame in Arab dress' (Edwards 2000: 120). It is striking to see how this Orientalist myth was reversed during the twentieth century. As

Karen Armstrong suggests, the post-Christian West saw itself as sexually liberated compared to sexually repressed Islam, and as such Islam is frequently denigrated as a sexually repressive religion (Armstrong 1992: 230).

Another image of American political Orientalism, not considered by Sha'ban, is that of the 'barbarian' Oriental. A good example of this trend is Susanna Rowson's 1794 play *Slaves in Algiers*. While one initially expects the play to handle the serious topic of slavery in the context of the United States, the entirety of the play takes place on North African soil. The main topic of Rowson's theatrical production concerns the plight of 'white' Americans held as slaves in the 1790s by the 'barbarian' Algerians. Rowson never acknowledged that the Moroccan government (one of the so-called Barbary States) was among the first countries in the world to diplomatically recognise the newly independent United States.[12] Even if one disregards this oversight, the fact that Rowson singles out the practice of slavery in Algiers already constitutes Orientalism in action. Indeed as Darby argues 'various forms of forced labour remained common in Europe and America until well into the nineteenth century: assignment of convicts in Australia, black slavery in the USA, serfdom in Russia, and impressed service in the British Navy could all be compared with slavery in North Africa, and not necessarily to the advantage of the West' (Darby 2003: 126).

Slaves in Algiers' Orientalist discourse is built into a constructed narrative about an imagined enemy, through the creation of a threatening image of the 'other'. The barbarity of North Africans is constantly invoked in the tales of captivity, which cast them as demonic, amoral and inhuman. Yet these same tales never questioned the institution of slavery in America, which was economically dependent upon black slavery from Africa. If slavery was uncivilised in North Africa, was it not equally uncivilised in America? At the same time, *Slaves in Algiers* effectively creates a new form of national and racial identity in a transatlantic context; this discourse served to reinforce feelings of superiority among the American public in relation to the 'other'. The very notion of Barbary captivity emphasises the victimisation of the Christian and the inhumanity of the Muslim. This shaped the mind-set of Americans regarding the Muslim Orient in general, and this was reflected in the immense success of James Riley's 1815 captivity story, *Sufferings in Africa*.[13] Through these narratives, America inherited the ancient ideological schisms between Christianity and Islam.

Their supposed animosity was reflected in economic struggles over trade and shipping rights. This 'had been framed in Europe as a fight between Christian knights and Islamic pirates in which both sides justified enslaving each other' (Baepler 2004: 219). Islam was often constructed as the 'alien' in the construction of Western identity. It serves as the other against which Westerners have struggled to organise a collective self (Hurd 2003: 26–27). In addition, these narratives helped create a sense of political unity against non-western outsiders. This in turn justified the establishment of a huge American navy with a global reach. This political ploy is confirmed by Jared Gardner, who argues that the conflict with the 'Barbary' pirates served to deflect attention from the sharpening tensions between Republicans and Federalists. He states that 'all sides could unite in abhorring the pirates, and Federalists and Republicans alike used the cause to unify Congress and the public in support of the establishment of a navy ... At a time when the nation had much more serious threats to confront, the Algerian captive and the exotic, "oriental" background of this first American "war" united the nation in outrage and indignation' (Gardner 1998: 32–33).

Contemporary Orientalism

In 1798, convinced of their own superiority and authority, Napoleon and his troops invaded Egypt. This historical episode has been described as a 'turning point for Orientalism' (Kolluoglu-Kirli 2003: 100), and 'the start of modern Orientalism' (Said 1979: 120). In fact, this invasion provided the formative moment for the discourse of Orientalism and opened the door to European domination of the Orient, prompting Said to observe that 'with Napoleon's occupation of Egypt, processes were set in motion between East and West that still dominate our contemporary cultural and political perspectives' (Said 1979: 41–42).

There are three main reasons for regarding this late-eighteenth-century event as the start of modern Orientalism. Firstly, Europe at the time of Napoleon's Egyptian invasion had progressed beyond the zealous religiosity of the Crusades, and the Biblical framework previously devised to interpret the Orient was no longer in vogue. People were no longer divided into Christian and heretics, and new classificatory terms such as 'Asiatics' were introduced (Said 1979: 119). This shift in classification redefined Europe's engagement with the Orient from 'the narrowly religious scrutiny by which it had hitherto been examined (and judged) by the Christian West' (Said 1979: 120). Yet this secularisation did not lead to the complete abandonment of the old religious concepts; they were simply 'reconstituted, redeployed [and] redistributed in the secular frameworks' (Said 1979: 120). As Said points out, this occurred because the impulse of modern Orientalism was religious, and the old supernaturalism had been naturalised (Said 1979: 121).

Secondly, Napoleon's invasion of Egypt is important because it represents a 'truly scientific appropriation of one culture by another' (Said 1979: 42). In contrast to the older Orientalism, which relied on imaginary narratives and unusual tales of voyagers, this time it was the power/knowledge nexus that led the modern Orientalist endeavour, as one hundred and fifty handpicked scientists, artists and engineers (known as the savants) accompanied the 55,000 troops of the Napoleonic expedition (Smith 2006). Those 'chemists, historians, biologists, archaeologists, surgeons, and antiquarians' were, according to Said, 'the learned division of the army' (Said 1979: 83–84). They 'provided a scene or setting for Orientalism, since Egypt and subsequently the other Islamic lands were viewed as the live province, the laboratory, the theatre, of effective Western knowledge about the Orient' (Said 1979: 43).

Thirdly and most importantly, Orientalism moved from the cultural sphere to the political, becoming intertwined with imperialism. As Said explains, 'European awareness of the Orient transformed itself from being textual and contemplative into being administrative, economic and even military (Said 1979: 210). Orientalism, and more particularly its 'corporate' offshoot, informed Western political involvement in the Orient, preparing the ground for, and sustaining, Western imperial hegemony over Oriental regions. Thus, the new relation between the West and the Orient was based on power and dominance, and Orientalism served as the ideological vehicle for dominance over the Orient. The apogee of this hegemonic relationship was reached in 1914, when colonialism claimed about 84 per cent of the earth's surface (Said 1993: 8). In order to administer these newly acquired spaces, colonial authorities further encouraged Orientalism's development and institutionalisation.

From the mid-twentieth century, a pivotal geo-political shift affected Orientalism. As a consequence of World War II, the United States replaced Europe as the world's dominant region. Orientalism became an American enterprise rather than a European one, and its institutionalisation was conducted through the development of 'Area Studies' (Kolluoglu-Kirli 2003: 107). Said argues that area studies, and especially those devoted to Middle East and Islamic studies accumulated knowledge upon Orientalist assumptions. Subsequently, stereotypes about Islam and Arabs were transmitted from one generation to another, and were able to survive revolutions, world wars, and the literal dismemberment of Empires (Said 1979: 222).

Inheriting the Western Orientalist apparatus has had a direct impact on American policy makers' perceptions. It has prompted the tendency to underestimate the peoples of the region, and to dismiss their legitimate nationalist aspirations.[14] Hence the Truman Doctrine (1948) and the Eisenhower Doctrine (1957) were directed not just against the communist bloc, but also Third World national liberation movements that aspired to achieve national independence. In Iran, this point was illustrated by the overthrow of the democratically elected Mohammad Mossadegh by the CIA in 1953. In *All the Shah's Men*, Stephen Kinzer, depicts Mossadegh as a nationalist leader whose entire political career was shaped by two ideas: placing Iran on the path of democracy and establishing Iranian control over Iranian resources. Yet, Mossadegh's national dream was swiftly repressed, and the US sent a clear message to the Middle East that it was less interested in democracy than in compliant regimes. The CIA-restored Shah was celebrated as an 'enlightened' and 'modern' ruler by the *London Times*, while its counterpart *New York Times* provided an Orientalist-tainted editorial judgement[15] (Chomsky 1992: 50).

Edward Said has traced the continuation of Orientalist thought among American academics. A case in point was Harold W. Glidden's 1972 article in the *American Journal of Psychiatry* entitled the 'Arab World'.[16] In four pages, he made generalisations about 100 million people and 1,300 years of history, and purported to uncover 'the inner workings of Arab behaviour.' They were said to be conformist, hierarchical, egoistic, dishonest and prone to violence and revenge. There were within academia some attempts to correct this distorted image. For example, Albert Hourani's *A History of the Arab Peoples* (1991) provided a fourteenth-century overview of Arab peoples. His approach is methodical and meticulous and emphasises the contextual background required to understand the rich history of an entire people and culture (especially the important Arab contributions to world civilisation in the areas of science, architecture and philosophy). Hourani's work examined the gap between the Arab period of early Islam and the modern era. He also corrected the stubbornly resistant stereotype that Arabs were a bunch of rural Bedouins by highlighting the rich urban legacy of Arab culture in cities such as Fez, Tunis, Cairo, Damascus and Baghdad.

Despite this contribution, essentialist Orientalist discourse became omnipresent within American literature and the mass media. Arab identity was reduced to Islam and Islam to a religion of fanatical incitement. During the 1970s Said observed that while 'it is no longer possible to write learned (or even popular) disquisitions on either "the Negro mind" or "the Jewish personality," it is perfectly possible to engage in research, such as "the Islamic mind," or "the Arab character" (Said 1979: 259–262). A good example of this trend was *The Arab Mind* (1974), written by Zionist scholar Raphael Patai. He used psychological and cultural generalisations to claim that Arabs' alleged backwardness was rooted in mental configurations. They are said to have a 'sense of marginality which never allows an Arab to detach himself from his traditional culture' (Tuastad 2003: 592). Patai died in 1996, but his book was revived in 2002, just in time for the war in Iraq. This time, it was tagged as 'the bible of the neo-cons on Arab behaviour', and was said to be a 'required reading' by US policy makers and military personnel in order to understand Iraqi behaviour (Hersh 2004: 42). Writing the foreword of this new edition, army colonel Norvell B. De Atkine says that Patai's book informs his briefings for military teams deployed to the Middle East. In his view, the book deciphers the Arabs' 'seemingly irrational hatred' and 'rejection of Western values' (Patai 2002: x-xviii).

Patai's book recalls the works of another contemporary Orientalist, Bernard Lewis, prolific author and political commentator on the Middle East. Described as the *New York Times* reviewer and 'doyen of Middle Eastern studies', Lewis gained major prominence after the Al Qaeda suicide bombings of September 11 2001. Various reports referred to his close ties with Deputy Secretary of Defense Paul Wolfowitz and other senior figures in the Bush administration.[17] Edward Said was Lewis' most outspoken critic, and had clashed with him over previous decades (as exemplified in a famous 1982 exchange in *The New York Review of Books*).[18] Said's criticism of Lewis, was not that he was ignorant, but that he was arrogant and contemptuous of Muslims, and disguised political agendas within scholarship. In an interview, Said went as far as to call Lewis a scholar-combatant, alongside Fouad Ajami and Daniel Pipes (Said 1991).

Lewis' bestselling book *What Went Wrong* (2002) re-affirmed ideas he had expressed since the publication of *Islam and the West* (1993), namely that democracy and modernity are incompatible with Islam; that Muslims feel humiliated because of the West's superiority, and that Muslims are nostalgic for the ancient past. As is habitually the case with Orientalist scholarship, Lewis ignores the historic Western role in Middle-Eastern affairs, as exemplified by the legacy of colonialism or the occupation of Arab territories by Israel (only mentioned once in *What Went Wrong*). For him, these are merely illustrations of a vicious 'blame game', in which Arabs/Muslims, while not wanting to learn from the 'infidels', gratuitously project their failures into criticisms of European imperialism and American policies concerning Israel (Lewis 2002: 151–160). Lewis avoids any serious contextual analysis of the ongoing crises in the Middle East. This shortcoming is highlighted by as'ad Abu Khalil who criticised Lewis for deriving his assessment of the Palestinians' political predicament from a de-contextualised interpretation of a ninth-century Arabic manuscript (Abu Khalil 2002: 18). This kind of essentialist presumption undermines Lewis' scholarly understanding of Middle-Eastern affairs. Some of Lewis' critics like Nader Hashemi believe that Lewis tries to project a line back to medieval and early Islamic history, so that the impact of the British and French colonialists, and the repressive rule of many post-colonial leaders are ignored' (Hirsh 2004).

However, by highlighting Lewis' shortcomings, I do not adhere to the so-called Occidentalist[19] thesis, which tends to blame the 'West' entirely, while exonerating Arabs and Muslims from their due responsibilities within particular crises. In this regard, I endorse Said's view that:

> the absence of democracy and the culture of violence that now are prevailing in the Arab world are Arabs' responsibilities to rectify, but because the West has important even massive interest in the Arab world and as it regularly intervenes to protect

those interests ... a certain responsibility for what is taking place, and continues to occur there, must also be borne by the West. (Said 1992)

These comments reflect the views of other scholars, such as the Moroccan philosopher Mohammed Abed Al-Jabri, who contends that Arabs can fully enter the age of technology, participate in production, and aspire to express their role in the world, but only once they succeed in building a model of Arab unity based on social justice and democracy. This prescription did not prevent Al-Jabri from highlighting various external obstacles, such as American hegemony and the role of Israel in obstructing Middle Eastern development (Fritsch-El-Alaoui 2005: 47–48).

But nuanced voices, such as Al-Jabri's, had little public opportunity to press their point, whereas Lewis' ideas underpin respected canons of knowledge about the Middle East. He conceived of a 'Clash of the Civilizations' decades before Samuel Huntington. At a Middle East conference at Johns Hopkins University in 1957, he declared that 'we shall be better able to understand this situation if we view the present discontents of the Middle East not as a conflict between states or nations, but as a clash between civilizations' (Glass 2004). At that time, he did not have the ear of American policy makers, who were busy containing the Soviet Union. Moreover, Washington had still some credibility in the Middle East (despite its role in toppling the nationalist Iranian prime minister in 1953). The United States prevented colonial powers France and Britain from returning to the Middle East (during the 1956 Suez crisis). As Glass observes, Lewis' reference to the Christendom-Islam split found an audience among American Cold War warriors only when they lost their Soviet nemesis (Glass 2004).[20]

During the 1950s and 1960s, the United States sought to counteract communist and nationalist forces by building diplomatic connections with Middle Eastern regimes (Saudi Arabia, Jordan, Morocco, and Pakistan). In 1955, The Central Treaty Organization (CENTO, or the Baghdad Pact) was established to include Iraq, Turkey, Pakistan, and Iran, as well as the United Kingdom. CENTO's main goal was to contain the Soviet Union along its south-western frontier. As a result, the United States established communications and electronic intelligence facilities in Iran, and began operating U-2 intelligence flights over the USSR from bases in Pakistan.

At the same time, the Soviet Union stepped up its efforts to gain local allies in the Middle East, and slowly succeeded in gaining a strong foothold in the region (Egypt until 1974, Syria, Iraq after 1958, Algeria, Libya after 1969, Southern Yemen etc.). As result, Washington perceived that a majority of Arab states were on the side of the enemy. This consolidated the United States – Israel alliance, which further alienated the peoples of the Middle East. From the 1970s, the relationship between the United States and Middle Eastern states was strained by the 1973–1974 Arab oil embargo, the Iranian Revolution of 1978–1979, and the Iranian student takeover of the American Embassy in Tehran. The ensuing hostage crisis, which fatally damaged Carter's presidency, contributed to the election of Ronald Reagan to the White House. He was determined to compensate for Jimmy Carter's alleged lack of leadership, and came to office with the Middle East high on his agenda (Crenshaw 1995). Ironically, since the mid-1970s, the United States encouraged Islamism[21] as a counter-weight to communist influence in the Middle East (Marquand and Andoni 1996). Ronald Reagan even invited the leaders of the Afghan Mujahedeen to the White House praising them as 'the moral equivalent of America's founding fathers' (Al-Azm 2004: 115).

However, Reagan also rhetorically threatened Libya and Iran and all those who supported them. As a result, there was a marked increase in acts of political violence from Middle Eastern militant groups, and far more Americans were killed during the 1980s than the 1990s (Lizza 2004). For example, following the US military intervention in Lebanon (29 September 1982), suicide bombers attacked the US Embassy in Beirut (18 April 1983), killing sixty-three people. Later that year (23 October 1983), a 12,000-pound bomb destroyed the Marine barracks in Beirut killing 241 Americans – the most deadly terrorist strike against the United States until September 11 2001. Other violent incidents[22] combined with US military interventions in Lebanon (1983) and Libya (1986), along with covert actions against Iran, further soured relations between the United States and its Middle Eastern detractors. This heated environment fuelled, according to Burke III, a 'new Orientalism' with a new object of fear and study: Islam. By the end of the 1980s, the mass media had established a simplistic monolithic Islam opposed to the West.

Accordingly, Bernard Lewis published in 1990 an *Atlantic Monthly* article entitled 'Roots of Muslim rage'. He reduced complex political, economic and social dynamics to a simplistic leitmotif: the 'rage' of Muslims at 'us' happens because 'what is evil and unacceptable [to them] is the domination of infidels over true believers' (Lewis 1990: 53). Such over-simplifications ignore particular political grievances in the Middle East by framing all resentments in terms of religious difference and conflict. The resuscitation of such prejudices became a discernible pattern after Western politics lost its 'other' with the collapse of organised communism (Turner 2002: 109). Saddam Hussein's invasion of Kuwait in 1990 provided the perfect pretext for a new American geo-strategic objective: reshaping the Middle East so as to control energy sources. Oil and construction companies supported this objective as did neo-conservatives and pro-Israel lobbyists imbued with Orientalist ideas.

By the early 1990s, neo-conservative ideas and attitudes had become a political force in the United States. Declarations of American exceptionalism and the desire to employ military power permeated Washington's political elites (Halper and Clarke 2004: 67). Geopolitical interests in the Middle East brought together neo-conservative doctrine and the prejudices of Orientalist scholarship. This bond rests upon 'a hatred of Arabs and Muslims, an identification with Israel, and racism towards decolonized "Third World" people of the global South, who are seen as inferior, primitive [and] backward' (Abdulhadi 2004: 85–86). An important consequence of the neo-conservative–Orientalist convergence was the resurgence of crude medieval-style rhetoric, highlighting the opposition between Islam and Christianity as a looming problem for the West. Samuel Huntington best exemplifies this outlook. In *The Clash of Civilizations*, he declares that the possibility of dangerous clashes between East and West rests upon the fundamental differences that exist between two civilisations – 'The West and the rest – and more specifically 'between Muslim and Asian societies on the one hand, and the West on the other' (Huntington 1997: 183). Huntington presupposes that the West's global power is diminishing, and argues that rearmament strategies are necessary.

Initially, the academic community soundly criticised Huntington's book on numerous grounds. Some authors maintained that civilisations should be thought of as processes or tendencies rather than as fixed and bounded essences (Cox 2000). In this regard, Edward Said explains that 'Huntington ... wants to make "civilizations" and "identities" into what they are not: shut-down, sealed-off entities that have been purged of the myriad currents and counter-currents that animate human history.' He went on to observe that 'this history not only contains wars of religion and imperial conquest but also expressions of exchange, cross-fertilization and sharing' (Said 2001). Similarly, Ishtiaq Ahmed deplores how Huntington's worldview downgrades human purpose to tribal instincts which negate 'the long and arduous struggle of human beings to transcend the bounds of race, religion, caste, sect and language'. For Ahmed, the 'clash of civilisations' thesis denies the notion of universal human rights and the spirit of internationalism and global solidarity that humanity has long struggled to achieve (Ahmed 2003).

From an international relations perspective, some academics remarked that foreign policy decisions were made by governments, not civilisations (Abrahamian 2003: 530). Others put forward evidence which falsified Huntington's thesis. Islamic Iran, for example, has sided in recent years with Orthodox Christian Russia against the Muslim republic of Chechnya. Iran also took the side of Orthodox Christian Armenia against Muslim Azerbaijan, while backing Hindu India in its confrontation against Muslim Pakistan (Cornell 1998: 51). Showing the empirical shortcomings in Huntington's thesis, Chiozza meticulously researched all the conflicts that took place from 1946 to 1997, including the first eight years of the post-Cold War era. The findings of this study reveal that disputes between groups belonging to different 'civilisations' are in general less likely to happen, while countries belonging to the same civilisation are more conflict prone (Chiozza 2002).[23]

Huntington's book exemplified how Orientalist treatments of Islam pervaded popular literature during the 1990s. For example, in *God Has Ninety Nine Names: Reporting from a Militant Middle East* (1996), Judith Miller (who has covered the region for 25 years for the *New York Times*) provides accounts of Egypt, Saudi Arabia, Sudan, Algeria, Libya, Lebanon, Syria, Jordan, Israel, and Iran. Yet despite her extensive experience in the region, Miller's account is full of double standards. When referring to pro-American regimes such Saudi Arabia or Jordan, Miller legitimises their crushing of internal opposition by depicting such actions as a 'strategic decision'. She also comments that it was 'natural that the king, or any ruler, would try to survive' (Miller 1996: 340–341). Yet, the repressive deeds of an anti-US regime, such as Syria, are depicted as 'state terrorism' (Miller 1996: 15–16). Miller omits local contextual analysis by classifying Arab rulers in terms of their distance from Washington. In the case of Egypt, Miller does not consider the political, economic and social grievances behind the rise of violent political movements there. For Miller, only Arab tradition and mentality can explain turmoil in the region. In this regard, she repeats Lewis' claim that Arabs like to avoid blame for their circumstances 'by spinning elaborate conspiracy theories' (Miller 1996: 355). Miller described the American-supported Egyptian ruler Hosni Mubarak, who has a poor human rights record, as 'a patriot who wanted only the best for Egypt,' and stated that she 'found his candour disarming' (Miller 1996: 44).

Another example of 1990s Orientalist writing is Benjamin Barber's *Jihad vs. McWorld*. In my view, Barber's chapter on Islam is a more sophisticated version of the Lewis/Huntington paradigm. Undeniably, Barber conducts a good analysis of the correlation between global corporate capitalism and fundamentalist movements throughout the world. Yet, when he handles the issue of Islam, Barber regurgitates classic Orientalist themes. He states:

> although it is clear that Islam is a complex religion that by no means is synonymous with Jihad, it is relatively inhospitable to democracy and that inhospitality in turn nurtures conditions favourable to parochialism, anti-modernism, exclusiveness, and hostility to "others," the characteristics that constitute what I have called Jihad (Barber 1996: 204).

Critics of Barber, reproach to him his lack of evidence (Barber refers only to the Quran and seventh-century Medina) and the fact that he omits the events of the last 100 years. Khaldoun Samman argues that 'an individual living in 1850 would not be able to recognize the same Islamic real estate some 70 years later, no matter how much he read the Quran' (Samman 2005: 166).

The preceding examples demonstrate how Orientalism continues to pervade the prevailing knowledge/power nexus albeit in more subtle ways. After the fall of the Soviet Union, the American global posture gave pre-eminence to the Middle East for various strategic reasons. Therefore, the official discourse drew upon Orientalist rhetoric as a way to establish an Arab/Islamic 'other'. Past imagined narratives became associated with present populations in the Middle East, and ancient myths were refashioned to identify Islam and Arabs as a single cultural entity, without internal complexities, and most importantly without any systemic relationship to the larger world. Contemporary Orientalism continues to focus on the Arab/Muslim Orient and has legitimised US imperial policy since the suicide bombings of September 2001.

Definitions and discourses of terrorism

According to the Oxford English Dictionary, the words 'terrorism' and 'terrorists' were first used in 1795 to characterise state violence in post-revolutionary France. Thus, the systematic use of terror was initially understood as a coercive technique or method of subjection used by rulers to control the people. In the nineteenth-century, the term 'terrorist' was rapidly extended to groups or individuals that carried out violent actions and assassinations against ruling elites. Such victims of assassinations included the French President Sadi Carnot (1894), Empress Elizabeth of Austria (1897), the Spanish Prime Minister Antonio Canova (1897), the Italian king Umberto I (1900), and the President of the United States William McKinley (1901). In that period, terrorism was already the leading preoccupation of politicians, police chiefs, journalists, and writers (Laqueur, 1996).

Despite evidence of terrorist tactics within ancient Israel,[24] there is a tendency to associate terrorist actions with Arabs and Muslims irrespective of evidence (Wilkins and Downing 2002: 419). Thus, according to the chronology of terror compiled by Dobson and Payne (1986), the first hijacking of a plane was conducted by Palestinians in July 1968. Yet, this allegation contradicts findings of the American Federal Aviation Administration stating that 79 hijackings occurred worldwide between 1930 and 1967. A notorious hijacking happened in 1956, when the French authorities hijacked a plane carrying the leaders of the Algerian Liberation Front (FLN), including Ahmed Ben Bella, the first president of post-independent Algeria (Falligot 2001).

It is interesting to note that the term 'terrorism' only started to occupy a prominent place in the media and academia after 1967 (Guelke 1995: 2). The 1967 Six-Day war in the Middle East, in which Israel militarily defeated three Arab countries, led Palestinian groups to undertake armed interventions for themselves. After 1967, Palestinians who had lost their entire homeland to Israel resorted to highly mediatised violent actions. It should be remembered that the 'armed struggle' was carried in the name of socialist liberation, which also attracted numerous educated urban youth in Western Europe and elsewhere. Baader Meinhof, for example, was the most active left-wing armed group in West Germany. This group, founded in 1970, voiced the resentment of German leftist students against 'capitalism' in Germany, and the alliance with Washington during the Vietnam War. The Italian Red Brigades (formed in 1970 and still operational today though considerably diminished) sought to create a revolutionary state through armed struggle and to separate Italy from the Western Alliance. Other European groups resorting to political violence expressed nationalist and ethnic grievances. Thus, the Irish paramilitary group PIRA (commonly referred to as IRA) fought to end Northern Ireland's status within the United Kingdom and create a united Ireland by violent means (until the 1998 Good Friday agreement). Likewise, the Basque paramilitary group ETA sought to create a socialist state for the Basque people in the Basque Country, independent from Spain and France. In Latin America: the Colombian group FARC, which is still operational today, was established in 1964 as the military wing of the Colombian Communist Party. Similarly, during the 1960s and 1970s, the Tupamaros in Uruguay (known as the MLN) used urban guerrilla tactics against Uruguay's oppressive military dictatorship.

After 1967, the widespread use of political violence generated numerous of books and articles with the term 'terrorism' in their title. Norman Provizer, the author of two major bibliographies on terrorism, pointed out that over 99 per cent of the general works on terrorism had been published from 1968 (Guelke 1995: 2). Frequent use of the term 'terrorism' did not reflect any scientific precision. Indeed, there is no universally agreed upon definition of terrorism. One approach defines terrorism as

> a particular use of violence for political ends, where the violence is intended to create a psychological reaction in a person or group of people – the psychological target – to make them act in a way which the attacker desires (Drake 1998: 53).

Another definition defines terrorism as 'the victimization of unarmed civilians in an attempt to affect the policies of the government that leads those civilians' (Carr 1997). One of the most serious academic attempts to find an appropriate definition of terrorism was undertaken by Schmid and Yongman in their monumental work, *Political Terrorism* (1984). These experts on terrorism listed some 109 definitions. Their attempt to narrow all of these definitions into one resulted in the following statement:

> Terrorism is an anxiety-inspiring method of repeated violent action, employed by (semi-) clandestine individual, group, or state actors, for idiosyncratic, criminal, or political reasons, whereby – in contrast to assassination – the direct targets of violence are not the main targets. The immediate human victims of violence are generally chosen randomly (targets of opportunity) or selectively (representative or symbolic targets) from a target population, and serve as message generators. Threat- and violence-based communication processes between terrorist (organization), (imperilled) victims, and main targets are used to manipulate the main target (audience(s)), turning it into a target of terror, a target of demands, or a target of attention, depending on whether intimidation, coercion, or propaganda is primarily sought. (Schmid and Yongman 1984: 5–6)

From an official perspective, this definition is problematic because it includes the violence inflicted by the armed forces of nation-states alongside that perpetrated by non-state or sub-state entities. In any case, no matter what the general definition is, terrorism is not simply an expression of violence; it is an act of politics by those who declare that no other channels of political engagement exist (Flint 2003: 161).

In theory, there is a difference between armed forces and non-state organisations: state forces in principle respect war conventions that limit violence against civilians, while sub-state organisations eschew these conventions. In practice, however the difference is not clear-cut. Deliberate terrorising of civilians by conventional military forces is often the norm. Accordingly, terrorism can be defined as 'the systematic use of coercive intimidation against civilians for political goals' (Norris et al. 2003: 6). This definition does not leave out state actors. Examples in this regard abound; the Japanese invasion of Nanking, the London blitz, the Allied bombing of Germany and the atomic bombing of Hiroshima and Nagasaki, all targeted civilians in the hope of shattering morale. This is synonymous with the exercise of terrorism. From World War II onwards, mass bombing of civilians has become an essential tool of military strategy. In this regard, it has been suggested that these same strategies encouraged the adoption of terrorism by non-state groups (Carruthers 2000: 164).

Hence, terrorism is a word, which is deployed rhetorically and selectively for given purposes. For example, the attacks upon civilians in Nicaragua by the US-supported 'contra' rebels of the 1980s claimed over 3000 civilian lives. They were never denounced by American mainstream media as terrorism. Again, the massacre of over 2000 Palestinian civilians in the Sabra and Shatilla refugee camps in Beirut in 1982 is rarely referred to as terrorist activity, and the alleged perpetrators of that massacre, members of the Lebanese Forces and their supporters in the Israeli military, are rarely called terrorists (Kapitan and Schulte 2002: 172). Inconsistency of usage is further exacerbated when former 'terrorists' become elected politicians, and/or sometimes central figures on the global political scene; Nelson Mandela, Menachem Begin, and Yasser Arafat all made the transition from being regarded as terrorists to being recognised as statesmen and peacemakers. In fact, they all have been awarded the Nobel Peace Prize and Mandela in particular is considered to be a paragon of moral leadership.

To avoid the inconsistencies and the polemics behind the term 'terrorism', I prefer to adhere to Noam Chomsky's comprehensive yet short definition. For him, terrorism refers to 'the threat or use of violence to intimidate or coerce.' This definition is opportune because it incorporates all kinds of terror. Herman (1982) had previously made the distinction between state terror, which he termed 'wholesale terror', and the terror of isolated individuals and small groups which he termed 'retail terror'. Herman argues that the latter had been overemphasised notwithstanding the pain and suffering which resulted. This allows official manipulations of public fears and the 'engineering of consent' (Herman 1982: 212).

As argued earlier, any understanding of terrorism depends on the definition, which in turn depends on the perspective. Some academics identify four ways of talking about terrorism: official, alternative, populist, and oppositional. The official perspective tends to be the most prevalent. It 'represents the set of views, arguments, explanations and policy suggestions advanced by those who speak for the state' (Schlesinger et al. 1983: 2–27). The key official definers of terrorism are government ministers, conservative politicians and top security personnel. For them, terrorism is an extreme form of criminality with no political significance (Schlesinger et al. 1983: 2–7). Consequently, terrorism represents illegitimate political violence as opposed to the legitimate force used by the state. This stance allows official authorities to label all attempts to change the status quo by coercive means as terrorist manifestations. This delegitimises national liberation movements, as well as social economic revolutions (Weinberger 2003: 65–66). Labelling is part of the war of ideas that accompanies overt hostilities; 'terrorism' is thus a term designed to vilify opponents. This label automatically discredits any individual or group to which it is affixed; it places them outside the norms of acceptable social and political behaviour. Terrorists by definition are people who cannot be reasoned with.[25] The labelling process is an ideological exercise which turns state violence into a legitimate act of war, and 'terrorist' operations into acts of gratuitous brutality (Meeuf, 2006).

In *Policing the Crisis*, Hall argues that the mass media lend legitimacy to the views of official sources, and thus serve to symbolically reproduce the institutional order of society. Official authorities are primary definers, able to set agendas; they 'command the field [and] set the terms of reference'. Moreover counter-definitions are usually denied access, or fitted into the dominant agenda, leading to 'strategic areas of silence'. The state may be rhetorically challenged as in investigatory journalism, but the 'prevailing tendency is to reproduce, amidst all their contradictions, the definitions of the powerful, of the dominant ideology' (Hall et al. 1978: 59, 65–66). To this end, the media tends to consolidate the ruling ideology by criminalising various forms of dissent. As a result, coverage of political violence becomes a ritual, which always features condemnation from politicians and community leaders, the stories and grief of the victims, and the reaction of the government.

Media organisations thereby find themselves constrained to adopt a 'counter-terrorist' stance, facing popular and possibly legal sanctions if they fail to comply. In the case of the IRA and Northern Ireland, former British Prime Minister Thatcher criticised the BBC and independent programs for allowing interviews with republican groups. She did not want their views disseminated to a wider public. Thus, in October 1988 the British government imposed a broadcasting ban; several named Irish organisations, including the IRA, Sinn Fein, the UDA and UFF could not be heard speaking on television and radio (this ban lasted until September 1994). The ban turned out to be farcical; for example, when Gerry Adams was Member of Parliament for West Belfast, he could appear on television in that capacity, speaking about housing, roads or schools, but he could not address political matters on behalf of Sinn Fein. He could be seen and his views reported, but his voice could not be broadcast (Schlesinger et al. 1983: 23–27).

In the United States, every president from Carter to George W. Bush labelled and externalised various forms of political violence. After the suicide attacks of 9/11, the discourse on terrorism became far more prominent. It is undeniable that these attacks constituted an unprecedented attack on American soil, in which thousands of people died and landmark buildings crumbled. September 11 witnessed one of the most dramatic media spectacles in history. Hundreds of TV cameras and commentators throughout the world focused on downtown New York, as graphic images displayed panic scenes of wounded and dazed people fleeing. Almost immediately American television news drew upon the discourse of patriotism to describe the atrocity. American news media relied heavily on elite sources, and the frames that they conveyed, to mobilise public support. Initial US news coverage did not even open a debate about whether or not to go to war or how best to respond.

In this regard, Karim H. Karim observed that on September 11, 'most experts interviewed responded to security matters and did not seem interested in the larger political, social and economic causes of the attacks.' Consequently, the focus was primarily on the immediate reaction rather than on the larger issues (Karim 2002: 105). Similarly, Robert McChesney has challenged the pre-eminence given to the official perspective over others in mainstream news stories after 9/11:

> in a case like the current war on terrorism, where the elites and official sources are unified on the core issues, the nature of our press coverage is uncomfortably close to that found in authoritarian societies with limited formal press freedom (McChesney 2002: 95).

The aftermath of the 9/11 attacks witnessed moves toward information control by the Bush administration, as well as a journalistic inclination towards 'patriotism' rather than impartiality. This impacted greatly on the ability of reporters to do their job properly. The reporters and commentators dispatched to comment on the events of September 11 became propaganda conduits for the military rather than independent analysts. Personalities such as John McCain, Henry Kissinger, Lawrence Eagleburger, James Baker, and Jeanne Kirkpatrick, immediately described the attacks as an 'act of war' and called for military retaliation, a line that dominated media discourse for a considerable time. The frame proposed by the administration, namely the 'War on Terror', was not especially new despite the fact that September 11 is often referred to as 'the day that changed the world' (Campbell 2002: 12). Indeed the 'War on Terror' idiom was first declared in 1981 when the Reagan administration targeted 'state-sponsored terrorism' with particular reference to Nicaragua.[26]

The political complicity of the US media with ruling elites has also economic dimensions. Indeed, since the mid-1980s media ownership is increasingly concentrated. This state of affairs led media critics Herman and Chomsky to propose their propaganda model in *Manufacturing Consent*. In this perspective, the concentration of media ownership reinforces the mainstream media's dependence on elite information sources. Large news media institutions may also participate in propaganda campaigns helpful to elite interests (Herman and Chomsky 1988: 303). Media content undeniably reflects the pressures and priorities of owners. McChesney argues that 'their constant drumbeat for profit, their concern with minimizing costs and enhancing revenues, invariably influences the manner in which news is collected and reported' (McChesney 2003: 306). Furthermore, McChesney notes that budget-cutting on journalism has had a negative impact, 'it has meant a relaxation or alteration, sometimes severe, of professional news standards' (McChesney 2003: 309). Other studies confirm that news media have economic motivations to align with government leaders in times of crisis (Hutcheson et al. 2004).

Immediately after 9/11, alternative perspectives to the official discourse were virtually absent in American mainstream media. In general, the alternative perspective is advanced by civil libertarians, liberal academics, journalists and some politicians. While alternative views do not fundamentally challenge official assumptions about the legitimate use of violence, they do consider the impact of excessive repression on the rule of law and democratic rights (Schlesinger et al. 1983: 2–27). The absence of alternative perspectives immediately post-9/11 is related to the fact that terrorism was represented as beyond law. Irene Porras gives an insightful analysis on this matter:

> To say anything about terrorism or terrorists, it turns out, is to be caught in a normative bind: one must either be for or against terrorism. In terrorism discourse, if I am not explicitly against terrorism then I am necessarily for it. There is no middle ground, no ambivalent position available. Not to condemn terrorism is to condone it, and to condone terrorism is to be morally as bad as a terrorist. Indeed to publicly sympathize with terrorism may itself become a terrorist offence. Thus I find that there is really only one legitimate position that I may hold vis-à-vis terrorism and terrorists. I must think terrorism a great evil. (Porras 1995: 298–299)

So generally speaking, there was little discussion in mainstream media about domestic legal mechanisms and virtually no focus upon international law. When they were mentioned, 'legal responses were condemned as a failed policy that provided terrorists with too many procedural safeguards' (McMillan 2004: 391). The official perspective's devaluation of legal procedure as a response to terrorism has been highlighted by many authors (Chomsky 2001; Porras 1995; Zulaika and Douglass 1996). By disregarding the dimension of law, official terrorism discourses rely upon political violence to reaffirm the legitimacy of the Western state and the boundaries of the Western community (Porras 1995). Just as Orientalism constructed an image of the self in contrast to that of the 'other', so the official discourse on terrorism positioned the state as barrier against outside forces. Annamarie Oliverio has argued in *The State of Terror* that terrorism has become the ideal means to write 'the script for historical interpretations of national identity and political sovereignty'. The end of the Cold War and the disappearance of the rival communist 'Evil Empire', means that the discourse of terrorism is an alternative means for constructing national identity (Oliverio 1998: 6, 37). This, in turn, unleashes even further violence against outside forces both at home and abroad.

Nonetheless, there were some attempts to provide an alternative discourse on terrorism. Al Jazeera exemplifies this endeavour (this will be discussed in more detail in later chapters). The internet too has proved to be a mine of alternative discourses on terrorism. Indeed, this period witnessed an increase in blogs that discussed the prospects of war in the Middle East. Those opposed to the war pointed to the perceived shortcomings of the mainstream mass media in regard to informing the public of the possible dangers, risks and threats associated with the American military actions (Allan 2004: 358). One of the bloggers exemplifying this trend was Christopher Allbritton, who travelled to Iraq thanks to contributions from his readers. From there, he filed daily stories and responded to e-mail queries from his readers (Allan 2004: 359). The purpose of Allbritton's blog was to provide an alternative perspective on the conflict.

The populist discourse on terrorism was noticeably present in the media post-9/11. Populism has been defined by Daniele Albertazzi and Duncan McDonnell as

> an ideology which pits a virtuous and homogeneous people against a set of elites and dangerous 'others' who are together depicted as depriving (or attempting to deprive) the sovereign people of their rights, values, prosperity, identity and voice (Albertazzi and McDonnell 2008: 3).[27]

The populist perspective insists that combating terrorism and restoring order requires a tough and uncompromising response. This perspective calls for a 'full-blooded' war against terrorism aimed at restoring order by whatever means necessary. It has been suggested that war is the 'supreme populist moment' (Steinert 2003: 266). Such populism enlists the greatest number of co-citizens to work for a shared goal, thereby leading to a militant form of national unity. Examples of such discourse proliferated after 9/11. In the *New York Post*, a day after the attacks, columnist Steve Dunleavy wrote: '... kill the bastards. A gunshot between the eyes, blow them to smithereens, poison them if you have to. As for cities or countries that host these worms, bomb them into basketball courts' (Mokhiber & Weissman 2001). Likewise on Fox News, Bill O'Reilly said on his show The O'Reilly Factor (17 September 2001) that 'the US should bomb the Afghan infrastructure to rubble – the airport, the power plants, their water facilities, and the roads.' He added that the people of any country are ultimately responsible for the government they have. O'Reilly then went on to say: 'the Germans were responsible for Hitler; the Afghans are responsible for the Taliban. We should not target civilians. But if they do not rise up against this criminal government, they starve, period'.

Finally, the oppositional perspective is put forward by those who perform or support acts of politically motivated violence in support of given objectives. Adherents of political violence try to gain respectability in the public sphere through statements, briefings, staged events, publications and murals. In place of terrorist discourse, they use alternative terms such as 'guerrilla', 'liberation army' or 'freedom fighter'. The Irish Republican Army (IRA), for example, used terminology which promoted the group as a legitimate army with military structures and ranks. The IRA had an 'army council', 'brigades', 'battalions', 'companies' and 'active service units'. Members held ranks such as 'commander', 'brigadier', 'quartermaster' etc. The IRA commonly described members, who were serving time in prison for violent acts, as 'POWs' or as 'political prisoners' (Cooke 1998: 7). The oppositional perspective can also include people who explain the 'terrorist' viewpoint without supporting their methods. Robert Fisk and John Pilger provide some of the best examples of this perspective. Other examples include Robert McChesney, Noam Chomsky, Edward Said, and Tariq Ali. However, this outlook receives only minor mass media exposure (Schlesinger et al. 1983: 22–27). Yet again, these authors can be read on the internet, worldwide. In fact, the internet has provided an opportunity for even more radical views to be accessed by a wide public. For example, the Iraqi Resistance website[28] has actively reported and explained the views and motives of the local Iraqi fighters. It also includes galleries of photos, showing overwhelmed American troops, and as is usual for this type of communication, images of triumphant opposition forces.

In sum, one can say that all these perspectives on terrorism actively seek the attention of media. Some of these perspectives overlap, and writers might use a combination of perspectives (i.e. populist/official, alternative/oppositional). It is evident that the official perspective gets most of the attention, while the populist perspective is prevalent and serves its purpose of domestic unity (especially when the American military goes to war). The institutional tendency of the news media to filter out anti-elite perspectives explains the marginalisation of alternative discourses on terrorism[29]; oppositional perspectives received little if any coverage after 9/11. However, alternative and oppositional arguments were somewhat represented on the internet and via transnational satellite channels.

Terrorism and Orientalism

The hegemonic discourses of 'terrorism' and Orientalism closely resemble each other. In both cases, the nexus of knowledge and power operates through discourse. For example, 'Corporate Orientalism' makes statements about [the Orient], produces dominating definitions of it and rules over it (Said 1979: 3). Similarly, the counter-terrorist intelligentsia produces knowledge about terrorism that is always amenable to elite agendas of control. Resemblances between the two began at the definitional level. Like Orientalism, much research on terrorism provides little more than generalisations, and reductionist historical chronologies (see for example Ascher 1986; Laqueur 1977). In addition, many works serve only to demonise the term 'terrorism', while constructing highly malleable definitions that could include all kinds of dissenters against the state (Clutterbuck 1975; Jenkins 1985; Nacos 1994; Wilkinson 1986). In this regard, Lon Troyer observes: 'definitional ambiguity is not an unfortunate state of affairs for the discourse on terrorism – it is its tactical strength'. In his view, 'the malleability of the term allows for its opportunistic application, frequently for the purpose of differentiating state violence from other, insurgent forms, thus rendering the violence and the politics of opposition groups illegitimate simultaneously' (Troyer 2001). Similarly, Pat Lauderdale has observed that political motives are behind the practices that maintain, create, and change the definition of terrorism (Oliverio and Lauderdale 2005: 154).

As with Orientalism, official discourse on terrorism has affinities with the Gramscian notion of hegemony. Indeed, Antonio Gramsci initially used the concept of 'hegemony' to conceptualise the ability of the modern state to rule over its citizenry. According to him, hegemony refers to 'an order in which a certain way of life and thought is dominant, in which one concept of reality is diffused throughout society, in all its institutions and private manifestations' (Quoted in Altheide 1987: 163). Gramsci expressed the view that intellectuals often gave credence to the ideas of the ruling class. This insight helps us to understand the role of think tanks dealing with the issue of terrorism. They adhere almost exclusively to governmental theses, omitting any attention to social relations of domination, which might underlie outbreaks of political violence. Yet, as with Orientalists, the counter-terrorist intelligentsia monopolises knowledge about the subject under review, and makes public discussion of counter-hegemonic political views dangerous if not impossible.

The hegemonic discourse of counter-terrorism also resembles Orientalism in that both employ de-contextualisation and de-historicisation techniques. In a compelling 1988 article entitled 'Identity, Negation and Violence', Edward Said noted the way these techniques have been built into the counterterrorist discourse. In this regard, Said found out that those rhetorical tendencies waned little over time. For example, in the official discourse concerning Irish resistance to British rule, little difference exists between the recommendations of Robert Louis Stevenson in 'Confessions of a Unionist' (1888) and the suggestions of his 1988 editor Jeremy Treglown. Both recommend a full use of force in facing the Irish opposition regardless of any context (Said 1988: 49). This avoidance of context and history in writings about terrorism precludes any questioning of the term 'terrorist' itself. One cannot seek any 'root causes' because this would render the commentator an apologist for violence. The hegemonic strategy that is recommended by the counter-terrorist intelligentsia is 'to act as if the term [terrorism] refers to a confirmed reality that, like obscenity, you know when you see it' (Troyer 2001). Another similarity between Orientalism and the official discourse on terrorism is their positioning of the 'other'. Just as Orientalism reproduces power relations vis-à-vis the external 'other', so counter-terrorism reproduces power relations vis-à-vis the internal 'other'. Just as Orientalism represents the mirror image of the Western self, so terrorism represents the antithesis of liberal democracy. In both cases, 'otherness' is the focal point.

As I will cover in Chapter 6, the rise of neo-conservatism as a major political force in Washington contributed to linking the terrorist discourse with the Middle East. Indeed, since the 1980s, neo-conservative quarters made constant interventionism in the Middle East a cornerstone in the US defence strategy. In subsequent strategic documents drafted by neo-conservatives, such as *Rebuilding America's Defenses: Strategy, Forces and Resources for a New Century* (2000),[30] terrorism is identified as the primary enemy for the United States. Yet surprisingly for such a strategic text, vagueness characterised the new enemy. Indeed, this document considers that the 'enemy is not a single political regime or person or religion or ideology. The enemy is terrorism' (p. 5). This vagueness allowed every enemy of the US administration to be associated with the term 'terrorist'. This substantiates the claim of critics who have long regarded 'terrorism' as merely a label affixed to those opposing central authority at home and abroad. 'Without defined shape, or determinate roots', Derek Gregory writes, the mantle of 'terrorism' can now 'be cast over *any* form of resistance to sovereign power' (Gregory 2003: 219, original emphasis). It was then no surprise that the first post-9/11 initiative of the Bush Administration was to silence the oppositional perspective at home, Attorney General John Ashcroft stated that critical voices 'only aid terrorists' (Carter and Barringer 2001). Subsequently, media flak (to borrow the term of Herman and Chomsky) vilified anti-war dissenters, critical researchers, and globalisation activists. Furthermore, pressure was exerted upon academic circles to close down serious discussion about the role of US foreign policy in inciting political violence worldwide. A neo-conservative association, namely the *American Council of Trustees and Alumni*, accused critical academics of 'giving comfort to America's enemies' (Lockman 2004: 256).

Externally, countering 'terrorism' became the pretext for waging wars of domination. This was particularly striking in the case of the PNAC, which sent an open-letter on 20 September 2001 to President Bush [stating] 'even if evidence does not link Iraq directly to the attack, any strategy aiming at the eradication of terrorism and its sponsors must include a determined effort to remove Saddam Hussein from power in Iraq' (Calabrese 2005: 159). Echoing the official frame, a mass-mediated demonisation process within the United States targeted not only the group responsible for the attacks, but the Islamic civilisation as a whole. Islam was depicted as being culpable for such attacks, and media audiences, especially in the western hemisphere, were constantly reminded of the backwardness, brutality and irrationality of everything Arab or Muslim. At this point, one can say that Orientalism and the official institutional discourse on terrorism reached a state of fusion. The result was a proliferation of an 'alarmist' literature, which included such publications as: Bernard Lewis, *The Crisis of Islam* (2003); Steven Emerson, *American Jihad: The Terrorists Living Among Us* (2003); Daniel Pipes, *Militant Islam Reaches America* (2003); Robert Spencer, *Islam Unveiled: Disturbing Questions about the World's Fastest Growing Religion* (2002); Serge Trifkovic, *Sword of the Prophet* (2002); and Anonymous, *The Terrorist Hunter* (2003).

These writings adhered to medieval style Orientalism, and their recommendations were often aggressive. Authors such as Podhoretz called for the United States to remake the entire Middle East region by 'forcibly re-educating the people' to follow the thinking of America's leaders (Podhoretz 2002). These views undeniably hold racist connotations; these gained credence from the sensationalist reporting of Islamic fundamentalist movements (Michael 2003: 715). While Western societies have long struggled to impede anti-Semitism, few made analogies between those attitudes and the spread of Islamophobia. An exception perhaps was Anne Norton, who observed that 'scholars familiar with the language of anti-Semitism will find [the writings about Islam] reminiscent of older, long-dishonoured texts'. She went on to say that 'the careful fabrications, the language of blood libel, the calls for violence in the name of defence, all are present here' (Norton 2004: 210–211). Numerous writers contributed to the alarmist literature after 9/11, one of them, namely Daniel Pipes, clearly exemplifies the fusion between Orientalism and counter-terrorism discourses. Considered to be a Middle East scholar after writing *In the Path of God* (1983), Pipes lectured at several prestigious universities, and enjoyed frequent media access. He was a signatory of the Project for the New American Century, and served as a counter-terrorism analyst on the 'Special Task Force on Terrorism and Technology' at the US Department of Defense. Pipes stated that:

> I approach the subject of Islam and politics from within the Orientalist tradition of European and American scholarship [...] [since] the fact remains that the Western academic study of Islam provides the *only* basis for an analysis of the religion in relation to political life. Certainly, the Orientalist tradition *cannot* be replaced by the recent profusion of writings by social scientists and journalists. [emphasis added] (Pipes 1983: 24)

As argued earlier, the synthesis between Orientalism and counter-terrorism produced a discourse positioning both the 'other' within the West (embodied by the Muslim minorities) and outside the West (embodied by the Muslim World). Echoing nineteenth-century and early-twentieth-century Orientalism with its explicit racist imagery, Daniel Pipes wrote back in 1990:

Fears of a Muslim influx have more substance than the worry about Jihad. Western European societies are unprepared for the massive immigration of brown-skinned peoples cooking strange foods and maintaining different standards of hygiene [...]. Put differently, Iranian zealots threaten more within the gates of Vienna than outside them. (Pipes 1990)

After 9/11, these attitudes were reiterated. In *Militant Islam Reaches America* (2002), Pipes demonised Muslims within the United States by claiming that Muslims in America had adopted the ambitious agenda of converting all non-Muslims and replacing the American Constitution with the Koran.[31] Employing the counter-terrorist discourse, Pipes warns in the introduction to the 2002 edition of *In the Path of God* that '[t]he preservation of our existing order can no longer be taken for granted; it needs to be fought for,' and calls for the need to 'adopt a tough line' against 'the ultimate enemy in the war on terrorism' (Pipes 2002: xi). For him, Muslims represent

> 'a basically hostile population'. Therefore, there should be no mercy for Muslim civilians during military strikes. He argued that the distinction between terrorists operating in the name of Islam and ordinary Muslim 'moms and dads' ... is a true and valid distinction, but it goes much too far, and if adhered to as a guideline for policy, it will cripple the effort that must be undertaken to preserve our institutions (Pipes 2002: 102, 124).

It is true that the intensity of this discourse has become marginalised over time, particularly after the public outcry against human rights abuses committed in the name of the United States in various detention camps worldwide (e.g. Guantanamo Bay, Abu Ghraib). In this regard, American non-governmental organisations, such as Human Rights Watch, have protested against the lack of legal status and physical condition of detainees. In its 2003 world report, Human Rights Watch issued a strong criticism of the Bush administration:

> On the anniversary of the September 11 attacks, President George W. Bush asserted, as he had throughout the year, that the United States campaign against al Qaeda was a fight for freedom, the rule of law and human dignity. Nevertheless, many of the steps taken by the U.S government to protect the

> country against terrorism belied the very principles the president pledged to defend. Over the past year, the country witnessed a persistent erosion of basic rights, including the right to liberty. The executive branch sought to circumvent legal restraints imposed by international human rights law and the Geneva Conventions, as well as the US Constitution. It sought to shield its conduct from public scrutiny, disdaining democratic principles of public transparency and accountability, and to deny the courts any meaningful role in protecting citizens and non-citizens alike from arbitrary detention. (Human Rights Watch 2003 [electronic version; no pagination])

The fact that military officers acted as interrogators, prosecutors and defence counsel, judges, and executioners, fuelled the scepticism about the fairness of the trials conducted in Guantanamo. These protests cooled the rhetoric stemming from the Orientalist/counter-terrorist nexus. For example, *New York Times* columnist Thomas Friedman urged George W. Bush to 'just shut it down', calling Guantanamo 'worse than an embarrassment' (Friedman 2005: A23). Eventually, the hard-line official discourse on terrorism loosened up, especially as civilian fatalities mounted in Iraq and Afghanistan. As subsequent chapters show, Al Jazeera fuelled international opposition against the Orientalist/counter-terrorist nexus.

To sum up, Orientalism is a discourse that originated during medieval times. It began as religious rhetoric but then evolved into an academically oriented discipline. Numerous scholars considered that the latter was deeply flawed and needed radical reform. Professor Edward Said was a primary contributor to this debate through his major work *Orientalism* (1979), which demonstrated that Orientalism functioned to serve political ends, and more especially imperialist endeavours. He also contended that Orientalists constructed narratives and images that assumed Western superiority over the other, thus producing a false description of Arabs and Islamic culture.

Gradually, Orientalism's range extended from Europe to the United States. American Orientalism developed its own constructions of the Orient, which were primarily based on biblical references that considered Americans as God's chosen people. This led to alignment of the will of God with the national objectives of the United States. In addition, captivity narratives of American sailors in North Africa had a deep impact on

American popular consciousness. Consequently, America inherited the ancient ideological schisms between Christianity and Islam.

When the United States became a superpower after World War II, the American Orientalist apparatus influenced American policy makers' perceptions. The legitimate nationalist aspirations of newly independent countries in the Middle East as well as in Africa, Asia and Latin America were swiftly dismissed. American containment strategies were thus directed not just against the communist bloc, but also against nationalist movements. This state of affairs strained the relationship between the United States and Middle Eastern states. Events, such as the Arab oil embargo (1973–1974), the Iranian Revolution (1978–1979), and the Iranian student takeover of the American Embassy in Tehran, as well as violent actions perpetrated by Palestinian militants gave more momentum to Orientalist discourse within American literature and the mass media. As a result, Islam was often constructed as an external threat to Western identity and interests. In addition, leading Orientalist scholars also adopted the counter-terrorist rhetoric.

The term 'terrorism' carries numerous inconsistencies of usage. It is a word, which is deployed rhetorically depending on who wants to apply it. From an official perspective, terrorism represents illegitimate political violence as opposed to the legitimate force used by the state. It is employed by this perspective to reaffirm the legitimacy of the Western state and the boundaries of the Western community. In other words, just as Orientalism reproduces power relations vis-à-vis the external 'other', so counter-terrorist discourse effectively reproduces power relations vis-à-vis the internal 'other'. A fusion of the Orientalist discourse and the counter-terrorism discourse occurred after 9/11 within American mainstream media organisations. Initially, alternative perspectives to the official discourse were publicly invisible because terrorism was represented as beyond law. As a result, the image of Islam and the Arabs became popularly associated with terrorist threats to the West and liberal democracy. However, this rhetoric started to cool somewhat after the exposure of widespread abuses by the American military in their prosecution of the 'War on Terror'.

3

CNNI Framings of Middle East Conflict, 1991–2001

CNN history

Cable News Network (CNN) was the unexpected idea of entrepreneur Ted Turner.[1] In 1976, he had said, 'I hate the news; news is evil'. Eventually, however, Turner saw the opportunity to combine idealism with commercial opportunity. He realised that a high profile new media network could cool world tensions and make money at the same time. As a sailboat racer, he had made trips to Cuba and the Soviet Union, and thought that giving a voice to 'other' countries could make international relations much warmer. In his view, the 'the most angry people in the world are those who do not get listened to' (Flournoy and Stewart 1997: 17, 24, 27).

CNN was launched on 1 June 1980 as America's news channel; satellites were used to deliver its programmes to cable operators around the country. Upon launching, Turner vowed that 'we won't be signing off until the world ends. We'll be on, and we will cover the end of the world, live' (Ainsworth 2000 [electronic article; no pagination]). With start-up costs of $34.5 million, this venture was financially risky, as the markets did not appreciate the potential revenues. Indeed, only 1.7 million of American households received the services of this new 24-hour news channel; far fewer than were needed to make a profit. Initially, media competitors labelled CNN 'the Chicken Noodle Network'. However, Ted Turner had recognised the transformation

CNNI Framings of Middle East Conflict, 1991–2001

brought by the proliferation of cable television channels. The cable industry generally used the CNN phenomenon to 'convince Americans that it was time to pay for the TV that had always been "free"' (Schechter 2000).

The first big test for CNN came in the form of the 1980 presidential elections. This was a disaster, CNN crews were poorly prepared and its brand was still unknown to politicians. In addition, the broadcast networks refused to include CNN in the pools covering the White House. Only a justice order compelled them to do so. However, politicians soon realised the publicity value of a 24/7 news channel. Before then, Ted Turner lost even more money launching Headline News, a second 24-hour news network. After a few years, Turner had spent more than 70 million dollars keeping CNN and Headline News afloat. This situation changed as more channels became available on cable (ESPN, HBO, Nickelodeon etc.), and as more viewers subscribed. Eventually, CNN reached four out of five US cable homes; a situation which exponentially increased CNN advertising revenues to $56.5 million in 1985 (Flournoy and Stewart 1997). By the mid-1980s, as CNN and Headline News were growing, Ted Turner decided to create more cable news and entertainment networks. In 1985, CNN and Headline News domestic signals were combined to create CNN International (CNNI). Some studies indicate that CNN International has effectively contributed to the creation of a global public sphere that has had a deep impact on political communication (Volkmer 1999). In *CNN: News in the Global Sphere*, Ingrid Volkmer thoroughly examined the *World Report* programme. This broadcast is a contribution of TV stations from all over the world which sent their reports. These were compiled by CNN in a special programme. Before long, *World Report* gained overwhelming viewership worldwide, as it allowed a diversity of perspectives in relation to current affairs.

But it was the capacity to cover live events that allowed CNNI to become a world brand of global news programming. In fact, CNN changed the whole news industry (Ainsworth 2000). Ted Turner, himself came up with various ideas such as airing diverse thematic programmes modelled on a magazine style. For instance, *Time* magazine featured half an hour of politics and *Sports Illustrated* provided news and sports with images. These basic formats added entertainment value to the news channel. In addition, CNN revolutionised the use of graphics, camera angles, and the background monitor screen. It invented new formats for news presentations, such as the 'newsflash'. Most importantly, CNN gave special prominence to breaking news stories and unlimited live coverage. This projected a sense of liveness and instantaneity, as well as a sense of watching first hand primary sources (Volkmer 1999: 130–132; 138–141). These innovations attracted global audiences, while also impressing other media organisations. During its first 10 years, it covered important events such as the Solidarity strife in Poland, the Falkland Islands War, and the Salvadorian Civil War (Hickey 2001: 88). CNN also reported upon top level meetings between world leaders, the explosion of space shuttle Challenger (1986), the Tiananmen Square riots (1989) and the fall of the Berlin Wall (1989). Some observers argue that CNN's contribution to the collapse of the Soviet Bloc was substantial (Campbell 2000: 11). But the most important manifestation of the CNN phenomenon happened during the Gulf War of 1990–1991. During that major international crisis, CNN became the channel of communication between the warring parties, and the instant chronicler of the conflict (Moisy 1996: 7). CNN's high-tech tools, such as 'flyaway dishes',[2] and the ingenuity of its reporters, such as Peter Arnett, deeply impressed audiences around the world. The general result was described by *Time* magazine as 'an exceptional and perhaps unprecedented, live account of the start of war from inside an enemy capital' (Zelizer 2002: 71). By early 1991, CNN had earned its reputation of 'the war channel' (Campbell 2000: 11). Its audience probably exceeded a billion worldwide (Hall 1997: 33).

High profile war coverage throughout the 1990s led some commentators to talk of the 'CNN effect'. In 1992, the US intervention in Somalia was said to have been triggered by the impact of CNN on policy makers (Cohen 1994:10). In the aftermath of the ill-fated mission to capture Somali warlord Farah Aideed, dead American soldiers were dragged through the streets of Mogadishu. A Black Hawk helicopter was gunned down, and the resulting action led to the killing of 18 Rangers (75 others were wounded), and the capture of one American pilot. CNN correspondents on the ground sent to their headquarters images of the captured pilot, combined with video images of a dead US soldier being dragged through the streets of Mogadishu amidst cheering Somali crowds. It has been asserted that the domestic impact of these images effectively ended the US mission to Somalia (Baum 2004: 218).

References to the 'CNN effect' reflected the perceived impact of the 24-hour news coverage upon decision makers. In this regard, some authors regarded television in general and CNN in particular as the driving force of the American foreign policy agenda. The interventions in Iraqi Kurdistan in early 1991 and Somalia in December 1992 were cited as evidence of this. Some politicians expressed their irritation about this situation. Former Defense Secretary James Schlesinger, for example, argued that the United States was formulating foreign policy in response to 'impulse and image' (Livingston 1997). Former US diplomat George F. Kennan, one of the artisans of the Cold War, lamented in an article to the *New York Times* that American policy had become 'controlled by popular emotional impulses, and particularly ones provoked by the commercial television industry'. For him, this state of affairs had circumvented traditional policy making channels in both executive and legislative branches (Kennan 1993: A23). On the other hand, the 'CNN effect' enabled NGOs and other non-state actors to advocate just causes though the media (Girardet 1995; Rotberg and Weiss 1996). During the mid-1990s, regional conflicts in Asia and Africa put approximately 42 million people at risk of disease and starvation (according to UN figures). Therefore, NGOs involved in humanitarian issues hoped that vivid television coverage of these crises would attract the attention of US foreign policy makers and other media.

However, a series of content analysis studies demonstrated that stories about humanitarian crises, while framed by journalists, were circulated only when political elites had decided to intervene according to their own timing (Livingston and Eachus 1995; Mermin 1997: 403). In this regard, Philip Seib (2002) argues that the much-vaunted 'CNN effect' is largely wishful thinking. He points out that various media and conflict studies indicate that American news coverage of conflicts tends to propagate the policy of the US administration (especially in conflicts involving American troops). This tendency reflects journalistic dependence on official sources (see Hallin and Gitlin 1993; Herman and Chomsky 1988; Kellner 1993; Mowlana 1992).

In the new millennium, CNN was still a major news provider worldwide. However, because of a gigantic merger between AOL and Time Warner (January 2001) and the departure of its pioneer Ted Turner, CNN began to experience some media fatigue. The AOL and Time Warner merger led a 10 per cent reduction of CNN staff. This evidently reduced the capabilities of CNN. After the earthquake that shook Seattle in 2001, CNN's crew took ten hours to arrive, much too late compared to their competitors. But the merger was not the only reason for CNNs ratings decline, there was increasing competition from rivals MSNBC and Fox News, in addition to local and regional cable channels, such as New York 1. Internationally, BBC World Service and Deutsche Welle were also major competitors. Nevertheless, CNN remained a major domestic and international news provider. As such, it was the first network to break news of the September 11 attacks.

According to a press release from Time Warner, CNN reached more than 150 million television households in over 212 countries as of 2000. Furthermore, the CNN Group was available to more than 800 million people worldwide, thanks to its six cable and satellite television networks (CNN, CNN Headline News, CNN International, CNN-fn, CNN/SI and CNN en Español), its two radio networks (CNN Radio and a Spanish version CNN Radio Noticias), and its 11 websites on CNN Interactive and CNN Newsource (TimeWarner.com, 2000).

CNN framing of the 1991 Gulf War

By 1989, the United States administration was faced with multiple internal challenges, a growing national debt, a shrinking job market, and loss of social services. Saddam Hussein's invasion of Kuwait on 2 August 1990 provided the opportunity for a military intervention, which 'temporarily assuaged this malaise and loss of national self-esteem through a display of US power abroad' (Husting 1999: 162). The prosecution of war was also an opportunity to unify the American people around the flag through values, such as pride, prestige, and patriotism.

In this context, the Kuwait invasion and its consequences represented the first major post-Cold War international crisis. It therefore attracted global attention from global news agencies and news providers, particularly CNN (Mawlana et al. 1992). This was also the first war to be covered live on television, a distinction which caught the attention of media critics and social scientists. Much academic research centred upon the primacy of global television news, particularly CNN. Throughout the Gulf crisis, CNN performed the role of witness, diplomatic messenger and military tool. According to Claude Moisy, for the first time in history, 'a television network became an active participant in the development of a major international crisis' (Moisy, 1996: 4). In the lead up to conflict, CNN was watched and used by American politicians Iraqi officials, UN leaders, Soviet intermediaries and other world leaders.[3] As the war unfolded, CNN became the favoured conduit of US information warfare specialists. The network had a technological edge over its competitors; reporters were equipped with small lightweight cameras, portable up-links, digital editing facilities and mobile satellite telephones.

For propaganda purposes, military elites used CNN to make the war a sort of a 'staged event'. Examples of this symbiosis abound. The start of the air campaign for example was scheduled for American prime-time television. Thus audiences knew through CNN that 'Desert Storm' had begun even before the Pentagon announced this formally (Van Tuyll 2002: 234). Media planning was such that the military knew, months in advance, the types of stories the press would cover during the different phases of the campaign. Israeli academic Gabbi Wolfsfeld is adamant that media coverage was designed according to the military script: in the build-up phase, the focus was on the human everyday experiences of American soldiers. During the air campaign, emphasis was to be on the cleanliness and efficiency of the hi-tech weapons (Wolfsfeld 1997: 133).

This script did not only involve CNN. For every major news media outlet, the information warfare paradigm was irresistible, particularly so when the political discourse concerning Gulf War issues was monolithic (Pan and Kosicki 1994: 120). According to Professor of linguistics, George Lakoff, the deployment of classic fairy-tale narratives in framing the issues was tremendously powerful, especially the 'self-defence story' and the 'rescue story'. Thus, the administration claimed that Saddam Hussein was threatening America's oil supply and way of life, such that self-defence was deemed necessary. The Kuwaiti baby atrocity stories[4] were designed to prompt the rescue story (Lakoff 2003). These story frames were reinforced by the fact that reporters conformed to the Pentagon's pooling system; a practice that skewed discussion toward the Pentagon's agenda.

Military framing

Research into media coverage of conflicts demonstrates that American television overwhelmingly relays the perspectives of the Pentagon (O'Heffernan 1993; Paletz 1994). During the 1991 Gulf crisis, American television coverage avoided questioning military operations and policy, overwhelmingly relayed the Pentagon's perspective and showed elements of jingoism. Ella Shohat and Robert Stam observed that 'newscasters spoke of Iraq as the 'enemy', as if they had personally joined the armed forces' (quoted in Fritsch-El-Alaoui 2005: 154). Such coverage overemphasised the precision of military bombings, but underemphasised the suffering of innocent Iraqi civilians and the destruction of non-military targets (Paletz 1994: 282). A study by Hallin and Gitlin concluded that CNN's coverage of the war was in tune with other mainstream news media organisations. The primary themes were American prowess, the power of American technology, and the courage of American soldiers (Hallin and Gitlin 1993: 414). Hallin and Gitlin's content analysis showed that images of tanks, planes, missiles, and American soldiers constituted a high percentage of television time (p. 420). In contrast, anti-war rallies hardly ever appeared in television network coverage.

Military framing fully appears in the CNN documentary *Desert Storm: the Victory* (1991). In a thorough analysis of this docudrama, Michelle Kendrick (1994) identified a clear beginning (the day after the 15 January deadline[5]), a middle (the switch from the air war to the ground), and an end (a cease-fire after 100 hours of ground war). The docu-drama was subdivided under chapter headings; 'The Air War', 'The Ultimatum', and 'The Hundred-Hour Ground War'. The entire video presents the war through the 'eyes' of military technology. As a result, certain technologies were positioned as the main protagonists of the narrative. Patriot missiles for example were described as 'the first heroes' of the war (Kendrick 1994: 140). This fetishism of military weaponry presented the war as a videogame, with numerous 'smart bombs' hitting targets with disconcerting ease (Kellner 1992: 374). The sanitised nature of the video game narrative was a primary goal for military propagandists. Television coverage of the Vietnam War had involved some gruesome images, particularly during the Tet offensive (1968). This time, the Pentagon decided that the imagery associated with 'Desert Storm' would be totally different. This was to be a 'bloodless, humanitarian and hygienic' war (Der Derian 2001: xv).

On CNN's video a few dead bodies were shown, but these were Iraqis only and individually unrecognisable. Seasoned war correspondent John Pilger pointed out that the war as a whole was often reported as a technological wonder with remarkably few casualties. Yet, despite being one of the most covered wars in history, few journalists reported the truth, still widely unknown, that a quarter of a million Iraqis were wantonly slaughtered or died unnecessary deaths (Pilger 1998: 144). Pilger's argument was that Gulf War coverage was worse than sanitisation, it was the masking of an atrocity, and journalists were part of the process.

Sanitisation and masking are dominant features of CNN's video. For example, in the section entitled 'The Hundred Hour Ground War', CNN omitted to mention that the largest battle took place well after the cease-fire. In this 'engagement', US bombers destroyed 247 Iraqi tanks and more than 500 military transport vehicles, while they were retreating. CNN and other mainstream media organisations did not fully investigate how the military actions contravened the rules of war. Joyce Chediac argues that this episode is a war crime because it violates the Geneva Conventions of 1949 (Common Article III) which outlaws the killing of non-combatant soldiers (Chediac 1992: 91). According to the ex-US Attorney General, Ramsey Clark, 'the United States intentionally bombed and destroyed civilian life, commercial and business districts, schools, hospitals, mosques, churches, shelters, residential areas, historical sites, private vehicles and civilian government offices' (Clark 1991 [Electronic article; no pagination]).

At an afternoon Pentagon briefing on 1 March General Thomas Kelly said that American troops had 'killed an entire army' even though President Bush had declared a cease-fire on 28 February. The next day, CNN described the future episode as the 'highway of death'. Independent journalists, such as Robert Fisk, who ventured into the highway leading from Kuwait City to Iraq, about thirty kilometres from the Kuwaiti capital, saw the scale of the massacre. They raised the point that that the use of force was disproportionate because the Iraqi forces were retreating. They also pointed to the fact that there were also innocent civilians on the highway. The significance of this incident was diluted by CNN anchors. They reminded the viewers about stories of Iraqi atrocities in Kuwait. Shortly afterwards, CNN changed the story. This time, the Iraqi convoy in question was said to be composed of stolen vehicles full of contraband goods, as to insinuate that the looters got their due punishment (Kellner 1992: 407). European media took a more critical stance; BBC's Stephen Sackur, for example, raised questions about the legitimacy of this military action.

Occasionally, CNN did mention Iraqi civilian casualties, but only within the reports of New Zealand born CNN correspondent Peter Arnett. His live reports from Baghdad contradicted the standing military framing of the war. Most controversially, Arnett reported from the site of a baby milk factory bombed by the coalition. His testimony and the visual footage contrasted with the military claims that missile and bombing strikes were surgical. Arnett also reported on the destruction of the Amiriya shelter in Baghdad (13 February 1991). Gruesome images of civilian bodies being extracted from the rubble disturbed the Pentagon's meticulously constructed myth of a clean and sanitised war. However, some members of Congress described Arnett as a propaganda mouthpiece for Saddam Hussein (Evans 2004: 36). Arnett's broadcasts did not alter the general patterns of military framing. In the aftermath of the baby milk factory incident, mainstream media again adhered to the explanations provided by military sources, especially General Powell. He stated at the daily Pentagon press conference that 'it is not an infant formula factory ... it was a biological weapons factory, of that we are sure'.

Apart from the influence of sources, self-censorship prevented images of civilian casualties from being broadcast on television networks. Furthermore, 'issues' of taste and decency became fashionable in newsrooms, and graphic images were heavily edited (Taylor 1992: 113–114). As a matter of fact, Western journalists tend to refrain from displaying pictures of their own; this restraint does not extend to the bodies of the 'Others'. In *Body Horror* (1998), John Taylor explains that news media representations of foreign bodies reinforce Western ideas and culture. Thus, viewed from an American perspective, the carnage of Al-Amiriya – as described by Arnett – never impacted upon American public perceptions of the war.

The Orientalist frame

Stereotypes of 'otherness' based on religious and cultural difference tend to flourish in times of war. In earlier conflicts, this process took the form of atrocity stories designed to demonise the enemy. In World War I, for example, Britain and France propagated false stories about Germans bayoneting babies on their way through Belgium. During the military build-up prior to 'Desert Storm', Iraqis were demonised in the same way. The fabricated story of the Kuwaiti babies removed from their incubators and left to die circulated all around the world. This story was accepted at face value by major American media outlets, including CNN (Kellner 1992: 429).

Atrocity stories appeals to national self-identification processes and externalises other nations or cultures involved in the conflict. It makes the binary opposites of good vs. bad and civilised vs. barbarian easier for audiences to accept. In the case of conflicts involving Western and Middle Eastern nations, the Orientalist frame is readily available; there is 'a rich reservoir of Arab stereotypes ... drawing on myths and beliefs of the past' (Rolstrup 1996). Mainstream media coverage also tends to pass through the prism of deep cultural difference between West and Islam.

Throughout the Gulf conflict, Saddam Hussein was portrayed as a dangerous tyrant and a villain. Yet, there was no differentiation between Saddam Hussein and the state of Iraq. American and Western audiences were constantly reminded about his ruthless rule and Iraq's aggression against its neighbours. This demonisation campaign was so potent that in January 1991 public opinion polls revealed that many Americans considered Saddam Hussein an evil that had to be uprooted by all means (Hoynes 1992: 311). Of course, there was no reference to the fact that Saddam Hussein had been an ally of the West for a long period of time, and that his weapons were the provenance of Western arsenals (Rolstrup, 1996).

In 'Desert Storm', the Oriental was fully positioned as the 'other' in relation to American national identity. In this context, Abouali Farmanfarmaian has identified many racist expressions that were used by the media during the 1991 Gulf War. Labels such as 'niggers' and 'sand-niggers' were frequently employed by soldiers in media interviews. This suggested the prevalence of 'a racial link that implicitly emphasized Western values and only thereby managed to generate unanimity in outrage against an outside evil, Iraq' (Farmanfarmaian 1992: 112). The entire Gulf conflict was pervaded by depictions of 'good' and 'evil'. Thus American soldiers, shown in emotional farewell scenes before their missions, were personalised and humanised, whereas Iraqis were considered as a pestilence to be removed (Liebes 1992: 52).[6]

Another Orientalist theme, which was prominently featured in CNN's coverage, was the binary contrast between American and Oriental women. Despite the fact that women constituted a scant 6 per cent of US troops in Saudi Arabia, the image conveyed was that of progressive, even post-feminist, democratic American women, in contrast to their veiled and oppressed Oriental counterparts (Husting 1999: 164). While this construction held some truth in regards to Saudi Arabia (a major American ally in 1991), it was completely erroneous in the case of Iraq (the targeted enemy). According to Human Rights Watch, Iraqi women have enjoyed more rights under Saddam Hussein than many of their Middle Eastern counterparts (Human Rights Watch, 2003). The Iraqi Provisional Constitution (drafted in 1970) formally guaranteed equal rights to women and other laws specifically ensured their right to vote, attend school, run for political office, and own property. As a result, Iraqi women played an active role in the political and economic development of Iraq. Iraqi statistics revealed that in 1976 women constituted approximately 38.5 per cent of those in the education profession, 31 per cent of the medical profession, 25 per cent of lab technicians, 15 per cent of accountants and 15 per cent of civil servants. Moreover, during the Iran-Iraq War (1980–1988), women assumed greater roles in the civil service and the general workforce (this reflected the shortage of working age men). The Human Rights Watch briefing paper points out that the Gulf conflict and its aftermath worsened the position of women and girls. They were greatly affected by the economic consequences of the UN sanctions, and lacked access to food, health care, and education (Human Rights Watch 2003).

CNN framing of the US intervention in Somalia (1993)

While I mentioned earlier the American intervention in Somalia in the context of the 'CNN effect', it is also important to consider the perspective of humanitarian intervention.

The concept of humanitarian intervention

The principle of 'humanitarian intervention' has a long history within Western political thought. In *A Few Words on Non-Intervention* (1859),

John Stuart Mill argued that the whole doctrine of non-interference with foreign nations should be reconsidered, especially when those nations were under 'barbarian' rule. In Mill's view, barbarians would surely benefit from the intervention of 'civilised' powers. One derivative of this discourse is the French *mission civilisatrice* (the civilising mission), which was the guiding rationale of French colonial rule in Algeria, West Africa, and Indochina. However, 'humanitarian interventions' had also been conducted by Western powers to support Christian minorities in the Mediterranean against their Muslim rulers (e.g. Greece in the 1820s, the Lebanese Maronites in 1862). By contrast, the plight of non-Christians attracted no such attention from Western decision makers or publics in that period (Shaw 2007: 354).

Nevertheless, the concept of humanitarian intervention disappeared for a while, until the aftermath of World War II, when European liberals aspired to establish a system of corrective security mediated through international law and organisation. However, as the Cold War intensified, the force of these ideals weakened. They only regained momentum when extensive fighting led to famine and great suffering in Southern Nigeria (1967–1970). As the Western media covered these developments, the atrocities that were depicted triggered heated debates, as well as calls for activism from European intellectuals. The NGO Médecins Sans Frontières (MSF) was created in this context; they argued that humanitarian catastrophes might call into question the sovereignty of states. However, following the 1991 Gulf War, in which the United Nations under heavy American pressures authorised a 'humanitarian intervention'. MSF termed these events 'armed charity'. They warned associated NGOs that they must 'eschew all collaboration – let alone integration' into these new state-run ventures (MSF 1993: 111–124).

On 9 December 1992, Operation 'Restore Hope' in Somalia represented the first large-scale 'peace operation' since the 1991 Gulf War. The official purpose was to avert a humanitarian disaster in the famine stricken and increasingly lawless Republic of Somalia (following the demise of the Somali President Siad Barre). However, the real designs behind this military operation are still unclear. Major decision makers such as President Bush Sr, Secretary of State James Baker, and General Colin Powell (Chairman of the Joint Chiefs of Staff) have long refrained from offering any hints about their intentions (Fox 2000).

When the Clinton administration took over (20 January 1993), there were immediate attempts to frame the operation in humanitarian terms. Anthony Lake, the then national security adviser, gave a speech in fall 1993 titled *From Containment to Enlargement*, in which setting 'a humanitarian agenda' was featured as a major foreign policy priority (Lake 1993).

The Orientalist frame

The tragedy unfolding in Somalia was soon interpreted through Orientalist lenses. The explanations offered by the media establishment, including CNN, were framed by assumptions designed to boost the American self-image. Thus, the Somali civil conflict was portrayed in terms of 'tribalism'. This generic explanation ignored the complexities of status, class, and race. On 8 December 1992, CNN reported that 'the crisis in Somalia has been caused by intense clan rivalries, a problem common in Africa, but here carried out with such violence, there is nothing left of civil society, only anarchy and the rule of the gun'. On the same night, CNN's star anchor Christiane Amanpour outlined how the CNN staff were paying local clans for protection. A few days later (12 December 1992), a CNN story referred to a 'clan leader' ousted in a 'clan uprising'. This had triggered 'clan warfare' characterised by 'anarchy' and 'a confusing patchwork of clan fiefdoms' (Besteman 1996: 121).

Yet in the midst of this rhetoric, nothing was said about the American support for the former Somali dictator Siad Barre. During the Cold War, he confronted Ethiopia, the Soviet ally. The United States provided military assistance, which was also used by Siad Barre to quell dissent inside Somalia. And American-provided development money was used by Barre's regime to buy the support of local elites, including tribal chiefs (Besteman 1996: 127). These events fuelled the regime-cultivated tribalism. However, historical evidence reveals the simplicity of this argument. From 1978, the former Somali dictator, began humiliating and massacring his own clan in a systematic way.

After the military intervention, tribalist themes were reinforced by American political elites. President Bush Sr pointed to the responsibility of the 'warlords controlling the ports' and emphasised that there was also a 'difficulty separating these warlords one from the other'. Similarly, US

Press Secretary, Marlin Fitzwater described Somalia's tragedy as involving 'vast numbers of people … suffering and dying from famine caused by a senseless civil war.' He went on to depict the situation as a 'manmade famine' caused by 'armed bands … stealing and hoarding food as well as attacking international relief workers.' These comments invoked the early-twentieth-century image of the 'primitive savage', in which the enemy 'other' is not just a leader or leaders, but the people and their culture (Butler 2002: 2–3).

The Orientalist assumption underlined tribalism discourse was that Somalis were savages for most of their history; they had been brought into the civilised world by Italian and British colonisation, but with the civil war, Somalis were in danger of relapsing into the darkness of history (predating colonisation) (Besteman 1996: 122). This suggests that colonial interventions enormously benefited Africa, whereas historical evidence points to the complete opposite (Jones 2004). In short, it appears that without the legacy of the white man, Africa reverts into savagery and backwardness. CNN's visual framing consolidated this Orientalist narrative. This occurred in the aftermath of a battle in Mogadishu, in which 18 men were killed, over 70 wounded, and one captured (3 October 1993). The latter, Chief Warrant Officer Michael Durant was videotaped by his Somali captors and was shown in obvious physical discomfort. Worse, CNN broadcast footage of dead American soldiers being dragged through Mogadishu streets by Somali mobs. Cori Dauber explains the connotative meaning of such images:

> The bodies are surrounded by Somalis of all ages and both genders, none in clothing that can be identified as specifically military uniforms. Thus the argument is made that it is the general population of that country that has turned against us. Once again we are in a chaotic environment where combatants cannot be easily distinguished from non-combatants, and where the very people we came to help are the ones killing our troops. (Dauber 2001: 656)

Both the narrative and the visual framing, while hinting at the irrationality, backwardness and barbarism of the Somalis, omitted an important fact. The US military decision to hunt Aideed and his fellow clan leaders contributed to the conflict in Mogadishu (Butler 2002: 11).

CNN and the 'War on Terror' (2001)

While earlier attacks against American interests (World Trade Center (1993); Pan Am 103 (1988); embassies in Kenya and Tanzania (1998); the Alfred P. Murrah building (1995)) were framed as 'criminal investigations', the attacks of September 11 2001 were framed as a 'War on Terror' (Ryan 2004: 364). In *Projections of Power: Framing News, Public Opinion, and US Foreign Policy* (2003), Robert Entman explains how the US administration imposes its framing of events upon media organisations. This occurs through a 'cascading activation' model, whereby interpretive frame of news content are established by senior political elites and flow downward. According to Entman, it is difficult for the media to resist these particular frames, particularly if there are no meaningful intra-elite divisions also flowing downwards. The 'War on Terror' frame was available and believable to a country in search for a secure frame of reference. Frames simplify the situation at hand: they offer a simple definition of the problem, establish its boundaries, and promote a course of action (Kinder 1998: 167–197). With the 'War on Terror' frame, the attacks of 9/11 were simply interpreted as the terrorists' hatred of the United States because of its freedoms and affluent way of life (McChesney 2002: 92). This enabled President George W. Bush and surrounding elites to translate the expected retribution into the waging of wars in the Middle East. Here, the "War on Terror" frame was readily accepted by CNN. In fact, they offered no meaningful analysis, context or historical background in relation to the 9/11 attacks (McDonald and Lawrence 2004). For instance, CNN did not mention Washington's own covert and overt actions that had contributed to anti-Americanism internationally and in the Middle East. Nor did it discuss the array of national and international responses to Al Qaeda terrorism. Violent retaliation was accepted as the sole course of action without question.

This lack of analysis can be explained through the paradigm proposed by Shanto Iyengar. He points out that television news reporters usually frame terrorism in episodic rather than thematic frames. During the 1980s for example, the huge coverage given to terrorist acts focused episodically on specific acts without providing any connection whatsoever with their broader context (Iyengar 1991: 2, 14). Thus, CNN's breaking news of September 11 used episodic titles in its coverage i.e. 'Attack on

America', then 'War on Terror', and finally 'Strike against Terror'. They also used certain keywords repetitively. Reynolds and Barnett (2003) conducted research on the first 12 hours of CNN's coverage after the attacks. They found out that the word *war* was used to describe the attacks 234 times. In addition, CNN anchors commonly referred to 'America' instead of the United States; words like 'freedom', 'justice', and 'liberty' were used as simple descriptors of America and its ideals. Within these patriotic terms of reference, CNN journalists also made atypical references to 'God' and the need to 'pray' or for 'prayer'. Symbolic comparisons to Pearl Harbour were also made. CNN reporters described the attackers as cowards and madmen. Overall, stories of bravery, patriotism, camaraderie, sacrifice, and the love for New York formed the basis of CNN coverage. It was also the first network to display patriotic images of American flags flapping in the breeze, while its celebrity anchor Lou Dobbs was the first journalist to wear an American flag lapel pin (Aday et al. 2005: 8–9). This kind of coverage gave little space to the huge anti-war protests in the US and Europe (Chattarji 2004: 3).

CNN's total adherence to the official rhetoric was described by Douglas Kellner as 'a stunning collapse of a respectable news organisation into a vehicle of conservative ideology' (Kellner 2002: 150). The network echoed the dominant militaristic discourse, which considered the attacks to be an 'act of war'. Accordingly, military retaliation was proposed as the inevitable policy response. CNN relied less upon journalists than upon experts, analysts, and consultants to interpret news events. The prevailing 'War on Terror' frame carried by CNN served to construct the national identity of the United States as the hyper-masculine, heavily militarised, world hegemon, which employed war to solve its problems while ensuring continuous American public support (Saso 2005: 1).

After the 9/11 attacks, the Orientalist frame was employed by official sources and establishment media to differentiate foes from friends, and to reinforce the constructed linkage between Islam and terrorism. So when President Bush openly declared 'You're either with us or against us',[7] this message was translated in context by the media by expanding the notion of the 'enemy' to all Muslims, whether living in the Middle East, or living in the West (Ruigrok and van Atteveldt 2007: 68–69). One striking aspect of the Orientalist discourse post-9/11 was the unfavourable comparison of women's status. Women of American Caucasian origins were positioned as the standard for judging the lives of Afghan women (who had survived three decades of foreign invasions and civil wars). CNN used this sub-frame when it broadcast *Inside Afghanistan: Beneath the Veil* (2001); a documentary which attempted to trace the history of Taliban restrictions on women in Afghanistan.[8] This documentary represents a textbook example of the binary construction of the 'uncivilised East' vs. the 'civilised West'. Miriam Cooke argued that this documentary's powerful emotional framing was used to gather additional support for the war and reinforce images of otherness associated with Afghanistan (Cooke 2002: 228).

The notion of women as victims has a long history within Western culture's symbolic repertoire[9] This discourse resurfaced during the war on Afghanistan. Mainstream media adopted the 'saving brown women' sub-frame to reinforce the idea that Oriental women 'would not have a future unless the forces of the good and civilized West defeated the forces of the evil, barbaric, male-dominated East' (Rowe and Malhotra 2003: 19). There were many criticisms of the Burqa; the women's veil that has long been used by the ethnic Pashtun (the main ethnic group in Afghanistan). At no point did CNN mention that the Burqa was not a Taliban invention. Nor was there any reference to various anthropological studies suggesting that the Burqa in the Afghan context conveys meanings associated with women's modesty or respectability (Abu-Lughod 2004: 785).

The routine employment of Orientalist imagery and discourse allowed the government media strategists to frame the war as a benevolent intervention on behalf of Afghanistan women. This was a clear attempt to invoke support for military intervention by pitching Western feminism against Oriental fundamentalism. This opposition informed Presidential communications; for instance, the First American Lady Laura Bush stated after the fall of Kabul: 'Because of our recent military gains in much of Afghanistan women are no longer imprisoned in their homes; they can listen to music and teach their daughters without fear of punishment; the fight against terrorism is also a fight for the rights and dignity of women' (Radio Address by Mrs Bush 2002). Another presidential communiqué titled 'Progress on the War on Terror' (22 January 2004), reiterated the same 'saving brown women' sub-frame by stating that 'Afghan women are experiencing freedom for the first time' (White House 2004: 3).

CNN and information dominance

CNN duly participated to the strategy of information dominance initiated by the Pentagon. In the aftermath of the September 11 2001 attacks, CNN offered training to Army Psyops crews. Reports suggest that personnel belonging to the Fourth Psychological Operations Group (Fort Bragg) received training as interns at CNN's Atlanta headquarters. Some sources hinted that these military personnel were involved in news production, although CNN rebuffed the accusation (Macdonald 2007: 156). As mentioned earlier in Chapter 2, during the military intervention in Afghanistan, when reports emerged about civilian casualties, the Pentagon immediately bought exclusive rights for extremely high resolution satellites, denying the circulation of any photos depicting Afghan civilian casualties (Campbell 2001). This trend was followed by CNN, which decided to avoid reporting Afghan civilian casualties altogether. Instead, its reporters were instructed to constantly repeat that the 'war is in response to a terrorist attack that killed close to 5,000 innocent people in the US' (Bleifuss 2001 [electronic article; no pagination]).

CNN was also a vehicle for the Pentagon's perception management efforts. Indeed, most of the analysts invited to comment on the network had close connections to the Pentagon.[10] In his book *How CNN Fought the War*, Major General Perry M. Smith (Ret.) related his experience as a full-time military analyst during the 1991 Gulf War. This account reveals how the Pentagon translated their perception of events into television reportage. Smith mentioned that he would routinely contact former colleagues at the Pentagon to get their views on the conflict. He also admitted being lobbied by Pentagon officials along the following lines:

> We're trying to get something done here, but we are stuck. It would be great if you could raise the issue on CNN. That might help us get some important things done more quickly.

Smith confessed he became part of the Pentagon's propaganda effort when he suggested on CNN that 'Saddam Hussein was losing the military war, but winning the propaganda war on the issue of civilian casualties' (Smith 1991: 24). These instances clearly show that by relying on sources with close ties to the Pentagon, CNN served as their propaganda channel.

Through their pseudo independent analysis, these sources not only generated news coverage favourable to the military perspective, but they also contributed to a news environment which made it easier for policy makers to advocate an aggressive and interventionist foreign policy agenda (Domke 2004).

In short, CNN is a major international television news provider, and a pioneer of 24-hour news networks. The Atlanta based news organisation has developed large viewership by diversifying delivery methods (satellite, cable and internet). It also provided audiences worldwide with quality coverage and analysis. CNN had also achieved numerous scoops in its long list of achievements. As such, it was the primary news television that covered live from Baghdad the 1991 Gulf War. Since the latter was a defining episode in the American–Middle Eastern relationship, the leading role played by CNN in this war justifies its choice as object of this study. Furthermore, CNN's influential Somalia coverage led numerous authors to speculate about the existence of a 'CNN effect'.

In both of these conflicts, CNN employed Orientalist and military frames. CNN's coverage of 'Desert Storm' set the template for this kind of coverage. It covered American troops from a human perspective, whereas Iraqis were demonised and dehumanised. Similarly, military framing provided a sanitised account of the war, which wrongly conveyed the impression that bombings and missile strikes were clean and surgical. In Somalia, the stakes were different and so was the framing, which focused on socalled 'humanitarian intervention'. Yet, even in this case, the Orientalist clichés predominated; the world was divided into the good guys (the Americans) and the bad guys (the others). This binary division moulds the different ethnicities and political forces in the Middle East into one undifferentiated form. By doing so, CNN provided a fixed and immutable picture of the Middle East and absolved the United States from any responsibility for its hegemonic role in the region.

4

The Origins of Modern Arab Nationalism

The Arab world consists of 358 million people in 25 countries and territories straddling North Africa and Western Asia. Most of the Arab population lives in cities and towns, while 5 per cent are pastoral nomads living in the deserts (Crystal 1987). The rise of Arab civilisation from the seventh century was linked to the emergence of Islam. A few decades after the death of Muhammad, the Prophet of Islam (AD 632), the Umayyad Dynasty came into power in Arabia (AD 661). The new regime eventually stretched across North Africa, Spain, Central and South Asia. But unlike the previous reign of the Four Rightly Guided Caliphates,[1] the Umayyad rulers favoured the Arabs over other ethnicities. This led to numerous uprisings, most particularly in Persia. By AD 750, subsequent insurgencies had shifted the balance of power inside the realm of Islam from the Arabs to the Persians (the Turks gained the ascendancy from 1075 onwards). Up until the twentieth century, Arabs were usually relegated to a secondary role even though Arabic remained the *lingua franca* of the Islamic Caliphate.

Over the centuries, Arab consciousness transcended regional and religious identifications. For Albert Hourani, the renowned fourteenth-century Arab Philosopher Ibn Khaldun exemplified this consciousness. According to Hourani, Arabs lived in 'a world where a family from southern Arabia could move to Spain, and after six centuries return nearer to its place of origin and still find itself in familiar surroundings, [they] had a unity which transcended divisions of time and space; the Arabic language could open the door to office and influence throughout that world; a body of knowledge, transmitted over the centuries by a known chain of teachers, preserved a moral community even when rules changed' (Hourani 1991: 4). Sati' al-Husri, one of the main Arab nationalist philosophers, regards the Arabic language and the common history of Arab peoples as the defining pillars of Arab nationalism (Barakat 1993: 34). Citizens within Arab countries carry a sense of historic accomplishment achieved through a millennium of achievements in fields as varied as politics, military knowledge, economics, arts and sciences.[2] The diverse dynasties that ruled the Arab world as a single entity for extended periods instilled a sense of common history.[3] The free circulation of peoples, especially traders and scholars, from one end of the Arab world to the other for more than a millennium (until the advent of European colonialism) fostered a collective memory. However, some theoreticians of Arab nationalism, such as Abd al-Aziz Duri, consider that it was Islam, which had 'unified the Arabs and provided them with a message, an ideological framework, and a state,' (Barakat 1993: 35). As a consequence, the identities of Arabism and Islam, traditionally inseparable and used interchangeably, illustrate the Arab concept of *umma* (nation).

As the nineteenth century approached, the Ottoman Empire confronted continuous European expansion. Ottoman defeats in the Caucasus and Central Asia[4] paved the way for Western imperialism in that area and destabilised the Arab region. This became obvious after Napoleon's invasion of Egypt in 1798 and the French occupation of Algeria (formerly an Ottoman territory) in 1830. In its final days, the Ottoman State was itself dominated by Turk nationalists, who sometimes forcibly imposed the use of the Turkish language in predominantly Arab regions. This state of affairs led to the creation of Arab nationalist movements; they first appeared in Syria and Lebanon, and were primarily led by Arab Christians. In *The Arab Awakening* (1938), George Antonius chronicled the crucial role played by Arab Christians in stirring up Arab nationalist feelings against Ottoman rule. Originally therefore, Arab nationalism was primarily directed against the Turks, not against the West (Kramer 1993:180).

Turkey supported the Axis powers during World War I, and this enabled greater cooperation between the Allies and Arab nationalists. It has often been asserted that modern Arab nationalism began when the Allies promised support to Cherif Hussein's campaign for a united Arab state. This pledge was offered on the condition that the Arab tribes mobilised against the Turks[5] (Antonius 1938: 153–157). However, the pledge proved to be a mirage. Following the defeat of the Turks in 1918, the Arabs found themselves separated in newly created colonies, mandates and protectorates arranged by French and British officials. The Sykes–Picot Agreement secretly negotiated in 1916, divided the Arab lands in Arabia and the Levant into zones of French and British colonial influence. The Arabs' situation was further complicated when British Foreign Secretary Arthur James Balfour issued a letter to Lord Rothschild in 1917, promising Britain's support for the establishment of a Jewish state in Palestine. This letter became known as the Balfour Declaration, the precursor of Israeli nationhood in 1948 (Stork 1972: 9–13).

Meanwhile, other Arab regions aligned with the Ottoman Empire were transferred to Colonial rule (Libya to Italy, the rest of North Africa, Syria and Lebanon to France; Egypt, Sudan, Palestine, Iraq, Arabia, and Aden to the British). The imposition of Western designed borders on the Arab world inevitably provoked deep resentment. In 1931, Sir Walter Smart, Oriental counsellor at the British Embassy in Cairo, denounced the division of lands that were ethnically, linguistically and economically homogenous into unpractical states (Kedourie 1976: 260). Boundaries between the newly designed nation states were indeed often arbitrary. They were mostly the work of junior colonial administrators such as T.E. Lawrence and Gertrude Bell (Henry et al. 2003: 297). With such measures, the Western colonial powers turned the tide of Arab nationalism against them (previously this nationalism was directed against the Turks).

As Western-established borders obstructed the political and economic development of the newly created Arab entities, Arab intellectuals developed a pan-Arab consciousness. Politically, the shared objective was to unify the Arab peoples of the Middle East under the banner of a single state (modelled on the pledge of Sir Henry McMahon to Cherif Hussein in 1915). Later, pan-Arabism became a sort of 'macro nationalism, or the projection of micro nationalism onto the larger geographical area, based on common interests (religion, culture and race) as the basis of aspiration for political entity' (Tibi 1981: 44). Under the impulse of the Christian Syrian ideologue Michel Aflaq, the 1943-created Baath Party (Renaissance Party) was the first to promote a version of Pan-Arabism that would unify Arab peoples into one single state. Accordingly, the Baath movement advocated three main principles: 'Arab unity based around Arab ethnos (rather than around religious identity through Islam); socialism; and a willingness to use, if necessary, revolutionary rather than democratic action through, for example, military coups to promote Arab unity and socialist goals' (Henry et al. 2003: 297). In the heated political atmosphere of World War II, many parties promoting Arab nationalism, such as the Baath party, were inspired by German nationalism.[6] For instance Sati' Al Husri considered the unification of the Arabs under one state to be the supreme goal. This necessitated the subordination of the individual will to the national will (Dawisha 2003). Just as German and Italian nationalism sought to unite Germany and Italy in the nineteenth century[7] pan-Arab nationalism aimed to unite the Arab nation. By the end of World War II, pan-Arabism had gained wide popularity in the Middle East. Consequently, the Western Colonial powers and especially Britain, decided to co-opt pan-Arab proponents instead of confronting them. British foreign affairs officials thus supported the formal creation of the Arab League in March 1945.[8] The league was established in Egypt under British occupation. Several studies highlight Britain's discrete role in shaping the structure of the inter-state Arab organisation (Doran 1999; Kedourie 1976; Kramer 2000). Pro-British Egyptian leadership of the Arab League would ensure the continuation of British military presence in the Middle East.

Nasser and the apogee of pan-Arabism

British plans to co-opt the ideals of pan-Arabism through the Arab League were soon obstructed by a major political development; the 1953 coup of Colonel Gamal Abdel Nasser against Faruk the pro-British monarch of Egypt. Nasser had served as a high ranked Egyptian officer during the 1948 War, following the creation of Israel. The subsequent defeat of several Arab armies by superior Israeli forces proved to him that the newly independent Arab states suffered from disunity and under-development. To overcome these weaknesses, Nasser and other advocates of Arab nationalism sought the realisation of two ideals: Arab renaissance and pan-Arab unity (Kramer

1993: 190). Later, secular and socialist understandings of these ideals were also adopted.

Nasser's detractors saw in pan-Arabism a means of political opportunism. They point to the fact that Nasser was primarily an Egyptian nationalist, who was affiliated with jingoistic organisations such as Young Egypt. The wars he waged in the name of pan-Arabism were described as a 'duty imposed by self-defence' (Jankowski 2002: 30–31). From this perspective, Nasser's pan-Arab call to political unity could be construed as a cynical way to barricade behind the Arab world for security purposes (Jankowski and Gershoni 1995: 134–135). But regardless of these criticisms, it is indisputable that Nasser strongly opposed Western interference in the region. Thus, he exploited the Cold War political atmosphere by playing the Eastern bloc against the Western powers.

In September 1955, Nasser concluded an arms deal with Czechoslovakia, a close ally of the Soviet Union; a move that irritated Washington. Western powers reacted by withdrawing their pledge of monetary assistance for the building of the Aswan Dam. His purpose was to irrigate potential farm land and to introduce electricity to rural Egypt. Nasser was initially approved a World Bank loan, but after the Czechoslovakian arms deal, the United States and Britain obstructed the loan, pushing Nasser toward the Soviet Union. Aligned with the communist bloc, relations between Nasser and the West soon deteriorated. Nasser stood up against neo-colonial schemes in the region, such as the Baghdad Pact (1955),[9] and initiated a major international crisis by nationalising the Suez Canal (26 July 1956), which was owned by British and French investors. Nasser's status in the Arab world was enhanced; he gained worldwide recognition as a champion of decolonisation in Africa. At the 1955 Asian-African Conference (also known as the Bandung Conference)[10] held in Indonesia, Nasser reached the height of international recognition, becoming the friend of Prime Minister Jawaharlal Nehru of India and President Tito of Yugoslavia.

With Suez nationalisation, the armies of Britain, France, and Israel sought to occupy Egypt. This military operation ended in fiasco after strong criticisms from both the United States and the Soviet Union. This episode strengthened Nasser's pan-Arab claims. His support for socialist independence movements throughout the Middle East and Africa brought Third World acclaim. However, his decision to engage further on behalf of the Soviet Union against the clients of Washington in the region (especially the Gulf monarchies) led to the disastrous Egyptian intervention in Yemen (1962–1967);[11] a costly adventure for the Egyptian military (McNamara 2000). Hence, when Israel launched the Six-Day War in 1967, the overstretched Egyptian forces were crushed. This humiliating defeat combined with the death of Nasser (1970) set back the cause of Pan-Arabism. Nonetheless, these ideals remained alive at the popular level. Nasser had skilfully used radio and television broadcasting to spread pan-Arab sentiments (Danielson 1998: 113–114). The Egyptian revolutionaries, while seizing power from King Faruk, announced their first communiqué from Cairo Radio on 4 July 1953. This communiqué was inserted within a half-hour radio programme called *The Voice of the Arabs*. Nasser gave orders to upgrade this programme into a major radio feature. *The Voice of the Arabs* started broadcasting for 18 hours each day across the Arab world (James 2006b). Cairo Radio soon succeeded in mobilising the Arab populace. Its contribution toward the anti-colonial struggles in North-Africa and Yemen has been well documented (James 2006a). *Voice of the Arabs* reached its zenith during the mid-1950s, as new low-cost transistor radios became available in cities and villages. Combining highly emotive anti-colonial rhetoric with music from renowned Arab female singers such as Umm Kalthoum,[12] Cairo Radio became a pan-regional phenomenon.

Nasser's communication strategy bypassed the illiteracy that plagued the Arab world.[13] Illiteracy meant that classical Arabic was in steady decline, whereas local dialects flourished. There has always been a gulf between formal Arabic and the different local dialects, which vary even within particular countries. A Moroccan would never be able to understand an Iraqi if both use their respective dialects to communicate. But because of Nasser's communication prowess, Egyptian movies, radio broadcasts, and television serials gave Egyptian cinema Arab pre-eminence for more than half a century, turning the Egyptian dialect into the Arabs' new *lingua franca* (Shafik 1998: 85–86). This provided the Arabs once again with a commonly understood language; an important prerequisite in developing national consciousness (Anderson 1991: 44–46).

The Arab transnational media and pan-Arabism

In the decades after decolonisation, some Arab governments, especially those of North Africa could not easily revert to the Arabic language. In 1968, Algerian President Boumedienne announced that 'without recovering that essential and important element which is the national language, our efforts will be vain, our personality incomplete and our entire body without a soul' (Mostari 2005: 43). Yet despite political commitment, the 'Arabization programmes' often faced hostile reactions from people previously educated within colonial educational institutions. There was also a shortage of the qualified personnel needed to achieve linguistic re-conversion. After the Algerian government decided to dismantle the colonial language as the first language of education and administration in the late 1960s, Arabic was only slowly introduced in schools, starting with the primary schools, and then in social science and humanities subjects in high schools. Two decades later, Arabic finally became the primary medium of communication in the secondary schools and several university programmes. Other Arab countries, such as Morocco and Tunisia, knew similar developments. Therefore, one can say that classical Arabic language regained its vitality in the entire Arab world only from the mid-1980s onwards. In these circumstances, there were opportunities for pan-Arabist discourse. These opportunities were underpinned by common historical, linguistic and cultural experiences reinforced by migration flows. Furthermore, the Arab anti-colonial struggle was often a transnational activity (e.g. Moroccan, Algerian and Tunisian nationalist leaders were based in Egypt); a trend further reinforced by Nasser's foreign policy orientations. Hence, shared history and modern collective concerns meant that Arabs had an established transnational basis for political debate (Lynch 2003: 59).

In this light, one can appreciate the proliferation of transnational Arabic newspapers and magazines, and the steady increase in their readership throughout the Arab world. Arabic newspapers based in London, such as *Asharq al-Awsat* (launched in 1978) and *Al Hayat* (Launched in 1988), were able (with technological developments in design, transmission and text) to simultaneously print their papers from many hubs in the Middle East and worldwide. During the early 1990s, *Al Hayat* for example printed in London, Frankfurt, Cairo, Bahrain, Beirut, New York and, occasionally Marseille. As such, they could access readers throughout the Arab Diaspora. In 2005, *Al Hayat*'s combined print run was between 160,000 and 170,000, and *Asharq al-Awsat* around 200,000.[14] Both these newspapers were the preferred tribune for liberal intellectuals (before satellite television and the internet). The off-shore Arab press adhered to a broad pan-Arab discourse in order to cater for its readership in the Arab world (Schleifer 2004).

Yet despite these tangible developments, Arab print media still operated in precarious economic circumstances against the constant interference of governments, political players and ideologically lauded partisans (El Affendi 1999). Former American ambassador to Yemen and specialist in Arab media, William Rugh, classified Arab journalists prior to the 1990s into three categories: The 'mobilisation press' controlled by revolutionary governments (Libya, Syria, Iraq, and Sudan), the 'loyalist press' which mostly belonged to the private sector but answered to governments (e.g. in the Gulf States), and the 'diverse press' which reflected diverse partisan politics but was subjected to subtler pressures (Lebanon, Morocco, Kuwait etc.) (Rugh 2004: 30–91). The overall situation was succinctly summarised by Ibrahim Nawar, head of the Arab Press Freedom Watch (APFW), who observed that 'freedom of expression is not something on offer in the Arab world' (Nawar 2000).

Arab journalists have always had to carefully contemplate the 'red lines' established by authoritarian governments. Issues associated with the ruling institutions and their interests, national traditions, and predominant ideologies, were all classified under the sacrosanct title of 'national security'. On this basis, governments implemented a wide range of restrictions supervised by censorship departments and intelligence agencies. These restrictions have included the refusal to issue visas, the blocking of news sources, and the seizure of publications. Furthermore, Arab journalists have frequently been singled out through monitoring, deportation and personal threats. This led many publications to conduct self-censorship (Amin 2002: 128). Even offshore printed media, such as *Al Hayat* and *Acharq al-Awsat*, were subject to political pressure from Arab regimes. Jihad B. Khazen, former senior editor of both publications, wrote about the pressure from Arab officials not to publish certain information. He observed that the Arab media was controlled by an official 'system of denial'. In cases of non-compliance, ban and seizure were the usual sanctions.[15] For instance, *Al Hayat* was banned in certain Arab countries 60 times in 1994, 35 times in 1995, and 20 times respectively in 1996 and 1997 (Khazen 1999: 87–92).

But this state of affairs was about to change. Indeed, in the early 1990s, private Arab transnational satellite broadcasters (primarily Saudi-owned), such as the Middle East Broadcast Corporation (MBC)[16] (1991) and The Arab Radio and Television (ART)[17] (1994), began their operations in the Arab world, and successfully won audiences over. MBC catered to more than 130 million Arabic speaking people around the world (1996 estimations), while ART (later to become a pay per view television network) had claimed by 2007 about 10 million subscribers (Allied Media Corp. 2007). Transnational satellite broadcasting significantly reinforced the pan-Arab identity. Under new technologies of transmission, local regimes could no longer imprint their so-called 'national values' upon their subjects. By transcending borders, satellite broadcasts were able to circumvent national controls. Thus, Arab rulers (who are mostly non-elected and authoritarian) could no longer preserve their monopoly on information. During earlier decades, government-controlled television was the defining feature of local and regional broadcasting in the Arab region. Accordingly, television news was no more than a 'mouthpiece for government policies vis-à-vis national, regional, and international issues and events' (Ayish 2002: 138, 140).

Arab satellite channels thus provided Arab intellectuals with the necessary platform to discuss Middle Eastern issues on a pan-regional level; a trend reinforced by the introduction of the internet. As a result, Arab opinion leaders started talking to each other as never before. Due to the declining cost of dishes and sophisticated programming, which rivalled government-owned channels, satellite television had become the preferred choice to millions of Arab viewers. Subsequently, satellite television networks, such as Al Jazeera, free-view newspapers on the Internet, and instant mobile texts, have enabled citizens throughout the Middle East to share opinion outside of state censorship. This has facilitated communal consciousness and the reconstruction of Arab identity in the Arab world, despite the opposition of official apparatchiks, who have long relied upon regional illiteracy to minimise scrutiny of their policies. In one instance, a senior Yemeni official spoke of his surprise when he went to the countryside to hear local villagers speaking of issues such as privatisation and globalisation. When he asked about their source of information, he was told it was from watching Arab satellite television, including Al Jazeera and MBC (Ghareeb 2000: 399).

Evolution of the pan-Arab discourse

Nasser, the Baath party (in Syria and Iraq) and other Arab nationalist movements sought pan-Arab political unity, by force if necessary. Nasserist and Baathist perspectives were very critical of Arab state entities. They were regarded as 'deviant and transient' because they obstructed the construction of a larger Arab nation. This objective grew out of the commitment to Arab consensus (i.e. that Arab leaders are expected to act collectively on important Arab issues). Egypt was regarded as central to the Arab system (it was the most populous Arab country, and host of the Arab League), and the Palestine cause was strongly emphasised (Sirriyeh 2000: 54–56). Pan-Arab discourse was imbued with socialism and secularism and left no particular room for Islam. Islamists often received harsh treatment from Nasserist[18] and Baathist[19] regimes.

From the early 1970s, pan-Arabism became an authoritarian doctrine. The Baath party, for example, relied on security forces to govern Syria and Iraq at the expense of human rights. In the meantime, Nasserism declined as social force with the death of its leader, while pan-Arab Palestinian movements lost their appeal after continual in-fighting and disastrous political choices.[20]

When the American military campaign against Iraq took place in 1991, pan-Arabism's appeal was at its lowest point. Islamist movements benefited from this decline in what constituted a major shift in Middle-Eastern politics (Kepel 2002). Previously, Islamist movements had barely survived within Arab societies, but opposition to the 1991 Gulf War rallied Islamist opposition throughout the Arab world. Mass protests were organised by Islamist parties from Casablanca to Jakarta. Such parties became more visible in the politics of societies as diverse as Morocco,

Egypt, Jordan, Kuwait, Turkey, Indonesia, and Malaysia.[21] As pan-Arabists and Islamists felt the danger of the American hegemony, they decided to cooperate.

The pan-Arab discourse and Al Jazeera (1996–2001)

The First Gulf War (1991) was a crucial episode in the development of Arab media. This was the first time that Arabs had seen a war against fellow Arabs through the 'enemy's lenses', as CNN was the sole instant chronicler of that conflict. This exposed the shortcomings of Arab state-owned television networks. Saudi television, for example, failed to mention Iraq's invasion of Kuwait for more than 48 hours. Such media were also ineffective in 'selling' their patrons' alliance with Washington. This situation compelled the wealthy Gulf States to consider an upgrade in their broadcasting networks (Schleifer 2004). Consequently, Saudi-sponsored satellite broadcasters grew rapidly, as stations such as MBC (1991), ART (1994) started transmitting. These were entertainment-focused in 1994. The Saudi government proposed the establishment of a 24/7 news channel and founded the satellite network ORBIT.[22] For this purpose, ORBIT commissioned the BBC to produce Arab-World Television. For the BBC board, this was a way to penetrate the wealthy Gulf States market. This initiative foundered after the BBC aired some critical programmes about the Saudi Royal family. Eventually, ORBIT-BBC was terminated in April, 1996 (Richardson 2003). One hundred and fifty former staff members of BBC Arabic, who had been trained for the ORBIT project, were made redundant. One fired journalist offered a business proposal for a professional 24-hour Arabic news channel to the Qatari government. Coincidentally, Qatar, under a new Emir, was undertaking a modernisation campaign, and had just liberalised censorship practices. This opened the way for professional television journalism and public affairs programming (Schleifer 2003).

Understanding Qatar's history and geo-politics places the Al Jazeera phenomenon in context. Since the nineteenth century, Qatar had been threatened by the expansionist clans governing neighbouring Bahrain and Saudi Arabia. Military excursions from the Al Khalifa clan (Bahrain) and the Al Saud (Saudi Arabia) were frequent. Ultimately, Qatar's survival depended on the intervention of British colonial forces (led by Colonel Lewis Pelly). In 1916, Qatar was designated as a British protectorate.

The foreign policy course of modern Qatar was shaped by tensions with neighbours, and the patronage of foreign powers. Tensions were especially sharp with Bahrain[23] and with Saudi Arabia. Occasionally, military skirmishes took place (this occurred in 1986 between Qatar and Bahrain coastguards). Similarly, serious border incidents between Qatar and Saudi Arabia almost led to military confrontation in September 1992.[24] In 1995, their relationship deteriorated when Qatar objected to the Saudi candidate, who was about to take over the position of secretary general of the Gulf Cooperation Council (GCC).[25] In the meantime, Sheikh Hamad Bin Khalifa Al-Thani ousted his father as Emir of Qatar. Hoping to exploit this situation, Saudi Arabia, Bahrain and the United Arab Emirates welcomed the deposed Emir of Qatar Sheikh Khalifa (Cordesman 2003). In response, his son established economic ties with Israel. In October 1995, he signed a letter of intent to supply Qatari gas to Israel. Ties between Qatar and Saudi Arabia further worsened in February 1996, when a Saudi-backed coup was foiled in Qatar (MEES 1996).

Qatar is a very rich country, holding the third-largest natural gas reserves in the world estimated at 15 billion barrels (2.4 km^3). Its per capita income is the highest in the Middle East ($39,607 as of 2005) and among the highest in the world. However, Qatar is also a tiny country with a population of 589,000 (2001 census) of which less than 200,000 are native nationals. Qatar is in fact the smallest Arab state (Sakr 2001: 56). Being extremely rich, yet vulnerable, compelled the Qatari rulers to think about efficient insurance strategies. One of these is obviously Western patronage. However, this possibility extends to its neighbours as well. Qatar's new Emir, Sheikh Hamad, sought to create a comparative advantage over its neighbours through media development. This would give Qatar a distinctive voice, and change its image from that of a little-known Gulf oil producer to a major player in the international community. Thus, within four months of his takeover, Sheikh Hamad ended press censorship, and soon afterwards abolished the Ministry of Information. Also, he agreed to the local 24-hour relay of BBC programmes in Arabic and English on FM radio (a first in the Arab world). It was against this backdrop that the Qatari government invested $150 million for the establishment of Al Jazeera in November 1996. However, the Qatari government was careful to avoid any national recognition with the Al Jazeera logo. The Emir also insisted that the $150 million investment was to be a five-year loan rather than a gift (Sakr 2001: 56–57). Therefore, despite being launched as a state-financed satellite channel, the Qatari government's subtle distancing made Al Jazeera look like a BBC type model rather than a state-controlled Arab network (Schleifer 2001).

Al Jazeera and the establishment of a new Arab journalistic culture

Before Al Jazeera, 'Arab news media resembled the desert: barren, boring, oppressive and repetitive' (Lynch 2005a: 40). Arab viewers were bombarded by footage detailing their rulers' trips inside and outside their countries, without any coverage regarding plans and policies. Communication was always top-bottom, rather than the opposite. As the mouthpiece of local regimes, Arab media never approached political, social, economic, or religious subjects which were deemed sensitive. Al Jazeera immediately challenged this environment by launching talk shows that were fast paced, innovative, and daring. At the forefront of the change was Faisal Al-Kasim, a Syrian Druze with a PhD in English literature. He had worked for the BBC Arabic Radio and Television as producer and anchor of news programmes. Al-Kasim became famous as the presenter for *Al Ittijah Al Mo'akis* (The Opposite Direction), a weekly talk show that helped to forge Al Jazeera's reputation. In this programme, Al-Kasim would spend the first two minutes posing questions that reflected opposite positions on a chosen topic. He would then open the debate on some of the most sensitive issues in Arab society. The format of this show, namely two guests representing two opposite sides of an argument, was novel in the Arab media.

From the very beginning in November 1996, the show stirred up controversies over political, cultural, and religious controversy. On politics, 'The Opposite Direction' regularly featured opponents of Arab regimes, most particularly Egypt, Syria, Algeria, Morocco, Tunisia, Jordan, and the Gulf states. At the end of 1998, the talk show featured a debate between a Jordanian official and a Syrian intellectual on the 1994 Jordanian–Israeli

Peace Treaty. The Syrian directly questioned the legitimacy of the Jordanian state by claiming its formation had been designed to absorb Palestinians displaced by the creation of Israel in 1948. In response, the Jordanian Ministry of Information cancelled the accreditation of the Al Jazeera news staff in Amman (Sakr 2001: 120). 'The Opposite Direction' also irritated the Kuwaiti government when it hosted a debate between a Kuwaiti newspaper editor and a renowned pro-Iraqi Palestinian journalist on the issue of UN sanctions against Iraq. Both guests criticised the Kuwaiti regime for its endorsement of the sanctions. Immediately afterwards, the Kuwaiti information minister flew to Qatar to complain. He was told that the government was not involved with Al Jazeera's news content. On 27 January 1999, the programme hosted a debate about the ongoing Algerian civil war. The oppositional representative clearly gained the upper hand at which point the Algerian government cut the electricity supply to the capital Algiers (and some other cities), to prevent the programme from screening. Abdullah Al Nafisi, a Kuwaiti intellectual, was the guest of the same talk-show on 13 July 1999. He launched a salvo of criticisms against the Gulf monarchs, and attacked the Saudi clergy for ignoring major issues such as royal corruption. The Saudi authorities responded by pressuring on Al Jazeera. Saudi officials even intimidated the only Saudi member of Al Jazeera to leave the network (El-Nawawy and Iskandar 2002: 117, 119). Yet, Al-Kasim's talk show knew no boundaries. Even Qatari government policies constituted no red line for the daring Syrian anchor. He hosted a debate on Qatar's rapprochement with Israel; a policy that was openly criticised on the programme by a professor of political science at the University of Qatar (Al-Kasim 1999).

Beyond politics, Al-Kasim's programme regularly featured controversial anti-religious personalities. On 31 December 1996, For example, 'The Opposite Direction' hosted an episode with the Egyptian scholar Nasr Hamed Abu Zeid (the local equivalent of Salman Rushdie). That was the first time that Abu Zeid had appeared on television; he was so vilified by religious authorities that no Arab television network dared to interview him. Abu Zeid took full advantage of the opportunity and vehemently attacked his detractors. In a similar incident in 26 October 1997, Al-Kasim invited Sadeeq Jalal Al-Azm, professor of philosophy at the University of Damascus, to challenge renowned Muslim scholar, Yousuf al-Qaradawi. The latter was put on the defensive as Al-Azm ridiculed the fundaments of religious thought; a previously unthinkable occurrence on Arab television. Other prominent Arab anti-religious thinkers, such as Lafif Lakhdar, Aziz Lazma, and Rifaat Saeed appeared on the programme, amidst opposition from religious institutions.

While the aforementioned exchanges reveal the degree of freedom enjoyed by Al Jazeera's anchors,[26] they also drew criticism from foreign and Arab observers. The Qatar–based channel was said to encourage sensationalism in order to increase audience share. The response of Al Jazeera's journalists was to highlight that critics had confused the network with the views of talk-show guests (Zednik 2002:4). Al Jazeera's talk-shows simply allowed scholars and political opposition figures the opportunity to articulate their views publicly. Al Jazeera's philosophy totally contrasted with that of elite controlled, Saudi-funded competitors (Bahry 2001; Sakr 2001: 55). By serving as a forum for opposition groups, and by airing controversial debates, Al Jazeera exposed the misdeeds of the local regimes. Institutionalised corruption in the monarchical regimes and widespread human rights abuses in the militaristic regimes were equally criticised. Scholars such as Kai Hafez hailed Al Jazeera as the only satellite television service in the Arab world to deal with sensitive political, social, and religious issues (Hafez 1999: 75). Other academics, such as John Alterman, noted that Al Jazeera had obliged Arab politicians to become attentive to public opinion more than in the past (Alterman 1998).

Al Jazeera's news gathering and news presentation techniques were also innovative. The Qatar based channel introduced new methods of editing and graphic design. It also pioneered new delivery formats in the region by coordinating different in-studio and satellite-relayed real time interviews (Ayish 2002: 149). Consequently, Al Jazeera set the standards of news reporting in the region. State operated media organisations were obliged to open up, upgrade the training of their staff, and even advocate the lifting of censorship. Arab private networks were pushed to include serious current affairs debates in their programming. The result was undeniably beneficial to the viewers; they received diversified programmes and tasted freedom of expression for the first time (Al-Hail 2000). Yet, with these innovations came heavy consequences. Al Jazeera's anchors became persona *non grata* in many Arab countries, and Al Jazeera offices were forcibly closed throughout the Arab world.[27] At various times Tunisia, Morocco, and Libya have recalled their ambassadors from Doha in protest against Al Jazeera coverage. Strained relationships with Arab governments also affected advertising. The Saudi government discouraged regional companies and multinationals alike from doing business with Al Jazeera. Accordingly, PepsiCo, General Electric, and many other multinational corporations cancelled advertising campaigns. As a result, Al Jazeera received only a meagre part of its revenues from advertising. Other Arab transnational satellite networks earned 90 per cent of their revenue from this source (Zednik 2002). Thus, Saudi-owned MBC earned 91.5 million dollars from advertising in 1999, while Al Jazeera, with its 35 million watchers, earned only 8 million dollars during the same year (Sakr 2001: 114).

Despite these difficulties, Al Jazeera's contributions to Middle Eastern journalistic culture were unprecedented. It was the first network to have an investigative agenda in a political environment characterised by official secrecy. With its show, *Sirri lil-Ghaya* (Top Secret), Al Jazeera's journalist Yosri Fouda tackled many issues for the first time. Modelled on BBC's *Panorama*, 'Top Secret' scored many scoops, such as the investigation of the 1999 crash of Egypt-Air flight 990.[28] This episode attracted much popular interest primarily because the numerous Egyptian television channels kept silent about it, while the US media spread many premature speculations. Yosri Fouda's programme managed to prove the technical impossibility of the pilot suicide theory. On 9 November 2000, Fouda ran an investigative piece which linked the use of depleted uranium during the 1991 Gulf War to the spread of cancer and birth defects in southern Iraq. Helped by Christopher Busby, a renowned British scientist, Fouda's investigation broke new ground. It preceded similar findings by European journalists, who were enquiring about the mysterious illnesses that had affected NATO soldiers (Fouda 2001).

Similarly, In October 2000 Al Jazeera launched a 15-hour documentary dedicated to the Lebanese Civil War. Viewer ratings rose throughout the Middle East, as the war was explained systematically with passion and intrigue. Despite criticisms from the major protagonists, people throughout Beirut and elsewhere gathered to watch each episode. Yet again, such openness was resented by some Arab journalists. In an interview with Al Jazeera's director Mohamed Jassem Al-Ali, the Arabic newspaper Al Wasat, was asked whether the documentary had aggravated past wounds. Al-Ali responded that it wasn't the first time they had 'tackled issues that others considered to be a taboo, subjects for which people think that the time is not yet appropriate'. He then declared 'to those people, I answer that the timing will not be suitable any day, and thus this excuse should not remain like a sword aimed at us' (Gabriel 2002).

Arguably, Al Jazeera's most significant innovation was in the area of war reporting. In December 1998, the Qatar-based satellite channel gained an impressive scoop by reporting on the American/British joint bombing campaign 'Desert Fox'.[29] It was the only international media organisation to have reporters inside Iraq who could provide live broadcasts of this military operation (Bahry 2001). It has been asserted that Al Jazeera's coverage pushed the US military to shorten the timeframe of their 'Desert Fox' operations (Sheikh 2003). During this crisis, CNN relied partially on footage from Al Jazeera for their coverage. Thus, only a few years after the 1991 Gulf War, Arab and international viewers depended on Al Jazeera rather than CNN to see exclusive images of important military events.

It was the second Palestinian uprising (also called *al-Aqsa Intifada*) that really gave Al Jazeera a major international profile. On 28 September 2000, Israeli Prime Minister Ariel Sharon, surrounded by hundreds of Israeli riot police, visited Al Haram Mosque in Jerusalem (the third holiest place in Islam). This visit was perceived as a provocation by the worshipers. Their angry reaction led to a major police intervention. The day after Sharon's visit, following Friday prayers, riots broke out in the West Bank and Gaza. In a short period, dozens of Palestinians were killed by the Israeli army and thousands were injured. Al Jazeera, along with other Arab transnational networks, seized this opportunity to obtain maximum coverage for the Arab world. To this end, Al Jazeera did not hesitate to air graphic footage of death and demolition in the West Bank and Gaza. These images were not screened by Western television networks and this enhanced the reputation of Al Jazeera as a credible and reliable source of information in the Middle East. The Qatar based channel subsequently devoted much airtime to cover the plight of the Palestinians. This included debates and documentaries about the Intifada. Academic Mohamed Zayani observed: 'More than any other channel, Al Jazeera has capitalized on the importance of the Palestinian question. It has [...] provided instant coverage of the events and aired detailed reports on the latest developments, [and] shed an unpleasant light on the practices of Israel in the Middle East' (Zayani 2005: 171).

With this coverage Al Jazeera viewership in the occupied territories increased considerably. An October 1999 survey found that 32.8 per cent of Palestinians 'watched and trusted' the network compared to only 1.4 per cent who said the same about CNN (Lynch 2003: 64). Al Jazeera's audience support was higher than that of any other network. As part of their reportage, the Qatari-based channel frequently investigated the inefficiency, abuse and corruption of the Palestinian Authority. This infuriated Arafat's officials, who twice shut Al Jazeera's Ramallah bureau in protest (Shaulia 2005). Al Jazeera also invited Israeli decision makers to participate in panel programmes. Previously, no Israeli (official or otherwise) had ever been interviewed[30] in any Arab media outlet. Al Jazeera was the first to break this taboo, a move that drew considerable criticism from Palestinian radical movements. Many Israeli officials welcomed Al Jazeera's approach. For example, Gideon Ezra, former deputy head of the General Security Service (GSS) commented favourably on the fair hearing he was given by Al Jazeera. Nonetheless, other Israeli decision makers complained about the tone of Al Jazeera's coverage and its likely impact on Arab populations. In a Washington speech, Shimon Peres, the Israeli foreign minister, criticised Al Jazeera. This was covered by the network (Miles 2005: 95-96). Peres criticised Al Jazeera's use of the word 'martyr' to describe Palestinians killed in the Intifada (uprising) against Israel. He also criticised the avoidance of the expression 'suicide bombing' in the Palestinian context. Against this, it should he noted that most (if not all) of the other Arab satellite networks could be criticised on the same grounds. Some scholars attribute these semantic patterns of coverage to cultural factors (Barkho 2006).

Al Jazeera and the pan-Arab discourse

Many academics considered Al Jazeera's coverage of the 2000 Intifada as a major contribution to the pan-Arabist revival (Schneider 2000; Kraidy 2002; Amin 2004, Zayani 2005). In fact, this coverage attracted the largest audience in the history of Arab broadcasting, and gave the Intifada its pan-Arab dimension. Viewers from Morocco to Oman came to share the experiences of Palestinians confronting the Israeli military machine. The image of the young Mohammed Al-Durrah being shot by Israeli troops on 30 September 2000 gained international prominence. The video footage was provided by freelance cameraman Talal Abu Rahma, who worked for French television channel, France 2. Al Jazeera's repeated broadcasting of Al-Durrah's death became a rallying symbol for anti-Israel opposition throughout the Arab world. This recreated a pan-Arab sense of 'imagined community' (Anderson 1991).

In the aftermath of the 1991 Gulf War and the subsequent growth of American hegemony over the Middle East, pan-Arabist and Islamist leaders decided to open a dialogue. The first gesture was made by the ruling Sudanese Islamist leader Hassan Al-Turabi. He organised in April and August 1991 rounds of conferences named Popular Arab Islamic Conference (PAIC) in Khartoum (Sudan). Attended by delegates from 45 States, the conference sought to reconcile the various pan-Arab and pan-Islamist groups. The New joint purpose was to oppose America's 're-colonization of the Islamic world' (Lesch 2002: 203).[31]

Al Jazeera's journalists provided a platform for both pan-Arabs and pan-Islamists to exchange ideas and principles. This editorial stance was enabled by the fact that many Islamist opinion leaders, such as Tarek El-Bishri[32] and Fahmy Howeidy,[33] were themselves former pan-Arabists. Earlier, hard-line Islamist rhetoric, viewed pan-Arabism as a Western import, encouraged by Orientalists and colonialists to divide and weaken the Muslims by separating Arabs from different ethnic groups. The new approach favoured reconciliation and mutual cooperation. For example, Tarek El-Bishri wrote: 'it is a duty of every Muslim to work for the revival and support for Arab unity' (Bishry 1998: 52). Pan-Arabist leaders also softened their positions by voicing respect for the role of Islam in Arab society. Their former ideals of political unity were abandoned in favour of an abridged version of pan-Arabism, which merely articulated cultural, social and economic bonds. It is this version of pan Arabism that became evident in Al Jazeera's coverage.

The 'Desert Fox' campaign (1998) and the second Palestinian Intifada (2000) were presented on Al Jazeera as Arab crises, rather than Iraqi and Palestinian issues, respectively. Media research confirmed this trend. Mohammed Ayish showed in an exploratory study, that 73.3 per cent of Al Jazeera's coverage was pan-Arab in orientation (Ayish 2001). This orientation allowed the Qatar-based network to expand its geographical reach, in the sense that its coverage of issues of interest to most Arab peoples increased its presence all over the Middle Eastern market. They provide what the public wants and reflect public opinion across the Middle East (Kifner 2001). Thus, one can say that editorial orientation of Al Jazeera conveniently met its market-driven strategy.

Al Jazeera's recruitment also followed the aforementioned direction. While the Qatar-based satellite channel recruited anchors, correspondents and staff from every Arab country, most of journalists originated from countries surrounding Israel (Palestinian territories, Jordan, Lebanon, and Syria). Historically, pan-Arabism was strongest in these regions, especially among the Palestinian people. Palestinian nationalism was itself strongly tinged with pan-Arabism.[34] Journalists were often influenced by pan-Arabism, as this world view pervaded in the education system and organisations. A good example is the Tunisian journalist Mohammed Krichane, who joined Al Jazeera in 1996 after working for the BBC and Radio Monte-Carlo. Apart from his daily appearances on the new network, he wrote articles for renowned pan-Arab newspapers such as *al-Quds al-Arabi*. Abd El-Bari Atwan, the influential editor of this newspaper, was often invited to discuss events on Al Jazeera's various talk-shows.

Yet unlike Nasser's revolutionary *Voice of the Arabs*, Al Jazeera's pan-Arabism adapted to modern realities. It did not advocate any unity guided by political authoritarianism; rather it promoted civil solidarities across Arab societies by making public argument accessible. Al Jazeera promoted a new culture of communication, which embraced dialogue and tolerated dissent. This contemporary version of pan-Arabism circumvented the repressive measures which had been implemented by national dictatorships to disrupt local traditions of the Arab public sphere.[35] Therefore, Al Jazeera helped to build a pan-Arab public sphere (Chapelier and Demleitner 2004; Lynch 2003). Al Jazeera's official motto, namely *Al-rai wa rai al-akhar* (The Opinion and the Opposite Opinion), spread the idea that viewpoints of others should be respected and discussed peacefully (Bahry 2001).

Another key contribution of Al Jazeera concerns its empowerment of women. The recruitment of many women anchors, gave them visibility within Arab public space. The courage, professionalism, and dedication of Al Jazeera's women correspondents became openly recognised throughout the Arab world, and this soon affected local politics. For example, two years after the launch of Al Jazeera in 1998, women in Qatar were allowed to stand as candidates and to vote in municipal elections for the first time. Forty seven per cent of Qatari women voted in these elections (Al-Hail 2000). Overall, after its inception in 1996 Al Jazeera became an island of open debate and information amidst a sea of oppression and censorship. Previously suppressed political debates, about all sorts of issues and among different political persuasions, became commonplace in the Arab world.

Al Jazeera in the aftermath of September 11

After 9/11, Al Jazeera assumed an unprecedented global profile. The Al Qaeda attacks increased the demand for sensational imagery and militant rhetoric. Subsequent statements by Osama bin Laden on Al Jazeera were highly sought after by other networks. Al Qaeda itself well understood the dynamics of media coverage (Lynch 2006). Previously, Al Qaeda's propaganda was hardly visible, but it was nonetheless active. Its main centre was located in London, under the pseudonym 'Committee of the Council and the Reform', and was coordinated by Khalid al-Fawwaz (arrested in 1998). Al Qaeda viewpoints were also spread through periodicals and Internet websites (such as azzam.com). Occasionally, Osama Bin Laden granted interviews to international journalists, such as Peter Arnett, Robert Fisk, Peter Bergen and Abdel Bari Atwan.[36] By having his videos broadcast on Al Jazeera, Bin Laden and his network maintained their profile. Al Jazeera's graphic coverage of American air-strikes in Afghanistan and the circulation of bin Laden's videotapes quickly became a public relations crisis for the Bush administration.

The use of Al Jazeera's platform enabled Al Qaeda to reach the transnational Arab audiences, and gain the attention of Western news media (Lynch 2006). The Qatar based satellite station also benefited from the worldwide attention. It should be noted that Al Jazeera was not the first network to be approached by militant groups. For example during the hijacking of the TWA 847 flight to Beirut in June 1985, the leader of the Lebanese Shiite militant group (AMAL) was in constant contact with the American network ABC. He appeared regularly on its news shows, and even participated in negotiating the story of the day. This infuriated some of the hostages, who referred to ABC as the 'Amal Broadcasting Corporation' (a reference to the name of the militia) (Cohen-Almagor 2005: 392). Similar arrangements were entered into by the *New York Times*, which published letters from the Unabomber, and CNN which ran interviews with Bin Laden in 1997 and again in 2002.[37]

Prior to 9/11, Al Jazeera was neither for, nor against the United States (Jasperson and El-Kikhia 2002: 9). In fact, Washington initially praised Al Jazeera for its democratic influence upon the Arab world (Schleifer 2005). Paradoxically, Al Jazeera's vulnerability derived from its commitment to the provision of extremely opposed viewpoints, however controversial. The Qatar based channel lined up Iraqi Baathists against Kuwaiti nationalists, pro-Iranian Shiites against pro-Saudi Sunnites, religious fundamentalists against ultra-secularists, Kurds and Berbers against pan-Arabists. Therefore, juxtaposing Al Qaeda's rhetoric with the US official communication was never intended to be an anti-American exercise. Bin Laden was simply another extreme voice open to criticism by detractors. This nonchalance was reflected in many Al Jazeera interviews. Omar Al-Issawi, one of the channel's founders stated in this regard: 'we do not believe in a blackout on Bin Laden. We know that if we do not broadcast that somebody else will' (Al-Issawi and Patiz 2003).

Al Jazeera was used to broadcasting controversial views and was not necessarily sympathetic toward Al Qaeda. The network would always scrutinise Al Qaeda discourse by bringing cohorts of analysts and commentators after every controversial broadcast. Whenever Al Qaeda released a tape, Al Jazeera allowed critical analysts from across the Arab political spectrum to provide a lengthy discussion. The militant group was denied any monopoly over political discourse and the shortcomings of its arguments were highlighted. Furthermore, Yusuf al-Qaradawi, the widely popular Islamist figure that regularly appeared on Al Jazeera's *Religion and Life*, fiercely criticised Bin Laden's brand of Islam (Lynch 2006). And, while airing interviews with Taliban representatives in Afghanistan, Al Jazeera allowed the expressions of anti-Taliban views. Warlord Abdurrab Rasul Sayyaf, whose support was pivotal for the pro-American post-war Afghan government was given airtime (Waxman 2001).

Al Jazeera also regularly invited American spokespeople. The best performed guests were, predictably, American diplomats who spoke Arabic, such as Christopher Ross and Alberto Fernandez. They appeared to be convincing in response to Al Qaeda's claims. Al Jazeera maintained a permanent reporter at the US Central Command (CENTCOM) in Qatar to relay the military perspective concerning the 'War on Terror'. Official accusations that Al Jazeera was a 'mouthpiece for terrorists' were not supported by evidence. As a matter of comparison, Al Jazeera aired five hours of Bin Laden videotapes over a four-year period; live broadcasts of President Bush exceeded 500 hours (Miles 2005: 360). Other research shows that over 90 per cent of all official statements screened on Al Jazeera over a one year period after 9/11 were made by American officials or their allies (Wildermuth 2005).

American frustration with Al Jazeera was driven by three related factors. From a military perspective, providing access to anti-American militants undermined media strategies associated with psychological operations. From a political perspective, the Bush administration sought to restrict debate regarding American foreign policy choices. Thus, alternative voices were seen as a threat to this course of action. The diplomatic battle for hearts and minds across the Muslim World was also threatened. By providing airtime to anti-American voices, Al Jazeera hampered America's public diplomacy throughout the Middle East.

Military and political considerations

After the 1991 Gulf War, military operations were no longer considered as a series of ground/air/sea manoeuvres. As the military entered the information age, warfare became a fast-paced confrontation of words and images. Subsequently, major news media organisations (and television in particular) were perceived as a 24-hour wartime player. Control of media content was deemed to be a paramount requirement to prevent the spread of information which might undermine the public will for wars. Reporters and news organisations were no longer considered to be dispassionate observers but potential friends or foes. This shift made the media environment itself a battlefield. Accordingly, the US military regarded the management of public information, the control of media sources, and the outright manipulation of public opinion as routine wartime objectives.

The grand strategy of information warfare aims to deny, exploit, influence, corrupt, or destroy the adversary information. In terms of tactics, one can differentiate between proactive and reactive tactics. The proactive side is encapsulated by the 'spectator sport warfare' paradigm, whereby Western citizens have become spectators rather than participants. From this perspective, war becomes a spectacle, which involves entertaining videogame-like sanitised images, which blur the distinction between truth and reality, factual information and propaganda.

On the reactive side, the Pentagon spin doctors identified a set of uncrossable red lines. These included coverage which questioned the justice of the American cause and commentary which might undermine the relationships within American brokered coalitions. Also redlined was news content with might undermine support or morale at home; and compromise the secrecy of military plans (Bessaiso 2005: 156). Clearly, therefore, American concerns about Al Jazeera were, *a priori,* military in origin. As subsequent analysis will show, the Qatar based channel regularly contravened the redline boundaries established by the Pentagon's information warriors.

As noted in the previous chapter, the Pentagon sought to buy exclusive rights for extremely high-resolution satellites covering Afghanistan in order to censor any photos of Afghan civilian casualties. This sanitisation was successful on American television networks, which rarely showed footage of 'collateral damage'. When they did so, they would reiterate that the war on Afghanistan was in response to the atrocity of the 9/11 attacks (Pintak 2006: 41–42). However, Al Jazeera contradicted this frame with vivid footage of personal suffering and human tragedies occurring within Afghanistan. Images of death and desolation associated with the bombing campaign were received by millions of viewers worldwide (Jasperson and El-Kikhia 2002: 7).

At the same time, Al Jazeera's critical scrutiny of the Bin Laden tapes and philosophy strengthened their legitimacy as a reliable television network vis-à-vis the 'War on Terror'. For the most part, they were not caught in the mutual clash of fundamentalisms. However, by broadcasting the Bin Laden videotapes, Al Jazeera presented multiple challenges to American officials. The Pentagon spin doctors had chosen names such as 'enduring freedom' and 'Infinite Justice'[38] to label their campaign, (suggesting that liberty and justice awaited the Afghan people). Yet, Bin Laden framed the war on Afghanistan as a 'religious war', taking advantage of a gaffe from

President Bush, who used the word 'crusade' in one of his speeches.[39] The Bin Laden videotapes also included threats that the war will continue as 'terrorist war', and that the 'storm of airplanes will not be calmed'. These threats, which were relayed by US media, directly hit the morale of the American people, provoking uproar within military and security circles. Al Jazeera's journalists also exposed occasional American military setbacks in Afghanistan. For example, Tayseer Alouni reported that two aircraft had been destroyed by Taliban forces. His report was accompanied by pictures of the debris, forcing the Pentagon to retract earlier denials (Bessaiso 2005: 157, 165). There is no doubt that Al Jazeera constituted a major difficulty for the Pentagon's 'War on Terror' media strategy. This state of affairs compelled the military elites to try and reduce the Arab Satellite Channel's influence internationally and in the Middle East.

The US president George W. Bush announced a zero-sum ultimatum for all the nations of the world, when he declared before a joint session of the US congress on 20 September 2001: 'every nation, in every region, now has a decision to make. Either you are with us, or you are with the terrorists.' This binary discourse left no room for alternative voices or analyses, and this was made very clear by Ari Fleisher the White House spokesman, who told journalists to be 'very careful about what they say'. Withholding information, censorship, and intimidation of media dissenters were intended to win the propaganda war within the United States and overseas. Yet, the reports of Al Jazeera from Afghanistan meant that US news media relied on a foreign source for its news feeds. This was in itself a major development. Indeed, 10 years earlier, global audiences had relied on CNN and its New Zealand-born reporter Peter Arnett to obtain on-the ground footage from Baghdad. In 2001, the world relied on Al Jazeera to get footage of the war on Afghanistan. For the first time in modern history, the Arab channel offered a worldwide, non-western perspective, on major international events. Al Jazeera's growing influence prompted American liberal news media to quote the Arab channel whenever they wanted to challenge the official perspective. El-Kikhia observed this development: 'in the climate after 9/11, no one wanted to be critical of what the Bush administration was doing. Being able to say "according to Al Jazeera," the media could say something without actually being the ones to say it' (Browne 2003: 25).

All things considered, it is a fact that many in the Arab world resented the unjust Ottoman administration in the years preceding World War I. This state of affairs planted the seeds of a new discourse promoting transnational Arab nationalism based on common interests. The end of the war and the victory of the allies saw the transfer of Arab lands into Western hands. The subsequent colonisation and partition of Arab territories increased pan-Arabism's popularity in the Middle East as it called for the unity of the Arab people. After World War II, pan-Arabism became the ideology of choice for several post-colonial regimes in the region (Egypt, Syria, and Iraq).

In Egypt, the Nasser regime was adept at using communication methods to reach out to the wider Arab community in support of anti-Western policies (such as backing the Algerian independence movement against France). The use of simple Arabic words in Egyptian television, radio, and print media, combined with entertainment programmes, amidst pan-Arab news framing, gave a wide appeal to the ideological framework promoted by the Nasser regime. This format moulded the Arab transnational media that appeared later in Beirut, and then in London (after the start of the Lebanese civil war). Accordingly, Arab transnational radio stations and newspapers targeted the wider Arab populations from Morocco to Oman as well as the Arab diaspora in Europe. Saudi Arabia supported numerous Arab transnational media initiatives to enhance its international status. However, a Saudi row with the BBC foiled their joint project for a news satellite network (Orbit). Qatar's Emir was approached to save the project, and Al Jazeera was born under Qatari patronage.

The BBC-trained journalists, who constituted the backbone of Al Jazeera, introduced a new journalistic culture to the Arab world. They adopted a daring editorial line which left no political taboos, and gave priority to debates and talk-shows featuring guests from across the political spectrum. After decades of state pressures and censorship, the freedom brought by Al Jazeera reinvigorated the Arab public sphere in many ways. Firstly, Arab audiences could view genuine discussions related to matters of collective concern, in which every subject was expected to be tackled. Guests were free to express their opinions on air as they had never done before. This has transformed an Arab political culture which had previously featured speakers bowing to official spheres and avoiding sensitive issues. Secondly, Al Jazeera reaffirmed the centrality of politics in the Arab public sphere, whereas other satellite competitors were solely concentrated on entertainment. As such, the Qatar based channel renewed emphasis on issues that were central to pan-Arab politics such as the Israel–Palestinian problem. As a result, Al Jazeera obliged Arab politicians to become more attentive to public opinion. Finally, Al Jazeera incorporated the increasingly influential Arab Diaspora into the Arab public sphere by discussing their own problems and by getting their feedback on the predicaments faced by the Arab world generally.

Al Jazeera's brand of pan-Arabism is a soft one. Unlike the authoritarian Nasserite and Baathist pan-Arab ideologies, the Qatar based network did not aim to create violent revolutions in the Arab world, or to push for forcible unifications in the region. Instead, they believed that the best way to reinforce pan-Arab solidarities was by making public argument accessible on a transnational level. Thus, freedom of speech and freedom of thought and empowerment of minorities would guarantee a culture of dialogue that would strengthen the transnational Arab public sphere.

Al Jazeera's journalistic culture created numerous problems for Arab regimes. The Qatari government was subsequently entangled in a web of diplomatic rows. The start of the 'War on Terror' in late 2001 brought a new set of problems for the Doha-based network. The American neo-conservative elites had embarked on a geo-strategic remoulding of Middle East foreign policy objectives, starting with Afghanistan and Iraq. As it provided a propaganda critique of American official communication efforts, Al Jazeera was identified by US political and military decision-makers as an enemy mouthpiece.

5

The Prospect of War in Iraq: Frames, Propaganda, and Debate

Why Iraq?

At the end of World War II, President Roosevelt met the King of Saudi Arabia, Abdulaziz Al Saud, and signed agreements that established a long-lasting American presence in the Middle East.[1] This presence grew to the point where the CIA played a key role in overthrowing the Mossadegh government of Iran. Their nationalisation of the British owned oil industry in 1953 had upset Anglo-American oil interests. Consequently, the CIA (with the active participation of the British MI6) removed Mossadegh from power on 19 August 1953 (Campbell and Keylin 1976: 205). From 1973, when the OPEC cartel of oil-producing countries dramatically increased oil prices, a small group of Washington insiders known as neo-conservatives advocated direct control over the Middle East region. They became influential within the Pentagon under the Presidential administrations of Ford, Reagan and Bush Senior. During the presidency of George W. Bush, neo-conservative figures filled the most influential advisory positions. Examples include Dick Cheney (US vice-president), Donald Rumsfeld (defense secretary), Paul Wolfowitz (deputy defense secretary), Richard Perle (chairman of the Pentagon Defense Policy Board), and William Kristol (founder of the neo-conservative think-tank, the Project of a New American Century (PNAC) (George 2005: 185–187).

The Prospect of War in Iraq

Under George W. Bush, official attitudes toward Iraq reflected the PNAC ideology. Their stated goal was 'to promote American global leadership' through 'military strength and moral clarity.' With these words, the PNAC envisioned America as a global hegemon which ought to become an empire (Altheide and Grimes 2005: 624). One should recall that on the eve of the 1991 Iraq War, PNAC issued a document, drafted by the likes of Elliot Abrams, Paul Wolfowitz and Richard Perle, entitled 'Defense Planning Guidance' which argued that the United States should be the sole twenty-first-century superpower. As pointed out in Chapter 3, this would happen by conducting pre-emptive wars to prevent the emergence of potential challengers. Interestingly, this document also called upon the United States to safeguard 'access to vital raw materials, primarily Persian Gulf oil' (Public Broadcasting Service 1992). Therefore, it was clear that the neo-conservatives, even before the formal inception of the PNAC in 1997, considered the invasion of Iraq indispensable and unavoidable. So, it was not surprising to see eighteen PNAC affiliates sending an open letter to President Clinton in January 1998, urging him to:

> enunciate a new strategy that would secure the interests of the US and our friends and allies around the world. That strategy should aim, above all, at the removal of Saddam Hussein's regime from power. (PNAC 1998)

Senior PNAC figures positioned themselves as primary opinion makers on matters concerning Iraq. They served as government officials, inner cabinet members, presidential advisers, journalists, and publishers. Consequently, PNAC members were key news sources whose claims were not openly challenged. Because reliance on official sources was part of journalistic routine, mainstream news institutions played a pivotal role in the 'war programming'[2] that occurred during the American invasion of Iraq.

The events of September 11 gave full momentum to PNAC projects. According to John Pilger, some high-ranked PNAC members had been longing for a catastrophic event on the scale of Pearl Harbor that could be used as a catalyst to reshape foreign policy. The attacks of September 11 2001 were thereby described as 'the opportunity of ages' (Pilger 2002: 19). The climate of fear which eventually prevailed enveloped political leaders and journalists, who were ready to do anything for the sake of protecting the United States. This was the ideal environment for PNAC to set in motion its agenda regarding Iraq. Richard Clarke, President Bush's advisor on terrorism until March 2003, confirms that the plan to attack Iraq was prepared before the attacks of September 11. In his book *Against All Enemies: inside America's War on Terror,* Clarke stated that following 9/11, the main topic discussed by the US Department of Defense was Iraq:

> I expected to go back into a round of meetings examining what the next attack could be, what our vulnerabilities were, what we could do about them in the short term. Instead, I walked into a series of discussions about Iraq. At first, I was incredulous that we were talking about something other than getting Al Qaeda. Then, I realized with almost a sharp physical pain that Rumsfeld and Wolfowitz were going to try to take advantage of this national tragedy to promote their agenda about Iraq. Since the beginning of the administration, indeed well before, they had been pressing for a war with Iraq. (Clarke 2004: 30)

Similar observations were made by seasoned reporter Bob Woodward, who said that Secretary of Defense Donald Rumsfeld immediately linked Iraq to the September 11 attacks regardless of evidence:

> Before the attacks, the Pentagon had been working for months on developing a military option for Iraq ... Any serious, full-scale war against terrorism would have to make Iraq a target – eventually. Rumsfeld was raising the possibility that they could take advantage of the opportunity offered by the terrorist attacks to go after Saddam immediately. (Woodward 2002: 49)

Richard Clarke's observations from this period are important because they reveal the motivations of key people within the US administration. According to Clarke, meetings involving senior neo-conservative figures produced five justifications for war: the first was about completing the unfinished business of the 1991 Gulf War by overthrowing Saddam Hussein. Second, attacking Iraq would eliminate its threat to Israel – the most important American ally in the region. Third, building a democratic state in Iraq would serve as an example to the region. Fourth, a pro-American Iraq would accommodate troops formerly stationed in Saudi Arabia. The presence of large American bases there had encouraged opposition to the Al-Saud regime. Finally, overthrowing the Iraqi president would enable the establishment of another compliant oil-producing state (Clarke 2004: 265).

From the 'War on Terror' to the 2003 Iraq War

Linking Iraq to the September 11 2001 suicide attacks was the purpose of a sustained communications exercise. Initially, government and military elites were preoccupied with the 'War on Terror' in Afghanistan. Immediately after the September 11 attacks, the United States implemented a vast communication programme aimed at diminishing international criticism of its Middle East policies. The Bush administration turned initially to public relations advisors, the Rendon Group, who fashioned immediate replies to Al Qaeda and Taliban statements over the 24-hour news cycle. As indicated in the previous chapter, the Rendon Group helped to establish the Coalition Information Centres (CIC) in Washington, London and Islamabad, as a way to cover all time zones, in opposition to the presence of Al Qaeda and the Taliban (DeYoung 2001). The CIC prepared daily press releases and responses, and undertook opinion poll research across the Middle East. They also arranged interviews for key American officials with major Arab Networks.

On 2 October 2001, the Bush administration also appointed Charlotte Beers as Undersecretary of State for Public Diplomacy and Public Affairs to undertake the 'branding of US foreign policy' (Rich 2006: 31–32). Beers' strategy was formulated in marketing jargon: to build a brand (America), and sell this brand to a target audience (the Arab 11-year-old), by using an emotionally appealing message (freedom) (Figenshou 2006: 85). But while Charlotte Beers was successful in commercial marketing terms, selling 'Uncle Sam' to the Middle East was a different matter altogether. Beers' attempts to address anti-Americanism through promotional videos about Muslim life in America and simplistic brochures on terrorism were unsuccessful.[3] Opinion polls conducted after 9/11 in predominantly Arab and Muslim nations showed that anti-American sentiments were still prevalent. The General Accounting Office, the auditing arm of the

Congress, confirmed this state of affairs when it declared in a report that the $1 billion budget spent annually by the Bush administration to polish America's image in the Middle East had largely gone to waste (Weiser 2003). Subsequently, Charlotte Beers resigned on 3 March 2003.

After the Afghanistan campaign, the Rendon Group was asked to develop a marketing plan for the upcoming war in Iraq. The groups is thought to have told Defense Secretary Donald Rumsfeld to fix in the public mind a link between terror and nation-states (rather than focusing exclusively on fluid, ad hoc groups such as Al Qaeda) (St-Clair 2007). The *New York Times* reported in 19 February 2002 that the Pentagon was using the Rendon Group to develop a new propaganda agency, the Office of Strategic Influence (OSI). The latter was used by the Pentagon to coordinate factual news releases, foreign advertising campaigns and covert disinformation programmes designed to plant pro-American stories in international media. Private firms were sometimes used to achieve these objectives (Campbell 2003). However, after OSI's classified proposals were leaked to the media amidst controversy,[4] White House officials announced, on 26 February 2002, that the office had been shut down (Allen 2002). Secretary of Defense Donald Rumsfeld remained adamant that the same programmes and practices intended for OSI would proceed under other names (Rumsfeld 2002). What the American administration and its different communication branches did not understand was that the source of anger within the Middle East was American foreign policy itself. American support, for Israel against the Palestinians, oppressive dictatorships in the Arab world, and the invasion and occupation of Muslim countries such as Afghanistan, had generated widespread popular hostility. At this time, Naomi Klein declared that, 'America's problem is not with its brand – which could scarcely be stronger – but with its product' (Klein 2002 [electronic version; no pagination]). Accordingly, Marc Lynch noted the feeling among Arabs and Muslims was that their views were not being taken seriously. Any dialogue between the United States and the Arab world was always one-directional and top-bottom. Almost every Middle East peace plan was drafted in Washington without any serious consultation with Arab leaders, much less with the Arab public (Lynch 2003). This can be seen as a counter-productive attitude in regard to a region steeped in anti-colonial resentment.

The Prospect of War in Iraq

Such political grievances could not be resolved with officially sanctioned, simplistic advertising campaigns. In any case, American communication blunders during the 'War on Terror' had already generated negative attitudes among Arab and Muslim audiences. These discomfitures prompted the United States to intensify its public diplomacy effort within Arab world. However, as I have mentioned the Voice of America in Arabic was ineffective (it had only an audience of some 2 per cent in the Middle East). It was replaced in March 2002 by Radio Sawa ('together'), an Arabic entertainment and news station covering the entire Middle East. Its aim was to encourage favourable Arab perceptions toward the 'American way of life' (Van Ham 2003). Another addition was Al Hurra ('The Free One'), an American backed television network, which was intended to compete against Al Jazeera. As the previous chapter discussed, Al Jazeera had assumed a global profile after the attacks of September 11 2001, when Osama Bin Laden's videotaped interviews were broadcast. The Arab network frequently invited less extreme guests with viewpoints critical of the American foreign policy. Although US officials were invited to appear on Al Jazeera, as was the case with Christopher Ross (former US ambassador to Syria and US State Department counterterrorism coordinator), favourable treatment could not be assumed. When Ross appeared on *Al Ittijah Al Mo'akis* (The Opposite Direction), he received a salvo of destabilising questions from Al Jazeera's talk-show host Faisal Al-Kasim (El-Nawawy and Iskandar 2002).

Al Jazeera's focus on human tragedies in Afghanistan contrasted with the American media's occasional acknowledgement of 'regret' over the 'rare' and 'accidental' 'collateral damage' (Scraton 2002). At the same time, Al Jazeera continued to broadcast Al Qaeda's videotapes, and eschewed the 'War on Terror' slogan in favour of 'the so-called War on Terror'.[5] The terminology used by Al Jazeera, which included terms such as 'resistance' and 'occupation', irritated the Presidency and the Pentagon. Accordingly, they increased pressure upon Al Jazeera as well as the Qatar authorities. Subsequently, Al Jazeera's office in Kabul was destroyed by an American air attack on 13 November 2001. At first, US officials said it was an accident, but General Tommy Franks later admitted Al Jazeera's building in Kabul was deliberately targeted as 'a known Al Qaeda facility' (Pintak 2006: 159). Other intimidation tactics against Al Jazeera included the

US capture of Sami Al-Haj, a Sudanese cameraman who worked with Al Jazeera during the Afghan campaign.[6] However, such punitive measures only increased Al Jazeera's popularity and reputation for independence in the Arab world and beyond.

Framing the Iraq War

After the Afghan War, the Bush administration used the media, both domestically and internationally, to market its Iraq policy. Three important claims were endlessly repeated: Firstly, the Iraqi regime had continued to store, produce, and develop biological, chemical, and nuclear 'weapons of mass destruction' (WMDs). Secondly, there were covert links between the Iraqi government and members of the Al Qaeda network (Iraq was thus implicated in the terrorist attacks of September 11 2001). Thirdly, Iraq constituted an imminent threat both to its neighbours and to the United States (Kellner 2003; Altheide 2005: 626–627).

According to Sheldon Rampton and James Stauber (2003), these claims did not have to be accurate. All that mattered was that high-ranked officials in the Bush administration persistently declared them to be true. Relentless repetition through the media would eventually persuade the public. A report issued by the Committee on Government Reform in March 2004 stated that President Bush, Vice President Cheney, Secretary of State Colin Powell, and National Security Advisor Condoleezza Rice made 81 statements about Iraq's nuclear activities and 84 statements about Iraq's chemical and biological weapons capabilities in over 125 separate appearances between March 2002 and January 2004. The same report observed that key government figures had made 61 misleading statements concerning the strength of the Iraq-Al Qaeda connection in 52 separate public appearances. John MacArthur observed that 'Bush's PR War' required a compliant press to repeat almost every fraudulent administration claim about the threat posed to America by Saddam Hussein (MacArthur 2003: 62). The American public soon believed that Saddam Hussein and Al Qaeda had joined their forces against the United States; a conviction which was strengthened by presidential speeches. For instance, on October 2002, President Bush declared that Saddam Hussein was 'a man who, in my judgment, would like to use al Qaeda as a forward army' (Rampton and Stauber 2003: 95).

Meanwhile, counterclaims were dismissed by the White House and received little media coverage even if they were made by senators or congressmen. Views which expressed caution, restraint, and the need for further inquiries by weapons inspectors were simply rejected. Worse, analyses originating from credible intelligence sources showing that Iraq had no WMDs were discarded. For example, Charles Duelfer, a renowned WMD expert with more than ten years field experience in Iraq, declared in July 2002 that there were no fissionable materials. He acknowledged that the Iraqi regime had a nuclear weapon programme prior to the 1991 Gulf War, but noted that this was terminated as part of a cease-fire agreement with the United States. In October 2004, Duelfer's official report to the Congress re-confirmed that Iraq had no stockpiles of WMDs, no weapons to give to Al Qaeda, and no viable programmes to resume making weapons.

Yet, the dominant official frame until 19 March 2003 was the inevitability of war and America's preparation for it (Altheide and Grimes 2005: 617). Within this frame, simple themes were repeated by military and political elites, especially the demonisation of Saddam Hussein. Demonisation served to channel negative feelings against the Iraqi nation. As I have indicated previously, academic Georges Lakoff has observed that the 'nation as person' metaphor is a key device in positioning other nations against the United States. In this context, Lakoff identified two central narratives: the 'self-defence story' and the 'rescue story'. According to him, the story always has a hero, a crime, and a villain. The villain is inherently evil and irrational. If the hero cannot reason with the irrational villain, he has to defeat him and save the world (Lakoff 2003b). The self-defence story prior to the start of the 2003 Iraq War focused on Saddam's connection to Al Qaeda and terrorism. Apparently, weapons of mass destruction, allegedly developed by Iraq, would fall into the hands of Al Qaeda. The rescue story focused on saving the Iraqi people and bringing democracy to the region (Hiebert 2003: 245). These narratives emphasised Iraq's repression of its people, Iraq's harbouring of international terrorist organisations and Iraq's defiance of UN resolutions. These claims were central components of the Bush administration's communication strategy (Altheide 2004).

The base simplicity of the Bush administration rhetoric has been succinctly summarised by James Moore and Wayne Slater:

> We are good. Iraq is bad. We love freedom. They do not. A clear, accessible message for an electorate too busy to read deeper into the story. The language must not be bloody. It is regime change. Not war. Clean and antiseptic. More of a procedure than a battle. (Moore and Slater 2003: 287)

All officials associated with the Bush presidency deployed the language of 'good' and 'evil'. This language derives from a religious neo-conservative lexicon, which justifies the construction of an American empire on exceptionalist grounds (Halper and Clarke 2004). The term 'evil' enables smear campaigns because it insulates the surrounding rhetoric from counterargument and rational challenge (Windt 1992). President Bush described the September 11 2001 attacks as 'evil, despicable acts of terror', and then said that 'today, our nation saw evil, the very worst of human nature'. Bush's speech writer David Frum commented that the term 'evil' was useful in securing popular support from conservative audiences in the 'Bible Belt' (Frum 2003: 140).

Crucial in the making of the Iraq War was Secretary of State Colin Powell's speech at the UN Security Council on 5 February 2003. His presentation was prominently covered in international media. Many journalists drew comparisons with the American stance against Soviet missiles in Cuba during the 1960s.[7] In his presentation, Powell used 45 visual 'pieces of evidence' to reiterate the aforementioned neo-conservative case for intervention. However, Powell's rationale for war was not convincing at all for important members of the United Nations Security Council such as France, Russia and China. They vetoed American and British diplomatic attempts to issue a UN mandate for war against Iraq. Investigative reporter Seymour Hersh was also unconvinced by Powell's case for war. In particular, he pointed out that documents alleging transfers of uranium from Niger to Iraq were faked. According to Hersh, 'one member of the UN inspection team who supported the American and British position arranged for dozens of unverified and unverifiable intelligence reports and tips – data known as inactionable intelligence – to be funnelled to MI6 operatives and quietly passed along to newspapers in London and elsewhere' (Hersh 2003: 42–43). In Hersh's view, the CIA always knew that the documents were falsified.

Hersh affirmed that Powell never saw the actual documents even though his speech was partly based on this data (Hersh 2003: 43). Overall, Hersh argues that American and British fabrications about Iraq's nuclear power programme were designed to counteract international criticism of the prospective invasion. Nonetheless, American mainstream media promoted the viewpoint of their administration. For instance, CNN portrayed war as the simplest and most favoured outcome to the crisis. They opposed the extension and deepening of WMD inspections (as sought by France, Russia, Germany, China and others) (Lundsten and Stocchetti 2005: 10). On the other hand, the potential consequences of invasion were left unexplained. CNN journalists seemed to regard the political discussions and diplomatic negotiations taking place in the United Nations as preparations for war.

Lundsten and Stocchetti argue that CNN did not simply cover the Powell presentation at the UN; it actually promoted the case for war. Journalists, such as Jim Clancy and Zain Verjee, never questioned the allegations that Saddam Hussein supported Al Qaeda and possessed weapons of mass destruction. And, they quickly split the different parties into 'friends' and 'foes' depending on whether they adopted or rejected the Bush administration's stance. Lundsten and Stocchetti provide an example of this from Zain Verjee's interview on 5 February 2003 with the editor of *Al-Quds Al-Arabi*, Abdel Bari Atwan. As soon as the latter expressed scepticism toward Powell's arguments, the interview went sour:

ZAIN VERJEE (CNN ANCHOR):	'The issue of al Qaeda link to Iraq: what did you make of that?'
ABDEL BARI ATWAN (AL-QUDS AL-ARABI):	'I believe this is the Secretary of State's weakest point'
ZAIN VERJEE (CNN ANCHOR):	'We have seen a lot of visual evidence that most people, some at least would say was compelling ... Are you convinced by those intercepts that Iraq is hiding weapons that Iraq is deliberately not cooperating?'

At this point, Atwan stated that more time should be given to UN inspectors to actually verify the information provided by Powell. The information he presented was not deemed convincing enough to justify a war. Visibly annoyed by Atwan's response, CNN journalist Zain Verjee cut short the interview:

ZAIN VERJEE 'Unconvincing to you Abdel Bari Atwan [*turning*
(CNN ANCHOR): *away visibly annoyed*]. We'll continue to check in
with you as we dissect the body of what Colin Powell
had to say this day at the UN Security Council'.
(Lundsten and Stocchetti 2005: 10–11)

Two months before the start of the conflict, CNN introduced its Iraq coverage with the words, 'Showdown: Iraq' (similarly Fox used 'Target Iraq: Disarming Saddam', MSNBC used 'Showdown with Saddam', and NBC Nightly News used 'Countdown: Iraq' and 'Target: Iraq'). Jack Lule has observed that the slogan 'Showdown: Iraq' frames the situation as a final confrontation, a reckoning between Iraq and the United States. This metaphoric framing is deeply rooted in the American psyche; in frontier times, gunmen faced each other off to settle their differences. Here, the metaphor complements portrayals of President George Bush as a cowboy figure from Texas. Lule also observes that 'Showdown' dates back to the placing of poker hands face-up on a table to determine the winner. In any case, the 'Showdown' metaphor suggested that the situation in Iraq was inevitably headed toward a confrontational conclusion (Lule 2004: 183).

In 2003, 15 February was a day of protest mobilisation called 'The World Says No to War'. This involved millions of people in 800 cities around the world. In Rome, the protest involved around three million people, and is listed in the 2004 Guinness Book of World Records as the largest anti-war rally in history. Also noticeable was the strength of anti-war sentiment in the London march, when approximately one million people marched in London, making this the largest ever demonstration in Britain. Another 100,000 to 200,000 protested on 22 March 2003, setting a record for a wartime demonstration in Britain. In the United States, according to the television network CBS, protests were held across 150 US cities (Chan 2003a). In New York, demonstrations drew between 300,000 people and one million (according to organisers' estimates) (Hauben 2003). Police on horseback charged protesters, preventing many of them from joining the officially approved rally on First Avenue. These events were mostly downplayed by American mainstream media. However, Al Jazeera focused on them, discussing their significance in numerous newscasts and talk shows; a response which confirmed the anti-war stance of the Qatar based channel.

In the meantime, media pundits and Pentagon Officials were talking openly about their upcoming 'Shock and Awe' strategy. This rhetoric came into the public realm when the co-inventor of this military strategy, Harlan Ullman was interviewed on *CBS Evening News* two months before the war (24 January 2003). Developed at the National Defense University, 'Shock and Awe' focused upon the psychological destruction of the enemies' will to fight (rather than the physical destruction of their military forces). Ullman stated: 'We want them to quit. We want them not to fight.' To this end, 'Shock and Awe' would rely upon an initial barrage of precision guided weapons. As Ullman further explained, this would have a simultaneous effect:

> You're sitting in Baghdad and all of a sudden you're the general and 30 of your division headquarters have been wiped out. You also take the city down. By that I mean you get rid of their power, water. In 2,3,4,5 days they are physically, emotionally and psychologically exhausted. (Chan 2003)

Finally, on 18 March 2003 – on the eve of hostilities – the US administration announced that the war would be waged by a 'coalition of the willing'. Instead of emphasising the fact that 98 per cent of the military forces involved come from America and Britain, the Bush administration named 30 countries which were prepared to be publicly associated with the war (BBC 2003a). The 'coalition of the willing' was fragile propaganda because most of the named countries[8] offered no concrete support,[9] and several of them had no army at all.[10] This state of affairs later prompted American filmmaker Michael Moore to re-describe the campaign as the 'coalition of the coerced, bribed and intimidated' (Moore 2003: 73).

Counter-perspectives from the Middle East

Many Arabs and Muslims were unprepared for the attacks of September 11 2001 and could scarcely believe how they were orchestrated. Even when Osama Bin Laden publicly claimed responsibility, many people in the Muslim World refused to believe he was the mastermind. Many believed that American intelligence agencies could have used high-tech devices to fabricate the Bin Laden videotapes (CNN.com 2001). The rushed decision by the Bush Administration to invade Afghanistan was met with disapproval in the Middle East and Asia. In a Gallup poll conducted in nine predominantly Muslim nations (Indonesia, Iran, Jordan, Kuwait, Lebanon, Morocco, Pakistan, Saudi Arabia, and Turkey), 77 per cent of those interviewed, said that American intervention in Afghanistan was morally unjustifiable (Gallup.com 2002). Echoing these concerns, Egyptian intellectual Fahmy Howeidy wrote in Cairo-based *Al Ahram* that:

> It's been more than 40 days and they've kept bombing the Afghan people. This will violate the image of the United States in the Arab world. (*Al Ahram*, 1 December 2001)

Meanwhile, prominent Christian fundamentalist leaders such as Jerry Falwell, Jimmy Swaggart, Pat Robertson, and Franklin Graham, exploited the fallout from the attacks to label Islam a religion of hate and terrorism (Gillespie 2003). These offending remarks which reflected already existing prejudices within television, cinema and White House rhetoric, further alienated large segments of public opinion throughout the Middle East. Subsequently, opinion polls showed that only 6 per cent of Iranians, 6 per cent of Indonesians, and 13 per cent of Saudis believed that western nations respected Arab Islamic values (Gallup.com 2002).

The justifying themes for the American invasion of Afghanistan, followed by Iraq, were mostly rejected by senior Arab intellectuals, journalists, and politicians. For instance, the claim that America ought to spread democracy by force, if necessary, was disbelieved. Riyadh Al-Hajj, columnist for the Palestinian daily *Al-Quds*, argued that democratic reform must come from within, not from outside. He wrote:

> There is a need for essential and genuine change [in the Middle East], deep change that is not cosmetic. Change is possible, and has great potential, but only if it emerges from our own will – not out of striving to please the US (*Al-Quds*, 18 December 2002)

The attempt to link the democratisation agenda with the 'War on Terror' and the upcoming war in Iraq, met vast opposition among Arab publics. Opinion polls conducted in 2002 in Egypt, Saudi Arabia, Morocco, Jordan, the United Arab Emirates, and Lebanon showed that fewer than 10 per cent believed that democratic ideals drove American foreign policy.

Instead, a majority of Arab respondents believed that oil appropriation, the Israeli alliance, and weakening the Muslim world were the real objectives of the Bush administration (Telhami 2007).

Numerous Arab commentators also highlighted what they perceived as double standards in the American rationale. For example, Salameh Ahmad Salameh wrote in the Egyptian daily *Al-Ahram*:

> America cannot act for reform in the Arab world as long as it tramples the rights of the Palestinian people underfoot and deploys its forces in the region to wage war on an Arab state [Iraq], regardless of the world consensus that the allegations regarding weapons of mass destruction are not the reason, while it remains silent about the existence of nuclear weapons in Israel. (*Al-Ahram*, 19 December 2002)

Other commentators, such as Dr Maya Al-Rahbi, writing for the Syrian website *Akhbar Al-Sharq*, rejected the liberation theme promoted by the Bush Administration. In an article titled 'A Letter from an Arab Woman to Colin Powell', she wrote:

> The Arab women, Mr Powell, are not stupid enough to believe your promises that you want to liberate them. Even if they truly need it, let it not be your way ... The Arab women say to you: 'Take your hands off our homeland and our existence; we want nothing to do with you, for better or for worse ... Leave us alone' [...] The group of women for whom you sketched out a rosy future during meetings between them and Ms. Cheney in the bosom of your civilization do not represent Arab women at all. No Arab woman with any common sense would be tempted [to adopt] the democracy to which you claim to adhere and want to export to us, when your history is terrifyingly rife with racism and discrimination ... The system of overseeing your citizens, which you invented today, claiming defence [against terrorism], is no different than the security apparatuses in the countries to which you say you will bring democracy and civilization. (Al-Rahbi, 23 December 2002)

Even intellectuals supportive of America (such as Dr Fahd Al-Fanik), found it difficult to accept the Bush administration's arguments for war. Al-Fanik wrote in the Jordanian daily *Al-Rai*:

> It will be difficult for the US to convince the Arabs that America's policy is balanced and just, and that it is not Israel's strategic ally ... and even more difficult to persuade the Arabs that the US is not applying sanctions on the Iraqi people but only on Saddam Hussein, and that it will wage war against Saddam Hussein alone and not on Iraq. Similarly, it will be difficult for the US to deny that it is planning to conquer Baghdad, the capital of the Abbasid state and the symbol of Arab honour, which is a new humiliation of the Arabs and Muslims in the world ...[11] (*Al-Rai,* 17 December 2002)

These opinions reflected large segments of Middle Eastern public opinion. Unsurprisingly, Arab anti-war activists joined the world movement against the imminent invasion of Iraq. On 18 December 2002, the International Campaign against US Aggression on Iraq (ICAA) organised a two-day meeting at Cairo. Attendees included high profile Arab activists and political figures, such as former Algerian President Ahmed Ben Bella. The latter demanded that Arabs organise huge demonstrations against the Iraq invasion. One of the organisers, Amin Eskander said that this meeting was a step towards coordinating with international anti-war and anti-globalisation activists (Bishr 2002).

As part of world protests against the war, demonstrations took place across the Middle East. Within repressive pro-US regimes, they were difficult to organise.[12] Nevertheless, in Cairo fairly large demonstrations, which included both secular politicians and Islamists, took place on 1 February 2003. Meanwhile, tens of thousands gathered in Sana'a, Yemen, while other protests bubbled up in other regional states, such as Bahrain, Lebanon and Sudan. A few weeks later, further protests took place in the Middle East. On 10 March, hundreds of thousands marched in Rawalpindi, Pakistan to denounce the upcoming war. The same day, 200,000 Syrians protested in Damascus, and half a million Indonesians rallied in Jakarta.

CNN and Al Jazeera: Organisational issues preceding the war

Observing that war was imminent, CNN and Al Jazeera stepped up their preparations for coverage. More advanced technology was available in 2003

The Prospect of War in Iraq

than during the 1991 war, when news reports relied upon large satellite systems. Devices, such as small DV cameras, Apple G4 laptops, portable videophones, and Inmarsat high-speed data Global Area Network (GAN) satellite phones,[13] had since become necessary tools for journalists. In addition, Iridium phones, networked into a system of low-earth orbital satellites, allowed journalists to be connected from any outdoor location. Small flyaway satellite dishes, palm-sized digital cameras, speedy laptops, and portable store-and-forward systems and nonlinear editors also enhanced broadcasting capabilities. As a result, small teams of war correspondents could send out their live reports from within moving troop formations or from stationary locations. Audiences around the globe followed the latest war developments in real time from their living rooms as well as on personal computers and laptops.

As an established brand in the global news market, CNN stands ready to swiftly mobilise and deploy crews and equipment anywhere in the world. These operations are supervised from CNN's headquarters in Atlanta, Georgia. However, after the AOL-TimeWarner merger of 2001, CNN cut costs and reduced budgets for international newsgathering (Turner 2004). Many foreign bureaus and news production facilities were closed, leading to an over-reliance on dispatched reporters to cover foreign affairs (Graber 2002: 342-380). Consequently, editors put extra pressures on correspondents. The constraints upon quality real-time coverage forced them to prepare their live reports as soon as they reached their destination. It was thus difficult for reporters to grasp the full context of the events to be covered. In the case of the 2003 Iraq War, CNN dispatched crews all around the Middle East (Israel, Jordan, Kuwait, Kurdish-controlled territories, embedded journalists with different fighting corps). To counteract any shortage of information from the Iraqi side, CNN ensured instant access to wire services, such as Reuters, Associated Press, and Agence France Presse. These wire services had numerous correspondents on the ground and were able to match the capabilities of CNN reportage. Furthermore, the Atlanta based channel struck news exchange deals with local stations in order to be able to out-source footage from Middle Eastern networks such as Al Jazeera.

Al Jazeera developed a different organisational framework of newsgathering. The network had financial support from the State of Qatar in the form of a loan that Al Jazeera needed to pay back after ten years of operation (on the assumption that it would have reached commercial self-sustainability). However, despite an increasing number of viewers, Al Jazeera did not reap the financial benefits of its popularity. As mentioned in the previous chapter, powerful Arab governments had persistently discouraged major businesses from placing advertisements on Al Jazeera. These pressures required the Qatar-based broadcaster to sell news footage for revenue. Subsequently, they sent crews to major Iraqi cities with the aim of obtaining dramatic and vivid footage, even when this was dangerous to acquire. Thus, Al Jazeera sent 30 staffers to Baghdad and placed others in Mosul, Basra. They had more reporters in Iraq than just about any other TV channel (BusinessWeek 2003). The expense of this exercise was reduced by technological advances allowing crews to broadcast from any location. Furthermore, because most of Al Jazeera's correspondents were new to the field, they earned moderate wages and offered very good value for money.

The highest echelons of political and military decision making in America were available to CNN. As a result, they were privy to military planning strategies. The development of 'embedded journalism' practices built a symbiotic inter-relationship, whereby CNN and other American news organisations would be allowed a better access to military operations in exchange for military control over information retrieved from combat zones. However, in the zero-sum environment of war, the Iraqi regime was to become wary of this arrangement; they restricted media access within the areas controlled by them. In contrast, Al Jazeera had built generally cordial relations with the Iraqis over the years, in spite of occasional misunderstandings. Therefore, Al Jazeera could expect a favourable access to the Iraqi-controlled areas.

Immediately preceding the war, CNN was wary of competition from other networks and most particularly from Fox News Corporation. In 2003, CNN was cited as the number one source for television news in America, over and above other major networks and cable rivals (analysis suggests that the peak growth of cable television core audience was reached at the time of the September 11 attacks and stalled thereafter). However, in 2002 Fox News had surpassed CNN in the ratings (1,014,000 viewers for Fox News vs. 721,000 for CNN) (Cable World 2003; Massing

2005). Commercially, this represented a worrisome trend for the Atlanta based network, although it was still able to market its multiple channels to advertisers (CNN International; CNNfn; CNN's airport news service etc.). The growing competition from Fox News – added to the costs incurred from the AOL – Time Warner merger, led CNN to abandon its traditional way of doing business. Instead of going for hard news, CNN began relying on studio discussions with analysts who interpreted the news (Loory 2005: 340). Another impact of the 'Fox effect' was CNN's drift towards a commentary/infotainment format, and the quest to hire 'recognisable journalists' in order to consolidate the brand. For example, CNN executives hired Connie Chung, a veteran journalist who covered Watergate, as well as anchor-woman Paula Zahn, and financial anchor Lou Dobbs (Campbell 2002: 1). Additionally, CNN also tried to emulate the tone and language of Fox News. After 9/11, CNN journalists started to wear pins with American flags. Their Standards and Practices Department sent out a memo to the different departments subsequent to the bombing and invasion of Afghanistan. This memo, in line with military objectives, suggested overlooking evidence of civilian casualties and encouraged an emphasis upon the Taliban leadership responsibility for the 9/11 attacks (Bleifuss 2001).

In the Middle East, Al Jazeera faced stiff competition from Al-Arabiya. The latter was established barely two weeks before the start of the Iraq War (3 March 2003) with Saudi funds (partly from the Saudi owned Middle East Broadcasting Center – MBC). Al-Arabiya was a Saudi vehicle to counter the increasing influence of the Qatar based Al Jazeera. Al-Arabiya director Abdul Rahman al-Rashed confirmed this fact during an interview with the New York Times in 2008 (Worth 2008). Al-Arabiya set out to outmanoeuvre Al Jazeera at its own game. The Saudi backed channel thus was very critical of the American led war, and provided access to insurgents and ex-members of the defunct regime. The establishment of Al-Arabiya was Saudi Arabia's response to Qatar's growing 'soft power'[14] in the region (Ruckower 2008: 6). Al Jazeera had given Qatar a counter to Egyptian and Saudi media outlets (the latter having quasi-monopoly over pan-Arab news coverage until then). Qatar thus became an important player in Middle Eastern politics; a role which a tiny state, with barely 200,000 nationals, could not previously have dreamt of. After decades of being ignored by other Arab countries, Qatar made itself indispensable in the Middle East. With this backing, Al Jazeera gained an enormous reputation in the Arab world and beyond as the most independent Arab media (Williams 2007: 7). Competition from Al-Arabiya made it impossible for Al Jazeera to revoke its anti-war editorial line. In a way, this was the Middle East equivalent of the relationship between CNN and Fox. The latter, with its patriotic fervour obliged CNN to respond accordingly. For Al Jazeera, having Al-Arabiya nearby projecting an independent Arab voice presented an incentive. Al Jazeera would need to perform at its best to remain the leading channel in the Middle East.

All in all, it is fair to say that while the American communication efforts were very efficient at home, they were fundamentally counteracted in the Middle East by Al Jazeera's news coverage and current affairs programmes. American officials tried to implement a series of measures to obstruct Al Jazeera, including the use of military force. This situation increased the international popularity of the Qatar based channel, and strengthened the resolve of its journalists.

Prior to the war, the US administration mobilised numerous claims which served to justify the invasion. These included the Iraqi government's alleged possession of weapons of mass destruction, and its alleged connection with terrorist networks. The constant repetition of these claims through different official sources generated a coordinated and constant barrage of information that ultimately won the approval of the American people for the war. From the 'War on Terror' to 'Shock and Awe', these claims mobilised the deep frames of Orientalism and counter-terrorism for the purposes of information dominance. Al Jazeera was obviously critical of this framing and its mobilisation. The network was therefore a major impediment to American war objectives. Viewed from the Middle East, American rhetoric leading to the wars in Afghanistan and Iraq proved to be unconvincing. Shapers of public opinion in the Middle East were quasi-unanimous that the American justifications for eliminating terrorism and promoting democracy constituted a façade that paved the way for military operations.

Finally, this chapter provided a general background on the news environments and preparations of CNN and Al Jazeera prior to the start of the war. Both channels committed resources to war coverage in the face of

The Prospect of War in Iraq

threatening competition from Fox News and Al-Arabiya respectively. The way these former channels set up their crews and their access to information from American and Iraqi sources, underpinned their patterns of reportage as the Iraqi conflict unfolded. In the following chapters, I employ framing analysis to examine the coverage of certain key events during the 2003 Iraq invasion. These events will incorporate the start of the war (in the episodes of 'Decapitation Strike' and 'Shock and Awe') and the end of the war (the bombing of the Palestine hotel and the fall of the Saddam statue).

6

Hostilities Begin: 'Decapitation Strike', 'Shock and Awe', and Contesting Realities

Figure 6.1: Real-time footage of CNN and Al Jazeera during 'Shock and Awe' (21 March 2003).

Context and chronology

The United States and the United Kingdom claimed that Iraq possessed weapons of mass destruction (WMD), which were threatening national and international security in the Middle East. The mainstream media in both countries repeated these claims in the absence of supporting evidence. In fact, Hans Blix, the lead UN weapons inspector, advised the UN Security Council on 7 March 2003 that Iraq was cooperating with inspections, and that a general conclusion could be expected within a few months (Blix, 2003). Nevertheless, the US Administration ignored Blix' report, announcing on 17 March 2003 that 'diplomacy has failed'. The weapons inspectors were thus advised to immediately leave Iraq (Voice of America, 2003). President George W. Bush then gave Saddam Hussein and his sons 48 hours to leave Iraq or face war.

Just before the expiration of President Bush's ultimatum, the CIA provided intelligence on the whereabouts of five key Iraqi leaders, including Saddam Hussein. President Bush authorised strikes against these targets, and declared war on Iraq soon afterwards. So, the war against Iraq began on 20 March 2003 at 02:34 GMT and was officially named Operation 'Iraqi Freedom'. Its first phase was called 'Decapitation Strike', and was carried out by forty Tomahawk cruise missiles and F-117A stealth fighters (CNN.com, 20 March 2003). Saddam Hussein appeared on Iraqi National Television three hours after the attacks in a taped interview. A second round of air strikes was then launched against Baghdad, and ground troops crossed into southern Iraq from Kuwait.

Iraqi army units retaliated by firing two 'Al Samoud' missiles and about five SCUD missiles into northern Kuwait, where coalition troops were assembled, but inflicted no casualties. Kuwait City was also subject to these attacks, but anti-missile batteries brought down two SCUDs, while others fell without causing any damage. Subsequently, American and British aircraft took off to hunt for Iraqi missile launchers. In the meantime, American and British artillery began shelling Iraqi troops on the Iraqi border. At 15:30 GMT US troops were told to prepare for combat, as Iraqis were reportedly burning oilfields south and west of Basra. About the same time, news broke that Turkey had given its airspace to coalition forces. At about 17:00 GMT, the coalition batteries intensified their shelling of Iraqi units across the border.

During the second day of hostilities (20 March 2003), Baghdad was again the target of coalition air strikes; several explosions rocked the city, missiles landed on the vicinity of presidential palaces, the Iraqi intelligence headquarters and several other buildings. Iraqi air defence crews fired against attacking aircraft without success. Coalition units launched an amphibious and helicopter assault on the Al Faw peninsula, which fell rather easily. Iraqi forces suffered numerous casualties and many prisoners were taken. This attack ensured coalition control over the oil infrastructure in that area. Other coalition regiments moved toward other southern Iraqi oilfields. Meanwhile, American submarines launched Tomahawk cruise missiles at various targets in Iraq.

American Marines entered Umm Qasr and declared the city under their control, although this was disputed by Al Jazeera. It then transpired that the Marines only controlled a small part of Umm Qasr (the city garrison surrendered one week later). British troops were now reported on the outskirts of Basra, and there were reports that the whole Iraqi 51st Division had surrendered. These reports were denied by Al Jazeera, whose reporter in Basra interviewed the division commander. In the air, coalition aircraft continued to attack key facilities in Iraq, while two airfields in western Iraq were captured by coalition commandos. At this juncture, CNN was asked to leave Iraq for carrying out 'propaganda activities'. On 21 March 2003, the Pentagon announced that the first phase of the war, namely 'Shock and Awe', had begun with heavy aerial attacks on key Iraqi targets. Baghdad experienced a major barrage and Saddam's presidential palaces were all hit by cruise missiles. Kirkuk, Mosul and Tikrit were also attacked. The Pentagon named this event 'A-Day' or 'Air Day'.[1]

For this research, tracing the start of hostilities is important because it introduced the war to American and global audiences. This period included enormous amounts of information warfare. Since 'Desert Storm' (1991), the US military had routinely incorporated media communication into their battlefield strategies. Military info-warriors devised their war plans to fit news media requirements. In particular, military strategies meshed with the strict production regimes, organisational routines and advertising orientation of the 24-hour news channels. The news media had been cued to expect an intensive bombing of Baghdad. Indeed, the plan for 'Shock and Awe' was deliberately filtered into the public realm as the co-inventor of this info-war strategy, Harlan Ullman, gave many pre-war interviews on the theory of 'rapid dominance'.[2] This entailed the use of dense aerial bombing to traumatise the enemy into believing that resistance was futile. The information warfare paradigm requires that hostilities be broadcast to millions around the world. Thus, 'Decapitation Strike' and the resultant 'Shock and Awe' bombing campaign was the subject of intense coverage. For that reason, anchors and political pundits spent an enormous amount of time from 20 to 21 March 2003 discussing whether or not President Bush had postponed the 'Shock and Awe' campaign, and if so why. This speculation advanced the narrative, and heightened anticipation, to the extent of creating a 'need' for the bombing campaign. This pattern was observable throughout mainstream American media, including CNN.

'Shock and Awe' was undeniably the defining event of the whole war. It enabled the US military to display their full might and latest hardware. The multiple 'firework' effects resulting from the intense bombings provided a major videogame-like spectacle, which thrilled and entertained American audiences. With the attention of television commentators from all around the world, American military and political elites could set the immediate agenda, command the field, and disseminate their frames for the conflict. However, as I will demonstrate, these frames were fundamentally contested by Al Jazeera.

'Decapitation Strike' vs. 'Assassination Attempt'

Scene establishments

For American television audiences, it was President George W. Bush who set the scene for the 'Decapitation Strike' during a four minute national address delivered on 20 March 2003 at 03:15 GMT (10:15 p.m. EST). He announced that coalition forces had been ordered to strike 'selected targets of military importance to undermine Saddam Hussein's ability to wage war'. These strikes would be the opening salvo of 'a broad and concerted campaign.' The different CNN anchors and correspondents, who spoke in the five minutes following Bush's address, such as CNN anchor Aaron Brown, CNN senior correspondent at the Pentagon Jamie McIntyre, and CNN senior White House correspondent John King, served to reiterate the major themes of the president's speech. For example, Aaron Brown stated that 'these are the early stages to disarm Iraq', that 'selected targets are being hit', and that the strike is meant to 'undermine the ability of Iraqi forces.'

Meanwhile, the following CNN trailers repeatedly stressed some of President Bush's key phrases.

'EARLY STAGES OF MILITARY OPERATIONS' BEGIN;
'MORE THAN 35 COUNTRIES' GIVING SUPPORT;

'PEACE OF TROUBLED WORLD' AT STAKE;
'WE WILL MAKE EVERY EFFORT TO SPARE CIVILIANS';
'SUSTAINED COMMITMENT' TO IRAQ EVEN AFTER WAR.

The size and font of these trailers made them unmistakably clear. They were constantly repeated during the course of Bush's speech. There were very few live images in the five minutes that followed Bush's announcement of the 'Decapitation Strike'. This may be explained by the fact that this operation was based on secrecy and swiftness. In any case, CNN established the first scenes of the 'Decapitation Strike' by relying more on talk than on imagery.

Al Jazeera went on alert after President Bush sent an ultimatum to Saddam Hussein demanding that he leave power and goes into exile. The ultimatum was due to end on Wednesday 19 March at 20.00 p.m. (EST). Therefore, Al Jazeera's correspondents in Washington covered major briefings and information coming from the American capital. Correspondents in Baghdad were also regularly asked from Al Jazeera headquarters to provide the latest developments. Al Jazeera's correspondent Majed Abdelhadi gave the first reports of anti-aircraft fire and explosions one hour and half after the end of the ultimatum (Thursday 5:30 a.m. Baghdad Time; 45 minutes before President Bush gave his address to the nation). Al Jazeera gave the speech live coverage and allowed local analysts to interpret its significance. Soon afterwards, Al Jazeera produced a major headline without voiceover tailoring Bush's speech for local audiences. The translated headline stated:

THE WHITE HOUSE HAS ANNOUNCED THAT THE AMERICAN PEOPLE MUST BE READY FOR A WAR THAT MAY LAST FOR SOME TIME AND CAUSE THOUSANDS OF VICTIMS

As hostilities escalated, the main anchor in the studio in Doha, Tawfiq Taha went back and forth to the numerous correspondents on the ground, Majed Abdelhadi, Diyar Al-Omari, and Mohammed Kheir Bourini. The fact that all of these correspondents wore helmets and bullet-proof jackets signalled the danger they faced. This danger was transmitted to the viewers; they were compelled to reflect upon how the local Baghdad population might cope with the imminent barrage.

At this juncture, Al Jazeera's anchors asked about the legality of the American attempt to assassinate a foreign leader without a formal declaration of war. Some of Al Jazeera's guest analysts put forward the argument that American law prohibited the assassination of foreign presidents; a prohibition which came in the mid-1970s after a review of the CIA methods by the Congress.[3] There was also a comment to the effect that 'Decapitation Strike' was an international war crime (since the actual strike had occurred before the formal declaration by President Bush).

'Decapitation Strike' unfolds

On CNN, three anchors; Aaron Brown, Jamie McIntyre, and John King summarised the main points of the President's speech, after which Jamie McIntyre gave further information about the strike. Aaron Brown opined about why the strike came much earlier than the planned full-scale bombing campaign. As there were no images of the target or clear-cut information on the military operation, Brown soon found himself in the unenviable position of speculating about the operation, using phrases and expressions that conveyed more uncertainty than knowledge. This can be felt in Brown's following comments:

> As Jamie reported, it appears to be an attack on a leadership bunker or a place where perhaps Saddam Hussein was. Perhaps he and the government of Iraq were hiding out, trying to stay safe ... attacked by cruise missiles. The United States government, the United States military has done this sort of thing before with less success. It's not an easy thing to do, and we won't know for some time if it was successful. It may be a long time ... (CNN, 19 March 2003)

Aaron Brown then turned to John King (CNN senior White House correspondent), who took the opportunity to summarise the presidential speech. Here, King played the role of official interpreter by insisting with the President that this was not a war on the Iraqi population, nor a war on Islam, but a war on Saddam Hussein and his regime:

> [The president] said the United States has no ambition in Iraq, it simply wants to free and liberate its people and remove a tyrant from power. The president making no secret that the goal is regime change. Also, a political message to the people of the United States, though. Mr Bush saying this conflict could be longer and more difficult than some predicted and would require a long and sustained effort to build up a new Iraq in the wake of this war (CNN, 19 March 2003).

Then, General Wesley Clark provided the military perspective on events. The general found it difficult to distinguish between his former job as NATO chief and his new role as military analyst at CNN. It was striking to see his routine use of the word 'we'. This gave the impression he was in charge of military forces.

> We've got continuous visibility over much of Iraq. We've got scouts forward. We've got special operations forward. We've got satellites. We've got aircraft. We've got moving-target indicators off those aircraft. So, when the Iraqis start to move their forces, we're going to see them. (CNN, 19 March 2003)

He also used the opportunity to do some advertising for CNN:

> Some of them may be in the headquarters plugged in and watching CNN. We always did watch the television broadcasts, CNN included, when we were there in Kosovo and Albania and so forth, because it is a source of up-to-the-minute news. (CNN, 19 March 2003)

There was talk of military objectives when CNN International correspondent Walter Rogers commented. The latter interviewed a captain of the 7th Cavalry, who did not miss the opportunity to reiterate official framings of the conflict:

> … we try to view ourselves liberating the people of Iraq and trying to remove that regime, not invading Iraq. And not fighting the people of Iraq … my troop, this squadron, the 3rd Infantry division have the best equipment in the world, and we're trained. (CNN, 19 March 2003)

Hostilities Begin

Later, Aaron Brown referred to the 'embed' programme, but instead of addressing the question of journalistic objectivity and independence, Brown discussed the programme in terms of whether it endangered the fighting units. The rationale of embedding itself was not the subject of examination:

> We know, many of you, when we start talking about where troops are, what troops are doing, get very nervous. And we do, too. The rules that we are operating under, rules that the Pentagon and news organizations around the world have agreed to is that, while our correspondents are embedded, they are in place, they will be free to broadcast or file. They won't be censored. But they do remain under the control, to some degree, of unit commanders as to whether they can file. And, certainly, at no time will we be discussing specifically where they are, specifically what they're going after. We are very – going to be very conservative on this. We are not interested in endangering a single life to get a story more quickly. (CNN, 19 March 2003)

Subsequently, CNN anchor Wolf Blitzer took over to absolve the US administration of any wrongdoing in their attempt to kill President Saddam Hussein.

> If you go after what are called command-and-control areas and the leadership, including the president of Iraq, happen to be inside those so-called command-and-control areas, it would not necessarily violate the prohibition that was incorporated by President Gerald Ford in 1977 that forbids assassination of foreign leaders. In a military kind of environment, when there is a war, US government lawyers have determined, if you go after the leadership, if you try to kill the command-and-control leadership in the course of a war, that is not necessarily a violation of that rule barring assassination. (CNN, 19 March 2003)

But undeniably the most important strategic framing in this broadcast hour came when CNN gave room to Senator Joseph Lieberman, who constructed some of the most resonant deep frames:

> This is all about one evil dictator who possesses brutal weapons, with which he will threaten and hurt a lot of people, including a lot of Americans, unless we take them away from

him ... Saddam has ruled by fear and has killed any number of people under him, himself, who have shown some disloyalty. So, if it becomes clear that he is gone, then you have to ask, what is the motivation for all those in the Iraqi military to continue to want to fight us? We are offering them a better way and a better life...we are standing together behind the American men and women in uniform, confident that they're going to achieve the victory that our security demands and the world's security demands ... Saddam Hussein would have used these weapons against us eventually, or given them to terrorists who would have. (CNN, 19 March 2003)

It is clear that Senator Lieberman's comment included two important deep frames, the Orientalist frame and the counter-terrorist frame. It also included the military meso-frame.[4] These frames were assembled as follows:

The Orientalist deep frame:
This is all about one evil dictator who possesses brutal weapons, with which he will threaten and hurt a lot of people, including a lot of Americans ...

...what is the motivation for all those in the Iraqi military to continue to want to fight us? We are offering them a better way and a better life ...

The military meso-frame:
We are standing together behind the American men and women in uniform, confident that they are going to achieve the victory that our security demands and the world's security demands.

The terrorist deep frame:
Saddam Hussein would have used these weapons against us eventually or given them to terrorists who would have.

It shall be recalled that Senator Lieberman was a prominent member of the Democratic Party. In the 2000 United States presidential election, Lieberman was the Democratic nominee for Vice President, running with presidential nominee Al Gore, against the Republican Candidate George W. Bush. However, in these comments, Lieberman reiterated the same themes promoted by President Bush. Accordingly, one can say that the strategic framing of the war reproduced a bi-partisan political consensus, and was not just an expression of President Bush's views. Equally important was the fact that the CNN anchors did not scrutinise Senator Lieberman's declaration. It was simply commented on, non-critically, in a way which legitimised the framings involved.

Meanwhile, Tawfiq Taha on Al Jazeera started the coverage on 19 March 2003 [22:30 EST][5] by raising the prospect that large segments of civilian infrastructure would be hit (as had been the case previously during the 1991 Gulf War). Questions were raised as to whether the Iraqi forces could mount stronger resistance compared to 12 years earlier. When news broke that the 'Decapitation Strike' had begun, Al Jazeera turned to its Iraqi correspondent in Baghdad, Diyar Al-Omari, who stated that the Pentagon had 'acknowledged violent Iraqi resistance'. As Al Jazeera's anchor, Tawfiq Taha, asked Diyar Al-Omari whether this was the most violent raid thus far. Diyar answered: 'As long as the Baghdad Bridge is still standing, the worst is yet to come' (Al Jazeera, 19 March 2003).

Diyar's correspondence was interrupted to cover events in Mosul, the Northern Iraqi city, also under attack. Al Jazeera's correspondent in Mosul, Mohammed Kheir Bourini, with an excited tone of voice, reported an American air raid over the city, and sporadic anti-aircraft gunfire. Then, Diyar Al-Omari was given another opportunity to speak and this time, he said that the Iraqi forces were much more experienced after 12 years of conflict with the United States. Diyar spoke about new methods implemented by the Iraqi anti-aircraft crews, who were said to be well trained, and who had forced American aircraft to flee the scene. He also spoke about a reward offered by the Iraqi regime to every soldier who succeeded in taking down an enemy plane.

Diyar Al-Omari (Al Jazeera's correspondent in Baghdad)
> Nonetheless, Iraqi anti-aircraft crews were doing their job for honour, duty, and country. I also came across reports that Iraqi forces have stopped an attack in the vicinity of Al-Nasiriya, a city which became a graveyard for American Tanks back in 1991, and was the real reason why the Americans agreed for a cease fire. (Al Jazeera, 19 March 2003)

Interestingly, in contrast to this national resistance frame, the editors back in Doha immediately relayed the commentary of US Colonel John Midvey from West Point, the renowned American Military Academy. He states that the ongoing air raid is a 'limited operation' and that it constitutes more of a 'message' to the Iraqi military that things are getting serious and that they had better overthrow Saddam Hussein for their own sake. Colonel John Midvey also says that these are mock raids designed for psychological warfare purposes. Tawfiq Taha from Doha, obviously unhappy with this comment, points out that these statements lack logic, since mock raids do not trigger the explosions that have been reported. Tawfiq Taha adds that the US military command has cancelled the day's briefing. In his opinion, this means that things are not going according to plan. Then, Tawfiq Taha from the studio in Doha asked Diyar Al-Omari, Al Jazeera's correspondent in Baghdad, to comment on Colonel John Midvey's opinion. Diyar repeats his commentary that anti-aircraft gunfire was still active, and that this obliges the US aircraft to fly far away. He also makes reference to the communiqué of the Iraqi Army stating that it has gunned down a few cruise missiles.

Immediately afterwards, Tawfiq Taha from Doha gave time to the other Al Jazeera correspondent in Baghdad Majed Abdelhadi. Appearing immovable with a helmet and bullet proof jacket, close to major targeted state installations in Baghdad, Majed Abdelhadi stated that anti-aircraft gunfire was initially very heavy despite the absence of visible planes, and that a missile had struck an area in his vicinity. Majed reported upon many local details, such as the fact that the lights in Baghdad were still switched on, in contrast to bombing raids in 1991. This comment was followed by an Al Jazeera camera providing an overview of the Iraqi capital, and the movement of cars on the bridge.

Majed then stated that millions of Iraqis had stayed home because of their fear of the expected heavy bombardment. In this regard, Majed Abdlehadi remarked upon the anxiety and fear that had affected the Iraqi population, as well as journalists on the ground, since the end of the US ultimatum. The body language of Majed was itself very expressive: he looked fearful and anxious. He was still giving his account, when without warning, the Iraqi anti-aircraft gunfire started to sound. The substantial background noise in the background, reminded the audience that war was indeed a very dangerous business.

'Shock and Awe' vs. 'Baghdad is Burning'

After a two day delay, the long expected 'Shock and Awe' bombing campaign was finally unleashed. It became clear that the delay was itself part of the plan, for the media heavily speculated during this period on why there was such a stoppage, asking about the time when 'Shock and Awe' would start. On CNN and other US networks, this speculation served the strategic purpose of publicising the war so as to create a desire for 'Shock and Awe' among US and international audiences. This was effectively the grand opening to the war narrative, the huge conflagrations caused by the bombing were meant to display 'Shock and Awe' as spectacle. American mainstream media focused on the magnitude of the bombings revealed by television, omitting almost everything else, including the actual consequences of the explosions on civilian populations. The purpose of this exercise was to demonstrate the military hardware and military might of the United States.

This opening episode could also be interpreted as retribution for what Americans experienced on September 11 2001. Like the 9/11 attacks, 'Shock and Awe' had a devastating impact on densely populated targets. The Pentagon had given notice of its intentions in the months preceding the war. Thus, in an interview given to CBS on 24 January 2003, Pentagon planner Harlan Ullman predicted that the Iraq blitzkrieg could approximate the devastation of the most intense bombing campaign; 'The sheer size of this has never been ... contemplated before,' the official boasted to CBS News, who added that 'there will not be a safe place in Baghdad. This 'would be a firestorm, a Dresden or Tokyo with 60 years of new technology' (CBS, 2003)

Baghdad experienced an enormous pounding from US missiles. Huge fireballs rocked the heart of the Iraqi capital, and the sky became filled with smoke. By dubbing this attack plan 'Shock and Awe', the Pentagon hoped to instil a mixture of trauma and admiration; in two days, over 800 cruise missiles were unleashed, more than were used in the entire 1991 Gulf War. But while many American audience members were awestruck by the barrage of bombing on key landmarks in Baghdad, Arab audiences would have been distressed to see a historic Arab capital treated in this way. In direct contrast to the slogan 'Shock and Awe',

Al Jazeera ran the headline: 'Baghdad is burning'. Images of explosion and conflagration would have been enough to infuriate the Arab audience. However, the actual headline 'Baghdad is burning' added another emotional dimension. Most importantly, these images and the headline were displayed without any accompanying commentary. This lasted about six minutes.

Scene establishments

On CNN, the headline for this operation was named 'Strike on Iraq', and the graphic design was distinctive, as it displayed this title on the flag of Iraq, which contains the slogan 'Allah Akbar' (Allah is great). Then CNN showed live (but infra-red and greenish) images of Baghdad. It was a dark night, lit only by what CNN described as Iraqi anti-aircraft fire. On some occasions, the camera tilted upwards to search for cruise missiles that may have been coming in, looking for targets in and around Baghdad. While these images offered no meaningful information, Wolf Blitzer, other anchors and analysts at the studio offered their own summation of the scene.

Eventually, sirens were heard, and the crackling sound of gunfire became louder. At this juncture, CNN's camera was stationary. Anchor Wolf Blitzer stated that these were 'live pictures to give our viewers some context'. Blitzer interrupted some of the journalists who were commenting by saying: 'Just listen a little bit to the sound of the gunfire, like if we are listening to explosions heard over Baghdad, just listen little bit more to this fire.' Split screens were used to show four images from different news organisations including Al Jazeera and Abu Dhabi TV. Basically, the images showed the same Baghdad locations which included governmental buildings being hit by bombardment. The by-line was entitled: Operation Iraqi Freedom; Baghdad activity now under way.

On Al Jazeera, Diyar Al-Omari was reporting live from Baghdad. He announces a new wave of American bombardments on the Iraqi capital. In the background, the sound of explosions and bombs was echoed. Buildings are bombed and suffer major damage. Iraqi anti-aircraft gunfire is seen sending flashes into the air. Majed Abdelhadi, Al Jazeera's other correspondent in Baghdad, was placed nearby the places targeted. As he commented on developments, explosions occurred only about 500 metres away, creating huge fires in the process. His cameraman panned upward to show the actual aerial bombardment and the falling of the missiles over the buildings in Baghdad.

'Shock and Awe' unfolds

Different narratives

During the initial unfolding of the 'Shock and Awe' attacks, Wolf Blitzer on CNN posed some questions about what was going on in the sky over Baghdad. He asked the same questions to everyone, starting with military analyst General (ret.) Don Shepperd. He explained in detail the source of the flashes appearing on the horizon:

> On the monitors there are no impacts goings on, at least in downtown Baghdad. But what I have seen is an obviously alerted Iraqi defence system with anti-aircraft fire going up in the air ... any of those shells, any single one of them, can bring down an American or coalition airplane, Wolf. So this is dangerous stuff. (CNN, 21 March 2003)

Soon after emphasising the danger presented by Iraqi anti-aircraft weapons, General Sheppered minimised its likely impact on American warplanes by focusing on the Iraqi radars' ineptitude.

> But I do not see any tracking fire. I do not see any fire that is tracing across the sky following an aircraft, indicating to me they are not seeing anything on, I have not seen anything that I can identify as a missile launch, indicating to me, again, that they are probably not seeing anything on the radar right now. (CNN, 21 March 2003)

After that, Blitzer decided to use his last war coverage experiences in Baghdad to reiterate the inadequacies of the Iraqi radar:

> Normally in the past, based on these kinds of experiences that I have covered over Baghdad, normally in the past the start of these kinds of anti-aircraft fire by the Iraqis, their radar may not be good enough. It seems like they are almost just shooting in

the air in a wild fashion, hoping to get lucky and shoot down a plane. But they have no real specific targets. Is their radar better than that? (CNN, 21 March 2003)

General Shepperd, once again, agrees with Blitzer's analysis and summarised the inferiority of Iraqi air defence capabilities.

> They are shooting into sectors, hoping that they will hit something, hoping that one of the airplanes will fly into it. That is all they can do. But much of this anti-aircraft fire is not radar-guided at all, so it does not depend upon radar. And that is the reason that U.S and coalition forces use the night, because if they can track you on radar, they can do that day or night. But if they cannot track you, then they must see you to fire accurately, and if they cannot see you, such as at night, then they are greatly hampered. (CNN, 21 March 2003)

Subsequently, Wolf Blitzer contrasts the Iraqis poor standard of radar with the superiority of US planes:

> We are seeing that tracer fire continue to go up, Iraqi anti-aircraft fire. They are shooting into the skies, hoping to get lucky, shoot down a US plane. In the past, those F-117A Stealth fighters, hard to detect. Certainly they fly pretty high, cruise missiles even harder to detect. (CNN, 21 March 2003)

At this stage, CNN announced the start of A-Day, the start of the aerial bombardment, the massive air strike campaign that has been dubbed 'Shock and Awe'. Wolf Blitzer:

> We have been told that this is the start of what the Pentagon is now calling A-Day, the letter A, the start of the aerial bombardment, a massive air campaign expected over the next 24 to 48 hours, perhaps as many as 3,000 so-called smart bombs, precision-guided weapons, laser-guided weapons as well as satellite-guided weapons ...
>
> CNN has confirmed the start of A-Day, the start of the aerial bombardment, the massive US air strike campaign that has been dubbed Shock and Awe, a campaign that was expected to last at least 24 to 48 hours. Iraqi anti-aircraft fire was firing

> almost randomly, wildly, into the skies, hoping to shoot down US planes, US Tomahawk cruise missiles. The – there is no indication any of that happened. We have been reporting that huge explosions have occurred in the outskirts of Baghdad, presumably explosions resulting from US bombs, US Tomahawk cruise missiles, and other sophisticated munitions. (CNN, 21 March 2003)[6]

While the CNN reported the starting of the aerial bombardment, journalists voiced their concern about the lack of briefings coming from the Pentagon about the development of the war. Wolf Blitzer (CNN anchor):

> We are standing by; in about half an hour from now, we are expecting a Pentagon briefing. The defense secretary, Donald Rumsfeld, the chairman of the Joint Chiefs of Staff, General Richard Myers, will be briefing reporters, presumably telling us some more about what we're seeing on our television screens right now. (CNN, 21 March 2003)

He then proceeds to gather some new information from various CNN correspondents including Bob Franken in Kuwait and Kevin Sites in Northern Iraq. Yet, these CNN correspondents did not provide any new information. Everyone seemed to echo the military frames, stressing the superiority of the US planes and hardware. Nothing was really said about the development of the conflict itself. Take for example the following comments by Bob Franken (CNN correspondent):

> There has been a parade of planes all day and into the night that's taking off ... they have a variety of fighter jets here. They have everything from the FA-18 to the F-16, both of them, of course capable of bombing ... these are ferocious planes. I have seen them on the battlefield, they shoot at something like 6,000 rounds per minute, or something like that, and literally can shred a tank ... (CNN, 21 March 2003)

However, with the lack of a supporting Pentagon briefing, correspondents could only speculate about possible battle plans, asking whether or not there was any change in the 'Shock and Awe' strategy. Anchor Barbara Starr goes on to assure viewers that the aerial bombardment will, in any case, carry on.

As the bombs actually fell over Baghdad, CNN anchors and guests expressed admiration. For example, John Burns (CNN Guest) considered this wave of bombardment as 'biblical' and 'an astonishing sight',[7] whereas Nic Robertson (CNN senior international correspondent) thought the event was 'Armageddon' and 'awesome'.[8] At one point, there was some acknowledgment of the human dimension involved. Freelancing from Baghdad, May Ying Welsh (Independent Journalist) said that Iraqis she had met were 'definitely' affected by the bombing. She also affirmed, contrary to reports from the Pentagon, that civilians lived near the government buildings under attack. Aaron Brown (CNN anchor) after long minutes of near jubilation acknowledged that the attacks were 'terrible ... if you're on the other end of them.' Similarly, Wolf Blitzer (CNN anchor) remarked that 'we can only imagine what terrifying state most of those people are presumably in'.

However, these expressions of concern were outweighed by other comments praising the precision of the US military operation. Such comments assumed that most Iraqi civilians were safe and that the US war effort revealed an elevated sense of humanity. For example, CNN military analyst Wesley Clark affirmed that 'Shock and Awe' was 'precision bombing ... not carpet bombing ... not directed at populated areas,' while Nic Robertson, who was at that time in Baghdad told CNN he 'felt safe during the bombing.' Sometimes, CNN anchors made unsubstantiated speculations. Thus, John Burns reported that during the 'Shock and Awe' bombardment in Baghdad, 'Iraqis wandered out of their homes, hotels, on the embankment on the east side of the Tigris, and went forward to the river to get a better look ... These people ... have an almost complete confidence that ... [the US military] have got the coordinates right.'

On Al Jazeera, the narrative of bombardment was entirely different. The imminent arrival of 'Shock and Awe' was announced by Dana Budeiri (Al Jazeera's correspondent in the Pentagon):

> The authorities in the Pentagon declared that the heavy attack of Baghdad, or what is called Operation Shock and Awe, will start at any moment. A briefing from General Myers is expected in less than an hour from now. This is an additional indication

that the expected attack will happen at any time from now onwards. In addition, it has been declared that the B 52 planes have departed from Britain on the way to Iraq. This gives the impression that a strike on Baghdad will happen very soon. (Al Jazeera, 21 March 2003)

In these comments, Al Jazeera's correspondent in the Pentagon provided an approach based on facts. Dana Budeiri characterised the operation as a 'heavy attack on Baghdad', preferring to discard the military appellation (she used the term 'what is called Operation Shock and Awe'). She referred to the fact that the briefing of the United Kingdom Ministry of Defence was scheduled shortly, and that the Bombardiers had left their British bases for Iraq. For her, these facts indicated the imminence of the Baghdad bombardment. Unlike CNN anchors and correspondents, Dana Budeiri did not refer to the might of the American war machine or the lethality of its equipment.

Immediately after Dana Budeiri's report, Al Jazeera became even more on alert. They provided up-to-the-minute coverage from Baghdad and Mosul. After a while, Al Jazeera anchors announced that the press conference with General Myers had started and that live coverage would take place. Baghdad correspondent Diyar Al-Omari commented on the increasing fire coming from the Iraqi defences and explained that American planes were flying at lower attitudes as they approached their targets.

At a given moment, as the pace and frequency of the bombing increased and the sound of the explosions amplified, Al Jazeera's anchors kept silent for about six minutes. The control room in Doha stopped all discussions and commentaries in order to emphasise the amplified sound of explosions. This silence was very meaningful; it conveyed feelings of sadness over the human losses that would result from such an intensive bombardment. After a while, Jumana Namur, the main anchor in Doha turned to Majed Abdelhadi in Baghdad for comment. The latter referred to the frequency and damage of the American air strikes thus far. He also gave an assessment of the Iraqi anti-aircraft response, and described the reaction of Iraqi civilians. He referred to the fact that Iraqi civilians were taking refuge inside mosques and praying to God for salvation.

Al Jazeera continued to televise the bombs hitting Baghdad with enormous explosions. Amplified sounds of these explosions accompanied the visual footage. Cameras revealed the multiple bombardments of various locations. The situation in Baghdad became unsafe for Al Jazeera crew members who quickly fled their position, but only after placing multiple remote controlled cameras facing toward the targeted locations. No commentary followed for some time, as the images were left to speak for themselves for about four minutes. In the intervening time, massive explosions were heard in the background. Cameras shook because of the constant bombardment. The televised images became all white as if thunder had struck the cameras. One hears the voice of journalists running away to hide. Adjacent edifices, which seem to be governmental buildings, were subsequently hit by bombs, and smoke covered the scene.

Adnan Charif (Al Jazeera anchor) in Doha could not describe the picture. One hears him whispering an Islamic prayer '*la hawla wala kouwat ila billah*' which literally means 'there is no movement or power except by Allah's will.' Such a prayer usually accompanies disasters. Then he commented:

> This is one of the biggest strikes on Baghdad ... This strike reminds us ... We don't want to talk about it ... Baghdad is burning ... what can we say more? [Silence] While watching these revolting images from Baghdad, we try to contact our correspondent in Baghdad. (Al Jazeera, 21 March 2003)

Anchor Adnan Charif continued his commentary:

> What can we say after these shocking images? This is a strike which allegedly intends to take out weapons of mass destruction from Iraq. What are these weapons used right now: aren't they weapons of mass destruction? This is a question that imposes itself in these moments, as we watch that scene with pictures and sound. The tongue is powerless to describe this situation. (Al Jazeera 21 March 2003)

Again Adnan tried to contact the Al Jazeera crew in Baghdad to get some additional information, but they had taken cover to avoid being killed by the massive bombing campaign. Soon afterwards, another huge explosion hit the same targeted place. Adnan then repeated his sarcastic question: 'aren't these weapons of mass destruction?' The whole sequence lasted about four minutes.

Soon afterwards, Jumana Namur, took over the anchor role, and posed a particular question for Al Jazeera's military analyst General (ret.) Saad Al Chazli. She asked him why the Americans were repeatedly trying to strike the same targets over and over. His answer emphasised the fact that the highest military priority in war is to flatten command and control stations. The next priority would be to hit the main infrastructure, such as power grids and water infrastructure etc. as this would destroy any will to resist from the Iraqi side.

Then, Anchor Jumana Namur went back over the issue of the Iraqi anti-aircraft response. She asked the General about whether anti-aircraft batteries could intercept missiles over the capital city Baghdad, and whether the coalition missiles were flying at a high or low attitude. General Chazli seemed puzzled by the fact that Iraqi anti-aircraft crews were unable to gun down any American missiles thus far. The questions of Anchor Jumana Namur indicate a pattern in which Al Jazeera tries to find shortcomings in the coalition military plans. This led her to ask General Chazli about whether this was going to be an easy and quick battle for the coalition forces, or whether Iraqi forces might make it harder for them. The General answered tactfully that there were still many unknowns surrounding the exact capabilities of the Iraqi forces.

Battle of frames

'Decapitation Strike'
It was clearly noticeable that the framings of reality contained in the speech of President George W. Bush were echoed in the CNN coverage. As a result, CNN carried the following frames: the Orientalist deep frame,[9] and the conflict meso-frame[10] (with all its sub-frames, namely the military sub-frame,[11] the liberation sub-frame,[12] and the pre-emptive war sub-frame[13]). The only exception is the religious frame,[14] which was emphasised by President Bush in his speech but did not find resonance in CNN's coverage.

The Orientalist deep frame was there from the outset; consider for example the judgment of CNN anchor Aaron Brown:

> Again, around the country now, there are all sorts of military operations waiting to move in on the borders. Ben Wedeman is in the northern part of Iraq. Ben is with Kurdish troops. This is part of the complicated ethnic and religious makeup of Iraq that, over the weeks that this war plays out, we suspect we'll spend a fair amount of time talking about, probably not the night for it now. (CNN, 19 March 2003 22:55 EST)

Brown's comment that 'this is part of the complicated ethnic and religious makeup of Iraq' illustrates the Orientalist deep frame. The fact that the Iraqi people include different ethnic groups and religions does not uniquely represent a 'complicated ethnic and religious makeup'. If we take the American people as an example, it is also very diverse and includes people from Caucasian descent, as well as from African, Latino and Asian origins. Hundreds of heterogeneous churches, synagogues, mosques and other sects proliferate throughout America, without anyone commenting that this is a 'complicated ethnic and religious makeup'. On the contrary, the dominant discourse will praise American diversity as 'cosmopolitan' rather than complicated.

Another comment which exemplifies the Orientalist worldview is the use of the term 'Arab Street' to describe the Arab public opinion. See John King (CNN senior White House correspondent):

> And in that, and in only four minutes, as you noted, the president touching on that important political message aimed at the citizens of Iraq and more broadly the Arab street across the Middle East. (CNN, 19 March 2003)

Traditionally, after World War II, the phrase 'Arab public opinion' was referred to in Western media. However, it was substituted during the struggle for independence with the belittling term 'Arab Street' (Zayani, 2008: 46). Underlying this phrase is the assumption that Arab public opinion is 'Oriental' in essence, and thus inherently hostile, emotional, and irrational. According to media scholar Mohamed Zayani, to employ the term 'Arab Street' is to insinuate vulnerability to easy manipulation and the inclination to follow a mob mentality; 'it suggests dangerous masses awaiting to rise up in anger and spill into the streets in response to a particular event or in a violent popular reaction against a particular incident' (Zayani, 2008: 47). Underlying this statement is the assumption that Arabs are only responsive to force not reason.

Another assumption carried by this phrase is that Arab and Islamic societies, by their nature, lack any public sphere within which to debate and discuss political issues. Such an assumption carries Orientalist prejudices. As academic Marc Lynch argued, 'the theoretical reduction of Arab public opinion to the Arab street systematically distorts accurate understanding of its dynamics' (Lynch, 2003: 56). In Lynch's view, this reductionism ignored the fact that 'the relatively unique transnational dimension of Arab public spheres has long and deep roots' and that 'the Arab world has decades of experience with political argumentation at the transnational level' (p. 59). This reductionist approach also overlooked the impact of new media, including satellite television stations, such as Al Jazeera, and the internet in reinvigorating the Arab public sphere.

Reinforcing otherness were other rhetorical techniques used by politicians on CNN. Historically, for example, the speeches of Presidents Bush (Senior and Junior) often contained the 'nation-as-person' metaphor. As I have explained previously, this tendency is revealed in George Lakoff's analysis of Gulf War media coverage in 1991 (see pages 79 and 127). One of the most widely used framing techniques was to conflate a given nation state with the personality of its leader. International relations, in this view, is akin to a neighbourhood whose inhabitants are categorised as villains, victims, or heroes. Thus, Iraq as state, regime, people, and territory become synonymous with Saddam Hussein. In this context, the 'nation as a person'[15] metaphor contrasted with some of the themes circulated by the Bush administration, particularly the assertion that this was not a war on Iraqis (or Islam), but solely a war on Saddam Hussein. However, the latter theme was not frequently employed.

There were also other comments on CNN which exemplify the Orientalist frame. For instance, Senator Joseph Lieberman provided the following comments:

Well, my thoughts, obviously, are with the American military who are there, hoping and praying for their success, right now hoping that this attempt at decapitation was successful, because, after all is said and done, this is all about one evil dictator who possesses brutal weapons, with which he will threaten and hurt a lot of people, including a lot of Americans, unless we take them away from him. I understand the odds against that decapitation working, but it might. And, if it does, all of us, including the Iraqi people, are going to be very fortunate…

Saddam has ruled by fear and has killed any number of people under him, himself, who have shown some disloyalty. So, if it becomes clear that he is gone, then you have to ask, what is the motivation for all those in the Iraqi military to continue to want to fight us? We're offering them a better way and a better life…

What we are doing here is not only in the interests of the safety of the American people, because, believe me, Saddam Hussein would have used these weapons against us eventually or given them to terrorists who would have. But this is – what we are doing here, in overthrowing Saddam and removing those weapons of mass destruction, taking them into our control, is good for the security of every nation in the world. And it is a task we are taking on. It is not a selfish task. It is a task of high justice and necessity and I'd say idealism in the best tradition of American principles and patriotism. (CNN, 19 March 2003)

By characterising Saddam Hussein as an 'evil dictator, who possesses brutal weapons,' a religious dimension is added to racial 'otherness'. The 'other' thus becomes a monster controlled by a malevolent force in need of exorcism (read military intervention) (Gunn, 2004).

In the subsequent CNN coverage, the pre-emptive war sub-frame complemented the military sub-frame. The latter focused on military prowess, praised the power of military technology and the courage of the troops. This sub-frame pervades a popular culture, which valorises violence (as news professionals acclimatise the public to the acceptability of war). Mainstream American media undeniably adhered to this sub-frame by featuring analysts with very close connections to the Pentagon. The Pentagon's military perspective was therefore always prominent. In the case of CNN, its main

Hostilities Begin

military analyst was General (ret.) Wesley Clark, the former head of NATO, and former chief commander of NATO troops during the War in Kosovo. General Clark's past credentials heavily influenced his commentary. As I have indicated, he always identified himself with coalition troops, and used the pronoun 'We' when discussing military situations. The following extract from General Wesley Clark reiterates the point:

> We've got continuous visibility over much of Iraq. We've got scouts forward. We've got special operations forward. We've got satellites. We've got aircraft. We've got moving-target indicators off those aircraft. (CNN, 19 March 2003 22:44 EST)

Although General Clark was hired by CNN in his capacity as an analyst rather than a military commander, his comments blurred the line between journalism and military discourse. Other military analysts on CNN's payroll included Retired Generals Don Sheppard and David Grange who gave a favourable spin to the military plans. The reproduction of military discourse was further revealed when on numerous occasions CNN's journalistic commentary incorporated aspects of psychological warfare. One important aspect is that of perception management; this combines 'truth projection, operational security, cover and deception and psychological operations' (Dearth, 2002: 2). To this end CNN, wittingly or unwittingly, contributed to the tactic of encouraging the Iraqi population to accept the war on the grounds that it was not the target of it. Aaron Brown (CNN anchor):

> I was saying the president was making a lot of the points that he has been making for a long time. This is not a war on the Iraqi population, not a war on Islam, it is a war on Saddam Hussein and his regime (CNN, 19 March 2003 22:35 EST).

Additionally, CNN coverage contributed to the psychological tactic of inducing Iraqis to surrender (on the grounds that American victory is guaranteed). Aaron Brown (CNN anchor):

> I don't think anybody, I suspect, on the planet doubts that the American forces will overwhelm, ultimately, the Iraqis and win this. It is a complicated process that comes after, putting Iraq together. (CNN, 19 March 2003 23:29 EST)

On Al Jazeera, coverage of the 'Decapitation Strike' was fundamentally different. The resistance theme was recurrent throughout their coverage. Unlike the American media for whom the outcome of the war was never in question, Al Jazeera's anchors recurrently asked whether Iraq would resist the coalition assault. Local correspondents tried frequently to assert that Iraqi forces would be better organised compared to the Gulf War in 1991.

The following comments made by Al Jazeera's anchors and correspondents within the first hour of 'Decapitation Strike' highlight the theme of resistance. Diyar Al-Omari (Al Jazeera correspondent in Baghdad):

> The Pentagon has acknowledged violent Iraqi resistance.
>
> ... new methods implemented by the Iraqi anti-aircraft crews, who are now well trained, obliged the US airplanes to flee the scene ... Iraqi forces have stopped an attack in the vicinity of Al-Nasiriya, a city which was a graveyard for American Tanks back in 1991...
>
> An official communiqué states that the Iraqi Army has gunned down few cruise missiles. (Al Jazeera, 20 March 2003)

Tawfiq Taha (Al Jazeera anchor):

> The US military command cancelled the briefing for journalists that day, this means that things are not going according to plan. (Al Jazeera, 20 March 2003)

During the early hours of 'Decapitation Strike', Al Jazeera's anchors sometimes framed the situation as if the 'barbarians' were at the gates of Baghdad. The 'barbarian vs. civilised' construction shapes the binary logics associated with Orientalism and Occidentalism.[16] In this case, the Occidentalist frame was employed to highlight the cruelty of invading armies and mobilise nationalist spirits.

The image of colonial powers occupying Arab lands has long traumatised Arab consciousness especially in the aftermath of the Sykes–Picot Agreement, signed by Britain and France in 1916. In one strike, Arab lands in Arabia and the Levant were divided into zones of permanent French and British colonial influence. Arab resentment rose further when Western Nations backed the establishment of Israel in 1948. In the subsequent Arab-Israeli Wars, local Arab regimes constantly invoked the Barbarian invader

Hostilities Begin

image to position Western Powers as necessarily hostile to Arab interests. In fact, pan-Arabism, as an ideology aimed to unify the Arab peoples of the Middle East under the banner of a large Arab single state, constructed the West (and later Israel) as the 'other'. However, although pan-Arabist diatribes might share some rhetorical elements with anti-Western Occidentalist harangues, there are wide differences between the two.[17]

The emergence of the Occidentalist 'otherness' frames within Al Jazeera's coverage during the early hours of bombardment was not surprising. It was Diyar Al-Omari, an Iraqi journalist, who stressed this frame most often. Al-Omari appeared affected by what was about to happen to his home country. In this respect, the impact of Barbarianism was set against nationalist sentiments in a perfect combination of oneself versus the other. This juxtaposition becomes clearer when nationalist sentiments are framed and mobilised by the notion of 'resistance'. After stressing the cruelty of the invading soldiers and praising the Iraqi soldiers who do their job for 'honour, duty, and country', Iraqis are called upon to resist. Thus, 'heroic' acts of defence are praised in ways which exaggerate their real nature.

Hence, unsurprisingly Al Jazeera focused upon the horrors expected from the bombing campaign. This contributed to the general sense of refusal against a war that the Qatar based channel considered illegal from day one. The illegality of the war was an important meta-frame for Al Jazeera's entire coverage. In this context, the notion of resistance was articulated by the behaviour and rhetoric of Al Jazeera journalists, who took full advantage of their 'un-embedded' status. The notion of resistance was also employed to counter the American/British official line that the campaign was going on as planned.

Also, Al Jazeera emphasised the human-dimension to war and this allowed them to invoke the 'injustice frame' and the 'victim frame' (Snow and Benford 2000: 615). In war zones, there is no doubt that civilians are the most exposed and vulnerable. Such vulnerability exponentially increases when battles take place inside cities, the more so when massive aerial bombings occur. It is then quite plausible to suggest that unarmed civilians are being victimised. Historic precedents, such as the London blitz, the Allied bombing of Germany and the fire-bombing of Tokyo, all entailed the destruction of civilian life. So, when Al Jazeera portrayed the Iraqi conflict in terms of its human dimension, victimhood and injustice inevitably came to the fore. Indeed, the Qatar based channel boasted that it followed this general editorial line; its managers openly declared that their channel 'put more concentration on the sufferings of the people after the attacks' (Figenschou 2006: 77).

Visual analysis
During the 'Decapitation Strike' sequence, CNN's footage lacked substantive context. During one hour, CNN's images came from an extreme wide-angled shot of Baghdad. Such images were captured from afar, using very long lenses. The still images appeared greenish because of the use of infra-red lenses. As the camera remained stationary, it conveyed none of the human dimension of Baghdad. The only movement seen was the occasional flashing of anti-aircraft gunfire. On some occasions, the images displayed came from archives, and showed cruise missiles launch-pads positioned in an unnamed aircraft carrier. Approximately, 95 per cent of the footage used by CNN during the 'Decapitation Strike' carried no human dimension. Iraqis were never at the centre of the visual coverage. American soldiers were also not the focus of the coverage at this stage (apart from one interview from Kuwait, and in one instance where American soldiers were shown preparing military airplanes on an aircraft carrier). So, the entirety of the coverage focused on Baghdad from afar. This gave the impression that Baghdad was a ghost town.

With the cameras placed far away, one could not determine what was actually happening on the ground. The Baghdad locations shown by the camera could not be identified. For a long period of time, all that one could see was something that looked like a mosque on the right side of the screen, and another construction that could not be recognised. Similarly, the footage did not show any bombing sounds or lights. Sometimes, other images of other locations in Iraq were displayed. However, these locations seemed quiet and did not convey any sense of the war taking place. At one time, the colour palette became very bright for about four minutes; this happened when the camera took an extreme wide-angled shot of a central Baghdad location while the anchor's voiceover accompanied the footage. After that, the footage brightness diminished.

Hostilities Begin

During the 'Decapitation Strike', Al Jazeera's camera positioning relayed an entirely different footage. Cameras depicted the neighbouring places in Baghdad from afar. Viewers were brought close to city life. On these occasions, the camera was regularly moving left and right, zooming-in, zooming-out to capture some of the nearby landmarks of the Iraqi Capital. As a result, residential buildings, public places, parks, mosques, and streets clearly appeared in the footage. Viewers could see cars moving in the background, as street lights embellished the city. The human dimension of Baghdad was thereby conveyed. The palette used by Al Jazeera contained bright colours, thus giving a lively feel to Baghdad. Due to this technique, the Iraqi capital looked romantic. This complemented those remarks from anchors and correspondents that sympathised with the plight of Iraqi people awaiting military attack. Additionally, Al Jazeera's correspondents on the ground conveyed the sounds of city life. At times, the correspondents were silent such that car horns and engine noise became clearly audible. Also, when the anti-aircraft gunfire started, it was loudly reproduced by Al Jazeera; thus emphasising for the audience the general sense of danger.

Keyword Analysis
The very title 'Decapitation Strike' employed by CNN originates from nuclear warfare theory. In this context, a 'Decapitation Strike' is a first strike attack that aims to remove the command and control infrastructure of the opponent, in the hope that their capacity for nuclear retaliation will be degraded or destroyed. By drawing upon cold war annals, and nuclear brinkmanship with the Soviet Union, the Pentagon aimed to build a connection between the military capabilities of Iraq, and the huge military might of the now defunct superpower. By so doing, the Pentagon could create a climate of fear among the American public concerning the purported availability of nuclear weapons in Iraq.

If one separates the two words 'decapitation' and 'strike', additional connotations arise. Thus, 'decapitation' has medieval roots as a method of punishment against rebels and dissidents. This method was also a state terror tactic; decapitations were generally conducted in public places in order to instil fear among the general public. 'Strike', on the other hand, generally connotes a military operation conducted from the air. Together, the two words semantically conveyed extreme deadliness, surprise, and sudden impact. Another frequently used military term was 'selective strike'. The term was used by CNN's Walter Rogers and John King during the first hour of 'Decapitation Strike' to describe the military operation conducted against the Iraqi President and high-ranked regime leaders. This phrase exemplified the sense of technological superiority and clean war. The term 'selective' implied that the American administration's removal of Saddam Hussein would save the Iraqi people a costly and bloody war. 'Selective strike' not only implied that American forces had the technological capacity to strike anytime and anywhere, but also that this was the only objective (rather than, for example, the control of Iraq's oil resources).

Another interesting phrase was 'real movie', which was employed by CNN Anchor Aaron Brown to describe the 'Decapitation Strike' sequence. He said: 'it is like a brief intermission in some terrible, but real movie' (CNN, 19 March 2003). This phrase exemplified the entanglement of reality and fiction. Academics, such as Robert Stam, have argued that television news inherits its discursive mode of operation from both cinema and journalism. Thus, Stam considers 'filmic procedures' to be vital to the process of making television news (Stam 1983: 33–34). In movies, the script tends to establish the star of the movie as well as the story line and the genre of the film. The plot then unfolds and reaches resolution by the end. The 'Decapitation Strike' sequence resembled the introductory segment of a movie. It attracted attention and introduced the star, namely George W. Bush, and the villain, Saddam Hussein. This segment also prepared the audience for the main course of action about to unfold; 'Shock and Awe'.

One more phrase of interest at this juncture is that of 'game plan'.[18] CNN anchor Wolf Blitzer use of the sports term was not new. Such terminology characterised the coverage of 'Desert Storm' in 1991; as Jim Castonguay observed: 'During the Gulf War the commentary of military and football analysts, and the methods deployed to illustrate and explain sports and the war, became almost indistinguishable' (Castonguay 1997 [electronic article; no pagination]). By talking of a 'game plan', Wolf Blitzer was packaging and selling military conflict as entertainment.

Another interesting key phrase was 'psychological warfare' which was employed by Christiane Amanpour.[19] The fact that 'Decapitation Strike' came early in the campaign and 48 hours before the massive bombing campaign was of major psychological importance from a military point of view. Psychological warfare is basically an attempt to alter the behaviour of people in enemy-controlled territory. In revealing without examination that the so-called selective strikes against Saddam Hussein and some of his regime members were accompanied by electronic warfare (the control of Iraq's radio broadcasting airwaves), CNN legitimises the widening domain of warfare. It shall be recalled that according to US Air Force documents, psychological operations are part of operation planning from the start[20] (Dearth 2002: 4).

As mentioned earlier, the term 'evil' was also used during CNN coverage.[21] This keyword illustrates the rhetorical dependence upon neo-conservatism; a worldview which states that 'the human condition is defined as a choice between good and evil' (Halper and Clarke 2004). From a strategic communication perspective, 'evil' is an extremely powerful word. It generates fear because it constructs the enemy as a monster controlled by a malevolent force (Gunn 2004). This in turn implies that a violent, military intervention is the only viable option. The use of the keyword 'evil' is a well-known technique for insulating one's own rhetoric against counter-argument and rational challenge (Windt 1992). As part of the demonisation process launched against the Iraqi leader, the phrase 'leadership bunker' was employed.[22] This invokes an association with another evil figure in history: Adolf Hitler. This phrase therefore provided further justification for the 'Decapitation Strike' episode and associated rhetoric.[23]

'Brutal weapons' and 'weapons of mass destruction' were phrases used to describe Saddam Hussein's purported arsenal. The inference was that possession of such weaponry would enable the infliction of terrible damage on innocent victims. This in turn connotes an image of a 'barbarian' Iraq. In reality, Iraq had been stripped of its defences, and could not threaten neighbouring countries, let alone the world's superpower. On the other hand, the United States possessed weapons of mass destruction as well as conventional firepower.[24] However, the 'politics of naming' enabled the United States to highlight its opponent's destructive tendencies, while fostering a righteous image of its own.

Last but not least, two keywords are of utmost importance, namely 'better way' and 'better life', which were employed by Senator Joe Lieberman.

He was the last political figure to intervene in this very important prime-time broadcast. He carefully chose his words to convey, domestically, the rationale for war. To this end, he played the Orientalist card. He advised the Iraqi military to surrender so that the United States could offer them a 'better way and a better life'. The underlying message was that Iraqis would never reach these ideals without America influence.

Al Jazeera's response to the 'Decapitation Strike' rhetoric centred on the keyword 'resistance'. Clearly, Al Jazeera's anchors and correspondents expected stiff resistance from Iraqi forces. The word itself has deep cultural resonance. Historically, rituals of resistance against invaders became testimonials of honour in the collective Muslim consciousness. Resistance also symbolises manly courage in the Arab world (Peteet 1994: 34). Thus, the Qatar-based network portrayed the Arab-Israel conflict and the War on Iraq as 'David vs. Goliath' struggles, whereby Arab forces in unfavourable situations continue to fight against superior foes. The keyword 'resistance' also resonates with the expectations of Arab audiences in times of foreign onslaught. This explains the tendency of Al Jazeera to romanticise acts of resistance, including those of its own journalists.

Another keyword commonly employed by Al Jazeera at this juncture was 'invasion'. Unlike the American television networks which adopted the appellation Operation 'Iraqi Freedom', Al Jazeera routinely referred to 'the war on Iraq' and 'the invasion'. These phrases reminded audiences that the war was regarded as illegal. Many nations, including European members of NATO, had rejected the American arguments for war. In the Arab world, Saddam Hussein's regime was not widely supported, however, most observers believed that he had complied with the UN resolutions and that Iraq had no weapons of mass destruction (a fact that was subsequently verified and acknowledged by the United States). The keyword 'invasion' suggests the illegal presence of a hostile foreign army, and hence contradicts the Pentagon's construction of the war as 'liberation' and 'Operation Iraqi Freedom'. Additionally within the Arab world, the invasion of Iraq and most particularly Baghdad brought to mind the sack of Baghdad in 1258. At that time, the Mongols led by Hulegu, grandson of Genghis Khan, massacred most of the city's inhabitants; a blow from which the Islamic civilisation never fully recovered.

Another keyword used by Al Jazeera was 'fear'. Whereas on American television the Iraqi foe was demonised, the Qatar based channel emphasised Iraqi feelings of fear and anxiety in light of imminent military bombardment. Essentially, fear is a feeling that is heightened by a threat. Al Jazeera addressed these feelings and thus helped Iraqis, who were demonised on American television, to regain their human dimension. Indeed, Al Jazeera placed its reporters near the locations to be targeted. Despite their own apprehension, these reporters, in effect, identified with the predicament of the Iraqi population.

'Shock and Awe'

CNN also conveyed a sense of the human dimension, although this only happened for a short time. This outlook was evident when CNN interviewed by phone the independent journalist May Ying Welsh in Baghdad. She related how Iraqi civilians had expressed their fear and anxiety to her.[25] She also described how the bombs shook the foundations of targeted buildings, and confirmed that many civilians living nearby had been killed during 'Decapitation Strike'.

> It was a really terrifying experience, I can tell you. And also, I mean, none of these buildings are just standing there by themselves. Civilians do live around these buildings. There are residential pockets near all kinds of buildings that are targets in the city. So from the first two nights of the bombing, which were relatively light, they had 37 civilian casualties. I do not know what the civilian casualties are going to be like now. (CNN, 21 March 2003)

Welsh's comments contradicted the routine military claims of surgical and clinical bombings. These claims were later reinforced by Defense Secretary Donald Rumsfeld when he declared that 'Shock and Awe' was the most humane bombing in history. During the US Department of Defense briefing on 21 March 2003, he stated that:

> The targeting capabilities and the care that goes into targeting to see that the precise targets are struck and that other targets are not struck is as impressive as anything anyone could see. The care that goes into it, the humanity that goes into it, to see

that military targets are destroyed, to be sure, but that it's done in a way, and in a manner, and in a direction and with a weapon that is appropriate to that very particularized target.[26]

Another interesting theme was the emphasis upon spectacular warfare. As I have outlined, from the beginning, the military sold 'Shock and Awe' as a spectacular and overwhelming display of military might which would destroy the will of the Iraqi side to fight. Researchers, such as Deborah Lynn Jaramillo (2006), argue that CNN and Fox News Channel positioned and packaged the 2003 US led war on Iraq for a domestic audience. In this context, she contends that war developments were streamlined into a filmic product which linked together narrative, style, ideology and commercial profits. CNN and other American television news networks mimic Hollywood filmmaking techniques to offer audiences the same formulaic entertainment they get from movies and other prime-time programmes.

During the 1991 Gulf War, the military had learned how to make their campaign a staged event for the major television networks. Thus, the American public knew through CNN that 'Desert Storm' had begun before the Pentagon's formal announcement (Van Tuyll 2002: 234). In addition, the US military info-warriors prepared, months in advance, the types of stories that would attract media coverage during the different phases of 'Desert Storm'. Strategic frames emphasising the cleanliness and efficiency of the American hi-tech arsenal were given special preparation (Wolfsfeld 1997: 133).

The notion of the war-as-spectacle, which thrills and entertains people, does not require the involvement of the population at large in the actual war effort. Their role is to express patriotic feelings in their living rooms (Castells 2000: 486). This, of course, entails close military involvement in news production (a theatre of war in its own right). Millions of dollars are invested in imaging and neural technologies to produce a 'militarized form of the image' (Mirzoeff 2005: 73). Subsequently, the borderline between truth and reality, factual information and propaganda is blurred, while bloodless and hygienic images have shrunk the gap between real wars and virtual wars (Der Derian 2001: xviii).

During 'Shock and Awe', Wolf Blitzer and other anchors contributed to the war-as-spectacle. While bombs rained on Baghdad, Blitzer and his colleagues appeared jubilant, as if they were watching fireworks. The following comments show this orientation. Wolf Blitzer (CNN anchor):

> The bombardment of Baghdad. The US blasts the city with deafening force. See how it unfolded on live television around the world. (CNN, 21 March 2003 17:00 ET)
>
> Here's a look at the bombing of Baghdad. Listen to this, Jamie. These are shots being fired now in Baghdad. I want our viewers to listen in. (CNN, 21 March 2003 17:36 ET)

Bob Franken (CNN correspondent):
> They are getting ready for an ear-shattering sound. Here comes another one. (CNN, 21 March 2003 17:02 ET)

At the same time, the psychological warfare sub-frame was a built-in feature of CNN coverage. It occurred after anchors and military analysts alleged that Iraqi forces were in disarray, that their commanders were negotiating their general surrender, and that Saddam Hussein was hit. In fact, Pentagon officials encouraged these speculations to generate discord among Iraqi rulers and to weaken Saddam Hussein's authority.

During the 2003 War on Iraq, Michael Ryan, a former editor for *Time*, observed that 'American media, essentially, have become an extension of the military psychological operations, with Rumsfeld hoping they can help to scare the daylights out of Iraq' (Kumar 2006: 62). At CNN, the views and frames of the military institutions were also conveyed by former military commanders such as General Wesley Clark and retired Air Force General Don Shepperd. In addition, embedded journalists with coalition military units conveyed and reinforced military frames. For Clark S. Judge, one of the White House spin doctors, the whole concept of embedding 'counts as the first major victory in the war in Iraq' (Judge 2003: B2). It counted as a victory because embedded journalists 'saturated the world's airwaves and newspapers with reports of the division's exploits and experiences in combat' (Plenzler 2004: 261).

The problem with embedding was not simply that military officials might spread disinformation through embedded journalists, or that journalists might sing the praise of the military. As Todd Morman has observed, the main problem was that embeds had access to a narrow range of war news sources. Because the military controls the transportation of reporters, they cannot determine where they go, what they see, and what they report. Consequently, embedded journalists 'have no way to check the validity of the second-hand information they are being given by military officials.' In Morman's view, 'this can result in an unusually narrow view of what is really happening on the ground' (Morman 2003 [electronic article: no pagination]).

It is clear that Al Jazeera's anchors could not bear to watch Baghdad being bombed so intensively. They and their reporters were imbued with deep pan-Arabist sensibilities, which tended to equate the bombing and invasion of Baghdad (a historic Arab city) with the desecration of an imagined sacral body. Hence, on many occasions during Al Jazeera's coverage, an implied parallel was drawn between 'Shock and Awe' and the Mongol sack of Baghdad in 1258. This parallel was also made by official Iraqi sources as well as by pundits invited to comment on other Arab media. This phenomenon has been compared by French sociologist Halbwachs with the process of retouching a painting, such that 'new images overlay the old' (Halbwachs 1952: 72).

As indicated in earlier chapters, the Middle East and North Africa have been shaped by Pan-Arabism; a form of cultural inter-nationalism that seeks to unify Arab peoples and nations. Pan-Arabism is classically opposed to colonialism and Western political interference in the Arab world. This ethos underpinned the coverage provided by Arab satellite news channels during the Iraq War. The prevailing perspective was that Arab sovereignty and heritage had been violated by the invasion of Iraq. Majed Abdelhadi (Al Jazeera correspondent in Baghdad) referred in his comments to 'people praying in mosques'. Likewise Adnan Charif (Al Jazeera anchor) uttered some Islamic prayers when the heavy aerial bombardment on Baghdad started.[27] This reveals how 'Shock and Awe' was depicted as a catastrophe striking Iraq. At one point, Al Jazeera's Adnan Charif referred to American bombs as 'weapons of mass destruction' because they had flattened whole Baghdad neighbourhoods. This war of words illustrated the fact that Al Jazeera was challenging CNN's framing of the conflict. It shall be recalled that the War on Iraq was justified on the premise that Iraq possessed weapons of mass destruction. By referring to the bombs and missiles used in 'Shock and Awe' as 'weapons of mass destruction', Al Jazeera's anchors showed their rejection of the US rationale for war (as well as the reproduction of this rationale on CNN and other television networks)

Visual analysis
The juxtaposed images at the start of this chapter were screened by CNN and Al Jazeera on 21 March at 5p.m. ET/10p.m. GMT. They reveal the huge explosions that rocked Baghdad during the massive aerial assault. The footage also shows luminous traces of Iraqi anti-aircraft fire. Al Jazeera's images were the most vivid and informative; they showed the impact of major explosions on the buildings. As the missiles and bombs landed, CNN often used Abu Dhabi television footage but the latter was not simply relayed; CNN edited the incoming images of bombardment in a fast paced way and seemed to use more images from distant cameras.

The bombardment was shown from various locations, and gave the audience wide shots of numerous explosions inter-cut with close-up visuals concerning the size, damage and combustion of the explosion. This editing style enabled the viewer to stay within the choreography of 'Shock and Awe' and to track the full scale of the strike. Any footage that did not show spectacular bombing or conflagration was trimmed out. A dissolve[28] was used to link the dramatic news segments. The result was a vivid sequence of bombardment, exactly as underlined in the title of 'Shock and Awe'.

The CNN trailers played a similar role:

LARGE EXPLOSION ROCKS IRAQ'S CAPITAL AND ANTI-AIRCRAFT LIGHT UP SKIES, AS LARGE-SCALE 'A-DAY' BOMBARDMENT OF IRAQ GETS UNDERWAY
SHOTS BEING FIRED OVER BAGHDAD
PENTAGON: BEGINNING OF THE SHOCK AND AWE CAMPAIGN
'SHOCK AND AWE' UNDER WAY
BOMBS FALLING ACROSS BAGHDAD
BAGHDAD UNDER HEAVY BOMBARDMENT

On Al Jazeera, numerous images showed the bombing of Baghdad. The huge sound of the explosions was amplified in the background. Multiple cameras revealed the impact of the bombardments from various positions in Baghdad. Al Jazeera's control room regularly abstained from commentary, leaving the images to speak for themselves.

The massive bombardment shook the cameras many times. The images depicted massive conflagrations, smoke and fires around all the locations covered. It is also interesting to note that Al Jazeera transmitted numerous publicity clips for its brand during these sequences. In one instance, a voice-over describes the professionalism of Al Jazeera news channel and its up-to-the-minute coverage of the war in Iraq. Unlike CNN, such publicity did not focus on the character of the anchors or correspondents. The clip's visuals revealed planes firing, missiles dropping, explosions, targeted places, and US soldiers.

In another instance, Al Jazeera screened a video recording of Saddam subtitled in English: 'Iraq has diligently implemented the 1441 resolution'. Another publicity break contained poignant music accompanying the aerial bombardment, and the ensuing explosions and fires.

Keyword analysis
On CNN, certain keywords and phrases with military connotations were constantly repeated. These included 'precision-guided munitions' and 'smart bombs.' The missiles' supposed precision and the bombs' smartness were regularly emphasised by the Pentagon info-warriors and CNN coverage. Such coverage disseminated the myth of a 'clean' war (in contrast to the old-style 'dirty war' reminiscent of guerrilla battles in the Vietnam jungles). The rhetorical emphasis on precision bombing presumes 'humane' destruction; even though, unacknowledged by info-warriors, the shells of some missiles were tipped with uranium contaminants.[29] The rhetoric of surgical strikes emanated from military and political elites who were also primary news sources. Indeed, in his news briefing shortly before 'Shock and Awe', Secretary of Defense Donald Rumsfeld pointed out that US weaponry had 'a degree of precision that no one dreamt of in a prior conflict'.[30] But in contrast to the Western weaponry deemed 'humane', 'surgical', and 'clinical', the weaponry deployed by the Iraqis was characterised

as wild, inefficient, disorderly, and irrational. For instance, Wolf Blitzer commented that the Iraqi anti-aircraft crews are 'almost just shooting in the air in a wild fashion, hoping to get lucky and shoot down a plane' (CNN, 21 March 2003).

During 'Shock and Awe', CNN anchors were directly inspired by the lexicon of sport. The wave of bombardment was described on CNN as 'literally awesome', 'just amazing', 'awesome', and a 'fireworks show'. These words, which are normally used during the coverage of major sports events, were used on CNN to mobilise viewer identification. Although sport and politics had long been mixed together, this tendency intensified during the Bush administration. Academics Mark Falcous and Michael Silk analysed the mediation of two major sporting events that took place in the first week of February 2002; the delayed National Football League (NFL) Super Bowl and the Salt Lake City Winter Olympics opening ceremony. They found out that sport in its mediated forms had become 'embedded in the cultural politics of "post 9/11 America".' As a result, sports' vocabulary was increasingly used to amplify the nationalist

Figure 6.2: CNN headline during 'Shock and Awe' (21 March 2003).

discourse. This discourse played a prominent role in re-constructing American identity through us versus them strategies (Falcous and Silk 2005: 60, 63).

Furthermore, the use of sports terms is a highly efficient perception management tactic. Indeed, CNN journalists were able to manage spectators' emotions in the face of images which revealed huge devastation. Judith Butler has stated that television news is about spectacle, what is seen as well as what is heard. Television news is also about what is 'felt' as well as what is 'known';

> To produce what will constitute the public sphere ..., *it is necessary to control the way in which people see, how they hear, what they see.* The constraints are not only on content – certain images of dead bodies in Iraq, for instance, are considered unacceptable for public visual consumption – but on what 'can' be heard, read, seen, felt and known. [emphasis added] (Butler 2004: xx)

In the context of 'Shock and Awe', the management of audience emotions was done by connecting this mortal environment with the terminology of sports (this conveyed the sense of intense competition devoid of human suffering or outrage). This exercise was made easier by the sanitised imagery which did not display the suffering of Iraqi civilians. To this end, CNN reiterated the humanitarian claim that the bombing would relieve Iraqis from the oppressive Hussein regime. This approach resolved a dilemma faced by the Pentagon, and observed by CNN Senior International Correspondent Christiane Amanpour. She declared in the period preceding the fall of Baghdad that 'the coalition troops want to be seen as benefactors not just as bombers' (CNN, 29 March 2003).[31]

Other keywords employed during the conflagrations were 'biblical' and 'Armageddon'. These words reflected the impact of Christian Zionism on American media and politics. It shall be recalled that the neo-conservative movement is a natural ally of Christian Zionism, and representatives of both movements rose to prominence under the Bush presidency. Christian Zionists believe, as exemplified by Pastor John Hagee in his book *Jerusalem Countdown,* that a confrontation in the Middle East is a necessary precondition for the battle of Armageddon and the Second Coming of Christ. According to this prophesy, the United States must join Israel in a struggle against Middle Eastern nations to fulfil God's plan for both Israel and the West. So the use of these keywords during the coverage of 'Shock and Awe' underlines the willingness of CNN to cue religious fervour for the Bush presidency's war agenda.

In contrast, as I have emphasised, Al Jazeera used a different set of keywords and phrases. Instead of using 'Shock and Awe', Al Jazeera's journalist Tawfiq Taha used the expression 'Baghdad is burning' when bombs and missiles started falling on Baghdad. Al Jazeera later used the by-line 'Baghdad is burning' dozens of times in conjunction with images of devastation. The images of havoc, conflagrations and fire without aural accompaniment spoke for themselves.

On at least two occasions,[32] Al Jazeera's anchors uttered religious phrases such as '*La hawla wa laa quwwata illaa billaah*' (There is no might nor power except by Allah's will). This is a common Muslim expression in the face of major difficulties. While this is a religious expression in essence, it is also part of non-religious parlance in the Muslim world. The employment of this phrase by Al Jazeera's anchors conveys the feeling that a major catastrophe is happening. This feeling directly contrasts with CNN's euphoric depictions of 'Shock and Awe' along with the 'liberation' message the Bush administration wanted to be transmitted across the Middle East.

Clash of frames

The 2003 Iraq War was undeniably an important chapter not only in the course of the Iraq War, but also in the Bush administration's 'War on Terror' (in the name of security, democracy, freedom and human rights). The start of this war was depicted differently by CNN and Al Jazeera. While CNN employed the military-inspired title 'Decapitation Strike' for the war prologue, Al Jazeera chose to frame the event as an 'assassination attempt'. CNN anchors and correspondents relayed the White House rationale for the attack, amidst speculative commentaries on the supposed locations of the Iraqi leadership. They also filled air-time with speculations that Saddam Hussein may have been hit. In addition, these speculations helped to construct a 'need' for the bombing campaign to get underway. In contrast, Al Jazeera anchors and correspondents denied that Saddam Hussein or any high ranked Iraqi official were hit during the first bombing. They downplayed the effectiveness of the first air strikes. They also hinted at their illegality by reminding viewers that the formal declaration of war was only issued once the raid was well under way. Therefore, the sequence was framed on Al Jazeera as an 'assassination attempt'.

In the first hour of the subsequent, and much heavier, aerial bombardment, there was again a sharp juxtaposition in CNN and Al Jazeera's coverage. For the former, the sequence was named 'Shock and Awe'; a climactic event in a spectacular war. The bombing of Baghdad was choreographed as an enjoyable fireworks display. In this context, CNN adopted, for the most part, a pro-military perspective which promoted the objective of Iraqi liberation, and the might of American firepower. Yet, there was no emphasis on the ongoing human consequences of the aerial bombardment. In contrast, Al Jazeera framed the sequence as 'Baghdad is burning'. This title was employed for hours at a time and was interspersed with footage of the ensuing destruction and civilian casualties. There were also moments of silence in Al Jazeera's coverage, as the control room regularly abstained from commentary, leaving the images to speak for themselves; silence was considered a more powerful statement as this implied grief over the loss of civilian lives.

There was undeniably a clash of terminologies between CNN and Al Jazeera. The following columns illustrate this:

Table 6.1: Table comparing the terminologies used by CNN and Al Jazeera during 'Shock and Awe'.

CNN's Terminology	Al Jazeera's Terminology
Operation Iraqi Freedom	Invasion of Iraq/War on Iraq
Decapitation Strike	Assassination attempt
Shock and Awe	Baghdad is burning
Liberation troops	Occupation troops
The Dictator/Saddam	President Saddam Hussein
Collateral damage	Carnage
Reconstruction of Iraq	Destruction of Iraq

In terms of deep frames, CNN's coverage reproduces the Orientalist frame which was particularly noticeable in Senator Joe Lieberman's statements. He boasted about the 'better way' and the 'better life' that America would offer to the Iraqis. Such remarks, combined with the liberation theme and the use of numerous rhetorical devices (e.g. the nation-as-person metaphor), underlined the supremacist perspective of the Orientalist frame. He presumed that the Orient would have no future, except if the civilised Occident defeated and dominated the Orient.

Al Jazeera, on the other hand, employed primarily a pan-Arabist frame with elements of Occidentalism. This former frame considered the bombardment of the historic capital of Iraq as an assault on the common Arab heritage. The anchors and correspondents of the Qatar-based broadcaster emphasised the human cost of the war. They also referred to religion and prayers to highlight the terrifying experiences of Iraqi civilians. In one instance, Al Jazeera anchor, Adnan Charif, directly challenged the Bush administration's rhetoric, describing the US missiles as weapons of mass destruction.

The coverage of CNN also included elements of US information warfare. The omnipresence of ex-Generals at the CNN control room in Atlanta effectively reproduced the militaristic discourse without scrutiny. CNN viewers were invited to identify with the Pentagon's military objectives whenever references were made about the lethality and precision of US missiles as well as the courage of American troops. The Pentagon's info-war strategy also downplayed references to war casualties, preferring instead to talk of 'liberation' and 're-construction'. In contrast, Al Jazeera's correspondents and guests emphasised the theme of resistance. For example, Diyar Al-Omari (Al Jazeera correspondent in Baghdad) referred to a battle in the 1991 Gulf War, in which Iraqi armoured divisions allegedly prevailed. Al Jazeera anchors frequently asked their military analysts whether Iraq would be able to resist the coalition assault, in contrast to CNN for whom the outcome of the war was never in question.

7

Journalists as Combatants: US Bombing of Al Jazeera's Office and the Palestine Hotel

Figure 7.1: Footage of CNN and Al Jazeera after the 8 April 2003 bombings in Baghdad (8 April 2003).

Context and chronology

Significant events took place after 'Shock and Awe' (21 March 2003) and prior to the 8 April bombings, which are described in this chapter. Although these events might seem unrelated, they reveal ongoing differences between CNN and Al Jazeera's conception of wartime journalism. After 'Shock and Awe', coalition forces asserted their control over key southern Iraqi cities. The heaviest battles took place on 23 March 2003 near the city of Nassiriya, a key crossing of the Euphrates river about 225 miles southeast of Baghdad. Marines battled Iraqi forces and suffered numerous casualties. Ten US Marines were confirmed killed after they ran into an ambush. Footage of British and American soldiers wounded and killed by Iraqi forces emerged; five were shown as prisoners of war and at least four were shown dead in what appeared to be a hospital room. The footage was shown first on Iraqi state television and then relayed by Al Jazeera on 23 March 2003.¹ The US military acknowledged that twelve mechanics were missing.

Nonetheless, coalition forces continued their advance from the south into Najaf and from the southwest into Karbala. The latter city witnessed an intense battle, following which one US Apache helicopter was captured, along with its two crew members. These events were reported by Al Jazeera on 24 March. Al Jazeera also reported on the same day that another American helicopter had been destroyed and that other coalition helicopters had come under heavy fire, with only two of them managing to achieve their objectives.

Evidence of Iraqi resistance contradicted the US military's promises of a swift and painless victory march into Baghdad. Therefore, the Pentagon's info-warriors had to rethink their Psyops strategy. The supposed ordeal of 19-year-old private Jessica Lynch became their major coup. On 23 March, she was travelling with the Army's 507th Maintenance Company when the convoy was ambushed after taking a wrong direction. After being injured in her legs and spine, Lynch was taken prisoner. Five of her comrades were also captured but held in separate locations. During the same ambush, eleven soldiers were killed. On 1 April, US Special Forces decided to rescue Private Lynch from the Iraqi hospital where she was being treated for her wounds. After the success of this operation, reporters were briefed at Centcom in Doha on the dramatic saga of Lynch's rescue.

The Pentagon turned this story into a stunning piece of news management.² Jessica Lynch was portrayed as a 'little girl Rambo', firing her gun down to the last bullet before being captured. She was then allegedly captured and 'tortured' by the Iraqis, only to be saved by a videoed commando type operation showing Jessica Lynch, draped in a US flag, being taken away in a helicopter (Compton 2004: 24–29). This compelling story featuring her ambush, alleged heroic resistance, and ultimate rescue became a major publicity exercise for the Pentagon.³ Michael Getler, from the *Washington Post*, commented on the sensationalised aspects of the story:

> Her rescue, filmed by the military and shown on television, came at a crucial time in the US offensive. It seemed to give

everyone a lift. The follow-up [*Washington*] *Post* exclusive about her actions and ordeal was a powerful additional element at the time. People remember that story. (Getler 2003: 10)

American networks eagerly embraced the story. On 2 April, CNN's Paula Zahn named the raid 'Saving Private Lynch', evoking parallels with Spielberg's movie. The brief footage of American soldiers carrying Lynch to safety was aired ad infinitum. CNN used graphic design and computer animation to simulate how the rescue might have happened. The Jessica Lynch story was designed to boost domestic morale in the United States. European and Middle Eastern audiences remained sceptical. In fact, Al Jazeera and other Arab media allocated only limited coverage; and after corroborating the Iraqi side of the story, including the medical staff that treated Jessica Lynch, they concluded that the American reportage was false.

At the same time, American forces encountered fierce fighting from small units of the Iraqi Republican Guard even on the outskirts of Baghdad (2 April 2003). In the south, coalition troops encountered heavy resistance which delayed their progress. To the surprise of Pentagon planners, Iraqi forces stationed in localities such as Umm Qasr, Basra, and Nassiriya fought staunchly. Consequently, there was a halt in the offensive, supply lines were stretched and coalition forces sustained numerous casualties. At this juncture, the Pentagon reshaped prevailing news narratives. Notwithstanding the Jessica Lynch coverage, televised images of US prisoners of war (POWs) and dead soldiers (shown on Iraqi National Television and Al Jazeera) replaced the euphoria of 'Shock and Awe'. Journalists started to question the military planning,[4] as this turn of events contrasted with the original promises of Pentagon officials that the Iraq campaign would be a 'cakewalk'.[5]

At this point, the international news media were openly speculating about the prospect of urban warfare inside Baghdad (especially once US forces took control of Saddam International Airport on 3 April). With the presence of hundreds of journalists in Baghdad, the Pentagon was fearful of a long lasting siege,[6] which would turn the war into a quagmire for US troops. This fear was heightened by international media, which occasionally voiced criticism concerning civilian casualties,[7] Against this background, Arab media continued to show stark footage of property destruction and wounded children. Arab journalists also interviewed Iraqi officials, such as Iraqi Information Minister Mohammed Saeed al-Sahhaf, whose perspective on events challenged the American narrative.

On Tuesday 8 April 2003, at about 6.30 a.m. (Baghdad Time)[8] two American air-to-surface missiles hit Al Jazeera's office in Baghdad. Reporter Tareq Ayyoob was killed and a cameraman wounded. Surviving Al Jazeera staff sought refuge at the adjacent villa of Arab satellite channel Abu Dhabi TV, which then came under US attack less than 15 minutes afterwards.[9] On the same day (8 April 2003), at about 11:45 a.m. (Baghdad Time) [3.45 a.m. ET], a US army tank fired into the 15th floor of the Palestine Hotel in Baghdad, (where almost all foreign journalists were based), killing two cameramen and wounding three media workers.

These events occurred just as US troops were attempting to control Baghdad. The military hierarchy would have been nervous about the prospect of negative coverage undermining their information management. The Pentagon was still experiencing the 'Vietnam Syndrome'; the belief that unpatriotic coverage contributed to military loss. Acknowledgement of these matters leads to the realisation that journalists and media outlets are themselves military targets. The numerous difficulties and dangers experienced by 'unilateral' journalists during the Iraq conflict, combined with the practice of embedding journalists with coalition troops, exemplify the information warfare paradigm. Embedded journalists are aligned with official military discourse at the same time as the communications and information systems of the 'enemy' have to be destroyed (Van Ham 2003: 440).

Story establishments

Notwithstanding CNN trailers, the first CNN anchor to report about the events in question was Carol Costello. This happened on 8 April 2003 at (8 April 2003 5:00 a.m. E.T.).

> Parts of central Baghdad erupted into an urban battlefield early today with US tanks and war planes taking on a high rise government building along the Tigris River. One of Al Jazeera's television reporters was killed by an air strike and a cameraman for Abu Dhabi Television narrowly escaped injury when his location was targeted. (8 April 2003)

Then, Carol Costello (CNN anchor) reviewed some skirmishes involving US Marines in southeast Baghdad. She also made reference to air raids conducted in Baghdad against a presumed hideout of Saddam Hussein. She also talked about video released by the Pentagon about an air raid against Iraqi leaders in Basra, including the home of an Iraqi General. After that, Costello returned to the main story of the day.

> The Arab television station Al Jazeera says one of its journalists was killed when a US air strike hit a Baghdad building housing Arab media. The journalist, identified as Tareq Ayyoub, was carried away from the wreckage in a blanket. Another Al Jazeera journalist was injured in the blast. The Pentagon denies it was targeting Al Jazeera.
> The Palestine Hotel in downtown Baghdad came under fire, too, today. We have reports now a Spanish reporter was killed. The hotel is known primarily as the home base for many international journalists remaining in the city. Several other journalists were wounded by what appears to be a shell hitting the 15th floor. The source of this fire is not yet known. (8 April 2003 5:04 a.m. E.T.).

In spite of the extreme newsworthiness of these events, CNN chose to air in full Private Jessica Lynch's reunification with her family at a news conference in Landstuhl, Germany. This took about 45 minutes. Subsequently, CNN gave airtime to Rym Brahimi their correspondent in Amman (Jordan) to get more information on the aforementioned incidents. Rym Brahimi expressed her sadness regarding the turn of events.

> Carol, this is a very sad day for us in the journalistic community. Two journalists have been killed. I was talking, indeed, to somebody who was just at The Palestine Hotel literally minutes before this hit against The Palestine Hotel, hit the 15th floor of the building, where the Reuters journalists had an office. (CNN, 8 April 2003).

She went on to describe the events and advanced the possibility that the firing had come from a tank (possibly two tanks) advancing on the Al-Jumhuriya Bridge. She then mentioned the possibility that there might have been an exchange of fire between the tanks and buildings in the vicinity of the Palestine Hotel.

> There's been an exchange of fire between those tanks and some buildings across the river from there. It's possible that one of these tanks may have been the one to hit the Palestine Hotel (CNN, 8 April 2003).

Rym Brahimi then went on to talk about the bombing of Al Jazeera's bureau, acknowledging that the deceased journalist, Tareq Ayyoub, had worked for CNN at some point, and that she knew him personally. She described him as a 'very hard working, extremely helpful colleague.' Afterwards, Rym Brahimi was pressed by Costello to endorse the official version of the incidents.

> Costello: Let's go back to The Palestine Hotel, because government sources say the media certainly is not being targeted. But we do understand that someone saw snipers on the roof and maybe that's why this explosion occurred.
>
> Brahimi: I can't comment on that. I don't know, I can't say whether or not that is accurate. I know that from the beginning The Palestine Hotel, from the beginning of the war, was the hotel where all the journalists were staying. There were very few journalists – in fact, I don't know of any journalists who at the eve of the war, when the war began, were still anywhere else but at the Palestine Hotel. (CNN, 8 April 2003)

Military spokespeople offered conflicting accounts of the incident; shortly after the attack on the Palestine Hotel, a CNN trailer quoted the Third Infantry Division's Commander, General Bouford Blount, as saying their tank had come under sniper fire from the hotel roof. Thus, the tank had fired at the source of the shooting. Then, Brigadier General Vince Brooks (Deputy Director of Operations – CENTCOM) made the following statement at CENTCOM, Qatar a news conference (covered by CNN at about 7:15 a.m. ET).

> Initial reports indicate that the Coalition force operating near the hotel took fire from the lobby of the hotel and returned fire and any loss of life, civilian loss of life or unintended

consequences, again, we find most unfortunate and also undesirable. (CNN, 8 April 2003)

But Brooks' explanation was met with scepticism by journalists present at the news conference, as is revealed in the following exchange between Geoff Mead (CNN Guest; Sky News correspondent) and Brooks:

Mead: If I can continue on the point you made there. If you're claiming the fire was coming from the lobby of the Palestine Hotel, why was the tank round directed at an upper floor? And what does that kind of marksmanship, or lack of it, suggest about the risks to civilians as your forces penetrate further into Baghdad?

Brooks: The response of fire is something that we always have to get more details as time goes on, first, specifically, where the fire was returned and what was hit and where the fire came from. So I may have misspoken on exactly where the fire came from. (CNN, 8 April 2003)

However, this version of events was disputed by journalists present at the news conference. They insisted that no gunfire had come from the hotel lobby, or from the hotel's surroundings. Brigadier General Brooks then stated:

> The action occurs when the action occurs – and everything thereafter is speculative or investigative. (CNN, 8 April 2003)

Al Jazeera chose to investigate the Palestine Hotel events by giving airtime to journalists who were there. The correspondents questioned the veracity of the US military's declarations. For instance, Spanish journalist Carlos Hernandez maintained that there had been no hostile fire against American tanks, either from the hotel, or from its environs. Another journalist, David Chatter, noted that more than 1,500 metre(s) separated the Palestine Hotel from coalition tanks on the bridge; far beyond the effective range of a rifle or a rocket-propelled grenade launcher. Other correspondents highlighted the military capacities and resilience of the Abrams Tank. They also stated that combat in the vicinity of the Palestine Hotel had ended two hours before the tank had fired. Crucially, Al Jazeera aired camera footage shot by journalists inside the hotel immediately after the attack. This footage showed images of Reuter's Taras Protsyuk, and Telecinco's Jose Couso covered in blood, along with other wounded journalists screaming for help.

Bombings aftermath: News events, feedback loops, and the battle over meanings

On 8 April, the dominant theme of Al Jazeera's coverage was that journalists had become targets in war. In this context, the meso-frame that predominated was that of the aggrieved victim. Al Jazeera described the death of its correspondent as the latest in a long history of attacks against the channel beginning with the Afghan campaign (in which Al Jazeera's office was also bombed). In Iraq, one of its cars had come under attack by US forces only two days before. And, two months prior to the attack Al Jazeera had given the location of its Baghdad office to the US military.[10]

The US bombing of Al Jazeera's premises and the shelling of the Palestine Hotel, where most un-embedded foreign journalists were staying, persuaded the network that journalists were being deliberately targeted. Against this backdrop, Al Jazeera reported at about 1.35 p.m. (Baghdad Time) what veteran BBC correspondent Kate Adie had been told by a senior Pentagon official before the war; that the military would not hesitate to target any broadcast satellite links, even if they belonged to journalists. In the same context, Al Jazeera aired statements by US Admiral Craig Quigley, to the effect that the Pentagon was indifferent to media activity in enemy controlled territory. Al Jazeera also informed viewers that in the early days of the conflict, they had been asked by the Pentagon to remove correspondents from Baghdad. In subsequent news segments, the Qatar-based channel aired footage from the French TV channel, France 3, which had filmed the US tank aiming and firing at the Palestine Hotel. The footage gave support to the view that there was no shooting coming from the Palestine Hotel. Al Jazeera's anchor and correspondents thereby argued that the tank fire was intended to curtail media scrutiny of military operations in Iraq. Consequently, as I have outlined, Al Jazeera's main news theme for this day was 'a black day in the history of journalism'.[11]

On 8 April (5 a.m. ET/ 9 a.m. GMT), Al Jazeera's anchor Jumana Namur mentioned the bombing of the Abu Dhabi TV office, and the death of Western journalists after their hotel was bombed. She added that American tanks had reached the centre of Baghdad and bombed government buildings and civilian neighbourhoods. She also referred to the incidents that happened five hours earlier, in which the Al Jazeera bureau was targeted. She made reference to the 'martyrdom' of Tareq Ayyoub, the correspondent in Baghdad. She also stated that Al Jazeera's cameraman Zouhair Nadhim had been wounded in the same incident.

In the meantime, the meso-frame which dominated CNN's 8 April coverage was that of the accident. But CNN faced a problem with this understanding of events. The view that the attacks on Al Jazeera and the Palestine Hotel were deliberate pervaded international news coverage. So instead of investigating the incident, CNN reviewed what international media had said about it. In the heated atmosphere leading to the Iraq War, there was huge resentment in the United States concerning the sceptical position of countries such as France, Germany and Russia. By highlighting what the media of these countries said about the incident, CNN insinuated that these media were biased because of their governments' stance toward the Iraq War itself. CNN also interviewed an Arab media editor to get the Arab perspective on the matter. But overall, instead of analysing the issue and factually allocating responsibility, the incident was framed as a mishap which was being used by anti-war quarters as rhetorical ammunition against the United States. The following comment from Anchor Aaron Brown illustrates the position adopted by CNN.

> When you ask the question how is the war being fought, the answer often depends on what channel you're watching and where in the world you are watching it. And today, the big story, it was a huge story around the world, was the loss of innocent life in Baghdad, not just the civilians. This time, of course, it was journalists as well. (CNN, 8 April 2003)

The fact that CNN correspondent Bruce Burkhart responded to this question by highlighting the nationality of the people (Russia, France, Germany, Arab) whose opinions were about to be beamed, suggests an attempt to discredit these opinions in advance for carrying an anti-war bias. Burkhart also made sure to emphasise the Pentagon's view that the passage of events represented a loss in the 'propaganda war'.

> It was the story in much of the world today, not the targeting of Saddam Hussein, but the alleged targeting of journalists. This Russian anchor starts the newscast by saying 'here is the most important event at this hour, which will be the major topic of our program, an American tank shot at the Palestine Hotel in Baghdad where the journalists are staying'. And a few moments later, in introducing their reporter in Baghdad, 'an American tank took dead aim at the Baghdad hotel where journalists are staying'. The Russian reporter said he was only one floor away from the explosion and gave a detailed account of the chaos and the carnage in the hotel and added this. 'I want to point out that this was not the first strike against journalists today the Americans have probably carried out. This is only the latest which we saw with our own eyes. This morning, we learned that America carried out an air strike against the offices of Al Jazeera'. And then, there was more. An interview with Al Jazeera's Moscow bureau chief; a profile of a Ukrainian cameraman who died in the mishap; the view in France was much the same. Here, the anchor says a building that has been deliberately targeted by a US tank, when everyone knows that only journalists were staying at this hotel. And in Baghdad, the reporter had this account. "On this balcony, a couple of moments before, a cameraman was filming a tank on the Liberty Bridge. And this tank, here it is, right at the moment it aims at the hotel ... From China's CCTV, the English language newscast, a much more subdued reaction. That seems to be consistent with what we've seen there since the war began.

Voiceover (images of the Palestine Hotel):

> The Pentagon said Iraqi snipers were believed to be operating near the Palestine Hotel, where the full Reuters staff were injured after a blast to strike an upper floor of the high rise. The Pentagon said it could not say if US troops were responsible for the blasts.

Bruce Burkhart (CNN correspondent):

> But in Germany, as in Russia and France, viewers got this view of the story. A reporter described how the hotel was occupied by most of the journalists and how everyone knew that. He then said, 'why was the building fired on anyway?' This is how the military explained it. 'We only returned the fire that was coming from the lobby of the hotel,' the translator quotes General Brooks. Then the reporter adds, 'Why then, of all things, was the 15th floor hit?' That remains unclear. *In the propaganda war being fought on TVs across the globe, this one has to go down as a loss for the US* (CNN, 8 April 2003; emphasis added)

Then CNN's anchor Aaron Brown questioned Abu Dhabi's TV chief news editor, Nart Bouran in an attempt to suggest that there was no clear-cut evidence that the US Forces had deliberately attempted to target the hotel. Brown sought to elicit the view that these events reflected an anti-Americanism that was deeply entrenched among Arab audiences.

Aaron Brown (CNN anchor):

> Nart, let me ask this question in two parts. Try and answer both. Do you believe that the Americans deliberately targeted journalists, part one, and do you think your viewers believe that Americans deliberately targeted journalists?

Nart Bouran did his best to answer these delicate questions, but having the earlier attack on Abu Dhabi TV taped on video,[12] the issue then became more than just a matter of opinion. The images reveal the surroundings of the Abu Dhabi TV villa/office just prior to the attack. The situation seemed quiet until the tank fired in direction of the hotel.

Nart Bouran (Abu Dhabi's TV chief news editor):

> Our correspondent was on the – just a couple of minutes on the roof, reporting to us live. And there was nothing happening there. We know the office. There's nothing there. And then, all of a sudden, we felt the small arms fire coming at us. And then from the tank, directly, because we'd have that all on camera. And then, they ran downstairs. There was nothing around us

to indicate that there was anything suspicious going around us. Otherwise, how could all of our correspondents be on the roof reporting at the time? As far as the other question is concerned, I think it's very difficult to convince people that this was not a deliberate act against journalists in that area. I think it's going to be very, very difficult.

Even then, Aaron Brown tried to cast doubt on this testimony and to reframe the issue in terms of soldier nervousness:

> Is it not a reasonable explanation that these tank commanders and soldiers on the ground see activity on the roof? They're nervous. They think sniper. And they take action?

Nart Bouran replied to these suppositions by emphasising that the locations of the correspondents were known to the whole world, and the 'accident' perspective was not really plausible.

> Yes, I guess the answer to that is yes and no. Because you can see our cameras. I mean, literally, our camera was targeted straight into the camera. We have been operating there for two and half years. This is not like it is a secret location. Everybody knew where we were. We've been broadcasting those live pictures to the whole world during the last almost three weeks now. I would assume anyone going to that kind of an operation in that kind of an area with all these position targeting smart bombs, and hitting specifically rooms where they think that people are – that they would know that this is an Abu Dhabi TV and Al Jazeera TV. And to be perfectly honest, in that vicinity, nothing else was hit except those two offices. (CNN, 8 April 2003)

On Al Jazeera, the aggrieved victim frame was reinforced by the constantly reiterated theme 'black day in the history of journalism'. This theme represented an opportunity for the network to openly criticise the coalition. This was done by using the footage of Abu Dhabi Television (Al Jazeera's bureau having been bombed). This footage depicted the three attacks (Al Jazeera, Abu Dhabi TV and the Palestine Hotel), while the voice-over of Diyar Al-Omari (Al Jazeera correspondent in Baghdad) commented as follows:

> A lot of questions behind the targeting by American and British forces of Arab and Western media: Why this targeting and who benefits from it? The first strike was directed against the office of Al Jazeera situated in the Dijla River in the middle of Baghdad. American and British tanks bombed the perimeters of the office, which led to the martyrdom of our fellow Tareq Ayyoub, and to the injury of many other workers in the office. The second strike was directed against the office of Abu Dhabi TV, which is situated near Al Jazeera's office and which was surrounded by American forces. The third strike was directed against the Palestine Hotel, where all foreign journalists work, resulting in serious casualties especially the cameraman working with Reuters who was filming the bombing of Al Jazeera office. Observers consider that these strikes targeted neutral media as they reported the war events. These objective media are now put in a situation of confrontation, where they face dangerous weapons in the absence of any reason. The search for a safe place becomes a hard task for the media, as the American and British forces do not differentiate anymore between targets, so everyone here is exposed to missiles that could be launched at any time. (Al Jazeera, 8 April 2003)

Then, Al Jazeera broadcasted the last report of Tareq Ayyoub, transmitted two hours before his death. He is shown facing the camera and wearing a helmet and a bullet-proof jacket. Ayyoub can be seen hiding from the bombardment, drawn, and scared by what is happening around him. His eyes tremble and his face expresses helplessness. During this time, Tareq Ayyoub reported that there had been a strange silence prevalent in Baghdad, in contrast to previous days.

> Is it the silence that comes before the storm? Or have the protagonists decided to give each other some time? Nobody knows the reason behind this silence. We were expecting the renewal of these clashes tonight in the earlier hours but until now there are no explosions as we have seen in the previous days, or like what happened yesterday in the morning when there was an

active air force activity, explosions, and anti-aircraft gunfire ...
(Al Jazeera, 8 April 2003)

Tareq Ayyoob went on to speculate that both Americans and Iraqi forces were playing a waiting game and that the spirit of resistance among Iraqis was still high. He said:

> Sadness prevails among the historic capital. Feelings of anxiety reign among people here after waves of incessant bombardment. The latter failed however to soften their determination. (Al Jazeera, 8 April 2003)

Afterwards, Al Jazeera showed the footage of other journalists wearing bullet-proof jackets with clear bolded inscriptions showing their media status. They were filmed while carrying a victim of the war. We later understand from the commentary that it was Tareq Ayyoub. The location looked chaotic and covered by smoke.

Then, to get more information, Al Jazeera's newsroom turned to its Baghdad correspondent Majed Abdel Hadi (Al Jazeera correspondent in Baghdad), who called the US missile strike and Ayyoub's death a 'crime'. Visibly upset, he added:

> I will not be objective about this because we have been dragged into this conflict ... We were targeted because the Americans do not want the world to see the crimes they are committing against the Iraqi people (Al Jazeera, 8 April 2003).

Because Al Jazeera's bureau was destroyed it relied on the footage from other channels such as Abu Dhabi TV. The latter showed images of a huge fire blazing from the Al Jazeera office. Al Jazeera correspondent Tayseer Alouni, who became known while covering the Afghan War, was seen carrying the wounded Ayyoub into a car. Maher Abdullah, another correspondent in Baghdad, recalled the bombing of the Al Jazeera bureau.

> One missile hit the pavement in front of us, ripping out windows and doors, while another one hit the generator (Al Jazeera, 8 April 2003).

Then, Al Jazeera turned to a media conference headed by Jihad Ali Ballout, a spokesman for the channel. He communicated to the international media what had happened in Baghdad. Jihad Ali Ballout said that Tareq Ayyoub, a Jordanian national was standing on the roof of the station's office just after dawn, transmitting a live broadcast from Baghdad when the building was hit by two missiles. Mr Ayyoub, in his mid-30s, was carried to a car by colleagues but died on the way to the hospital. Jihad Ali Ballout also said that An Iraqi cameraman, Zouhair Al-Iraqi, who had started work with the station several days previously, was wounded.

Afterwards, Al Jazeera went live to Amman in Jordan to get the reaction of Tareq Ayyoub's wife, Dima Tahboub. Visibly devastated, she stated the following:

> My husband died while trying to reveal the truth to the world, please do not conceal this fact under no circumstances: not for the sake of public opinion, not for the sake of American policy, not for the sake of British policy. Please be honest at least this time. For the sake of all those people who died: Innocent people, not military, not militia, not people in the army. Please tell the truth only this once. Thank you very much (Al Jazeera, 8 April 2003).

Al Jazeera also broadcast the memorial service of Tareq Ayyoub in his house in Amman. His family was present, including his mother, and daughter, as well as other family members and friends. Then, footage of the Al Jazeera office in Amman, where he was working, was shown. Feelings of sadness and anger were clearly prevalent among the attendance. Then, Al Jazeera showed a march of Jordanian journalists protesting against the death of Tareq Ayyoub. Some of the protesters were filmed holding the picture of Bush wearing a Nazi uniform with a Swastika in the background. Finally, a testimony from Yasir Abou Hilala, Al Jazeera's Bureau Chief in Amman, was aired. Yasir mourned his former colleague, praising his professionalism and courage.

Contrasting imagery

On CNN, visual imagery in relation to the three main incidents was relatively rare. Mostly, footage was taken from other international TV stations (e.g. Russian TV, Chinese TV), but this was not the main focus. Instead, CNN emphasised studio discussions and press conferences involving the US military, yet they still omitted visuals of the incident itself. In contrast, Al Jazeera used plenty of imagery (after the bombing this included footage supplied by Abu Dhabi TV). This contrast is revealed in the juxtaposition of images on the first page of this chapter. The images show footage of Al Jazeera and CNN on 8 April 2003 at 5 a.m. ET/ 9 a.m. GMT. The juxtaposition reveals that Al Jazeera provides live pictures of the attack against its premises (using footage from Abu Dhabi TV), whereas CNN at this stage used a trailer to inform viewers about the incident.

It should be noted that Al Jazeera tried to provide a comprehensive coverage on the attack against its Baghdad bureau. They provided a constant flow of images about the incident. Images of an American plane flying down in a firing position, dropping missiles and several bombs on its office were broadcast. Footage also showed a close-up of the Tigris river and the nearby Al Jazeera office being targeted. The explosions that rocked the office were heard in the background, while smoke was seen emanating from the location. There were additional images showing an American tank firing at the surroundings of the Al Jazeera office. Next, Al Jazeera aired footage of its correspondents and staff carrying the body of Tareq Ayyoob (see Figure 7.2).

Figure 7.2: Al Jazeera broadcasting footage via Abu Dhabi TV showing its crew members carrying the late correspondent Tareq Ayyoob (8 April 2003).

Later, Al Jazeera made sure to re-broadcast Ayyoob's most recent report as a way to commemorate his memory (see Figure 7.3).

Figure 7.3: Al Jazeera airing Tareq Ayyoob's last report to commemorate his memory (8 April 2003).

The source of Al Jazeera's footage was Abu Dhabi TV. When Al Jazeera's Baghdad bureau was hit, the latter recorded the immediate aftermath of the strike; however, its camera operator became a target soon afterwards. Subsequently, footage showed the camera losing balance, while the plane zeroed in the direction of its position, launching a couple of missiles.

When the ensuing attack on the Palestine Hotel took place, Al Jazeera aired footage showing an American tank on the Republic Bridge, near one of the presidential palaces, firing several times towards the Palestine hotel (see Figure 7.4). It was a wide shot that shows the tank and the targeted hotel. The film was obtained by Al Jazeera from French television (France 3), whose journalist was caught in the crossfire.

Afterwards, Al Jazeera showed footage from inside the Palestine Hotel; panic stricken international journalists were shown inside their offices.

Journalists as Combatants

Figure 7.4: Al Jazeera's footage showing a wide shot of the tank which targeted the hotel (8 April 2003).

A Ukrainian journalist, working for Reuters, was severely injured, while another journalist was wounded. The scene was bloody. Next, a female journalist was filmed shouting, as other people in the scene were trying to rescue the injured journalists.

In terms of keywords, Al Jazeera often referred to the phrase 'black day in the history of journalism'. For Al Jazeera, the fact that various international media were the victims of the coalition forces on the same day represented a transgression of the law of warfare. In their view, US forces had identified Al Jazeera as an enemy propaganda station which was transmitting disturbing accounts of Iraqi civilian casualties to a wide Arab audience. In this context, however, the bombing of the Palestine Hotel was counter-productive. Al Jazeera was able to claim 'victim status' and to attract the sympathy of international journalists and human rights groups. For instance, the watchdog group Committee for the Protection of Journalists (CPJ) demanded an investigation. In a letter to the US Defense Secretary, Donald Rumsfeld, the group stated that the attacks on correspondents violated the Geneva Conventions (Knightley 2003: 11).

Another keyword used by Al Jazeera was martyrdom. In Islamic jurisprudence, the martyr commits sacrifice for the sake of his or her community's survival. As a result, the martyr attracts admiration from the community and may expect substantial rewards in the afterlife. The fact that Al Jazeera presented this title to one of its journalists added a sacred dimension. The Arab network then became more than a standard news outlet; it was a symbol of resistance for all journalists targeted by bombs and missiles in defence of their community.

By contrast, CNN Correspondent Bruce Burkhart employed the 'propaganda war' theme. In one sense, this was a striking admission. In American popular culture, as in academia, propaganda was usually regarded with disapproval. Academics, Garth Jowett and Victoria O'Donnell have observed that 'to identify a message as propaganda is to suggest something negative and dishonest. Words frequently used as synonyms for propaganda are lies, distortion, deceit, manipulation, mind control psychological warfare, brainwashing, and palaver' (Jowett and O'Donnell 1999: 6). From this perspective, only totalitarian enemies – not democratic forces – were capable of resorting to propaganda. Yet, Burkhart depicted the United States as being implicated in, and losing, the propaganda war.

Rhetorically, CNN downplayed the bombing incidents, which had led to the death of three international journalists. These fatalities were considered as merely another accident resulting from the 'fog of war'.[13] Subsequently, CNN allocated less than half an hour to the story. Commentaries and discussions about the future of post-war Iraq received more prominent coverage. Burying issues is a commonly used crisis communication method. It is called 'masking' and involves 'image restoration strategies' in the form of excuses, blame-shift, defence and other defensive mechanisms (Benoit 1995). The way CNN dealt with the events in question exemplifies how issues can be downplayed or simply ignored. As Norman Fairclough has observed, media frames 'constitute versions of reality in ways which depend on the social positions and interests and objectives of those who produce them' (Fairclough 1995: 103–104). In this case, CNN adopted the US military standpoint that a tank had fired in self-defence against a sniper. On this account, the fatalities were regrettable but understandable. There was no effort made to link these events to wider issues concerning the treatment of un-embedded journalists in Iraq generally.

Such a stance recalls Shanto Iyengar's argument in '*Is Anyone Responsible?*' He argued that the media systematically deflected any criticisms of those in power by framing the news as 'only a passing parade of specific events, a "context of no context"'. He refers to this kind of coverage as episodic framing, whereby various news events appear entirely unrelated. Iyengar also contends that the episodic frame personalises the issues at stake. This 'prevents the public from cumulating the evidence toward any logical, ultimate consequence' (Iyengar 1991: 143).

While positioning the incident in this way, CNN also tried to infer that international media had over-reacted because of their anti-war bias. Here, it was noticeable that CNN focused upon reactions from countries such as France, Germany, and Russia. When CNN interviewed Nart Bouran, Abu Dhabi's TV chief news editor, it tried to convey the impression that this was another Arab 'conspiracy theory'. Resorting to this, deflected attention away from factual inquiry into the events and issues at hand. The key point here is that the first question 'do you believe that the Americans deliberately targeted journalists?' was not asked in isolation. The follow up question 'do you think your viewers believe that Americans deliberately targeted journalists?' suggests that Arab publics are possessed by subjective beliefs at the expense of rational enquiry.

Evidence concerning the bombing of Al Jazeera's office and the Hotel Palestine points to the likelihood of a deliberate act, not a conspiracy. The former building's position was well known to the Pentagon before the war and easily established through Global Positioning Systems (GPS) co-ordinates. This fact was reiterated by Al Jazeera's spokesperson Ibrahim Hilal; 'Our office is in a residential area and even the Pentagon knows its location,' he said. However, Hilal stopped short from saying that the attack was intentional (Cozens 2003). Nevertheless, previous events add weight to the deliberate attack thesis. The aerial bombing of Al Jazeera's Kabul office in 2001 was still vividly remembered. More importantly, on 7 April 2003 (one day before the attack on its premises in Baghdad), an Al Jazeera staff member was stopped at a US Marine checkpoint. After showing his papers, he was allowed to leave; a soldier apparently opened fire on his car as he drove away. Although he was not hurt, his car was badly damaged, and Al Jazeera understood that this was a message. One week earlier, the Sheraton Hotel in Basra, in which Al Jazeera correspondents were the only guests, had been aerially bombed despite the fact the location was known to the US military. While these correspondents were not hurt, the attack affected their ability to report (Gierhart 2008: 21).

Retrospective developments reinforce the suspicion that the 8 April attack on Al Jazeera's bureau in Baghdad was deliberate. On 23 November 2005, the British *Daily Mirror* noted that this bombing 'raises fresh doubts over US claims that previous attacks against Al Jazeera staff were military errors' (Maguire and Lines 2005: B2). Official leaks at that time strongly suggested that the targeting of the Qatar based channel was on the agenda of President Bush if not Prime Minister Blair.[14] The allegation that sniper fire had emerged from the Palestine Hotel was rejected by about 100 international journalists who were on the scene. Scepticism of the US military standpoint was strengthened when Brigadier General Vincent Brooks stated 'that while embedded journalists receive protection from the military, those who operate as non-embeds do so at their own risk.' Such declarations could only be interpreted as a threat to journalistic autonomy and media freedom. In this regard, it should be noted that while 3,000 journalists reported on the developments of the Iraq War, only 800 were embedded with coalition forces (Leaper, Löwstedt, and Madhoun 2003: 72–73). However, the existence of a large number of unilaterals may well have irritated the Pentagon's info-warriors. In this context, British journalist Martin Bell stated:

> Independent witnessing of war is becoming increasingly dangerous, and this may be the end of it. I have a feeling that independent journalists have become a target because the management of the information war has become a higher priority than ever. (Byrne 2003a [electronic article; no pagination])

It is a matter of fact that 17 media representatives died during the Iraq War. John Simpson, BBC world affairs editor, called upon 'the US government to investigate why more journalists were killed by American soldiers than by any other means during the Iraq war'. According to Simpson, the deaths of many of the journalists are due to what he called 'the ultimate act of censorship' that is embedding. Through this system, the Pentagon had journalists reporting its perspective, whereas those operating independently of US and British troops covered angles unwanted by the military (quoted in Byrne 2003b [electronic article; no pagination]). In this context, the International Press Institute (IPI) criticised the discriminatory way that unilateral journalists were dealt with by Coalition forces and details the complaints of press freedom violations: harassment, detainment, equipment confiscation, and deportation (Leaper, Löwstedt, and Madhoun 2003: 76).

The privileged access given to embedded journalists, and the discrimination suffered by unilateral un-embedded journalists reflected the practices of information warfare. More specifically 'information exploitation' and 'system destruction' are conventionally employed. The former practice involves activities, such as withholding information, omission, bifurcation and censorship, whereas the latter involves the destruction of 'enemy' information systems, including media outlets. Previous examples include the NATO bombing of Serbian Television during the Kosovo War (1999), which caused six fatalities among media workers.

During the Iraq conflict, information warfare practices influenced CNN's framing of the attacks against Al Jazeera's offices and the Palestine Hotel. Indeed, CNN never considered the issues of journalist safety and media freedom in relation to these military attacks. Rather, CNN embraced the accident version put forward by the Pentagon, and rejected the perspectives of other news media as subjective at best, and conspiracy theory at worst. On Al Jazeera, the attacks were especially significant. The Arab network had stood against restrictions on its activities in the Arab world. Its coverage of the Afghan War in the face of intimidation from the Bush administration only reinforced the image of Al Jazeera as a fiercely independent network. The continuation of such intimidation during the Iraq War suggested to Middle Eastern audiences that US foreign policy was hypocritical. On the one hand, the alleged purpose of the Iraq invasion was to establish democracy. On the other hand, Al Jazeera was criticised for holding a perspective different from that of the Bush administration. Thus, Al Jazeera's coverage expressed loudly what others said quietly, that the United States' support for democracy in the Arab world was not genuine. It is true that the Pentagon tried to build some bridges with Al Jazeera to reduce their criticisms. For instance, the establishment of Central Command (CENTCOM) in Qatar before the war enabled courtesy visits between Al Jazeera journalists and CENTCOM officials. After the war started, Al Jazeera put forward some of its journalists as embeds. It could not however communicate adequately with the US military. Amr El-Kakhy, Al Jazeera's sole embed with the US military during the war, later wrote of the mistrust he encountered:

> Actually there were a lot of misconceptions about Al Jazeera from different commands. I was told a lot of the troops said: 'Why should we have Al Jazeera? They are the enemy. It is the enemy's channel'. (El-Kahky 2004: 181)

Tine Ustad Figenschou notes that the US military respectively, 'courted, criticised, harassed, and eventually bombed Al Jazeera' (Figenschou 2006: 75). Internationally, therefore, Al Jazeera as such, became the subject of news media attention. The Qatar-based channel shrewdly capitalised on this situation. The Arab network profiled the attack on its office as a major event, stirring specific readings of what had occurred. It sought to establish the collective Arab understanding of the war. In this case, the understanding was that the channel was targeted for revealing the truth of the conflict.

Al Jazeera also played upon the emotional identifications of its audiences. The long moments dedicated to its dead journalist Tareq Ayyoub were especially significant. The impact of this coverage was reinforced by the fact that viewers were familiar with the Jordanian journalist's reports during the war. The human dimension resonated further when the channel interviewed Tareq's wife and attended the mourning in his family home. Al Jazeera's emotionally charged coverage of the incident was followed by tens of millions of Arab viewers. Al Jazeera's depiction of Tareq Ayyoub as a 'martyr' gave an Islamic touch to the mission of uncovering the truth. As explained earlier, a martyr in Islam is someone who manifests profound personal commitment to the general community. By naming the deceased a martyr, the Arab network called upon the Muslim imaginary to side with the channel. This naming also involved a subtle play of words: Martyr, or 'shaheed' in Arabic, literally means witness. In this context, Tareq Ayyoub was the witness of the war in Iraq. His killing was then witnessed by millions of viewers. Thus, this act of martyrdom would renew the strength of the community that witnessed the sacrifice.

But there was also another connotation to the message of martyrdom. The Qatar based channel had become a symbol of resistance. His journalists and anchors were targeted by bombs and missiles, as were members of Iraqi forces and other armed groups. So, by drawing upon this deep seated sensibility, Al Jazeera positioned its correspondent as someone who had sacrificed himself at the service of both the Muslim and pan-Arab imagined communities. As a result, the Arab network mobilised enormous popular support in the Arab and Muslim world. The mobilisation of this support was employed to stop the coalition targeting journalists and their locations. For its international audience, Al Jazeera emphasised that other journalists were also the victims of deliberate attacks on independent journalism. Through this frame, which draws a parallel between the attack on its bureau and the assault on the Palestine Hotel, the Arab network formed solidarity with human rights organisations and advocates of journalistic freedoms around the world.

Al Jazeera thus scripted a new narrative. The heroes were not resistance fighters or Iraqi soldiers, but correspondents who defended media freedom. They pursued the sacrosanct mission of revealing the 'truth' to the outside world. The villains were well established: they were the coalition forces who had violated the rules of protection available to the civilians, including journalists, within international humanitarian law.[15] By constructing an oppositional narrative, Al Jazeera ruined the original American script for the Iraq War. As outlined, the story of this war had distinctive Hollywood like features. The ensuing 'master war narrative' contained the following sequence: Shock and awe, triumphant heroes, victory and control (Schwalbe, Silcock and Keith 2005: 458).

Déjà vu

The events that unfolded on 8 April again highlighted a clash of frames between CNN and Al Jazeera. On CNN, the dominant meso-frame of the day was that of the accident, episodically reported. Although the attacks on journalists occurred three times in one day, they were constructed on CNN as separate episodes with no links to a broader picture. The events thus appeared as isolated accidents which absolved the US military of deliberate wrongdoing. Al Jazeera, on the other hand, explicitly linked the three attacks. At the same time, the Arab network adopted the meso-frame of the victim. This frame depicted the Qatar based channel as a victim of its quest to provide straightforward facts about the Iraq War. Such a frame resonated with audiences in the Middle East and Europe. Al Jazeera declared to its audiences that it was targeted because of telling the truth; the Qatar based network thus positioned itself as a source of propaganda critique and as a legitimate alternative source of information for media outlets worldwide. This positioning proved to be very successful. Al Jazeera could increase revenues by selling its footage all over the world. The channel won international acclaim for its incisive and daring coverage.

The events in question also revealed the dangers of information warfare for independent journalists. The embedding programme was at the heart of the Pentagon's quest to control information. Numerous studies have criticised the embedding programme, given that such reporters were not truly independent and depended on the military to file their stories (Bucy 2003; Ewers 2003; Kalb 2003). In this context, embed reporter Clive Myrie admitted to reporter John Kampfner in the BBC programme *Correspondent* that:

> As long as you are aware of that [that the military will try to look good in the eyes of the public] then you can begin to try and tell whatever story you are trying to tell in as objective way as you can, bearing in mind that the unit you are with is feeding you, dressing you, protecting you, whatever. (BBC2, 18 May 2003)

By its very nature, embedding could not provide audiences with the 'big picture.' Michael Wolff, a writer for *New York* magazine, observed:

> Eventually you realise that you know significantly less than when you arrived, and that you are losing more sense of the larger picture by the hour. At some point you will know nothing. (Wolff 2003: 6–7)

An additional criticism was directed towards the Pentagon's tendency to use embedded journalists as public relations conduits for the military perspective. For instance, Andrew Hoskins points out that:

> The journalists closest to the heart of battle itself ironically contributed mostly narrow and decontextualized snapshots of the war. Moreover the shrinking of the physical distance between embed and soldier was matched by a shrinking of the critical distance between journalist and story. In effect the Americans had successfully planted spokesmen and women for the Pentagon all over the battlefield. (Hoskins 2004b: 60)

Therefore, one can say that the Iraq War operations were transparently available to journalists while at the same time being the subject of official manipulation (Chouliaraki 2006: 261). Yet, in spite of its emphasis on information control, the Pentagon was shaken by the alternative information, analysis, commentary and worldview offered by international un-embedded journalists. Many of these journalists worked for Al Jazeera and other Arab television channels. They challenged the Pentagon's narratives piece by piece and offered counter-narratives of their own.

This contest was not to the Pentagon's liking. Their literature on information management specifies that any challenge to the strategy of information management is an obstacle to the war effort, which must be removed. Some media specialists, such as Philip Knightley (2003) and Nicholas Mirzoeff (2005), considered that the targeting of independent journalists signalled the end of any meaningful autonomy for war correspondents. The clear message to all unembedded journalists was to stop reporting alternative viewpoints during wartime, and especially those involving the United States.

The assault on independent media was denounced by media advocacy organisations. The International Press Institute (IPI) criticised the lack of protection provided to journalists. They considered that journalists, whether embedded or not, should be treated like civilians as stipulated in the Geneva Convention.[16] Similarly, the New York advocacy group Fairness & Accuracy in Reporting (FAIR) issued a media statement headed: 'Is killing part of the Pentagon press policy?' It stated:

> On April 8 ... US military forces launched what appeared to be deliberate attacks on independent journalists covering the war, killing three and injuring four others. In one incident, a US tank fired an explosive shell at the Palestine Hotel, where most non-embedded international reporters in Baghdad are based. Two journalists, Taras Protsyuk of the British news agency Reuters and Jose Couso of the Spanish network Telecinco, were killed; three other journalists were injured. The tank, which was parked nearby, appeared to carefully select its target, according to journalists in the hotel, raising and aiming its gun turret some two minutes before firing a single shell. (Fairness and Accuracy in Reporting 2003)

This targeting of journalists raised considerable opposition in many parts of the world. In Spain, the Spanish Minister of Defence Frederico Trillo asked for explanations from Washington. In Britain, Simon Walker, a spokesman at Reuters, confirmed that the agency had made a formal complaint to the Pentagon. Moreover, the press freedom organisation Reporters Sans Frontières filed a lawsuit in Spain against three American officers (Sergeant Shawn Gibson, Captain Philip Wolford, and Colonel Philip DeCamp) responsible for the attack on the Hotel, in which José Couso, a Spanish national, had died. Across Europe, such repercussions only added to anti-American tendencies fuelled by the Iraq invasion. In fact, an opinion poll conducted in 2003 by the Pew Research Centre, revealed that 57 per cent of interviewees in France, 55 per cent in Germany, and 62 per cent in Spain had an unfavourable view of the United States because of its war in Iraq (Pew Research Centre 2006).

On the whole, this chapter illustrates an unbridgeable conflict in interpretation. In a setting where journalists became casualties of war, Al Jazeera and other international news outlets argued they were victims of censorship, propaganda and military attack, while CNN and other American news outlets accepted the explanations of their military officials.

8

Liberation vs. Occupation: The Toppling of Saddam's Statue

Figure 8.1: Footage of CNN and Al Jazeera showing the toppling of Saddam's statue (9 April 2003).

Context and chronology

On 8 April 2003, foreign correspondents reported that US forces had advanced into the central neighbourhoods of the Iraqi capital. News reports also said that Kurdish fighters and US troops had extended their control of northern Iraq, including the cities of Kirkuk and Mosul. The advance into Baghdad was occasionally disturbed by sporadic fighting.

On 9 April 2003 at 9:00 a.m. (Baghdad Time), international journalists stationed at the Palestine Hotel received their usual briefing from Iraqi information ministry officials about where the journalists could go in Baghdad. This time however, there were no Iraqi militia men guarding the hotel. By 9:30 a.m. (Baghdad Time), foreign correspondents at the Palestine Hotel had noticed a mass departure of Iraqi males of fighting age from the north-eastern neighbourhoods of Baghdad. They were travelling on foot, carrying their belongings. Red chevrons, used by the Iraqi security forces, were also seen taking the same routes, although the drivers were this time wearing civilian clothes.

At 10:30 a.m. (Baghdad Time), reports indicated that looting was widespread in Saddam City, the large Shi'i neighbourhood. At an adjacent electrical supply depot, grown men piled whatever they could take on to forklifts and drove them to their homes. Earlier that morning, American tanks had quickly traversed the area and departed. At 11:00 a.m. (Baghdad Time), information spread that Marines had moved into the north of Baghdad, taking control of the last bridges across the Tigris. It became clear that the Iraqi regime had lost its grip on the city. In the meantime, the last officials of the Iraqi information ministry left the Palestine Hotel.

At 3:00 p.m. (Baghdad Time), small groups of Iraqis began drifting toward the Saddam statue in Firdos Square, on the eastern bank of the Tigris. This part of Baghdad was situated on the opposite shore to a conglomeration of security buildings, which had been bombed for three weeks by the US military. Shortly afterwards, American tanks appeared in the square. The crowds seemed to know what was expected of them. A man went up to one of the Marines, whose tanks now encircled the location, and asked for permission to destroy the statue. By 4:00 p.m. (Baghdad Time), American officers had told international journalists at the adjacent Palestine Hotel to visit Firdos Square. Iraqis were going to pull down the massive 12 metre statue of the President. This was one of Iraq's most recent sculptures erected in honour of Saddam Hussein's 65th birthday in April of 2002. Pulling the statue down was meant to show contempt for the Iraqi leader, and to affirm the triumph of coalition forces.

Toppling the statue proved to be a hard task. For about one hour and a half, the small crowd attacked the statue with little effect. The large metal plaque at the base of the statue was unmoved by the inefficient hits of sledgehammers and other rudimentary equipment. Iraqi men also secured a noose around the neck of the statue but were unable to tear it down. American troops, surrounding the square, joined in and used an armoured vehicle with rope to gradually pull down the statue. Marine Corporal Edward Chin of the 3rd battalion 4th Marines climbed up and covered the face with an American flag. The crowd reacted negatively, perhaps interpreting the

Liberation vs. Occupation

initiative as American triumphalism. The flag was quickly taken away, and replaced a few minutes later by the old Iraqi flag, to roars of approval. At about 6:50 p.m. (Baghdad Time), the Saddam statue finally came down.

This general sequence of events was evident on CNN and Al Jazeera. They both relayed the same footage, which was, however, edited differently. Initially, both CNN and Al Jazeera showed a small crowd. Yet, by the end there were more visual close ups on CNN, which conveyed the impression of a large crowd chanting, jeering and dancing around the fallen effigy, hitting it with their shoes in a symbolic gesture of contempt. On Al Jazeera, the edited footage showed more often the wider camera shots, which revealed pretty low numbers of Iraqis. This made the event appear less dramatic and spontaneous. This general difference is exemplified by the juxtaposed images in Figure 8.1. The pictures from CNN and Al Jazeera are representative of the pattern of coverage that both networks presented on 9 April 2003. CNN did sometimes use wide angle shots but not as often as Al Jazeera. The latter used closer shots but not nearly as often as CNN. One has also to bear in mind that large sections of those present on the Firdos Square that day were media workers. Nonetheless, from whatever perspective, the toppling of the Saddam statue was a major symbolic event.

From that episode onwards, the United States and the United Kingdom acted as the new masters of Iraq. On 15 April 2003, in a US brokered meeting, Iraqi representatives agreed to help build a new regime. It was the first step in the long task of setting up a new civil authority. On 1 May 2003, President Bush capitalised on the preceding events. From the upper decks of the USS Abraham Lincoln Aircraft Carrier, underneath a banner entitled 'Mission Accomplished', the American President declared that the coalition forces had prevailed in the Iraq War, and that major combat operations had ended. This closure proved to be ceremonial and premature; at the time of writing, violence in Iraq continues unabated.

The toppling of Saddam statue was chosen for this research because it clearly revealed a contest of frames. Al Jazeera had been bombed one day earlier with the loss of a correspondent. Consequently, they regarded the toppling of Saddam's statue as an arranged episode of defeat and humiliation. Al Jazeera emphasised that this was a staged event rather than a mass demonstration and highlighted the fact that Iraqis could not topple the statue without American tanks.

In contrast, CNN represented this event as the start of a new era. The symbols of the defeated regime had been overthrown. As Al Jazeera emphasised the staging of proceedings in Firdos Square, CNN anchors such as Paula Zahn insisted on the 'spontaneity' of the 'celebrations' in Firdos square. CNN also framed the event in terms of liberation and regime change. Some of its correspondents such as Christiane Amanpour compared this event to the fall of the Berlin Wall. Overall, CNN positioned the statue's fall as an important historical occasion; with anchor Paula Zahn commenting that the activity in the square was 'really extraordinary to watch'. Meanwhile Corporal Steven Harris (US Marine Corps) commented on CNN about the 'jubilation' shown by the Iraqi people in the square.

The supposed climax of the victory narrative was also an occasion for American networks to settle their accounts with Arab media. Thus, CNN linked images of the toppling statue, which symbolised Arab military defeat, to a defeat of the Arab media as well. For instance, Octavia Nasr, CNN correspondent, commented that:

> It is very interesting to see them try to apologize to their viewers ... And the Al Jazeera reporters, Abu Dhabi, Al Arabiya, LBC, all of them are trying to explain to their viewers that these celebrations are real. (CNN, 9 April 2003)

As this statement suggests, CNN anchors and correspondents expressed little sympathy towards the coverage of Al Jazeera and other Arab media. They were generally positioned as bad guys, who were providing a mouthpiece for anti-American rhetoric.

Scene establishments

On CNN, American soldiers and tanks were shown encircling the Firdos Square in Baghdad. Within this square, Iraqis appeared to walk without restrictions, and to interact peacefully with the soldiers. The latter appeared calm, patrolling the area, and eying the rooftops for any suspicious activity. Focus was then directed toward the reaction of Iraqis in the vicinity of the statue, with emphasis on their joy and cheerfulness. For almost one hour, cameras depicted Iraqis trying to bring down the statue using hammers and ropes. Initially, American tanks were pictured watching the square from a distance. After a long interval, Iraqi men were still unable to topple the statue. Some of them tried to climb to the top of the statue; others hit the statue with shoes and rocks. Eventually, American tanks started slowly moving towards the crowd.

The construction of the scene conveyed a strong message: The Iraqis are the ones trying to get rid of Saddam Hussein. The Americans were only there to provide support. In this context, CNN used certain rolling trailers and repeated them as needed to communicate the same message:

- Iraqis use rope and hammer in attempt to take down statue
- Coalition tanks move into Firdos Square in Baghdad
- Robinson: Some Iraqis shouting out 'thank you'
- Robinson: Mood in central Baghdad 'jubilant'
- People tearing down metal Saddam sign
- Iraqis climb tank to reach Saddam statue
- Iraqis target Saddam symbols in Baghdad
- Shots fired near Firdos Square in Baghdad
- Cheney: hardest battles could still be ahead
- Cheney: outcome is certain. The Iraqi people will be free

Studio discussions involving Paula Zahn, Simon Robinson and Christiane Amanpour interpreted the footage for the audience. Christiane Amanpour commented that this was 'one of the biggest shows of support we've seen yet.'

On Al Jazeera, the established scene was not entirely different. Video footage showed angry Iraqis shooting at statues of Saddam Hussein. They could be seen beating their shoes against a huge poster of the Iraqi president and tearing it down. Al Jazeera's footage then showed the full process of Saddam's statue being pulled down by an American tank in front of a jubilant crowd in Firdos Square. At given points in the coverage, the Qatar based channel showed the crowd as a large gathering, by zooming in on them. However, unlike some of its competitors, Al Jazeera did not use archive footage in its editing for negative purposes (Al Arabiya, for instance, aired two reports on the life of Saddam Hussein which concentrated on the poor decisions he took as President of Iraq). On the contrary, the Qatar based channel showed a video clip of the ousted Iraqi president being carried on his supporters' shoulders in the Al-Adhamiya district one day before. In addition, the commentary from the studio in Doha noted that the statue toppling lacked spontaneity.

On CNN, anchors and correspondents framed the event in terms of liberation, regime change and the making of history. Thus, Christiane Amanpour compared the event to the fall of the Berlin Wall. Numerous criticisms were directed at the ousted regime. Amanpour, for example, discussed the 'trauma' of living under the regime of Saddam Hussein, and characterised the statues as 'psychological tools' of dictatorship. Then, attention shifted to the events in the square; these were deemed 'really extraordinary to watch,' by anchor Paula Zahn.[1] Also, US corporal Paul Harris, speaking on the phone with CNN from Firdos Square, observed that there was 'a lot of jubilation' from Iraqis on the square. He estimated a crowd of about seventy.[23] Half an hour later, Simon Robinson (CNN guest) inflated this number to 1000.[4]

Liberation/US victory: Two narratives unfold

The CNN Iraqi liberation narrative was shaken when the American flag was put on the top of Saddam Hussein statue. This happened when First Lieutenant Tim McLaughlin passed the flag to Corporal Edward Chin, who then covered

Figure 8.2: Al Jazeera footage showing the American flag on the top of the Saddam statue (9 April 2003 10:41 ET).

Saddam statue's head with it. The flag remained there for about five minutes, and then Corporal Chin replaced it with a pre-1991 Gulf War Iraqi flag.

During the American flag incident, Barbara Starr, the CNN Pentagon correspondent, clearly noted: 'This is not a picture that the Pentagon wants to see ... The Pentagon has worked very hard to try and not show those images.' She added that these pictures could be very counter-productive as 'the US military knows these pictures are being broadcasted throughout the Arab world'.

Nevertheless, Barbara Starr (CNN's Pentagon correspondent) tried to justify this situation:

> I can tell you when the American flag went up; there was an almost audible gasp in some Pentagon offices here. This was not the picture the Pentagon wanted to see. Christiane is right, often in wartime soldiers undertake these signs of celebration when they believe they have achieved victory, and it may well be that this small group of troops was just going to put up that flag very briefly and take it down, but of course, not a good reaction of the people there in Baghdad. And the Pentagon has made it very clear, through General Tommy Franks, out to the troops in the field that this is not about the American victory over this country. This is about liberating this country. (CNN, 9 April 2003)

Afterwards, Starr highlighted the Pentagon's prevailing concern, namely the pockets of resistance in Northern Iraq. Then, in a positive tone, she drew attention to the fact that no aerial bombing had occurred in Baghdad, and that civilians were thereby spared.

> What is really interesting today, as you noticed, we haven't seen any aerial action over Baghdad. No bombs dropping from the air because there are so many civilians in the street. They are continuing to maintain air patrols ... they were fairly sure they wouldn't inadvertently kill civilians. (CNN, 9 April 2003)

After that, CNN anchor Paula Zahn's main concern was to counter the perception that coalition forces were occupiers. She repeated the same question to Starr for more clarification:

> Let's just come back to these sensitivities that the Pentagon brass had about the showing of that American flag ever so briefly on the top of Saddam Hussein's head. It now appears as though the pre-gulf war Iraqi flag come down. Once again, just for folks that might not have caught the first part of your explanation [Barbara Starr's explanation], talk about this concern about the perception that coalition forces are occupiers, at least that is the perception on some Iraqis' part, and they want to fight that perception. (CNN, 9 April 2003)

CNN correspondent Barbara Starr invoked an entirely oppositional frame (coalition troops as occupiers), and highlighted a major source of concern among the Pentagon info-warriors; depicting US troops as occupiers instead of liberators. For them, raising the American flag was counter-productive in terms of perception. The presence of an American flag on the battlefield framed the situation as victory vs. defeat rather than liberation vs. oppression; the former construction could inflame nationalistic passions among Iraqis.[5]

The American flag incident disrupted the Pentagon's information management efforts during an extremely mediatised juncture. It provided ammunition for critics of the war. For example, Arab satellite channel Al-Arabiya commented during the incident 'that it should have been an Iraqi flag'. This obliged Starr to shift her focus to the Arab media, which would, in her view, invariably misrepresent such images. Starr:

> What the Pentagon knows, what the US military knows, is these pictures are being broadcasted throughout the Arab world. They are being seen in the Arab world, and they are not being seen kindly, because of course, there are many sectors of the Arab world that genuinely believe that US military action in Iraq was not about liberation, but about occupation. There are many people in the Arab world that believe it was about the US military, for example, taking over Iraq's oil industry, all of that. The Pentagon has worked very hard to try and not show those images. (CNN, 9 April 2003)

In her attempt to justify the situation, correspondent Barbara Starr unwittingly mentioned some arguments adopted by those opposing the Iraq

Liberation vs. Occupation

War. This in itself could be interpreted as a defeat for the Pentagon info-warriors who usually ensure that one interpretation of reality predominates on American networks.

Moving away from the discussion of how the American flag had spoiled the approved narrative, Simon Robinson (*Time*) sought to restore that narrative.

> The Marines have attached a chain around the neck of Saddam, and now are reversing this large tank away from the statue and looks like- looks like it is about to go, as you said. When the American flag went up, there were no boos, but not much – not many cheers either. And then the pre-Kuwait war, pre-gulf war Iraqi flag was brought out, and there were cheers, a lot of clapping, cries. Of course, the Iraqi flag changed after the Gulf War. Saddam added a religious message in the middle of the flag. And the flag that was put up there was the old Iraqi flag, the flag I guess that older Iraqis remember from the days before Saddam. This tank is now reversing through a crowd of a few hundred people, perhaps a thousand people. Reversing away from the statue. I am not sure how far back it has to get before this statue will start toppling. It is late afternoon in Iraq. Next to, on the other side of the square, I can see, there is a large mosque, there is a large hotel behind me. And all around, Iraqi families out watching this momentous occasion in Baghdad and history.

Paula Zahn (CNN anchor):

> So you were saying, when the American flag went up for a very short period of time, there were no boos, but there was no cheering either, but it wasn't until the Iraqi flag was wrapped around the neck of Saddam, that there was real cheering going on?

Simon Robinson (*Time*):

> Exactly. Exactly. And they are now tightening – the statue is starting to topple – it is coming forward. They are winding in the chains, they are not moving the vehicle back, and they are just bringing it in, rather like a tow truck. And in fact, the left – the right leg has snapped, and the left leg is going as pieces of debris are coming off the statue, and now it falls. A cheer goes around the square. People are waving their hands. And the statue, the hollow

> statue of Saddam is left dangling from this marble splint. People now throwing objects at it, throwing rocks and pieces of anything they can find, throwing dirt up into his face. (CNN, 9 April 2003)

Zahn seemed to reconsider the American flag incident from a different perspective. Throughout this episode, she tried to make a clear distinction between the acts of 'irresponsible' Marines that opened up the claim of 'American occupation' and the US war command intention of 'liberating Iraq'.

Paula Zahn (CNN anchor) asking Simon Robinson (*Time*):

> I wanted to ask you a question about whether you were aware of any kind of command that went out to those Marines to bring that American flag down, because there is so much sensitivity about, perhaps, this being seen as a sign of occupation, not liberation? (CNN, 9 April 2003)

Robinson did not really have any confirmation that commanders had asked for the flag to be lowered.

> I am not sure in this instance, but I do know that during the campaign Marines have been told to take flags off vehicles. They were not allowed to fly the flags from the tanks or armoured personnel carriers or anything like that ... so there has definitely been directives from above not to be too triumphal about this whole thing. (CNN, 9 April 2003)

Zahn proceeded to focus on the climax of the liberation narrative; close ups of the crowd, sounds and images of a cheering populace. As the Marines had replaced the American flag with the pre-gulf war flag (which does not have the inscription 'God is great'),[6] anchor Paula Zahn focused on this when talking to Simon Robinson:

> A lot of symbolism at play here. You were saying that this is the pre-gulf war flag that is attached or they are attempting to attach to the base of what used to be the statue of Saddam Hussein. And I guess the one thing that is missing from this is what was added after the gulf war, which is a religious statement saying God is great. (CNN, 9 April 2003)

Al Jazeera had a different approach. The Qatar based channel was not convinced that the statue toppling signalled the end of the war. Indeed, in its headline news Al Jazeera anchor Adnan Charif claimed that despite the arrival of marine forces in Baghdad, the war might not be over. He quoted Vice-President Dick Cheney saying that he 'does not overrule the possibility of continued fighting in the days to come'. Nonetheless, Al Jazeera followed closely the events at Firdos Square. There were constant interactions between the studio in Doha and their correspondents on the ground (such as Maher Abdullah and Mohamed Ould Fal).

Al Jazeera's narrative contours were set by correspondent Mohamed Ould Fal. He offered a thematic commentary, linking the falling statue with the bombing of journalists the day before:

> The battle of the Palestine hotel that happened yesterday represented the last violent scenes of the American and Britain war in Iraq. What we see today is not as bloody as what happened during the black Tuesday. From yesterday to today, many things have changed, media is no longer the enemy of the Marines as was the case yesterday, and what appeared to be an American fiasco yesterday, was transformed overnight into a confident victory. When American tanks besiege a hotel where most of international media gather without any convincing reason, one wonders whether it was just a message to the world that the Yankees have reached the heart of Baghdad. Yet, this seems to represent only the preface to a surprise with a deeper significance, as the giant statue of the Iraqi President Saddam Hussein was still standing until this morning with potency, filling the space with pride and glory. The battle was not won, and so no time is better than this moment to spread the message that the coalition has reached the heart of Baghdad. This was to be followed by another message about the end of Saddam Hussein, through the toppling of his statue in a live scene witnessed by millions of television stations around the world. However, this operation was merely conducted by a few Iraqi youngsters assisted by American soldiers. In addition, this operation was full of mistakes, which in turn are full of meanings. Indeed, the Iraqis failed to bring down the statue of the President Commander in Chief Saddam Hussein. Their ropes and their

muscles failed. It was then up to the American soldiers to take in charge this hard mission.

> This scene represents the blurring of fact and fiction. Yet the American soldier coming on the top of a tank with his tall arm did not remember in the midst of this exciting victory that he is standing on the top of a land that is not American. Maybe he intended to be rude, or maybe he just misbehaved because of his lack of knowledge. All these excuses are worse than the insult itself and this remains the scene that will be recorded in history. And after the predicament of analysing the intention, the problem of interpretation remains: is this an American soldier hanging an American dictator? Or is it a foreign invader toppling the head of another nation? Isn't it that the flag used in this way usually honours the martyrs? And since when are criminals hanged with flags? To get out of this predicament in a decent way, it was remembered after a while that Iraq had its flag, and that there were Iraqi participants in this symbolic execution. However, another dilemma soon appeared as the flag associated with Saddam Hussein carries the expression of 'Allah is great', and for this reason it was to be replaced. So panic has prevailed, the president should be executed without any flag, he should be stripped from this honour. The final moment carried another development, which maybe created a hidden fear in the hearts of the Marines. The statue bent but did not fall easily and even after its fall, its feet remained entrenched in the Iraqi concrete, which lies in the heart of Baghdad. (Al Jazeera, 9 April 2003)

To summarise Al Jazeera's narrative, the toppling of the Saddam statue was an attempt to deflect attention from what had happened the day before when the US military attacked international correspondents. The events in Firdos Square were for the most part a media-friendly complement to US military propaganda. There was no doubt that the toppling of Saddam statue was staged. It was clear that the American forces were the ones pulling the strings, while Iraqi youngsters were merely extras. Accordingly, putting an American flag on the top of the statue was not an individual act, it was premeditated. The fact that the statue's feet remained in the concrete, symbolically meant that the US forces would not get rid of the Iraqi resistance easily.

Nonetheless, there was a noticeable tension in Al Jazeera's narrative between Saddam as American dictator and Saddam as symbol of resistance. Indeed, Al Jazeera correspondent Mohamed Ould Fal questioned the old alliance that linked the Iraqi dictator and successive American administrations, when he asked; 'Is this an American soldier hanging an American dictator?' By asking this question, Al Jazeera's correspondent Mohamed Ould Fal succinctly recalled memories of the CIA's role in Saddam's ascension to power (Morris 2003: A28; Sale 2003). The question also brought to mind the American support for Iraq during their war against Iran (1980–1988). At that time, US–Iraq relations were close, and high-level officials exchanged visits (Donald Rumsfeld was dispatched twice to Iraq in December 1983 and March 1984 as special envoy from President Ronald Reagan).[7] Subsequently, Iraq received American assistance through loan programmes. With improved credit standing, Iraq could obtain loans from international financial institutions. The United States also provided economic aid to Iraq in the form of agricultural products (Battle 2003; Dawoody 2006: 14–15).

Saddam Hussein ended his alliance of convenience with the United States on 2 August 1990, when his troops invaded Kuwait in response to a dispute over oil production.[8] Once America's ally, Saddam had become its bitterest enemy. This led other enemies of the United States to support his anti-imperialist rhetoric. From that time onwards, Saddam, once representing secular socialist values, increasingly portrayed himself as a devout Muslim. This allowed him to co-opt the conservative religious segments of society, thus building an image of himself as a model of anti-American resistance in the Middle East. The reversals which characterised Saddam's foreign policy might explain the tension in Al Jazeera's dual construction of Saddam as American pawn and anti-American resistance fighter. The latter frame underlay Mohamed Ould Fal's comment that 'the giant statue of the Iraqi President Saddam Hussein was still standing until this morning with potency, filling the space with pride and glory'.

Visually, CNN's footage of the toppling statue was shot from different angles and employed various camera movements. The camera was primarily focused upon the reaction of the Iraqis toward the Saddam statue, as well as their interaction with American soldiers. CNN showed American tanks on the top side of the camera frame, the statue in the middle of the frame, and the Iraqis in the down side of the frame. The composition of this high angle wide shot enabled the viewer to see the relationship between the three different elements in the frame; the Iraqis were hitting the statue with their shoes, and then American tanks came forward, and finally the Iraqis were seen cheering. Next, the American Marines gave the Iraqis a rope with which to topple the statue, but their attempt failed. The scene was dissolved and then the camera moved to a close-up of Saddam statue with a rope on its neck. The camera then panned to show the crowd and went back to the central, high angle, wide shot frame (comprised of American tanks, local Iraqis, and the beleaguered statue). Subsequently, the Marines used their M-88 Hercules tank recovery vehicle to secure a chain around the neck of the statue. At this stage, screen within screen choreography was employed to show the reaction of American forces towards the crowd, and to remind the audience that various signs, pictures and icons of Saddam were destroyed elsewhere at the same time.

As outlined, the chain was secured around the neck of the Saddam statue. First Lieutenant Tim McLaughlin passed an American flag up to Corporal Edward Chin, who then placed it over the statue's head. The flag remained there for about five minutes until Chin replaced it with a pre-1991 Gulf War Iraqi flag. This was draped through the chain around the statue's neck like a hankie. That flag came down, too, and the toppling of the statue commenced. The relevant footage included a front-on shot of the statue with people around it. The image then dissolved to a high angle shot of the Saddam statue on the floor. The Iraqi crowd was seen celebrating and humiliating the fallen statue, while journalists took pictures of the scene.[9]

Discussion and critique

CNN depicted the toppling of the Saddam statue as the climax of the Iraq campaign and as a successful conclusion for the coalition forces' journey. In fact, the Pentagon had prepared a master narrative for the 2003 Iraq War. There were occasional inadvertent references to this script, as when CNN anchor Wolf Blitzer observed in the first days of the war that a last-minute alteration to 'Shock and Awe' was 'totally unscripted' (CNN, 21 March 2003). In this storyline, reminiscent of Hollywood, the coalition undertakes the path of the Hero's journey.[10] This is a journey of multiple challenges and threatening opponents, in which the hero prevails to gain

Liberation vs. Occupation

the trophy at the end. French Philosopher Jean Baudrillard regarded the war in Iraq as synonymous with its filmic construction:

> What we are watching as we sit paralysed in our fold-down seats isn't *'like* a film'; it *is* a film. With a script, a screenplay, that has to be followed unswervingly. The casting and the technical and financial resources have all been meticulously scheduled: Including control of the distribution channels, these are professionals at work. In the end, operational war becomes an enormous special effect; cinema becomes the paradigm of warfare, and we imagine it as 'real', whereas it is merely the mirror of its cinematic being. The virtuality of war is not, then, a metaphor. It is the literal passage from reality into fiction, or rather the immediate metamorphosis of the real into fiction. The real is now merely the asymptotic horizon of the Virtual. (Baudrillard 2006 [Electronic article; no pagination])

From this perspective, the war narrative, as promoted by the Pentagon, had a predetermined beginning and end with a well-defined trajectory. The beginning of combat started with the 'Decapitation Strike' on 19 March 2003, and the closure of the narrative, as established by the Bush Administration, took place on 1 May 2003, when President Bush, aboard of the USS *Abraham Lincoln*, declared that 'major combat operations in Iraq have ended'. He wore a combat suit suggestive of the blockbuster *Top Gun*.[11] Between the start and the ending, the war narrative follows a linear sequence: shock and awe, conquering troops, hero (Private Lynch), victory (toppling of the statue), and control (Schwalbe, Silcock, and Keith 2005: 458). At times, there were tensions in this narrative between American victory and Iraq liberation

The 2003 Iraq War master narrative projected image-icons of the war, which were supposed to remain in the world collective memory. The toppling of the Saddam statue was arranged to join the lexicon of historic images, such as the raising of the flag on Iwo Jima (which was also staged[12]), the fall of the Berlin Wall, and the collapse of New York's Twin Towers. It is a matter of fact that collective memories are now extensively shaped by visual images; as Walter Benjamin observed, 'history decays into images, not into stories' (quoted in Der Derian 2005: 28).

The Pentagon worked to bring closure to the war narrative and to assert its victory and control over Iraq with a publicly memorable event.

As Barbie Zelizer argues, collective remembering has 'as much to do with identity formation, power and authority, cultural norms, and social interaction as with the simple act of recall' (Zelizer 1995: 214). In this context, one can draw similarities between the toppling of the Saddam statue and the destruction of the Lenin statues following the fall of the Soviet bloc. The *New York Times* reported on 11 December 1989 that thousands of Polish citizens attended the two-hour dismantling of a huge statue of Lenin in Krakow, Poland (New York Times 1989: A8). One can clearly see the striking similarity between these events and those described in this chapter. In fact, this analogy was explicitly invoked at a US Department of Defense briefing to all major US news outlets on 9 April 2003.

> The scenes of free Iraqis celebrating in the streets, riding American tanks, tearing down the statues of Saddam Hussein in the centre of Baghdad are breath-taking. Watching them, one cannot help but think of the fall of the Berlin Wall and the collapse of the Iron Curtain. We are seeing history unfold, events that will shape the course of a country, the fate of a people, and potentially the future of the region. Saddam Hussein is now taking his rightful place alongside Hitler, Stalin, Lenin, and Ceausescu in the pantheon of failed, brutal dictators, and the Iraqi people are well on their way to freedom.[13]

Playing with the dynamics of affective memory by establishing a similitude with the end of Soviet rule was a key objective of the Pentagon info-warriors. As Barbie Zelizer explains, 'collective memory thrives on remaking the residue of past decades into material with contemporary resonance; it is filled with reused and reusable materials' (Zelizer 1995: 217). Through the use of sophisticated depiction and display techniques, the toppling of the Saddam statue was supposed to appear as a major historical event. Collective memory related to war developments would then shrink it into a particular moment. Earlier episodes of the war such as 'Shock and Awe' intensive bombings, the resistance encountered, the civilian victims, and the attacks on unembedded journalists would be erased and replaced by an 'artificial memory' supplied by American mainstream media. Artificial memory emphasises the present real-live event at the expense of anything occurring outside. Commenting on this process, Andreas Huyssen argues that 'where the medium is presence and presence only, and presence is the live telecast of action news, the past will always necessarily remain blocked out' (Quoted in Hoskins 2004: 110, 123).

Unsurprisingly, CNN's coverage of the fall of the Saddam statue was imbued with the Orientalist deep frame. This had been a consistent pattern throughout the war particularly through the use of the 'nation-as-person' metaphor, which conflated Saddam Hussein with the state, regime, people, and territory of Iraq. News reports about getting rid of Saddam Hussein routinely employed this metaphor. This neglected the fact that the coalition bombs and missiles did not target solely that person. Thousands of people were 'hidden by the metaphor;' the United States apparently did not fight against them (Lakoff 2003). Through this metaphor, the Orientalist depiction of Saddam Hussein as the incarnation of evil, madness and irrationality was transferred to his countrymen.

The Orientalist deep frame was evident in CNN's coverage of Iraqis in the square. Their inability to take down the Saddam statue was imbued with a sense of ineptitude. CNN television coverage of the toppling statue transformed Iraqis into mere extras while the real accomplishment was attributed to American soldiers. Another Orientalist facet in CNN's coverage appeared during the reports of looting and plunder during the fall of Baghdad. Here, Iraqis were no longer shown as an oppressed people in need of liberation but, in harmony with Orientalist traditions, as a threatening and dangerous crowd. Visual evidence of large scale looting from people from all ages, including women and children, inevitably established a negative image of Iraqis in general. The participation of women and children in the looting conveyed an image of 'inborn barbarism' (Trivundza 2004: 489). This appeared to show the unbridgeable gap between the enlightened West and the barbaric Orient. The coalition soldiers were depicted positively as liberators of the people or as enforcers of law and order. CNN did not judge it appropriate to investigate the role of the US military in the spreading of chaos in Baghdad. They defended Iraqi strategic assets (oil fields, palaces, the Ministry of Oil and the Ministry of Interior) but did not prevent looting in other locations. In fact, no American media outlet, including CNN, considered the new authorities inability to stop highly organised acts of vandalism perpetrated at the archaeological museum and other historic sites (Trivundza 2004: 489–490).

Additionally, CNN coverage of the fall of the Saddam Statue exemplified the conflict frame.[14] Overall, this occasion was meant to demonstrate and celebrate the coalition victory for Iraqis and the world. American television networks were cautious not to show any excessive triumphalism on the airwaves; this was deemed by the Pentagon as counter-productive. Therefore, it was the Iraqi liberation frame, not the US victory frame, which was predominantly used by CNN. In this regard, Barbara Starr and guest Simon Robinson from *Time* magazine sought to differentiate between 'irresponsible acts' from individuals and the US Military High Command's commitment to 'liberate Iraq'.

However, placing a pre-Gulf War Iraqi flag on the statue could not erase earlier images of the American flag; the damage was already done. For Al Jazeera and other Arab media, the American flag incident exemplified American imperialism. Aware of this perception, CNN anchors and correspondents tried to portray US troops as unwise but not ill intentioned. Had CNN circulated more shots of images from a wider angle, showing Firdos Square from a broader perspective, this symbolic victory would have been less apparent.

Al Jazeera's visual and narrative positioning of the event emphasised the larger picture in terms of causes, consequences and responsibilities. Unlike CNN, Al Jazeera's coverage recalled the attacks it was subjected to a day earlier (as well as other attacks on international journalists at the Palestine Hotel). Al Jazeera's correspondent Mohamed Ould Fal highlighted the stark contrast between bombing foreign journalists one day, and then asking them to cover a staged episode the next. Awareness of this contrast shaped Al Jazeera's scepticism of the Iraqi liberation narrative and the staged symbolism of the toppling statue.

Al Jazeera's hostility to the coalition endeavour was amplified by the 'otherness' frame, whereby coalition forces were portrayed as an unwanted external threat. More specifically, the American military appeared as 'occupation forces'. They were creating 'havoc' in Baghdad by failing to prevent widespread looting. On this matter, Al Jazeera journalists and analysts were surprised to see the Iraqi forces collapse so quickly. They believed for a while that the Iraqi forces would resist within Baghdad and undertake urban guerrilla warfare. When it became clear that the Iraqi forces were no longer in control, and the shock of yet another defeat and humiliation by Western armies looked likely, Al Jazeera journalists resorted to speculations of conspiracy. Questions were raised about whether Saddam Hussein was not, in the end, an American agent, given the disconcerting easiness with which his army collapsed in every encounter with American troops.

While other Arab networks, such as Al-Arabiya, showed visuals of Iraqis burning a poster of Saddam, Al Jazeera stopped short of such coverage. Their pan-Arab deep framing had led to partial identification with the plight of the regime during the war. Al Jazeera could not easily change this position without irking its viewers. This explains why they showed Saddam being carried on the shoulders of his supporters one day prior to the fall of Baghdad. This was Al Jazeera's only visual footage of Saddam.[15]

Against this background, Mohamed Ould Fal and other Al Jazeera anchors looked for any development, no matter how small or symbolic, to lift the morale of Arab audiences. Thus, he described the whole statue toppling operation as a staged event in which only a small number of Iraqi 'youngsters' participated. Such a description implied that these youngsters were not mature enough to understand the situation and thus were prone to manipulation. The fact that the Iraqis failed to topple the statue obviously pleased Al Jazeera's anchor because the task fell back on the Marines at the end. This fitted with the Arab network narrative, which presented the episode as a staged event. By directly participating in the statue toppling, the Marines inadvertently revealed that the entire process was first and foremost an American endeavour, not a genuine uprising of the Iraqi people.

In fact, Al Jazeera's insistence on the lack of spontaneity proved accurate. One year later, in retrospect, Reporter David Zucchino revealed in the *Los Angeles Times* that the toppling of Saddam's statue was in fact a US Army psychological warfare operation, staged to look like a spontaneous Iraqi action. The article declared that:

> The early, iconic image of Saddam's statue being toppled in a Baghdad square was not a spontaneous act by joyous Iraqis. It was an Army psychological warfare operation that began when a Marine colonel chose the statue for its symbolism and the psychological team encouraged Iraqis to participate. In the end, a Marine vehicle dragged down the statue with a chain, but the

evocative image was indelible, because the military team filled the vehicle with cheering Iraqi children. (Zucchino 2004: A28)

Another aspect of Al Jazeera's reportage which proved to be valid was the symbolism of the statue's difficult fall. It came down slowly and messily, suggesting that the Americans had not achieved absolute victory. Correspondent Mohamed Ould Fal's observation that the 'statue bent but did not fall easily and even after its fall, its feet remained entrenched in the Iraqi concrete' delivered a central message; resistance was deeply rooted in the Iraqi nation. So despite the coalition's symbolic success in eventually toppling the statue, and their success in defeating the regular Iraqi army, Fal's comments inferred that the people of Iraq would continue fighting the occupation.

The day following the statue's fall, Al Jazeera anchors dressed in black to express their sadness about the occupation of Iraq. Their news bulletins carried the following headline: 'the fall of Saddam's regime ... Baghdad under occupation'. By contrast, CNN and American television networks interviewed pro-US Iraqis.

An image icon of the war?

As the finale of the war narrative, the toppling of Saddam's statue was arranged as an image-icon of the war and as a publicly memorable event. In this context, American news outlets drew analogies between this episode and events that followed the fall of the Berlin Wall. As on previous occasions, CNN and Al Jazeera provided contesting versions of the same event. The Atlanta based network adopted the Iraqi liberation narrative, whereas the Qatar based channel adopted the staged event narrative. From the same images, the two networks edited the footage in a way that supported their framing choices. Thus, CNN primarily used tightly cropped and/or close range camera shots to inflate perceptions about the number of Iraqis present at the square. This editing style also over-emphasised the jubilation of the crowd and their welcoming attitude to American troops. Al Jazeera usually employed wider camera shots of the square to reveal the smallness of the gathering.

The CNN Iraqi liberation narrative was shaken when the American flag was put on the top of the Saddam Hussein statue. This incident somewhat validated the perception of Arab media that the Iraq War was an American occupation. Aware of this, CNN anchors and guests tried to interpret the flag incident as the act of 'irresponsible' Marines, and to restore the original narrative. The latter included elements of the Orientalist deep frame, particularly the 'nation-as-person' metaphor. Orientalism was also at play when the toppling exercise transformed Iraqis into mere extras while the real accomplishment was attributed to American soldiers. Moreover, the reports of looting in Baghdad characterised Iraqis as a threatening and dangerous crowd.

In contrast, Al Jazeera's coverage always doubted the spontaneity of this event, and suggested that the Americans were pulling the strings. Al Jazeera also criticised the small numbers of Iraqis present, and questioned the episode's actual significance. Moreover, unlike CNN, the Qatar based network offered a thematic commentary by linking the falling statue with other events. This thematic approach created, however, a tension in its narrative between framing Saddam as a former US ally (and possible agent) or as a resister of occupation. However, because of its pan-Arab orientation, Al Jazeera generally favoured the latter interpretation and predicted Iraqi resistance against the American occupation.

Conclusion

The mobilisation of media bias works to reinforce or modify the attitudes and behaviour of audiences. This could be prompted by governmental authorities attempting to inflame patriotic feelings in favour of war. Similarly, military institutions may employ media strategies to demoralise the enemy and strengthen local morale. In the twentieth century, military propaganda became more sophisticated during the wide-ranging conflicts that took place during that period (i.e., World War I, World War II, anti-colonial wars of liberation). Elaborate ideological frameworks were designed to mobilise populations in favour of war. Established techniques included deception, information control, silencing dissent, as well as the manipulation of beliefs and language. Traditionally, within the United States, media organisations were very supportive of their government's war efforts. This situation changed during the Vietnam War, especially after the Tet offensive in 1968, when television audiences confronted the reality of war in Vietnam. Organised opposition to the war eventually involved some elites and media professionals. Popular support for the Vietnam intervention and confidence in the military diminished considerably. From the perspective of American commanders, it was the American media that had caused their debacle in Vietnam.

In the aftermath of this war, the Pentagon sought to develop a better strategy of media management. Early results were seen during the

US military interventions in Grenada (1983) and Panama (1989), in which media pool systems were implemented. But it was during the First Gulf War (1991) that the US military employed information dominance as an essential component of operational planning. The introduction of live war television coverage allowed the Pentagon to make war into a dramatic event for military purposes. Military sources shaped stories in anticipation of what the American news media would cover. These ranged from interesting personal testimonies from American troopers, to the lethality of hi-tech weaponry.

The Gulf War experience convinced the US military that information dominance was the way to achieve supremacy over all potential foes. The US military adopted doctrines that required the views and perceptions of national audiences to be shaped in accordance with military strategies. However, such practices could potentially undermine democratic processes and inflame cultural prejudices. In this context, making decisions about war and peace involved the most serious use of state power.

The preceding concerns proved to be valid. The Pentagon info-warriors demonised certain ethnic groups and played upon fears of the 'other'. Having led many military campaigns in the Middle East over previous decades, military propagandists readily exploited the fear of Arabs and Muslims evoked by Orientalist themes in American literature and the mass media. In this regard, the discourse of Orientalism participated in the creation of a hegemonic discourse that used the rhetoric of 'otherness' to justify political, economic and military expansionism. 'Otherness' implies a complex mechanism for social exclusion. It defines and secures one's own identity by distancing and stigmatising those who are different. Violent attacks perpetrated by Middle Eastern non-state actors appeared to justify the prevailing constructions of 'otherness'. Indeed, these attacks were interpreted through the prism of Islam, which was said to represent an external threat to Western identity and interests. Arabs and Muslims became the embodiment of both external and internal 'others'. The image of Islam and Arabs in American media discourse became associated with backwardness, religious fanaticism, and terrorism which threatened the West's freedom, economy, and culture. Historically, these rhetorical attacks preceded the bloody conflicts about to unfold. Indeed, there was a correlation between the demonisation of Islam and Arabs, and the subsequent wars of domination launched in the new millennium by the neo-conservative-inspired Bush administration.

Meanwhile, developments in the Middle East followed another course. After a century of Western colonial and neo-colonial designs, pan-regional feelings of resentment were common. While some Arabs and Muslims embraced Occidentalism, the mirror image of Orientalism, and refused anything associated with the West, other less vehement yet still oppositional viewpoints emerged. For example, pan-Arabist theoreticians called for the unity of the Arab people in the context of modernity and economic development. They borrowed many Western political principles, yet they also sought to resist the dangers of Western hegemony. As a Middle Eastern worldview, pan-Arabism also permeated Arab transnational media. Subsequent political developments shifted the hub of these media from Egypt to Lebanon and then to London. A Saudi-BBC project for an Arabic satellite news television network eventually folded and went under Qatari patronage in 1996. Al Jazeera emerged and immediately gave airtime to a range of religious, political and cultural viewpoints. Intellectuals, who in the past had no chance of featuring in public media, could express their opinions freely for the first time. This reinvigorated the Arab public sphere after decades of state censorship. It also renewed emphasis on key Arab political issues. Al Jazeera's brand of pan-Arabism was not based on revolutionary principles, but rather on public sphere principles. The network's rationale was that access to public argument on a transnational level would liberate Arabs and ultimately strengthen the transnational Arab public sphere.

Al Jazeera immediately filled a social need. Local audiences were not pleased with the type of coverage provided by leading global television networks. During the 1991 Gulf War coverage for example, Orientalist and military framing characterised the news coverage of CNN. The latter portrayed American troops as individual human beings, whereas Iraqis were dehumanised. Moreover, in tune with the Pentagon's communication strategy, CNN conveyed the incorrect impression that this war was clean and surgical. Similarly, in Orientalist terms, CNN's coverage of the 1994 American intervention in Somalia divided the protagonists into good guys (American troops) and bad guys (Somali warlords). This polarity moulded

Conclusion

the different ethnicities and political forces in the Middle East into one undifferentiated form.

The start of the 'War on Terror' in late 2001 put the Arab network under the international spotlight. Al Jazeera's criticism of American foreign policy decisions and official communication efforts was resented by leading members of the Bush administration, who branded the network as an Al Qaeda mouthpiece. From a communication point of view, Al Jazeera hindered the Bush administration efforts to promote its policies and actions to Arab audiences. The US communication strategy was devised by the Rendon Group and by the Undersecretary of State for Public Diplomacy and Public Affairs. These efforts were very efficient within the United States, but they proved inadequate to address Middle Eastern concerns. Because of Al Jazeera's critical news coverage and current affairs programmes, negative opinions toward the American foreign policy increased. This placed the Arab network, literally, in the line of fire of the US military. Shortly afterwards, during the Afghan campaign, Al Jazeera's offices were bombed.

After Afghanistan, the Bush administration concentrated its focus on Iraq. Numerous claims were persistently circulated by the administration's key figures among international media. These included Iraq's alleged possession of weapons of mass destruction, its threatening attitude to neighbouring countries, and its alleged terrorist connections. The mobilisation of these themes ultimately won the approval of the American people for war, but failed to convince Middle Eastern audiences. As the drums of war started beating, CNN and Al Jazeera stepped up their preparedness amidst threatening competition from Fox News and Al-Arabiya, respectively.

CNN and Al Jazeera covered all events of the 2003 Iraq War from markedly different perspectives. The general result was a multitude of competing and clashing frames, which underlined the role of the media as the public interpreter of events and as disseminators of 'packages for consciousness' (Hallin 1986: 13). Both networks gave their audiences specific cues for reacting to political developments. CNN adopted many Orientalist frames. Accordingly, Saddam Hussein was portrayed as a backward but dangerous Oriental and no differentiation was made between the Iraqi leader and the nation state of Iraq. Iraqis were absent most of the time from the CNN coverage. Depictions of them contained virtually no human dimension. They appeared mainly as a threatening crowd. CNN extensively covered widespread looting by Iraqis, without questioning the responsibility of the coalition forces for law and order. During the toppling of the Saddam statue, Iraqis were shown shouting and expressing their anger at Saddam and his era. Yet, they were depicted as unable to destroy the statue without the help of the US military crane. This appeared to underline the immaturity of the Oriental character (alongside stereotypes of violent behaviour and threatening attitude). In contrast, Al Jazeera portrayed the American-led war as direct aggression against an Arab nation. They used the pan-Arab frame to describe the war as an 'invasion', and after the fall of Baghdad as an 'occupation'. Al Jazeera focused on the human cost of the war and stressed the illegality of its prosecution. Overall, CNN was deeply imbued with Orientalist frames which portrayed Iraqis negatively, whereas Al Jazeera's deployment of pan-Arab frames did not necessarily entail the demonisation of Iraq's foes.

In terms of military control over the meanings of events, CNN clearly adhered to the Pentagon's choreography of the war narrative. Military inspired titles were used for the most important episodes (e.g. 'Decapitation Strike', 'Shock and Awe', 'Saving Private Lynch'). In particular, 'Shock and Awe' was conveyed as a climactic event and as an enjoyable fireworks display. Heavy reliance on US official sources significantly shaped CNN's war coverage as anchors and guests carried the military's version of events, including speculative commentaries and Psyops themes (e.g. Saddam Hussein was hit, whole Iraqi divisions were defecting, cities were surrendering). Also, CNN anchors and guests constantly referred to the lethality and precision of American missiles as well as the courage of American troops. During the toppling of Saddam's statue, CNN, alongside other networks, arranged the episode as a war finale and as a publicly memorable event. In this context, American news outlets drew analogies between this episode and events that followed the fall of the Berlin Wall. CNN primarily used tightly cropped and close range camera shots to inflate the number of the Iraqis present at the square. They also exaggerated the jubilation of the crowd to fit the Iraqi liberation narrative. On the other hand, throughout the war Iraqi casualties were either downplayed or buried under talk of 'liberation' and 'reconstruction'.

Al Jazeera's coverage effectively countered US Psyops-themed messages. They denied that Saddam Hussein or any high officials were hit during

Conclusion

'Decapitation Strike', which was conversely framed as an 'assassination attempt' by the Arab network. It also opposed the Pentagon's perspective during 'Shock and Awe' by focusing upon the ensuing destruction and civilian casualties. The entire opening sequence was framed as 'Baghdad is burning'. Moments of silence characterised the coverage and this conveyed a sense of grief over the loss of civilian lives. During the attacks that affected journalists on 8 April 2003, Al Jazeera reported on behalf of those who had died doing their journalistic duties. Subsequently, they positioned themselves as the champion of news media freedom in the face of censorious military practices.

Al Jazeera had some problems in terms of military sourcing. They relied extensively upon the military analysis of Retired General Saad Al-Chazli.[1] He often tried to emphasise that Iraqi forces could achieve their objectives, provided they used the terrain in their favour and their equipment to full potential (in contrast, for CNN the outcome of the war was never in question). There were other instances where the Arab network relied on dubious Iraqi information, and provided significant airtime to the Iraqi Minister of Information. However, Al Jazeera was able to balance these opinions by giving room to US military spokespeople and by covering CENTCOM and other Pentagon briefings. Therefore, one can say that, in comparison to Al Jazeera, CNN was more prone to manipulability by military Psyops.

But a question remains: did Al Jazeera provide a propaganda critique or was it simply a propaganda conduit for a different propaganda line? In my opinion, Al Jazeera's war coverage was not explicitly planned so as to represent participatory democratic ideals against militaristic discourse. The Arab network was first and foremost a news media organisation which aimed to attract audiences and generate profit. They were also not aligned with any particular social or political movement. It is true that Al Jazeera had provided airtime to Jihadists, social activists and facilitators of social change, but this was simply a reflection of Arab politics. For me, the Arab network did not intentionally set out an alternative news source during the Iraq War. They simply sought to outmanoeuvre the competition and provide good footage and credible information (so as to not loose viewership to their competitors). Consequently, when the war started they simply acted on professional premises, corroborated incoming pieces of information, and tried to put stories together. The Arab network had a large number of crew on location (unlike CNN whose news crew was expelled from Baghdad after the 'Decapitation Strike'). Al Jazeera correspondents understood the language and the culture, and thus provided a constant flow of valuable information and imagery to the control room in Doha. The negative reactions of the Bush administration and the barrage of criticism to which Al Jazeera was subjected, simply reinforced scepticism of American foreign policy objectives. The targeting of Al Jazeera's bureau became a major international media story. Such profile shaped Al Jazeera's image as a conduit of anti-war discourse. For media scholars, the Qatar based channel became identified as a major challenge to the dominant Western media discourse, and exemplified the contra-flow phenomenon, whereby international newsrooms imparted local and/or regional perspectives on major international events.

But being critical of the American side did not mean that the Arab network was reproducing messages crafted by the Iraqi information ministry. It is true that Al Jazeera anchors and correspondents generally showed some consideration to the Iraqi side, but they also criticised, at times, Iraqi military planning and operations. It should be noted that Saddam's regime twice shut Al Jazeera's offices in Baghdad during the war, and expelled one of its most renowned reporters, namely Tayseer Allouni on 2 April 2003.[2] As a result, Al Jazeera decided to suspend the work of all its correspondents in Baghdad, Basra and Mosul, while maintaining the broadcasting of live and recorded images received from its office in Baghdad.

In broad terms, this research has sought to analyse news frames in relation to the coverage of military conflicts in the Middle East. News frames influence worldviews and attitudes by emphasising specific beliefs, values, and facts, and endowing them with particular relevance in relation to given issues. In the context of the 2003 Iraq War, this study has uncovered the workings of US military propaganda. It has also shown how military propaganda practices worked in duo with framing processes adopted by American news media generally, and CNNI in particular. These practices were imbued with the deep frames of Orientalism and anti-terrorism. Here, it was noticeable that Arab news media, and particularly Al Jazeera, employed counter frames emanating from pan-Arabism which undermined the legitimacy of US military-media warfare on the global stage.

Conclusion

The originality of this study derives from the cross-cultural examination of how rival satellite television networks covered the same world event. The findings will, I hope, provide a platform for future studies concerning the mobilisation of media bias, and its contestation with regard to US interventions in the Middle East.

In this context, the phenomenon of frame formation is crucially important in explaining how conflicting news perspectives arise. As described in earlier chapters, frame formation depends on numerous factors, such as culture, ideology, professional values, bureaucratic norms, and economic interests, which combine to frame events within ideological, political and cultural contexts. In certain cases, this produces politically controversial representations of 'us' and 'them'. Such constructions align with hegemony theory, which considers the media as a terrain of struggle in which recurrent contests of representations take place. This contest happens between hegemonic discourses and their challengers from groups that lie outside dominant institutions (Kellner 2005: xv). In the case described here, Al Jazeera provided a powerful normative counter to the hegemonic, militaristic orientation of CNN.

Postscript

The Iraq War, which began on 19 March 2003 when a US-led coalition invaded the country and toppled the government of Saddam Hussein, continued for much of the next decade when an insurgency emerged to oppose the occupying forces and the newly instated Iraqi government. While the United States officially withdrew from Iraq in 2011, it re-entered the war once more in 2014 at the helm of a new coalition and under a new label. In the meantime, the insurgency and many dimensions of the civil armed conflict continue until now (July 2016).

After President Bush declared the end of major combat operations in Iraq on 1 May 2003, one of the major decisions by the occupying forces was the abolition of Iraqi ministries, institutions, and armed forces, as well as banning thousands of former Baath Party members from holding government jobs. Then, the US-led coalition formed the Iraqi Governing Council (IGC), which was composed of 25 Iraqi nationals. Their first task was to draft a new Iraqi constitution, under the authority of Paul Bremer. These measures gave the country's reins to a mix of Shiʻi political parties and armed militias, destabilising the situation further and fuelling a die-hard Sunnite opposition. By July 2003, the Commander of the US forces in Iraq acknowledged that his troops were facing a low-intensity guerrilla-style war. And despite the fact that Saddam's sons Uday and Qusay were killed in a gun battle in Mosul (13 July 2003), and that Saddam Hussein was himself captured near Tikrit (14 December 2003) and later executed by the new Iraqi government (30 December 2006), resistance to the US-led coalition and its Iraqi proxies continued unabated.

The policies adopted by the coalition on the ground have fuelled social violence and deep sectarian strife between different ethnic and religious groups. They also spread insurgency, which primarily targeted Coalition armies, especially during the 2004–2005 period. The insurgency also targeted police and military forces of the new Iraqi government, considered as collaborators with the enemy. The intensity of the insurgency during 2004 reduced the Coalition, when nine countries pulled their forces out. Later withdrawals continued, leaving the United States as the sole country with troops on the ground by mid-2009. In late February 2009, the new American President Barack Obama announced an 18-month withdrawal window for 'combat forces', leaving behind 30,000 to 50,000 troops to offer support and training to the Iraqi security apparatus.

The Iraqi insurgency subsequently escalated into a civil war in 2014 with the apparition of the Islamic State of Iraq and the Levant (ISIL, also known as ISIS) and its subsequent control of several areas in the Sunnite regions of Anbar, Mosul, and other regions in northern Iraq. This has resulted in reinforcing air bombardments by the United States and its allies, as well as the participation of Iranian troops on the ground.

The consequences of this war were disastrous for Iraq. In 2007, an independent British polling agency estimated total war fatalities to be over 1.2 million (Opinion Research Business 2007). In the same year, the Iraqi government reported that there were five million orphans in Iraq – nearly half of the country's children (US Labor against the War, 2007). The United Nations High Committee for Refugees estimated in 2008 that the war uprooted 4.7 million Iraqis (about 17 per cent of the population). Two million of them fled to neighbouring countries (UNHCR 2008).

The very high human and financial consequences have made the Iraq War the defining conflict of the twenty-first century, and a critical passage of American history alongside the Vietnam War. The mobilisation of media bias, which was an integral part of the game, has been retrospectively exposed. In 2008, *New York Times* Journalist David Barstow uncovered vital information concerning the relationship between military commentators and news networks. This revelation occurred after the *New York Times* successfully sued the Defence Department to gain access to 8,000 pages of e-mail messages, transcripts, and records describing years of private briefings, trips to Iraq, and Pentagon talking points. Barstow won the 2008 Pulitzer Prize for exposing *The Pentagon Military Analyst Program,* which was launched in early 2002 by then Assistant Secretary of Defence for Public Affairs Victoria Clarke to help sell a sceptical public 'a possible Iraq invasion'. The programme consisted of embedding Pentagon military propagandists into TV networks as commentators. This was a major information warfare tool for selling the war on Iraq to the American public. In a *New York Times* article titled 'Behind TV Analysts, Pentagon's Hidden Hand', David Barstow explains the modus operandi of this programme:

> Hidden behind that appearance of objectivity, though, is a Pentagon information apparatus that has used those analysts in a campaign to generate favourable news coverage of the administration's wartime performance, an examination by The New York Times has found.
>
> Records and interviews show how the Bush administration has used its control over access and information in an effort to transform the analysts into a kind of media Trojan horse – an instrument intended to shape terrorism coverage from inside the major TV and radio networks. Analysts have been wooed in hundreds of private briefings with senior military leaders, including officials with significant influence over contracting and budget matters, records show. They have been taken on tours of Iraq and given access to classified intelligence. They have been briefed by officials from the White House, State Department, and Justice Department, including Mr Cheney, Alberto R. Gonzales and Stephen J. Hadley.
>
> In turn, members of this group have echoed administration talking points, sometimes even when they suspected the information was false or inflated. Some analysts acknowledge they suppressed doubts because they feared jeopardizing their access.
>
> These records reveal a symbiotic relationship where the usual dividing lines between government and journalism have been obliterated.

Postscript

> Internal Pentagon documents repeatedly refer to the military analysts as 'message force multipliers' or 'surrogates' who could be counted on to deliver administration 'themes and messages' to millions of Americans 'in the form of their own opinions'. (Barstow 20 April 2008)

The Pentagon Military Analyst Program involved aforementioned CNN analysts, such as General Wesley Clark, General Don Sheppard, and General David Grange. Barstow's investigation also showed that numerous other military analysts participated in the programme.[1] The extent and scope of the programme only confirms that journalistic dependence on official sources allowed the militaristic discourse to permeate and undermine the public sphere. The programme also substantiates the power of the industrial-military-media complex in the United States. The latter has the capacity to integrate different propaganda, public affairs, military deception and psychological operations into specifically focused campaigns.

From their side, the Qatar-based network tried to reflect on the lessons learned from the Iraq War and the experience with the George W. Bush administration. Some of the outcomes were positive, as when Al Jazeera requested its Sudanese cameraman Sami Al-Haj[2] to head the network's newly established department: the Public Liberties and Human Rights Desk (1 May 2008). The desk's primary focus is to establish a specialised database for monitoring human rights abuses and to raise public awareness of particular cases and issues (Ajazeera.net 2008). Drawing on his ordeal, Sami Al-Haj proved to be a vociferous defender of journalistic freedoms worldwide, in association with renowned NGOs, such as the Committee to Protect Journalists (CPJ). This development reflects the Arab network's continued commitment to the rights and liberties associated with the public sphere.

Other outcomes were not as positive for the Qatar-based broadcaster. From 2004 onwards, Al Jazeera Arabic seems to have moved from its anterior position of advancing journalistic independence and giving a balanced airtime to the different forces (on the other hand, Al Jazeera English (AJE) continued providing a balanced coverage in general[3]). Al Jazeera Arabic's original official motto (the opinion and the opposite opinion) and initial editorial ethos, according to which all viewpoints should be respected and given airtime, seems no longer treasured, as particular viewpoints were provided considerable airtime at the expense of others. Some commentators criticised the Arabic network's hierarchy in the post-2003 period for further reinforcing the broadcaster's perceived sympathy towards the Muslim Brotherhood, which reflected in the often favorable coverage of this Islamist movement (Black 2011). In the view of several observers, the network's coverage of the Arab Spring also deviated from its early ambitions to provide balanced news coverage (Cherkaoui 2014). In fact, Al Jazeera Arabic has made many viewers question its veracity by taking the side of some activists (in Tunisia, Egypt, Libya, Yemen and Syria), while clearly ignoring others (such as in Bahrain and Oman) (*The Economist* 2013).

Ezzedine Abdelmoula, manager of research at the Al Jazeera Centre for Studies, disagrees with the above-mentioned perspective, arguing that Al Jazeera played a big role as 'agent of change' during the Arab Spring, to which the broadcaster has significantly contributed amidst the 'context of a changing landscape of Arab media and politics'. For him:

> The sudden eruption of the Arab spring took the channel by surprise. Like academics, intellectuals and politicians, the media also failed to anticipate the Arab revolutions. At least no one expected the events to be on that unprecedented scale. It is not common for small-sized protests to turn in no time to full revolutions in four countries with different social, political and historic experiences. These unfamiliar developments meant that the media would face serious challenges in performing consistent coverage. No matter how well Al Jazeera was prepared to cover big events, its coverage of the Arab spring showed some degrees of inconsistencies that, to some extent, damaged the channel's image and caused observers to question its credibility, balance and professionalism. (Abdelmoula 2012: 301)

All things considered, the close scrutiny of CNN and Al Jazeera during the War on Iraq was certainly pertinent in that particular case. However, one must acknowledge that significant changes happened in the news media landscape during the last decade, both within the United States and internationally. There is now more competition among news networks in the United States (CNN, Fox News, and MSNBC), and the latter two are strongly oriented toward partisan presentation of conservatives and

Republicans (Fox News) and Democrats and Liberals (MSNBC). While each network has pundits that don't align with this framework, the majority of the content is focused in one direction. Coverage of the Arab Spring, for example, was an improvement in comparison to the coverage of the Iraq War. US networks have provided a steady flow of storytelling images to American audiences, contributing to the public's understanding of the situation. It was suggested that CNN and Fox News' overall framing of the anti-Mubarak movement during the Egyptian uprising constituted a departure from Orientalist stereotypes, even if there were other frames at play (Guzman 2015: 14).

Yet again, there were other instances where cable news media failed to provide a balanced and unbiased coverage. For example, the former Libyan President Muammar Gaddafi's execution immediately became a very newsworthy event, receiving widespread coverage in international news media outlets. News accounts of Gaddafi's death were quickly accompanied by gruesome images showing the former president's bloodied body. A study of this particular event revealed that Fox News was inclined to display gruesome images that violated the dignity of the deceased, whereas CNN was less disposed to disregard ethical and professional guidelines (Yuval, Lavie-Dinur, and Azran 2014: 12).

Moreover, the post-US military intervention in Libya in 2011 found Fox News highly critical of the Obama administration and former Secretary of State Hillary Clinton. Fox provided considerable airtime to analysts and politicians who blasted the White House for its alleged lack of clear objectives. With the centrist consensus broken in a more fractured political situation, it could be argued that US cable news networks are less likely to serve as mere propaganda conduits for the US government and military, as CNN did in the 2003 Iraq conflict.

Finally, it is important to highlight the social media's significant role to convey news and visuals to audiences. While social media did not play a role in the 2003 Iraq War, they were ubiquitous during the Arab Spring. Numerous authors consider that a shift happened from an era of broadcast mass media to one of networked digital media; a shift that has altered both information flows and the way news organisations operate. This opinion has certainly merits as far as mainstream media outlets are concerned. They deploy social media to engage with viewers, expand viewership, and use key influencers as sources. However, when it comes to the actual impact of social media in mobilising collective action during the Arab Spring for example, a study reached a different conclusion. It revealed that social media 'did not appear to play a significant role in either in-country collective action or regional diffusion' (Aday et al. 2012: 21). Under this light, the interplay between broadcast news channels and social media mobilised popular support. In the authors' perspective, 'it is increasingly difficult to separate new media from old media. In the Arab Spring, the two reinforced each other. While Al Jazeera and other satellite television channels leaned heavily on Twitter and other social media' (ibid).

In any case, the new global media environment, which is characterised by the rise of social media and the widened competition among news outlets, means one thing for sure: information management practitioners face tougher days ahead!

Notes

Introduction

1. Mohamed Bouazizi (29 March 1984–4 January 2011) was a Tunisian street vendor who set himself on fire on 17 December 2010 in protest of the confiscation of his wares and the harassment and humiliation that he reported was inflicted on him by a municipal official and his aides.
2. See for example: Christensen 2011; Cottle 2011; Iskander 2011; Rane and Salem 2012; Smith 2011.
3. For more on this: Al Rasheed 2011; Colombo 2012; Kamrava 2012,
4. For example, the Qaddafi regime deployed anti-aircraft missiles against peaceful protesters, and bombarded Libyan cities and towns using fighter jets, tanks and destroyers, whereas the Egyptian police fired live ammonition at crowds, and used sniper fire and armored police trucks to kill about 1,000 Egyptians in just two days.
5. The period studied stretches from the start of the coalition's aerial bombardment (19 March 2003) until President Bush's declaration that major combat operations have ended (1 May 2003).

1 War, Propaganda, and the Mobilisation of Frames

1. Sun Tzu (personal name Sun Wu), a military strategist and general who served the state of Wu near the end of the spring and autumn Period (770–476 BC).
2. According to British historian Niall Ferguson, both German political and military officials, such as Adolf Hitler and General Erich Luddendorf, adopted this view (Ferguson 1998: 212).
3. The scenes of that movie represent the fierce and vicious battle that took place between the colonial French forces, under the authority of Colonel Mathieu, the character based on General Jacques Massu, and the Algerian guerrillas under the leadership of Ali La Pointe, who organised a network of armed cells and entrenched them within the Casbah, the Muslim section of Algiers. The strongest scene in the movie 'The Battle of Algiers' comes when three FLN (National Liberation Front) women wear Western clothes in order to infiltrate the European Quarter and plant explosives in two cafés and an Air France ticket office.
4. It is no coincidence that the Pentagon organised in 2003 a screening of *The Battle of Algiers*. Facing difficult times in countering insurgency in Iraq, they urged participating military and civilian experts to consider the issues at the core of the film – winning battles through brutal and repressive means without ultimately losing the war

for hearts and minds. See: Kaufman, M. T. (2003, 7 September). What Does the Pentagon See in 'The Battle of Algiers?'. *New York Times*.
5. During the World War II, despite the fact that the US military maintained a tight control on the media, patriotic feelings constituted a common platform for military and reporters. However, during the Korean War, reporters were no longer interested in merely conveying the official version of facts. This development prompted General MacArthur's decision to impose formal censorship. Yet this step was not entirely effective and numerous military operational details were leaked by reporters (Lafferty et al. 1994: 7–9).
6. Joint Pub 1-02, Department of Defense, *Dictionary of Military and Associated Terms*. Washington, DC: GPO, 23 March 1994.
7. In the 1991 Gulf War, the US forces waged an all out Psyops campaign. After dropping 29 million leaflets, and the considerable use of radio, loudspeakers and Commando Solo, 44 per cent of Iraqi army deserted i.e. approximately 80,000 soldiers.
8. An opinion poll showed that 64 per cent of the military officers strongly agreed or somewhat agreed that 'news media coverage of the events in Vietnam harmed the war effort'. See: Aukofer, F. & Lawrence, W. (1995). *America's Team, the Odd Couple: A Report on the Relationship between the Media and the Military*. Nashville, TN: Freedom Forum First Amendment Center), p. 31.
9. This quest was further reinforced whenever there was negative media coverage of US military operations such as Peter Arnett's Al-Amiriya coverage in 1991, or the Black Hawk incident that ended the US military presence in Somalia in 1994. These episodes were disastrous for the US military because of their impact on the American living rooms.
10. Wheatley, G. and Hayes, R. (1996) *Information Warfare and Deterrence*. Washington DC: National Defense University Press, p. 3.
11. Vallely, P. E., & Aquino, M. A. (1991). From PYOP to MindWar: The Psychology of Victory. In Cooper, W. (Ed.), *Behold a Pale Horse*. Sedona, AZ: Light Technology Publications, pp. 368–380.
12. BBC, The I bomb, (video 30 min, *BBC Horizon* 1995)
13. Szafranski, C. R. (November, 1994). Neocortical Warfare? The Acme of Skill. *Military Review*.
14. Molander, R. C., Riddile, A. S. & Wilson, P. A. (1996). *Strategic Information Warfare: A New Face of War*. Santa Monica, CA: RAND, p. 22–23.
15. Stein, G. J. (1996). Information Attack: Information Warfare in 2025. In *2025 White Papers: Power and Influence*. Maxwell Air Force Base, Alabama: Air University Press, pp. 91–114.
16. Abbreviation of the Military-Industrial-Media-Entertainment Network.
17. The *New York Times* reported in 19 February 2002 that the Pentagon was using the Rendon Group to assist its new propaganda agency, the Office of Strategic Influence (OSI). See: (Dao and Schmitt 2002: A1, A10).
18. Ten Serbian technicians and engineers died in this attack.
19. While in white propaganda the source is known and is usually official; in black propaganda it is concealed and a false source is suggested; in grey propaganda the source is obscured.

20. See: The White House, Office of the Press Secretary, 'Press Conference of the President and Chancellor Helmut Kohl', 9 February 1995, 8.
21. The Occidentalist frame refers to the ideology that tends to blame the 'West' in its entirety, while exonerating Arabs and Muslims from their due responsibilities.

2 Orientalism, Terrorism, and American Media Discourse

1. In 636, the armies of the Roman Emperor Heraclius were defeated in the Levant. Palestine was conquered in 636; Syria and Egypt in 640; Armenia in 693; North Africa in 698; and Spain in 711.
2. The First Crusade stemmed from the preaching of Pope Urban II at the Council of Clermont in 1095. Subsequently, Jerusalem was captured in 1099 and a series of crusader states established at Antioch, Edessa, Tripoli and Jerusalem. However, Jerusalem was recaptured by a Muslim army under Saladin in 1187. The crusaders were decisively defeated with the Muslim capture of Acre in 1291.
3. The Archbishop of Tyre describes as follows the crusaders' mass killing of Muslims and Jews in Jerusalem in 1099: 'regardless of age or condition, they laid low, without distinction, every enemy encountered. Everywhere was frightful carnage, everywhere lay heaps of severed heads […] It was impossible to look upon the vast numbers of the slain without horror; everywhere lay fragments of human bodies, and the very ground was covered with the blood of the slain. […] It is reported that within the Temple enclosure alone about ten thousand infidels perished'. Quoted in Stannard, D. E. (1992). *American Holocaust: The Conquest of the New World*. New York: Oxford University Press, p. 178.
4. Two of the main Muslim historians of that period, namely Ibn al-Qalanisi and Usama ibn Munqidh agree on that particular point. See Christie, N. G. F. (1996). 'The Presentation of the Franks in Selected Muslim Sources from the Crusades of the 12th Century'. M.Litt. dissertation, University St Andrews.
5. Quoted in *Macaulay, Prose and Poetry*, selected by G.M. Young (1957). Cambridge, MA: Harvard University Press, pp. 716–718.
6. According to Foucault, discursive practices delimit the field of objects, defining a legitimate perspective and fixing the norms for the elaboration of concepts. In order to produce a statement in a discourse, one has to adapt to the constraints, focus on a subject and claim authority: 'one would only be in the true if one obeyed the rules of some discursive "policy"'. See Foucault, M. (1971). *The Archaeology of Knowledge & The Discourse on Language*. London: Vintage, p. 224.
7. Foucault points out that: 'each society has its regime of truth, its "general politics" of truth: that is, the types of discourse which it accepts and makes function as true; the mechanisms and instances which enable one to distinguish true and false statements (…); the status of those who are charged with saying what counts as true'. See Gordon, C. (Ed.). (1980). *Michel Foucault: Power/Knowledge*. Hertfordshire, UK: Harvester Wheatsheaf, p. 131.
8. Edward Said supports this argument with numerous examples of racist and imperialist views contained in the Orientalist discourse. For example, Said analysed Arthur James Balfour's 1910 speech to the House of Commons, which claimed that

Egyptians 'are a subject race, dominated by a race that knows them and what is good for them better than they could possibly know themselves' (Said 1979: 35). Thus, Said explains that Balfour's supremacy was associated with British knowledge of Egypt and not principally with military or economic power.

9. The passage, in the English translation published by the Vatican, is as follows: 'Show me just what Muhammad brought that was new and there you will find things only evil and inhuman, such as his command to spread by the sword the faith he preached' (Pope Benedict XVI, 2006).
10. Lebanon's President is Christian by the terms of the Lebanese constitution despite the fact that the two thirds of the country's inhabitants are Muslims. Likewise, the Christian Coptic community in Egypt is well represented in power, and has many ministers which hold key jobs. They have enjoyed their religious and cultural freedoms since ancient times.
11. For example, the US President Theodore Roosevelt, a strong proponent of manifest destiny, intervened militarily in places as diverse as Cuba, the Philippines, Puerto Rico, and the Panama Canal zone, while invoking ideas of racial superiority to suppress 'minor' peoples (i.e. native Americans, Mexicans, Filipinos etc.).
12. The king of Morocco, Muhammad Ben Abdullah, officially recognised the American government in 1777, only a few months after independence. The United States established a consulate in Morocco in 1797.
13. Riley's story of despair and hope has influenced many American statesmen in history. When Abraham Lincoln listed the books that had most influenced him, one was *Sufferings in Africa* by James Riley. Riley's account of his life as a slave is thought to have influenced Abraham Lincoln's attitude toward slavery in the United States.
14. These aspirations were considered as 'manifestations of oil-inspired economic arrogance, anti-Semitic rabble-rousing, or oriental affinity for revolutionary despotism' (Little 2002: 314).
15. In its editorial of 6 August 1954, the *New York Times* wrote:

    Underdeveloped countries with rich resources now have an object lesson in the heavy cost that must be paid by one of their members which goes berserk with fanatical nationalism. It is perhaps too much to hope that Iran's experience will prevent the rise of Mossadeghs in other countries, but that experience may at least strengthen the hands of more reasonable and more farseeing leaders [...] (quoted in Chomsky 1992: 50).

16. See: Glidden, H. W. (1972). The Arab World. *American Journal of Psychiatry, 128*, pp. 984–988.
17. See: Buruma, I. (2004, October). Lost in Translation. *New Yorker*. See also: Gresh, A. (September, 2004). A L'Origine d'un Concept. *Le Monde Diplomatique*.
18. See: Lewis, Bernard, Orientalism: An Exchange, in *New York Review of Books*, no. 29, 1982, pp. 49–56.
19. Occidentalism is a recent field of study of the discourse constructing Europe or 'the West'. Bryan Turner states that Occidentalism rejects anything associated with

the West, which means the implicit abandonment of the heritage of modernity. See Turner, B. S. (1997). *Orientalism, Postmodernism and Globalism*. New York: Routledge.
20. Nonetheless, Orientalist ideas imbued news media and popular literature throughout the 1980s. For example, the former war correspondent David Pryce-Jones in *The Closed Circle: an Interpretation of the Arabs* (1989) claimed to show 'how Arab society functions'. According to him, Arab society and politics derive from the 'closed circle' of tribalism, excessive reliance on violence, self-aggrandisement, and other unsavoury characteristics. David Pryce-Jones asserted that 'there is no acceptable definition of a modern Muslim' (p. xi); 'an Arab democrat is not even an idealization, but a contradiction in terms' (p. 406); and 'Islam and representative democracy are two [...] incompatible ideals' (p. xi).
21. I define the term Islamist as follows: Organisations of dedicated and trained Muslims, who call on others to be more observant and who are willing to struggle against corruption and social injustice. See Esposito, J. L. (1998). *Islam: The Straight Path* (3rd ed.). Oxford: Oxford University Press, p. 170.
22. Examples include: the attack on a restaurant near an airbase in Spain which killed 18 American soldiers; the hijacking of TWA 847, in July 1985; and the Achille Lauro incident, in which Palestinian militants commandeered a cruise ship and killed a disabled American man.
23. Other researchers reached similar conclusions. For example, Ted Robert Gurr (1994) has employed systematic analyses to assess the validity of Huntington's perspective for explaining violence within states. His findings disprove Huntington's claims. Of the 50 most serious ethno-political conflicts being fought in 1993–1994, only 18 meet Huntington's criteria. In the Middle East, for example, only one active internal conflict (Palestinians in the Occupied Territories) was waged between peoples from different civilisations, while five (two in Iraq, and one each in Iran, Morocco, and Turkey) were within a single civilisation. Another study that tested Huntington's hypotheses regarding states' involvement in militarised interstate disputes between 1950 and 1992, concluded that states in four of the eight civilisations (singled out by Huntington) fought more among themselves than with states in other civilisations. See: Russett, B., Oneal, J. R., & Cox, M. (2000). Clash of Civilizations: Realism and Liberalism Déjà Vu? *Journal of Peace Research*, 37(5): 589, 602.
24. It is believed that during the Roman occupation of Palestine (around 67–73 CE), a Judean movement known as the *sicarii* began an indiscriminate war against its enemies. In this massive revolt against Rome, the *sicarii* would use terrorist tactics against their less zealous co-religionists. Violence included the burning of palaces, the torching of public archives and granaries, and the poisoning of wells. See: Weinberger, J. (2003). Defining Terror. *Seton Hall Journal of Diplomacy and International Relations*, (Winter/Spring), 64.
25. See, for example, the description of terrorists in Netanyahu, B. (1986) *Terrorism: How the West Can Win*. New York: Farrar, Straus, Giroux.
26. The faces conducting the new phase of the 'War on Terror' were also not new; John Negroponte, the overseer of the actual 'War on Terror' in Iraq, ran the operations against Nicaragua. Donald Rumsfeld, himself was Reagan's special envoy to the Middle East during Reagan's 'War on Terror' there. Likewise Elliott Abrams,

who was implicated in the Iran-contra affair, was appointed by Bush II 'to lead the National Security Council's office for Near East and North African affairs'. (Chomsky, 2003: 96, 106–107).

27. According to this definition, populism is not simply an offshoot of other ideologies (such as nationalism, neo-liberalism etc.). By claiming it reflects the pure and undiluted will of the people, populism can easily work with ideologies of both Right and Left.
28. http://www.albasrah.net/moqawama/english/iraqi_resistance.htm
29. Sometimes, the alternative discourse becomes prevalent when official counter-terrorist strategies have proved counter-productive.
30. This report was published by The Project for a New American Century (PNAC) in September 2000; one year prior to the suicide attacks of September 11.
31. In a previous article, Pipes asserts that '[t]he Muslim population in this country [the US] is not like any other group, for it includes within it a substantial body of people – many times more numerous than the agents of Osama bin Laden – who share with the suicide hijackers a hatred of the United States and the desire, ultimately, to transform it into a nation living under the strictures of militant Islam' (Pipes 2001).

3 CNNI Framings of Middle East Conflict, 1991–2001

1. Robert Edward Turner III was born on 19 November 1938 in Cincinnati, Ohio.
2. These are portable satellite dishes which can be easily assembled by two people.
3. On CNN and other media outlets, this period was commonly termed 'Desert Shield'. This operation was announced by President George H. W. Bush as a 'wholly defensive' mission to prevent Iraq from invading Saudi Arabia. Subsequently, US troops moved into Saudi Arabia on 7 August 1990.
4. The Kuwaiti government hired the public relations firm Hill & Knowlton to spread media stories that influenced the American opinion in favour of war against Iraq. For example, the firm arranged for an appearance before Congress members, in which a woman identified herself as a nurse working in the Kuwait City hospital, and told the members that Iraqi soldiers had pulled babies out of incubators and had let them die on the floor. This story was referred to by leading Congress and Senate members to support a military action against Iraq. Later, the Kuwaiti baby story was revealed to be a fabrication. The woman who had testified was in fact the daughter of the Kuwaiti ambassador to the United States (MacArthur 1992 58–60).
5. UN Security Council Resolution 678 dealt with the invasion of Kuwait by Saddam Hussein's Iraq. Voted on 29 November 1990, it gave Iraq a withdrawal deadline until 15 January 1991.
6. The Persian Gulf War has from this Orientalist perspective an antiseptic nature destined to clean the world from this sub-people. Edward J. Ingebretsen claims that constructing demons is part of some sort of 'pedagogy of fear', which is apparently a popular American narrative form. This narrative 'justifies otherwise unacceptable violence by de-humanising and demonising the other' (quoted in Gunn 2004).

7. http://archives.cnn.com/2001/US/11/06/gen.attack.on.terror/
8. The documentary depicted Sairah Shah's (a British television journalist of Afghan origin) returning to her father's birthplace in rural Afghanistan. Initially produced for Channel 4 in Britain in the spring of 2001, this documentary was first broadcast by CNN in the summer 2001. It was subsequently re-broadcast at the start of the Afghan campaign. It included gruesome images and sensationalist editing. For example, three Afghan girls related the story of their parents' murder and their subsequent rape. In another segment, images of three women bundled into the back of a truck, then thrown to the ground and shot point blank.
9. During the British colonial era in South Asia, there were many instances where women's issues, such as sati (the practice of widows immolating themselves on their husbands' funeral pyres), and child marriage were used as justifications for British expansionism (Abu-Lughod, 2004: 784).
10. Examples include personalities such as Senator John McCain, Henry Kissinger, Lawrence Eagleburger, James Baker and Jeanne Kirkpatrick.

4 The Origins of Modern Arab Nationalism

1. The Rightly Guided Caliphs or The Righteous Caliphs is a term used in Sunni Islam to refer to the first four caliphs that ruled after the death of the Prophet Muhammad. They are called so because they have been seen as model Muslim leaders by Sunni. They were all close companions of Muhammad, and their succession was not hereditary.
2. For extensive studies on the important scientific contributions by Arab/Muslim scholars see: (Pormann and Savage-Smith 2007) and (Zaimeche 2002).
3. The Omayyad Caliphate (based in Damascus; 661–750), the Abbasid Caliphate (based in Baghdad; 750–1258), and the Ottoman Empire (1299–1922) ruled an area that included most of the Arab countries as they are known today.
4. The Ottoman Empire was particularly weakened by the Russian annexation of Crimea (1783), Georgia (1800) and Baku (1806). Later Russian annexation of Central Asian territories such as Khokand, Bukhara and Khiva hit hard the status of the Ottoman Empire as a major player in the world stage.
5. In 1915, the British Government represented by Sir Henry McMahon promised Sherif Hussein (the leader of Mecca and King of the Arabs) Arab control over the whole of areas to be liberated from Turkey.
6. For instance the Mufti of Jerusalem and Palestinian Arab nationalist Mohammad Amin al-Husayni (1895–1974) fought against the establishment of Israel and closely collaborated with Nazi Germany during World War II. Similarly, in Iraq General Rashid Ali, who had the support of the Nazis, led a short-lived attempt in April 1941 to overthrow the pro-British Iraqi Prime Minister Nuri Said Pasha.
7. It should be noted that prior to the formal unification of Germany into a politically and administratively integrated nation state on 18 January 1871, there were numerous independent German states. The transition of the German-speaking states into one federated organisation of states occurred after numerous

attempts throughout history. Similarly, Italy was a patchwork of independent governments, either directly ruled or strongly influenced by the prevailing European powers such as Austria and France. Eventually, under the influence of unification leaders, such as Giuseppe Mazzini and Giuseppe Garibaldi, and after series of wars, Victor Emmanuel II became the first king of a united Italy in 1870.

8. The Arab League was initially founded by seven states (Egypt, Iraq, Syria, Lebanon, North Yemen, Saudi Arabia, and Transjordan). Some of these were still under formal occupation.
9. The Baghdad Pact (also referred to as CENTO for Central Treaty Organisation) was an alliance established in 1955 between the United States and the United Kingdom on one hand, and Iraq, Turkey, Pakistan, and Iran on the other.
10. The conference met on 18–24 April 1955 in Bandung, Indonesia, and was organised by Indonesia, Egypt, India, Pakistan, Sri Lanka, and Burma. This conference gathered 29 newly independent Asian and African states for the purpose of promoting Afro-Asian cooperation and opposing colonialism.
11. In 1962 a military coup overthrew the royalist government in Yemen. Nasser intervened to support the new republican government against the Saudi-backed royalists, who were attempting to regain control. This undertaking proved to be a great drain on Egypt's financial and military resources. At the height of its involvement, Egypt had 75,000 troops in Yemen. Egypt's intervention also increased inter-Arab tensions, especially between Saudi Arabia and Egypt.
12. Umm Kalthoum is still recognised as the Arab world's most famous and distinguished singer of the twentieth century (Danielson 1998: 199).
13. The Arab world inherited high illiteracy rates from the colonial era. For instance in Algeria, the proportion of literate to the general population plunged from 40 per cent in 1832 (prior to French colonization) to 5 per cent in 1962. Indeed, during the French colonial period in Algeria (1830–1962), French was considered as the language of instruction, and classical Arab was considered to be the reflection of ignorance and was therefore abandoned (Mostari 2005: 40–41).
14. http://www.allied-media.com/Arab-American/al_hayat_arabic_daily_newspaper.htm
15. For example, 14 publications were banned in Egypt in 2000. The order to close them down came in an administrative decree issued by the Governor of Cairo province.
16. MBC received direct financial support from Saudi Arabia's King Fahd. It was founded in London in 1991 by two private entrepreneurs, Sheikh Walid al-Ibrahim (a relative of King Fahd) and Sheikh Saleh Kamel (who will later set up ART). See: (Sakr 2001).
17. ART was founded by Sheikh Saleh Kamel and Saudi Prince Al-Waleed bin Talal. When it started in 1994, ART's offering consisted of four free-to-air channels: one general, one for sports, one for children and another showing only films.
18. Members of the Muslim Brotherhood (MB) were harshly repressed in Egypt during the reign of Nasser. Tens of thousands of alleged MB members were put in prison and tortured in two occasions (1954 and 1966). A few of their leaders such as Sayyid Qutb were hanged.

Notes to pages 102–107

19. As a result of a small-scale insurgency led by Islamists in Syria in 1982, the regime reacted by bombing with tanks and artillery the city of Hama, where some 25,000 people were killed according to Amnesty International estimates.
20. Three major disastrous mistakes were made by the Palestinian Liberation Organisation (PLO):

    Firstly, after the defeat of 1967, when the Palestinians felt they could no longer rely on Arab governments to retrieve back their territories. As a result, the Palestinians became very independent within Jordan. They virtually created a 'state within a state' in that country, eventually controlling several strategic positions. Open fighting with Jordanian state forces erupted in June 1970, and the Palestinians were expelled in great numbers from Jordan.

    Secondly, after having moved to Lebanon in the early 1970s, the PLO, encouraged by the weakness of Lebanon's central government, again operated as an independent state. This state of affairs destabilised Lebanese internal politics, leading to a civil war in 1975. This escalation led to a full-scale Israeli invasion which ended with their siege of Beirut (1982). As a result, Palestinian leaders and their armed contingent were expelled to Tunis (1983).

    Thirdly, during the Gulf War of 1991, the Palestinian leader Yasser Arafat decided to side with Iraq, alienating pro-US Arab states, which were the PLO's main financial backers. At the end of the War and the defeat of Iraq, the PLO was considerably weakened.

21. In Kuwait, Islamists become more involved in elections from 1992. In Turkey, two Islamist parties competed in elections and one of them (the Saadet or Contentment Party) won 48 seats in the 550-member Grand National Assembly. In Indonesia, several Islamist parties have shared power in a succession of fractious cabinets since the June 1999 elections; in Morocco and Bahrain, Islamists made notable gains in the parliamentary elections in the late 1990s and early 2000.
22. Orbit is a Pan-Arab satellite broadcasting network offering over 40 programming services including movies, live sporting events and news. It was founded by Saudi Prince Khaled bin Abdullah bin Abdel-Rahman, a cousin of King Fahd. This channel is currently owned by the Mawarid Group of Saudi Arabia.
23. Tensions originate from the borderline dispute concerning the Hawar Islands; a dispute that has persisted for over 60 years. The dispute was finally settled in March 2001 by the International Court of Justice, which ruled in favour of Bahrain.
24. This incident prompted Qatar to suspend a 1965 border agreement, which in fact had never been ratified. Other incidents in 1993 and 1994 led to a diplomatic row between both countries, and caused Qatar to boycott the November 1994 Gulf summit conference.
25. The Gulf Cooperation Council (GCC) is a trade bloc involving the six Arab Gulf states with many economic and social objectives.
26. Faisal Al-Kasim acknowledges this fact. He wrote: 'Al Jazeera's editorial policy is so lax that I am hardly ever given orders regarding programme content. The station has an even wider scope of freedom than the BBC Arabic radio, where I worked for ten years. I tackle issues that I never even dreamed of covering during my service at the BBC' (Al-Kasim 1999).

27. Saudi Arabia, Algeria and Tunisia bar Al Jazeera from their territory. The Jordanian authorities did the same after a guest on a debate programme criticised the regime in Amman, yet they revoked the decision later.
28. On 31 October 1999, EgyptAir Flight 990, a Boeing 767 flying between JFK Airport in New York City and Cairo, crashed into the Atlantic Ocean off the coast of Nantucket. The pilot, Gameel Al-Batouti, was suspected by US authorities of committing suicide and intentionally crashing the plane. Egyptian officials have strongly disputed that claim.
29. Operation 'Desert Fox' concerns the December 1998 bombing of Iraq. This was a major four-day air strike on Iraqi targets from 16 December to 19 December 1998.
30. Al Jazeera was not only the first Arab media to break the boycott of Israeli Officials; it is among the few in the Arab world that continue to conduct such interviews. See: Gentzkow, M. A., & Shapiro, J. M. (2004). Media, Education, and Anti-Americanism in the Muslim World. *Journal of Economic Perspectives, 18*(3), p. 117.
31. In December 1993, a third round of the *Popular Arab-Islamic Conference* was organised. It was attended by 500 delegates, with Turabi as its Secretary-General. All delegates resolutely opposed American hegemony in the Middle East.
32. Tarek El-Bishri is the author of 20 books on Islam and Arabism, nationalism, democracy and Nasserism, Egyptian politics under the British mandate, secularism and Egypt's judiciary.
33. Fahmy Howeidy is an Egyptian writer who specialises in Arab, Islamic and related political affairs. He joined the pan-Arab newspaper *Al-Ahram* in 1958. He was appointed as the Managing Editor of the Kuwaiti cultural monthly magazine, *Al-Arabi*, he then joined the London-based *Arabia* magazine. He has also published 16 books on issues related to Islamic thought and the state of the Muslim world.
34. The third article of the *Palestinian National Charter* states the following: The Palestinian Arab people has the legitimate right to its homeland and is an inseparable part of the Arab Nation. It shares the sufferings and aspirations of the Arab Nation and its struggle for freedom, sovereignty, progress and unity. For more on the charter, see: http://www.un.int/palestine/PLO/PNA2.html.
35. Arab public sphere traditionally existed in places such as coffeehouses in popular quarters, tribal *diwaniyat* (salons) and mosques (Lynch, 2003: 69).
36. In these instances, Al Qaeda reiterated its Manichean vision of a world divided between believers and infidels. Al Qaeda combines a heavy religious rhetoric with a political agenda that is in collision with US foreign policy. Topping Al Qaeda's grievances is the US military presence near Muslim holy sites. The stationing of US forces in the Middle East, particularly in the Arabian Peninsula near Muslim holy sites, was perceived as a trespass upon Islam's holy land. Also high among Al Qaeda's grievances was the longstanding American bias toward Israel, as well as the destruction of Iraq preceded by the devastating sanctions that killed one million Iraqi civilians (Bergen, 2002: 21–22, 98–101). To change the status quo in relation to these affairs, Al Qaeda opted for the use of armed means, including subversion and terrorism.
37. The 2002 CNN interview was conducted by Al Jazeera journalist, Tayseer Allouni. However, the Qatari-based channel found it was conducted in coercive conditions, and involved predetermined questions. This contravened Al Jazeera's code of ethics.

Notes to pages 117–131

38. The appellation 'Infinite Justice' was culturally insensitive toward millions of Muslims as they consider infinite justice to be the exclusive act of god.
39. President Bush said on 16 September 2001: 'this crusade, this war on terrorism, is going to take awhile.' But 'crusade' carries an extremely negative connotation within the Muslim world, because of the bitterness left after centuries of war against the medieval crusaders. For more on the controversy surrounding this, see: http://www.csmonitor.com/2001/0919/p12s2-woeu.html.

5 The Prospect of War in Iraq: Frames, Propaganda, and Debate

1. The meeting between US President Roosevelt and the Saudi King Abdulaziz took place aboard the USS *Quincy* in Egypt's Great Bitter Lake on 14 February 1945. President Roosevelt was interested in cultivating the friendship of Arab countries because of the need to protect US petroleum interests, but he also tried to persuade the Saudi King to acquiesce to a plan for Jewish emigration to Palestine.
2. As coined by Altheide and Grimes (2005).
3. These videos were not allowed to be broadcast in some countries, even within those close to the United States such as Egypt.
4. The *New York Times* reported on 19 February 2002: 'The new office has begun circulating classified proposals calling for aggressive campaigns that use not only the foreign media and the Internet, but also covert operations.... One of the office's proposals calls for planting news items with foreign media organisations through outside concerns that might not have obvious ties to the Pentagon ... General Worden envisions a broad mission ranging from 'black' campaigns that use disinformation and other covert activities to 'white' public affairs that rely on truthful news releases.... 'It goes from the blackest of black programs to the whitest of white,' a senior Pentagon official said.... Another proposal involves sending journalists, civic leaders and foreign leaders e-mail messages that promote American views or attack unfriendly governments' (Dao and Schmitt 2002).
5. In this it joined Reuters which proscribed the use of the word 'terrorist'.
6. Cameraman Sami Al-Haj was captured by pro-American Afghan warlords. Then he was sold for 5,000 US Dollars to US forces in Afghanistan in late 2001. He was held in extrajudicial detention in Guantanamo Bay in Cuba for over six years. He was released without charge on 1 May 2008 with two other detainees from Sudan.
7. For example, both the BBC (5 Feb. 2003 at 11:01 GMT) and CNN (5 Feb. 2003 at 15:15 GMT) compared the presentation of Secretary of State Powell with the one delivered by Ambassador Aldai Stevenson at an emergency session of the Security Council on 25 October 1962. During this session, Stevenson confronted the Russian Ambassador with photographic evidence of Russian missiles in Cuba.
8. The list of the 'the coalition of the willing' as identified in the US Senate's 27 March 2003 resolution included: Afghanistan, Albania, Australia, Azerbaijan, Colombia, Czech Republic, Denmark, El Salvador, Eritrea, Estonia, Ethiopia, Georgia, Hungary, Iceland, Italy, Japan, Latvia, Lithuania, Macedonia, Marshall Islands,

255

Micronesia, Netherlands, Nicaragua, Philippines, Palau, Poland, Romania, Slovakia, South Korea, Solomon Islands, Spain, Turkey, United Kingdom and Uzbekistan.
9. Only Australia, Denmark, Poland and Spain provided military forces.
10. Marshall Islands, Micronesia, Palau and Solomon Islands do not have standing armies.
11. This quote was translated from Arabic.
12. In many cases, the police outnumbered protesters such as in Egypt. See: Hassan, A. F. (2003). Police Outnumber Antiwar Protesters in Cairo [Electronic Version] from: http://worldpress.org/Mideast/922.cfm.
13. The Inmarsat GAN phone has the size of a small briefcase, including the antenna.
14. The term 'Soft Power' was first coined by Joseph Nye of Harvard University in his book, *Bound to Lead: The Changing Nature of American Power* (1991). Soft Power resides in the set of values, culture, policies and institutions which let other nations follow your leadership. This power is expressed through means such as diplomacy, strategic communications, foreign assistance, civic action and economic reconstruction and development.

6 Hostilities Begin: 'Decapitation Strike', 'Shock and Awe', and Contesting Realities

1. CNN's Wolf Blitzer first referred to A-Day on 21 March 2003 when interviewing CNN's military analyst General David Grange. He asked: 'We have been told that this is the start of what the Pentagon is now calling A-Day, the letter A, the start of the aerial bombardment, a massive air campaign expected over the next 24 to 48 hours, perhaps as many as 3,000 so-called smart bombs, precision-guided weapons, laser-guided weapons as well as satellite-guided weapons.' For the complete transcript, see: http://transcripts.cnn.com/TRANSCRIPTS/0303/21/bn.02.html.
2. See for example his interview on CBS Evening News (24 January 2003) which can be accessed online: http://www.cbsnews.com/stories/2003/01/24/eveningnews/main537928.shtml.
3. Following the Watergate Scandal, the United States Senate established the Select Committee to Study Governmental Operations with Respect to Intelligence Activities, chaired by Senator Frank Church in 1975. The committee investigated illegal intelligence gathering operations conducted by the CIA and the FBI. The Church Committee found five confirmed occurrences of direct US involvement in assassinations or assassination attempts against foreign leaders [Patrice Émery Lumumba – the first legally elected Prime Minister of the Republic of the Congo (killed in 1961); Rafael Trujillo – the dictator of the Dominican Republic (killed in 1961); Ngo Dinh Diem – South Vietnam's Prime Minister (killed in 1963); Iraq's President Abdul Karim Qasim (killed in 1963); Salvador Allende – the democratically elected President of Chili (killed in 1973)]. As a result of the Church Committee proceedings, President Gerald Ford formally issued the Executive Order number 11,905 in 1976. This document stated: 'No employee of the United States Government shall engage in, or conspire to engage in political assassinations'. President Carter and Reagan issued subsequent Executive Orders with minor

modifications to include in the assassination prohibition, contractors and the intelligence agencies (Johnson 1988: 426).
4. The military meso-frame is a sub frame of the conflict frame. It focuses on military prowess in times of war, praises the power of military technology and the courage of the troops.
5. Due to time zone difference, this occurred on 20 March 2003 at 3 a.m. GMT.
6. These quotes by Wolf Blizzer were made a few minutes apart. The second quote was made when CNN confirmed the actual attack.
7. John Burns (CNN guest, *New York Times*):

> It was an astonishing sight, even for those of us who have seen American air power unleashed in Bosnia and Kosovo, Afghanistan and, of course, in Baghdad itself back in 1991. It was something Biblical. It made you think of words like Beelzebub, and Milton. It was just astonishing to see an area of several square miles in an instant begin to explode everywhere. (CNN, 21 March 2003)

8. Nic Robertson (CNN senior international correspondent):

> I have not witnessed anything on this scale before. The multiple detonations, that almost, to be honest, Wolf, it had an Armageddon like feel to it, albeit in a limited area, multiple flashes, detonations that impacted your body, that blew the window open, that blew the plaster off the walls of the room I was in. It was massive, it was awesome, and for people who perhaps didn't have that same degree of knowledge of the weaponry and a certain knowledge that perhaps the location they were in wasn't about to be targeted, it certainly would have been shocking as well. It was – it was awesome is perhaps the only way to describe it, Wolf. (CNN, 22 March 2003)

9. To reiterate: the Orientalist deep frame refers to a form of representation that turns 'Oriental' lands and people into an epistemological construct that is easy to grasp and dominate.
10. The conflict frame emphasises conflict between individuals, groups, or institutions. Typically, this frame takes sides and determines the hero and the villain.
11. The military sub-frame focuses on military prowess in times of war. It praises the power of military technology and the courage of the troops.
12. The liberation sub-frame suggests that the purpose of the military conflict in Iraq was to liberate Iraqi citizens.
13. The pre-emptive war sub-frame suggests that the Iraq conflict was necessary as a pre-emptive measure to prevent the regime of Saddam Hussein from using weapons of mass destruction against the West or to transfer these to terrorist groups.
14. The religious sub-frame is based on 'manifest destiny', which conflates the will of God with the national objectives of the United States. This sub-frame implies that it is the will of God to export the American ethos to the rest of the world.

15. The 'nation-as-person' metaphor made it easy for the American troops and public to understand the rationale behind the war. Indeed, the metaphor personalised the war as one with the Iraqi dictator even though the war killed other Iraqis the United States was supposedly not at war against.
16. As discussed in Chapter 2, Occidentalism is the product of a discourse that constructs a monolithic image of 'the West'. It is the mirror image of Orientalism. Occidentalist views tend to depict everything coming from the West as moral arrogance and foreign ideological hegemony. For example, the influential Iranian intellectual Jalal Al-e Ahmad launched the concept of 'Westoxification' in the 1960s in order to describe the supposedly poisonous effect of Western civilisation on other cultures.
17. There is a large difference between pan-Arabism and Occidentalism. From a historic perspective, pan-Arabists were the allies of the Western Powers against the Turks in World War I (Arab nationalism was initially directed against the Turks because the Ottoman Empire implemented very unpopular policies in the Arab regions). Furthermore, Pan-Arabism drew inspiration from Western nationalisms. Early theoreticians of pan-Arabism, such as George Antonius and Michel Aflak, were directly inspired by the unification of the German and Italian states in the nineteenth century. In addition, pan-Arabists incorporated Western ideologies such as socialism in their programmes. What pan-Arabists rejected was the Western political interference in the Arab region, as exemplified by the 1916 Sykes–Picot agreements.
18. Wolf Blitzer (CNN anchor):

    Aaron, there's no doubt that the original game plan was for a day or two of concerted air strikes before the US ground forces which are amassed in the northern part of Iraq, would move in – the northern part of Kuwait, that is – would move in. (CNN, 19 March 2003)

19. Christiane Amanpour (CNN chief international correspondent):

    There has been a lot of psychological warfare. We have heard a lot about that, electronic warfare, and other kinds of psychological pressure to try to influence the Iraqi military not to fight and to take up non-offensive positions. (CNN, 19 March 2003)

20. At the operational level, psychological operations are conducted 'prior to, during, and following war or conflict to promote the commander's effectiveness'. (Department of the Navy 2000: 2)
21. Senator Joseph Lieberman:

    This is all about one evil dictator who possesses brutal weapons, with which he will threaten and hurt a lot of people, including a lot of Americans, unless we take them away from him. (CNN, 19 March 2003)

22. Aaron Brown (CNN anchor)

    As Jamie reported, it appears to be an attack on a leadership bunker or a place where perhaps Saddam Hussein was. (CNN, 19 March 2003)

23. In fact, this imagery was wrong. The Iraqi president was not fond of using bunkers because they were built by French engineers. Instead, he preferred the use of average villas as command and control structures, and changed them on a daily basis.
24. As a matter of fact, the US used nuclear bombs against Japan in World War II, deployed biological weapons in the Korean War, and used chemical weapons in the Vietnam War.
25. May Ying Welsh (Freelancer):

    I was able to speak with a woman who lives in the apartment building next to me. She told me, she was absolutely terrified. (CNN, 21 March 2003)

26. See Department of Defense News Briefing – Secretary Rumsfeld And Gen. Myers. 21 March 2003. The transcript can be found at: http://www.defenselink.mil/transcripts/transcript.aspx?transcriptid=2074.
27. This reflects a process whereby people experience a state of crisis but then turn to God for the crisis to be resolved. This rhetoric is very powerful in the Middle East for religion is deeply rooted in the common consciousness.
28. A dissolve is an editing technique in which a fade-in is superimposed on a fade-out. See: Mamer, B. (2008). *Film Production Technique: Creating the Accomplished Image* (5 ed.): Cengage Learning, p. 427.
29. During the conflict, numerous targets were hit by US A10 Thunderbolt aircraft, which are equipped with conventional missiles, but also with guns that fire rounds of depleted uranium (DU). The use of DU by coalition forces was confirmed by US Central Command on 26 March 2003. See: United Nations Environment Programme. (2003). Desk Study on the Environment in Iraq. Accessed on: 14 November 2009; http://www.unep.org/pdf/iraq_ds_lowres.pdf., pp. 80–81.
30. This was mentioned during the abovementioned Department of Defense News Briefing on 21 March 2003. See: http://www.defenselink.mil/transcripts/transcript.aspx?transcriptid=2074.
31. Amanpour's quote revealed some of the contradictions which underpinned the Pentagon's framing of the conflict. On one hand, the military frame depicted the might of the US war machine as in the bombardment of Iraqi cities. On the other hand, the humanitarian frame depicted American troops as benefactors helping the suffering Iraqis.
32. This phrase was employed twice by Adnan Charif (Al Jazeera anchor) on 21 March 2003.

7 Journalists as Combatants: US Bombing of Al Jazeera's Office and the Palestine Hotel

1. Al Jazeera aired a 30-second video of exuberant Iraqis celebrating over the corpses of two dead British servicemen. The anchor apologised for the 'horrific' pictures, explaining that 'it is in the interests of objectivity that we bring them to you.' Al Jazeera's editor-in-chief, Ibrahim Hilal later explained to the BBC the Arabic

Channel's editorial policy: 'Once we get a bit of information, we have to tell the whole world what is really going on inside this war even if it is horrible because this is part of our transparent job. What we are doing is showing the reality. We didn't invent the bodies; we didn't make them in the graphics unit. They are shots coming in from the field. This is the war.' For more on this, see: http://news.bbc.co.uk/2/hi/programmes/correspondent/3047501.stm.

2. In contrast to story allegations put forward by the Pentagon's info-warriors, Jessica Lynch was simply injured in a traffic accident. Her gun jammed and she never used it. Later, she was taken to an Iraqi hospital where she received care and was never subjected to torture. The doctor treating her was the one calling US authorities to let them know about her status and location. He also informed them that there were no Iraqi soldiers around.

3. Seven months after the rescue story broke, *Saving Jessica Lynch,* a movie based on Lynch's ordeal was aired on NBC. Its title referred to the 1998 Steven Spielberg film, *Saving Private Ryan,* an all-time blockbuster. The 9 November 2003 broadcast of *Saving Jessica Lynch* attracted a total audience of 14.9 million, ranking it 16th among the top 20 over-the-air television programmes for that week (*Entertainment Weekly*, 21 November 2003).

4. In a *Washington Post* article titled 'Clashes at Key River Crossing Bring Heaviest Day of American Casualties', questions were asked about the adequacy of the Pentagon strategies for this campaign. (Glasser and Chandrasekaran 2003: A1). Similarly, CBS Pentagon correspondent David Martin stated on 1 April 2003: 'There's beginning to be a credibility gap between what officials here in the Pentagon are saying about the progress of the war and what commanders in the field are saying.'

5. In an article for the *Washington Post* titled 'Cakewalk in Iraq', Kenneth Adelman, a national security official who served on the Pentagon's Defense Policy Board, promised that the invasion of Iraq would represent no problems for US forces (Adelman 2002: A27).

6. For example, Michael R. Gordon wrote an article for the *New York Times* titled 'Goal of US: Avoid a Siege'. In this article, he quoted an unnamed high-ranked Pentagon official as saying: 'The enemy is taking what forces he can muster and is ordering them back into the city. He is bringing in the Republican Guard for a last stand. We have been trying to kill anything that is moving toward the city. We don't want a big siege at the end of this' (Gordon 2003).

7. For example, Jo Wilding wrote an article for the *Guardian* titled 'Too many civilian casualties' in which she expressed criticism of the mounting civilian casualties as the result of US bombardment (Wilding, 29 March 2003).

8. This corresponded to 10:30 p.m. ET (the day before).

9. Abu Dhabi TV correspondent Shaker Hamed broadcast an emergency call for help: '25 journalists and technicians belonging to Abu Dhabi TV and Al Jazeera are surrounded in the offices of Abu Dhabi TV in Baghdad'. Hamed appealed on air to the Red Cross, the International Organization of Journalists, Reporters Sans Frontières, and the Arab Journalists Union 'to intervene quickly to pull us out of this zone where missiles and shells are striking in an unbelievable way' (Foerstel 2006: 98).

10. Omar Al-Issawi (Al Jazeera correspondent):

    What we know for sure is that two months ago, Al Jazeera communicated to the Department of Defense the exact GPS coordinates of our bureau in Baghdad ... the letter was addressed from our managing director to Victoria Clarke at the Department of Defense. (CNN, 8 April 2003)

11. This was the title of the first news item on Al Jazeera after the shelling of the Palestine Hotel (8 April 2003, 12:00 Baghdad Time). Al Jazeera Anchor Jumana Namur was the first to use it. The title was used in subsequent news segments all day long.

12. The attack on the Abu Dhabi TV premises took place at about the same time as the attack on Al Jazeera. At first, surviving Al Jazeera staff sought refuge at the adjacent villa of Abu Dhabi TV, which then came under US attack.

13. The fog of war is a term used to describe an ambiguous military situation. The term itself was used few times on CNN during its Iraq War coverage. For example, on 7 April 2003 Anderson Cooper (CNN anchor) stated: 'We'll try to check in with you a little bit later on. In the fog of war – and we have heard so much about the fog of war – things can go terribly wrong. It happened today in northern Iraq, where US special forces are working with Kurdish fighters' (CNN, 7 April 2003 00:00 ET).

14. On 22 November 2005, the UK's *Daily Mirror* newspaper revealed that a 'secret British government memo said British Prime Minister Tony Blair had talked President George W. Bush "out of bombing" Al Jazeera in April 2004.' The memo was leaked by civil servants who were subsequently charged in court under Britain's Official Secrets Act. Following the original report, British Attorney General Lord Goldsmith warned news outlets from publishing any further details about the memo, or else they would be prosecuted under the Official Secrets Act. For more, see: Kevin Maguire (23 November 2005), Law Chief Gags the Mirror on Bush Leak at: http://www.mirror.co.uk/news/top-stories/tm_objectid=16401707&method=full&siteid=115875-name_page.html.

15. The Geneva Convention IV and Protocol I (1949) protects civilian population, prohibits attacking civilian objectives, and insists that the conflicting parties take all precautionary measures to avoid civilian casualties and losses.

16. See: Protocols Additional to the 1949 Geneva Convention, Articles 50 and 79.

8 Liberation vs. Occupation: The Toppling of Saddam's Statue

1. Paula Zahn (CNN anchor):

    And from the bottom part of the screen, we can see several more people trying to scale up the base of that statue.
    Corporal Paul Harris:
      Yes.
    Paula Zahn (CNN anchor):
      This is really extraordinary to watch. (CNN, 9 April 2003)

2. Corporal Paul Harris:

   Well, I just see a lot of jubilation right now, especially when we first rolled in, and everybody's being patient, waiting for this rope to get round Saddam, and that's showing, you know, that we're taking it to him, we're going to keep taking it to him as long as we can. As long as he's here, we're not done. (CNN, 9 April 2003)

3. Paula Zahn (CNN anchor):

   How many people – we're looking at a shot now of it appears to be maybe some journalists and some Iraqi civilians standing underneath the statue of Saddam Hussein. How many people, would you say, are out there right now?

   Corporal Paul Harris:

   I'd say about at least 70. Everybody else is just around on the streets, talking to the Marines. (CNN, 9 April 2003)

4. Simon Robinson (Guest from *Time*):

   I'm on that square where you can see the statue with the rope around its neck. Looking at Marines, there are a lot of – I'd say there's around 1,000 Iraqis in all in the whole area. There's Iraqis picking little yellow flowers and coming up and giving them to Marines. A lot of the Marines, I think, are still nervous. (CNN, 9 April 2003)

5. It should be noted that the Pentagon faced a similar situation earlier in the war. During the battle of Umm Qasr, US Marines had raised the American flag there but were ordered to lower it down. At first CNN did not air news of raising the flag at Umm Qasr, but reported five hours later that the Marines had brought the flag down. CNN anchor Paula Zahn explained at that time that the Pentagon ordered the flag lowered out of respect for the local Iraqi citizenry (CNN, 21 March 03).

6. This flag had three stripes, of red, white, and black, with three green stars in the white stripe. It was adopted on 31 July 1963. The meaning of the three stars was interpreted as being the three tenets of the Ba'ath party motto, namely Unity, Freedom, and Socialism. It was altered on 13 January 1991 by Saddam Hussein. The words of 'God is great' between the stars were written in Saddam's own handwriting. This addition was supposed to garner wartime support from previously outlawed religious Iraqi leaders, and to garner support from the Islamic world against the United States.

7. During Rumsfeld's December 1983 visit, he met with Saddam, and the two discussed regional issues of mutual interest, shared enmity toward Iran and Syria, and the US's efforts to find alternative routes to transport Iraq's oil after the original routes were threatened by Iran. In his March 1984 visit, Rumsfeld discussed with Iraqi officials loans for Iraq, the alternative pipeline through Jordan, and the vigorous effort to cut off arms exports to Iran. Rumsfeld also conveyed to Iraq an offer from Israel to provide assistance against Iran; an offer which was rejected (Battle 2003).

8. Some authors highlighted the American responsibility in starting this conflict. The US ambassador to Iraq, April Glaspie, met with Saddam in an emergency meeting on 25 July 1990. In spite of the escalating tension between Iraq and Kuwait, Ambassador Glaspie maintained a conciliatory line with Iraq, indicating that the United States would not take any position on the Iraq–Kuwait boundary dispute and did not want to become involved. This ambiguous position was interpreted by many (including Saddam Hussein) as a green light for Iraq to settle his dispute with Kuwait in his own terms (Palast 2007: 79–82).
9. After the time-break in this footage, CNN put out a short edited version of the situation at Firdos Square. It consisted of Iraqis trying to topple the Statue, then Iraqis were seen celebrating, and finally the pre-gulf war flag was seen to envelop the head of the sculpture.
10. In books like *The Hero with a Thousand Faces* (1949), *The Inner Reaches of Outer Space* (1987) and *The Power of Myth* (1988), Joseph Campbell wrote about the story-telling structure he found while studying myths and legends of many cultures. He called this structure 'The Hero's Journey' because heroes seem to share the same journey across cultures, namely a journey of transformation which leads them through great movements of separation, descent, ordeal, and return.
11. The US news networks adopted the master narrative even in their web pages. CNN's 'War in Iraq' web pages put this notice at the top of the main page: 'This page was archived in May 2003 when President Bush declared an end to major combat'(CNN.com 2003).
12. Raising the flag on Iwo Jima is a historic photograph taken on 23 February 1945, by Joe Rosenthal. It depicts US soldiers raising the flag of the United States atop Mount Suribachi during the Battle of Iwo Jima in World War II. However, Rosenthal actually captured the second flag-raising event of the day. The first one, the real one, took place soon after the position was captured early in the morning of 23 February 1945.
13. A partial transcript of the briefing is available at: http://www.abc.net.au/am/content/2003/s828805.htm. An AFP press release is also reporting on the above-mentioned briefing, see: http://www.smh.com.au/articles/2003/04/10/1049567773284.html.
14. To reiterate, the conflict frame emphasises conflict between individuals, groups, or institutions. Typically, this frame takes sides and determines the hero and the villain.
15. One should, nevertheless, acknowledge the subtle anti-Saddam rhetoric of Al Jazeera's correspondent Mohamed Ould Fal; some of his comments may well have been understood as supportive of Saddam, however, when he referred to resistance this was not because of Iraqis' loyalty to Saddam, but because of the predominant feelings against Western occupation. His question about Saddam being an American dictator would have been picked up by large segments of viewers because this perception had been propagated for decades by Saddam's internal and external foes, and was quite widespread.

Conclusion

1. Al-Chazli belonged to the Nasser Era. He became an Egyptian war hero during the 1973 Arab–Israeli War when he successfully led the Egyptian Forces' breaching of the Bar Lev Line and crossing of the Suez Canal. This constituted at that time a major military breakthrough.
2. According to Sa'eda Kilani, 'One of Al Jazeera reporters in Iraq had been physically assaulted by former Information minister Mohamed Saeed As-Sahhaf for daring to broadcast events which cast the regime in an unfavorable light'. (Kilani 2004: 144–145).

Postscript

1. For a full list of military analysts involved in the programme, see: http://www.sourcewatch.org/index.php?title=Pentagon_military_analyst_program.
2. Sami Al-Haj was arrested during the war in Afghanistan by the US forces, and extra-judicially held in Guantanamo Bay for over six years without charge.
3. AJE has been broadcasting in English outside of the United States since 2006, and is not a mere English version of the original Arabic news channel. Although Al Jazeera Arabic and AJE answer to the same director general, and the two channels share content, AJE has its own managing director and director of news. Same observation goes to Al Jazeera America (AJAM), which was another offshoot of the Al Jazeera Media Network that was entirely dedicated to the American market. AJAM was launched on 20 August 2013 to compete with CNN, MSNBC, Fox News, and the likes. However, after persistently registering low ratings, AJAM stopped broadcasting on April 2016. While AJAM had several issues and struggled with television ratings, its online reporting and digital opinion sites have been successful, finding relatively large audiences among American news consumers (Greenwald 2016).

Bibliography

Abdel-Malek, A. (1963). Orientalism in Crisis. *Diogenes*, 44, 103–114.
Abdel-Malek, A. (1977). East Wind: The Historical Position of the Civilization Project. *Review*, 1(summer), 57–64.
Abdelmoula, E. (2012, 7 July). Al Jazeera's Democratizing Role and the Rise of Arab Public Sphere (doctoral dissertation, 2012). University of Exeter. Retrieved from https://ore.exeter.ac.uk.
Abdulhadi, R. (2004). Imagining Justice and Peace in the Age of Empire. *Peace Review*, 16(1), 85–89.
Abrahamian, E. (2003). The US Media, Huntington and September 11. *Third World Quarterly*, 24(3), 529–544.
AbuKhalil, A. A. (2002). *Bin Laden, Islam and America's New "War on Terrorism"*. New York: Seven Stories Press.
Aday, S., Farell, H., Lynch, M., Sides, J., & Freelon, D. (2012). Blogs and Bullets II: New Media and Conflict after the Arab Spring. *United States Institute of Peace*. Retrieved 2 July 2016, from http://www.usip.org/publications/blogs-and-bullets-ii-new-media-and-conflict-after-the-arab-spring.
Aday, S., Livingston, S., & Hebert, M. (2005). Embedding the truth: A cross-cultural analysis of objectivity and television coverage of the Iraq War. *Harvard International Journal of Press & Politics*, 10(1), 3–21.
Adelman, K. (2002). Cakewalk in Iraq [Electronic Version]. *Washingtonpost.com*, Retrieved from http://www.washingtonpost.com/ac2/wp-dyn/A1996-2002Feb12.
Ahiska, M. (2003). Occidentalism. The Historical Fantasy of the Modern. *The South Atlantic Quarterly*, 102(2/3), 351–380.
Ahmed, A. S. (2003). *Islam under Siege*: Oxford, UK: Polity Press.
Ahmed, I. (2003, 21 December). Debunking civilisational clash. *Daily Times*. Retrieved 24 September, 2006, from http://www.dailytimes.com.pk/default.asp?page=story_21-12-2003_pg3_2.
Ainsworth, D. (2000). 24-hour news through the looking glass [Electronic Version]. Retrieved from http://www.berkeley.edu/news/berkeleyan/2000/07/12/news.html.
Ajami, F. (2001, 18 November). What the Muslim World Is Watching. *New York Times Magazine*.
Alamdari, K. (2003). Terrorism cuts across the East and the West: deconstructing Lewis's Orientalism. *Third World Quarterly*, 24(1), 177–186.
Al-Azm, S. J. (2004). Islam, Terrorism and the West Today. *Die Welt des Islams*, 44(1).
Al-Hail, A. (2000). The age of new media: The role of Al Jazeera satellite TV in developing aspects of civil society in Qatar. *Transnational Broadcasting Studies*, 4.

Bibliography

Ali, A. (2000). Islamism: Emancipation, Protest and Identity. *Journal of Muslim Minority Affairs*, 20(1).
Ali, T. (2003). *Bush in Babylon: The Recolonisation of Iraq*. London: Verso.
Al-Issawi, O., & Pattiz, N. (2003). Al Jazeera, Radio Sawa Founders Report on Media in the Middle East. [Electronic Version]. Retrieved from http://www.international.ucla.edu/bcir/article.asp?parentid=5087.
Al Jazeera.net. (2007). Al Ittijah Al Mo'akis. Retrieved from http://www.aljazeera.net/NR/exeres/BE212265-7D56-420A-B99D-82D8624E6D41.htm
Al Jazeera.net. (2007). Hiwar Maftouh. Retrieved from http://www.aljazeera.net/NR/exeres/E66EBD87-4928-495B-979F-F3ADE06E4E87.htm.
Al Jazeera.net. (2007). Minbar Al Jazeera. Retrieved from http://www.aljazeera.net/NR/exeres/B998B21E-1875-437A-A041-E9FD8464FB19.htm.
Al Jazeera-Center-of-Studies (Ed.). (2007). *Islam and the West: For a Better World*. Beirut, Lebanon: Arab Scientific Publishers, Inc.
Al-Kasim, F. (1999). Crossfire: The Arab Version. *Harvard International Journal of Press/Politics*.
Allan, S. (2004). The culture of distance: on-line reporting of the Iraq war. In S. Allan & B. Zelizer (Eds.), *Reporting War: Journalism in War Time* (pp. 347–365). Oxon: Routledge.
Allen, B. (1993). *Truth in Philosophy*. Cambridge, MA: Harvard University Press.
Allen, M. (2002, 25 February). White House angered at plan for Pentagon disinformation *Washington Post*.
Allied-media. (2007). ART demographics [Electronic Version]. Retrieved from http://www.allied-media.com/ARABTV/ARTdemog.htm.
Almond, P. (2003). Western Images of Islam, 1700–1900. *Australian Journal of Politics and History*, 49(3), 412–424.
Al-Rahbi, M. (2002). A Letter from an Arab Woman to Colin Powell [Electronic Version]. Retrieved from http://www.thisissyria.net/2002/12/23/articles.
Al-Rasheed, M. (2011). Sectarianism as Counter-Revolution: Saudi Responses to the Arab Spring. *Studies in Ethnicity and Nationalism*, 11(3), 513–526.
Alterman, J. (1999). Transnational media and social change in the Arab world. Transnational Broadcasting Studies. Retrieved from http://www.tbsjournal.com/Archives/Spring99/Articles/Alterman/alterman.html.
Altheide, D. (1987). Format and Symbols in TV Coverage of Terrorism in the United States and Great Britain. *International Studies Quarterly*, 31, 161–176.
Altheide, D. L. (2004). Consuming Terrorism. *Symbolic Interaction*, 27, 289–308.
Altheide, D. L. (2006). Terrorism and the Politics of Fear. *Cultural Studies, Critical Methodologies*, 6(4), 415–439.
Altheide, D. L., & Grimes, J. N. (2005). War Programming: The Propaganda Project and the Iraq War. *The Sociological Quarterly*, 46, 617–643.
Amanat, A. (2002). Empowered through Violence: The Reinventing of Islamic Extremism In S. Talbott & N. Chanda (Eds.), *The Age of Terror: America and the World after September 11*. New York: Basic Books.
Amin, H. (2002). Freedom as a Value in Arab Media: Perceptions and Attitudes among Journalists. *Political Communication*, 19, 125–135.

Bibliography

Amnesty-International. (2000). AI on human rights and labor rights. In F. J. Lechner & J. Boli (Eds.), *The Globalization Reader* (pp. 187-191). Malden: Blackwell Publishers.

Andersen, R. (2006). *A Century of Media, A Century of War*. New York: Peter Lang.

Anderson, B. (1991). *Imagined Communities: Reflections on the Origin and Spread of Nationalism* (1983 1st Ed.). London: Verso.

Anderson, J. W. (1996). Conspiracy Theories, Premature Entextualization, and Popular Political Analysis. *Arab Studies Journal*.

Anding, K. M. (2003). The technology that helped bring the war in Iraq to your living room. [Electronic Version]. *Millimeter*. Retrieved 10 June 2009 from http://digital-contentproducer.com/mag/video_front_line/.

Anonymous. (2002). *Through Our Enemies' Eyes: Osama Bin Laden, Radical Islam, and the Future of America*. Washington, D.C.: Brassey's.

Antonius, G. (1938). *The Arab Awakening: The Story of the Arab National Movement*. London: H. Hamilton.

Aqtash, N. A., Seif, A., & Seif, A. (2004). Media Coverage of Palestinian Children and the Intifada. *International Communication Gazette*, 66(5), 383-409.

Arkin, W. M. (2002, 24 November). The Military's New War of Words. *Los Angeles Times*.

Armstrong, D. (2002, October). Dick Cheney's Song of America: Drafting a Plan for Global Dominance. *Harper's Magazine*.

Armstrong, K. (1992). *Muhammad, a Western Attempt to Understand Islam*. London: Victor Gollanca Ltd.

Asani, A. S. (2003). A Muslim American Reflects on Pluralism and Islam. *Annals*, 588.

Ascher, W. (1986). The Moralism of Attitudes Supporting Intergroup Violence. *Political Psychology*, 7(3), 403-425.

ASNE. (1999). *The local news handbook*. Reston, Va.: American Society of Newspaper Editors, Readership Issues Committee.

Aukofer, F., & Lawrence, W. (1995). *America's Team, the Odd Couple: A Report on the Relationship between the Media and the Military*. Nashville, TN: Freedom Forum First Amendment Center.

Ayish, M. (2002). Political Communication on Arab World Television: Evolving Patterns. *Political Communication*, 19.

Azran, T. (2004). *Contra-Flow in Global News? A Case Study of US Media's Representation of Al Jazeera*. Paper presented at the annual meeting of the International Communication Association, New Orleans. 27 May 2004. Retrieved on 26 May 2009 from http://www.allacademic.com/meta/p112587_index.html

Baber, Z. (2002). Orientalism, Occidentalism, Nativism. The Culturalist Quest for Indigenous Science and Knowledge. *The European Legacy*, 7(6), 747-758.

Bacevich, A. J. (2002). *American Empire: The Realities and Consequences of US Diplomacy*. Cambridge: Harvard University Press.

Badsey, S. (2000). *Interaction in the Kosovo Conflict March - June 1999*. Paper presented at the Political Studies Association-UK 50th Annual Conference, London.

Baepler, P. M. (2004). The Barbary Captivity Narrative in American Culture. *Early American Literature*, 39(2), 217-246.

Bibliography

Bagdikian, B. (2000). *The Media Monopoly* (6th Ed.). Boston, MA: Beacon Press.

Bahry, L. Y. (2001). The new Arab Media phenomenon: Qatar's Al Jazeera. *Middle East Policy*, 88(12).

Bai, M. (2005, 17 July). The Framing Wars. *New York Times*.

Bailey, T. D., & Grimaila, M. R. (2006). Running the Blockade: Information Technology, Terrorism, and the Transformation of Islamic Mass Culture. *Terrorism and Political Violence*, 18, 523–543.

Baker, S., & Martinson, D. L. (2001). The TARES Test: Five Principles for Ethical Persuasion. *Journal of Mass Media Ethics*, 16(2&3), 148–175.

Bankoff, G. (2003). Regions of Risk: Western Discourses on Terrorism and the Significance of Islam. *Studies in Conflict & Terrorism*, 26, 413–428.

Barakat, H. (1993). *The Arab World: Society, Culture and State*. Berkeley: University of California Press.

Barber, B. R. (1996). *Jihad vs. McWorld*. New York: San Val.

Barry, T., & Lobe, J. (2002). The Men Who Stole the Show. *Foreign Policy in Focus*.

Barstow, D. (2008, 20 April). Behind TV Analysts, Pentagon's Hidden Hand. *New York Times*. Retrieved from: http://www.nytimes.com/2008/04/20/world/americas/20iht-20generals.12156442.html.

Bar-Tal, D. (2005). Societal-Psychological Foundations of Intractable Conflicts. Retrieved 31 October 2007, from: http://www.tau.ac.il/education/homepg/bar-tal/Psychological%20Foundations%20Final%20long.doc.

Barthes, R. (1972). *Mythologies*. London: Paladin.

Barthes, R. (1977). *Image, music, text* (1987 Ed.). London: Fontana.

Bassiouni, C. M. (1981). Terrorism, Law Enforcement and the Mass Media: Perspectives, Problems and Proposals. *Journal of Criminal Law and Criminology*, 72, 1–55.

Batarfi, K. M. (1997, 27 March). Three American "Prestige" Newspapers' Stand toward the Arab-Israeli Conflicts: A Content Analysis of Editorials. Paper presented at the International Communication Division, AEJMC.

Battle, J. (2003). Shaking Hands with Saddam Hussein: The US Tilts toward Iraq, 1980–1984 [Electronic Version]. *National Security Archive*. Retrieved from http://www.gwu.edu/~nsarchiv/NSAEBB/NSAEBB82/.

Baudrillard, J. (2006). Virtuality and Events: The Hell of Power1. *International Journal of Baudrillard Studies*, 3(2).

Baum, M. A. (2004). How Public Opinion Constrains the Use of Force: The Case of Operation Restore Hope. *Presidential Studies Quarterly*, 34(2), 187–227.

BBC 2 (Writer) (2003). War Spin [TV]. In S. Smith (Producer), *Correspondent*: BBC2.

BBC. (2003, 21 July). CBS backs down on Lynch movie. Retrieved 16 October 2007, from http://news.bbc.co.uk/2/hi/entertainment/3083235.stm.

BBC. (2003a). US names 'coalition of the willing' [Electronic Version]. Retrieved from http://news.bbc.co.uk/2/hi/americas/2862343.stm.

BBC Website (2003, 24 May). Al Jazeera defends war reports. Retrieved from http://news.bbc.co.uk/2/hi/programmes/correspondent/3047501.stm.

Bellah, R. N. (1974). Civil Religion in America. In P. H. McNamara (Ed.), *Religion American Style*. New York: Harper and Row.

Bibliography

Bellamy, C. (2001). What is Information Warfare? In R. Matthews & J. Treddenick (Eds.), *Managing the Revolution in Military Affairs*. New York: Palgrave.

Bello, W. (2001). The American Way of War [Electronic Version]. Retrieved 25 October 2007 from http://www.zmag.org/bellowarway.htm.

Benford, R. D. (1993). '"You Could Be the Hundredth Monkey': Collective Action Frames and Vocabularies of Motive within the Nuclear Disarmament Movement". *The Sociological Quarterly*, 43(4), 509–526.

Bennett, W. L. (1990). Toward a Theory of Press-State Relations in the United States. *Journal of Communication*, 40(2), 103–127.

Bennett, W. L., & Lawrence, R. G. (1995). News icons and the mainstreaming of social change. *Journal of Communication*, 45(3), 20–39.

Bennis, P. (2003). *Before and After: US Foreign Policy and the War on Terror*. Moreton-in-Marsh, Gloucs: Arris Publishing.

Benoit, W. L. (1995). *Accounts, Excuses, and Apologies: A Theory of Image Restoration Strategies*. Albany, NY: State University of New York Press.

Berenger, R. D. (Ed.). (2004). *Global Media Go to War*. Seattle: Marquette Books.

Bergen, P. (2001). *Holy War, Inc.: Inside the Secret World of Bin Laden* (2002 Ed.). New York: Free Press.

Berinsky, A., & Kinder, D. (2006). Making sense of issues through media frames: understanding the Kosovo crisis. *Journal of Politics*, 68, 640–656.

Bessaiso, E. (2005). Al Jazeera and the War in Afghanistan: A Delivery System or Mouthpiece? In Zayani, M. (Ed.). *The Al Jazeera Phenomenon: Critical Perspectives on New Arab Media*. (pp. 153–170). Boulder: Paradigm Publishers

Best, S. (2000). Reading Ideology: An Evaluation of the Glasgow Media Group [Electronic Version]. Retrieved 11 December 2008 from http://shaunbest.tripod.com/id8.html.

Best, S., & Kellner, D. (2001). *Postmodern Adventure*. London: Guilford Press.

Besteman, C. (1996). Representing Violence and "Othering" Somalia. *Cultural Anthropology*, 11(1), 120–133.

Bhatnagar, R. (1986). Uses and Limits of Foucault: A Study of the Theme of Origins in Edward Said's 'Orientalism.' Social Scientist. In C. A. Breckenridge & P. v. d. Veer (Eds.), *Orientalism and the Postcolonial Predicament* (1994 Ed.). Pennsylvania: University of Pennsylvania Press.

Bishr, H. (2002). Arab, Western Activists to Send "Human Shields" to Iraq [Electronic Version]. Retrieved from: http://www.islamonline.net/english/news/2002-12/20/article08.shtml.

Black, D. (2004). Terrorism as Social Control. In M. Deflem (Ed.), *Terrorism and Counter-Terrorism: Criminological Perspectives*. Amsterdam: Elsevier.

Black, I. (2011) Al Jazeera boss Wadah Khanfar steps down to be replaced by Qatari royal. *Guardian*. Available at: http://www.theguardian.com/media/2011/sep/20/Al Jazeera-wadah-khanfar-replaced (accessed: 20 February 2014).

Black, J. (2001). Semantics and Ethics of Propaganda. *Journal of Mass Media Ethics*, 16(2&3), 121–137.

Blaufarb, D. S., & Tanham, G. K. (1989). *Who Will Win? A Key to the Puzzle of the Revolutionary War*. New York: Taylor and Francis.

Bibliography

Bleifuss, J. (2001, 9 November). Selling the War. Retrieved from http://inthesetimes.com/issue/26/01/editorial.shtml

Blix, H. (2003). Transcript of Blix's UN presentation [Electronic Version]. Retrieved from CNN.com.

Boyd-Barett, O. (2002). Doubt Foreclosed: US Mainstream Media and September 11, 2001. In D. Demers (Ed.), *Terrorism, Globalization & Mass Communication*. Washington: Marquette Books

Boyd-Barrett, O. (2004). Judith Miller, the *New York Times*, and the Propaganda Model. *Journalism Studies*, 5(4), 436.

Boyd-Barrett, O., & Rantanen, T. (Eds.). (1998). *The Globalization of News*. London. Thousand Oaks. New Delhi: Sage Publications.

Brewer, W. F., & Nakamura, G. V. (1984). The nature and functions of schemas. In R. S. Wyer & T. K. Srull (Eds.), *Handbook of social cognition* (Vol. I, pp. 119–160). Hillsdale, NJ: Lawrence Erlbaum.

Brown, G., & Yule, G. (1983). *Discourse analysis*. Cambridge: Cambridge University Press.

Brown, J. (2003). Why Uncle Ben Hasn't Sold Uncle Sam. *Counterpunch*. 8 April.

Brown, R. (2002). Information Operations, Public Diplomacy & Spin: The United States & the Politics of Perception Management. *Journal of Information Warfare*, 1(3).

Browne, J. (2003). Tuning In. *Sombrilla*, 20(1).

Bucy, E. (2003). Embedded reporting and narrow news: A matter of professional freedom and responsibility. *AEJMC Communication Theory and Methodology Division Newsletter*, 32(3), 3–5.

Burnett, N. (1989). Ideology and propaganda: Toward an integrative approach. In T. J. Smith (Ed.), *Propaganda: A pluralistic perspective* (pp. 127–137).

Burrett, R. (2004). Political Communication, Propaganda and Dissent – The British Tabloid Media and the Iraq Crisis in *University of Manchester Sociology Working Papers*, 40.

Buruma, I. (2004). The Origins of Occidentalism. *The Chronicle of Higher Education*. 50, 22(B10).

BusinessWeek. (2003). Al Jazeera: In an Intense Spotlight [Electronic Version]. Retrieved from http://www.businessweek.com/bwdaily/dnflash/mar2003/nf20030326_0570_db069.htm.

Butko, T. (2006). Terrorism Redefined. *Peace Review*, 18(1), 145–151.

Butler, J. (2003). *Precarious Life. The Powers of Death and Mourning*. London: Verso.

Butler, J. R. (2002). Somalia and the Imperial Savage: Continuities in the Rhetoric of War. *Western Journal of Communication*, 66(1), 1–24.

Byrne, C. (2003a). Iraq: The Most Dangerous War for Journalists [Electronic Version]. *The Guardian*. Retrieved from http://www.guardian.co.uk/media/2003/apr/09/pressandpublishing.iraq.

Byrne, C. (2003b). US soldiers were main danger to journalists, says Simpson [Electronic Version]. *The Guardian*. Retrieved from http://www.guardian.co.uk/media/2003/jun/27/Iraqandthemedia.bbc1.

Bytwerk, R. L. (1989). Western and Totalitarian Views of Propaganda. In T. J. Smith (Ed.), *Propaganda: A Pluralistic Perspective*. New York: Praeger.

Cable-World. (2003). Ratings. *Cable World*.

Bibliography

Calabrese, A. (2005). Casus Belli: US Media and the Justification of the Iraq War. *Television and New Media*, 6(2), 153–175.

Campagna, J. (2005). Arabic Satellite Channels and Censorship. *Transnational Broadcasting Studies*, 14.

Campbell, D. (2001). US buys up all satellite war images [Electronic Version]. Retrieved from http://www.guardian.co.uk/world/2001/oct/17/physicalsciences.afghanistan.

Campbell, D. (2003). Cultural governance and pictorial resistance: reflections on the imaging of war. *Review of International Studies*, 29(Supplement S1).

Campbell, J. C., & Keylin, A. (1976). *The Middle East*. New York: New York Times.

Campbell, K. (2000, 6/1). CNN turns 20. *Christian Science Monitor*, 92, 11.

Campbell, K. (2002, 25 January). TV news moves toward Hollywood star system. *Christian Science Monitor*.

Cappella, J., & Jamieson, K. H. (1997). *The spiral of cynicism: The press and the public good*. New York: Oxford.

Carey, A. (1997). *Taking the Risk Out of Democracy*. Chicago: University of Illinois Press.

Carr, C. (1997). Terrorism as Warfare: The Lessons of Military History. *World Policy Journal*, 13 (winter), 1–12.

Carruthers, S. L. (2000). *The Media at War*. New York: St Martin's Press.

Carter, B., & Barringer, F. (2001, 28 September). Speech and Expression; In Patriotic Time, Dissent is Muted. *New York Times*.

Casson, R. W. (1983). Schemata in Cognitive Anthropology. *Annual Review of Anthropology* 12, 429–462.

Castells, M. (2000). *The rise of the network society* (2nd Ed.). Oxford: Blackwell Publishers.

Castonguay, J. (1997). The Gulf War TV Super Bowl [Electronic Version]. *Bad Subjects*, 35. Retrieved from: http://eserver.org/bs/35/castonguay.html.

Cavanagh, J., & Mader, J. (Eds.). (2002). *Alternatives to economic globalization: A better world is possible – a report of the international forum on globalization*. San Francisco: Berrett-Koehler Publishers.

Cere, R. (2002). "Islamophobia" and the Media in Italy. *Feminist Media Studies*, 2(1).

Chalaby, J. K. (2003). Television for a New Global Order. *Gazette: The International Journal for Communication Studies*, 65(6), 457–472.

Chan, S. (2003a). Massive Anti-War Outpouring [Electronic Version]. *CBSNews.com*. Retrieved from http://www.cbsnews.com/stories/2003/02/16/iraq/main540782.shtml.

Chan, S. (2003b). Iraq Faces Massive US Missile Barrage; Plan Calls For Firing Up To 800 Cruise Missiles In First 2 Days Of War [Electronic Version]. *CBSNews.com*. Retrieved from http://www.cbsnews.com/stories/2003/01/24/eveningnews/main537928.shtml.

Chapelier, C., & Demleitner, A. (2004). Pioneering satellite TV channels energise Arab media market. *The Channel*, 7(4).

Chediac, J. (1992). The Massacre of Withdrawing Soldiers on "The Highway of Death". In R. Clark (Ed.), *War Crimes: A Report on US War Crimes Against Iraq*.

Bibliography

Cherkaoui, T. (2014). Al Jazeera's Changing Editorial Perspectives and the Saudi-Qatari Relationship. *The Political Economy of Communication*, 2(1), 17–32. Retrieved from: http://polecom.org/.

Cherribi, S. (2006). From Baghdad to Paris: Al Jazeera and the Veil. *The Harvard International Journal of Press/Politics*, 11(2), 121–138.

Chinni, D. (2003). Jessica Lynch: Media Myth-making in the Iraq War [Electronic Version]. *Journalism.org*. Retrieved from www.journalism.org/resources/research/reports/war/postwar/lynch.asp.

Chiozza, G. (2002). Is There a Clash of Civilizations? Evidence from Patterns of International Conflict Involvement, 1946–97. *Journal of Peace Research*, 39(6).

Chomsky, N. (1989). *Necessary Illusions: Thought Control in Democratic Societies*. Boston: South End Press.

Chomsky, N. (1992). *Deterring Democracy*. London: Vintage.

Chomsky, N. (2002). September 11 Aftermath: Where Is the World Heading? In P. Scraton (Ed.), *Beyond September 11th: An Anthology of Dissent*. London; Sterling, Va.: Pluto Press.

Chomsky, N. (2004). On Law and War. *Peace Review*, 16(3), 251–256.

Chomsky, N., & Herman, E. S. (1979). *The Political Economy of Human Rights. Vol1: The Washington connection and Third World fascism*. Montreal: Black Rose.

Chomsky, N., Mitchell, P., & Schoeffel, J. (Eds.). (2002). *Understanding Power: The Indispensable Chomsky*. Melbourne: Scribe Publications.

Chouliaraki, L. (2006). The aestheticization of suffering on television. *Visual Communication*, 5(3).

Christensen, C. (2011). Twitter Revolutions? Addressing Social Media and Dissent. *The Communication Review*, 14 (3).

Clark, R. (1991, 9 May). International War Crimes Tribunal: United States War Crimes against Iraq. Retrieved 9 November, 2007, from http://deoxy.org/wc/warcrim2.htm

Clutterbuck, J. (1975). *Living with Terrorism*. London: Faber and Faber.

Cmiel, K. (1996). On Cynicism, Evil, and the Discovery of Communication in the 1940s. *Journal of Communication*, 46(3).

CNN.com. (2001). Some Muslims view tape with skepticism [Electronic Version]. Retrieved from http://edition.cnn.com/2001/WORLD/asiapcf/central/12/14/gen.muslim.reax/index.html.

CNN.com. (2003). 'Decapitation strike' was aimed at Saddam [Electronic Version]. Retrieved from http://edition.cnn.com/2003/WORLD/meast/03/20/sprj.irq.target.saddam/.

Coe, K., Domke, D., Graham, E. S., John, S. L., & Pickard, V. W. (2004). No Shades of Gray: The Binary Discourse of George W. Bush and an Echoing Press. *Journal of Communication* 54(2), 234–252.

Cohen, B. C. (1994). A View from the Academy. In W. L. Bennett & D. L. Paletz (Eds.), *Taken By Storm: The Media, Public Opinion, and US Foreign Policy in the Gulf War*. Chicago: University of Chicago Press.

Cole, R. (Ed.). (1998). *The Encyclopaedia of Propaganda*. Armonk, NY: Sharpe Reference.

Coles, R. L. (2002). Manifest destiny adapted for 1990s' war discourse: Mission and destiny intertwined. *Sociology of Religion*, 63(4), 403.

Bibliography

Collins, S. (2002). NATO and Strategic PSYOPS: Policy Pariah or Growth Industry? In B. Hutchinson (Ed.), *Proceedings of the European Conference on Information Warfare and Security*. Reading: MCIL.

Colombo, S. (2012). The GCC and the Arab Spring: A Tale of Double Standards. *The International Spectator*, 47(4), 110–126.

Committee on Government Reform. (2004). Iraq on the Record: The Bush Administration's Public Statements on Iraq. Retrieved from www.reform.house.gov/min

Compton, J. R. (2004). *Shocked and Awed: The Convergence of Military and Media Discourse*. Paper presented at the International association for Media and Communication Research.

Cooke, M. (2003). Islamic Feminism before and after September 11th. *Duke Journal of Gender Law and Policy* 10.

Cooke, T. (1998). *Prepared for Peace, Ready for War? Paramilitaries, Politics, and the Press in Northern Ireland*. Cambridge, MA: The Joan Shorenstein Center for Press/Politics.

Cornell, S. E. (1998). Turkey and the Conflict in Nagorno-Karabakh: a Delicate Balance. *Middle Eastern Studies*, 34(1), 51–72.

Corry, J. (1996). Fancy man fever. *The American Spectator*, 54–55.

Cottle, S. (2011). Media and the Arab uprisings of 2011: Research notes. *Journalism*, 12 (5), 647–659.

Cox, R. W. (1992). Towards a Post-hegemonic Conceptualization of World Order: Reflections on the Relevancy of Ibn Khaldun. In J. N. Rosenau & E.-O. Czempiel (Eds.), *Governance without Government: Order and Change in World Politics*. New York: Cambridge University Press.

Cox, R. W. (2000). Thinking About Civilizations. *Review of International Studies*, 26.

Cozens, C. (2003). Al Jazeera claims military 'cover up' [Electronic Version]. *Guardian*. Retrieved from http://www.guardian.co.uk/media/2003/apr/08/iraq.iraqandthemedia2.

Crelinsten, R. D. (1987). Power and meaning: terrorism as a struggle over access to the communication structure. In P. Wilkinson & A. M. Stewart (Eds.), *Contemporary research on terrorism*. Aberdeen: University of Aberdeen Press.

Crenshaw, M. (Ed.). (1995). *Terrorism in Context*. University Park, PA: Penn State University Press.

Crumm, R. K. (1996). *An Air Force Policy for the Role of Public Affairs*. Maxwell Air Force Base, Alabama: Air University Press.

Crystal, D. (1987). *The Cambridge Encyclopaedia of Language* (1992 Ed.). Cambridge: Cambridge University Press.

Cunningham, S. B. (2002). *The Idea of Propaganda: a Reconstruction*. Westport, Conn.: Praeger.

Czege, H. W. d. (2006). Traditional and Irregular War. *Army*, 56(3), 12.

Dahlgren, P., & Sparks, C. (Eds.). (1991). *Communication and Citizenship: Journalism and the Public Sphere in the New Media Age*. London: Routledge.

D'Angelo, P. (2002). News Framing as a Multi-paradigmatic Research Program: A Response to Entman. *Journal of Communication*, 52 (4), 870–888.

Bibliography

Daniel, N. (1984). *Heroes and Saracens: An Interpretation of the Chansons de Geste*. Edinburgh: Edinburgh University Press.

Danielson, V. (1998). Performance, Political Identity, and Memory: Umm Kulthum and Gamal Abd al-Nasir. In S. Zuhur (Ed.), *Images of Enchantment: Visual and Performing Arts of the Middle East*. Cairo, Egypt: American University in Cairo Press.

Danielson, V. (1998). *The Voice of Egypt: Umm Kulthum, Arabic Song, and Egyptian Society in the Twentieth Century*. Chicago: The University of Chicago Press.

Dao, J., & Schmitt, E. (2002, 19 February). The Pentagon Readies Efforts to Sway Sentiment Abroad. *New York Times*.

Darby, R. (2003). Captivity and Captivation: Gulliver in Brobdingnag. *Eighteenth-Century Life*, 27(3).

Dauber, C. (2001). Image as Argument: The Impact of Mogadishu on US Military Intervention. *Armed Forces & Society*.

Dauber, C. E. (2001). The Shots Seen 'Round the World: The Impact of the Images of Mogadishu on American Military Operations *Rhetoric & Public Affairs*, 4(4), 653–687.

Daugherty, W., & Janowitz, M. (Eds.). (1958). *A Psychological Warfare Casebook*. Baltimore: Johns Hopkins University Press

Davidson, L. (2005). Christian Zionism as a Representation of American Manifest Destiny. *Critique: Critical Middle Eastern Studies*, 14(2), 157–169.

Dawisha, A. (2003). Requiem for Arab Nationalism. Middle East Forum. Retrieved 23 January, 2007, from http://www.meforum.org/article/518

Dawoody, A. (2006). Iraqi Notes: A Personal Reflection on Issues of Governance in Iraq and US Involvement [Electronic Version]. *Public Voices*, Vol. VIII. Retrieved from http://andromeda.rutgers.edu/~ncpp/pv/issues/8-2%20Final.pdf#page=14.

Dearth, D. H. (2002). Shaping the Information Space. *Journal of Information Warfare*, 1(3).

Deen, T. (2004). Arab nationalism tunes into Al Jazeera [Electronic Version]. *Asia Times*. Retrieved from www.atimes.com/atimes/Middle_East/FJ14Ak01.html

Department-of-Defense. (2003). News Transcript: DOD News Briefing – Secretary Rumsfeld and Gen.Myers. Retrieved from http://www.defenselink.mil/transcripts/2003/tr20030409-secdef0084.html

Der-Derian, J. (2001). *Virtuous War: Mapping the Military-Industrial-Media-Entertainment Network* Boulder, CO and Oxford, UK: Westview/ Perseus

Der-Derian, J. (2005). Imaging Terror: Logos, Pathos and Ethos. *Third World Quarterly*, 26(1).

Derian, J. D. (2002). The rise and fall of the Office of Strategic Influence [Electronic Version]. Retrieved from http://ics.leeds.ac.uk/papers/vp01.cfm?outfit=pmt&folder=10&paper=1751.

De-Vreese, C. H. (2005). News framing: Theory and typology. *Information Design Journal* 13(1), 51–62.

DeYoung, K. (2001, 1 November). US, Britain Step Up War for Public Opinion. *Washington Post*.

Diamond, L. (2003). Can Iraq Become a Democracy? *Hoover Digest*.

Dickson, S. H. (1994). Understanding media bias: The press and the US invasion of Panama. *Journalism Quarterly*, 71, 809–819.

Bibliography

Djait, H. (1986). *Europe and Islam*. Berkeley: University of California Press.
Dobson, C., & Payne, R. (1986). *War Without End*. London: Harrap Ltd.
Doran, M. (1999). *Pan-Arabism before Nasser: Egyptian Power Politics and the Palestine Question*. New York: Oxford University Press.
Dovring, K. (1959). *Road of Propaganda: The Semantics of Biased Communication*. New York: Philosophical Library.
Drake, C. J. M. (1998). The Role of Ideology in Terrorists' Target Selection. *Terrorism and Political Violence*, 10(2), 53–85.
Durant, A. (2008). 'The significance is in the selection': identifying contemporary keywords. *Critical Quarterly*, 50(1-2), 122–142.
Eaton, R. M. (2000). (Re)imag(in)ing Other 2ness: A Postmortem for the Postmodern in India. *Journal of World History*, 11(1), 57–78.
Economist.com. (2005). The rise of Arab satellite television [Electronic Version]. Retrieved from http://www.economist.com/displayStory.cfm?story_id=3690442.
Edwards, H. (2000). *Noble Dreams Wicked Pleasures: Orientalism in America, 1870–1930*. Princeton: Princeton University Press.
El-Bendary, M. (2003). Watching the war against Iraq through pan-Arab satellite TV. *Pacific Journalism Review*, 9, 26–31.
El-Bishry, T. (1998). *Bayna al-islam wa-al-uruba: fi al-mas'alah al-islamiyah al-mu'asirah (Between Islam and Arabism: On Contemporary Islamic Issues)*. Cairo: Dar al-Shuruq.
Eldridge, J. (Ed.). (1995). *The Glasgow University Media Group Reader: News Content, Language and Visuals*. London: Routledge.
El-Gody, A. (2006). Arab Media: Did it Cover the Same War. In S. A. Nohrstedt & R. Ottosen (Eds.), *Global War – Local Views: Media Images of the Iraq War*. Göteborg, Sweden: Göteborg University.
El-Ibiary, R. (2005, 6 April). Television Coverage of the 2003 US-Led Invasion of Iraq: Content Analysis of Al Jazeera and CNN. Paper presented at the 55 Annual PSA Conference, Leeds, UK
El-Kakhy, A. (2004). Trapped in the Media Crossfire. In W. Katovsky & T. Carlson (Eds.), *Embedded: The Media at War in Iraq*. Guilford, Conn.: Lyons Press.
Ellul, J. (1965). *Propaganda: The Formation of Men's Attitudes* (K. Kellen & J. Lerner, Trans.). New York Knopf.
El-Nawawy, M., & Iskandar, A. (2002). *Al Jazeera: How the Free Arab News Network Scooped the World and Changed the Middle East*. Cambridge: Westview Press.
Elster, J. (1985). *Making Sense of Marx*. Cambridge: Cambridge University Press.
Emorys, D. (1997). Radio Interview with Christopher Simpson. On *For the Record program series FTR-78*.
Entertainment Weekly. (2003). Get Smart [Electronic Version]. *Entertainment Weekly*. Retrieved 21 November from http://www.ew.com/ew/article/0,,543179,00.html.
Entman, R. M. (1991). Framing US coverage of International news: Contrasts in Narratives of KAL and Iran Air incidents. *Journal of Communications*, 41(4), 6–27.
Entman, R. M. (1993). Framing: Toward Clarification of a Fractured Paradigm. *Journal of Communication*, 43(4), 51–58.
Entman, R. M. (2003). Cascading Activation: Contesting the White House's Frame after 9/11. *Political Communication*, 20.

Bibliography

Entman, R. M. (2004). *Projections of Power: Framing News, Public Opinion, and US Foreign Policy*. Chicago: University of Chicago Press.

Epstein, E. (1973). *News from Nowhere: Television and the News*. New York: Random House.

Esposito, J. L. (1992). *The Islamic Threat: Myth or Reality*. Oxford: Oxford University Press.

Esposito, J. L. (1994). Political Islam: Beyond the green menace. *Current History*, 93(579).

Evans, H. (2004). Propaganda versus professionalism. *British Journalism Review*, 15(1), 35–42.

Everest, L. (2004). *Oil, Power and Empire: Iraq and the US Global Agenda*. Monroe, ME: Common Courage Press

Ewers, J. (2003). Is the new news good news? *US News & World Report*, 134, 48–49.

Fair. (2001a). Media March to War [Electronic Version]. Retrieved 17 August 2008 from http://www.fair.org/index.php?page=1853.

Fair. (2001b). Media Pundits Advocate Civilian Targets [Electronic Version]. Retrieved 17 August 2008 from http://www.fair.org/index.php?page=1675.

Fairclough, N. (1995). *Media Discourse*. London: Arnold.

Fairness and Accuracy In Reporting. (2003, 10 April). Is Killing Part of Pentagon Press Policy? Retrieved from http://www.fair.org/press-releases/iraq-journalists.html.

Falcous, M., & Silk, M. (2005). Manufacturing consent: mediated sporting spectacle and the cultural politics of the 'War on Terror'. *International Journal of Media and Cultural Politics*, 1(1), 59–65.

Faligot, R. (2001). France, Sigint and the Cold War. *Intelligence & National Security*, 16(1), 177–208.

Farmanfarmaian, A. (1992). Did you Measure Up? The Role of Race and Sexuality in the Gulf War. In C. Peters (Ed.), *Collateral Damage: The 'New World Order' at Home and Abroad*. Boston: South End Press.

Felman, M. D. (1992). *The Military/Media Clash and the New Principle of War: Media Spin*. Unpublished thesis presented to the Faculty of the School of Advanced Airpower Studies for completion of graduation requirements. Maxwell Air Force Base, Alabama.

Ferguson, N. (1998). *The Pity of War*. London: Penguin.

Feuilherade, P. (2003). Profile: Al-Arabiya TV [Electronic Version]. *BBC News Online*. Retrieved from http://news.bbc.co.uk/1/hi/world/middle_east/3236654.stm.

Fiest, S. (2001). Facing down the global village: The media impact. In R. Kugler & E. Frost (Eds.), *The global century* (pp. 709–725). Washington, DC: National Defense University Press.

Figenschou, T. U. (2006). Courting, Criticism, Censorship and Bombs: The Bush Administration's Troubled Relations with Al Jazeera Channel from September 11 to the War in Iraq. *Nordicom Review*, 27 (1), 81–96.

Fisher, E. (1978). Politics of Propaganda: The Office of War Information 1942-1945 [Review of book by Allan M. Winkler]. *The Review of Politics*, 40(3), 406–408.

Fisher, K. (1997). Locating Frames in the Discursive Universe. *Sociological Research Online*, 2(3).

Bibliography

Fishman, M. (1980). *Manufacturing the News*. Austin: University of Texas Press.

Fisk, R. (2005). *The Great War for Civilization*. London: Fourth Estate.

Fiske, J. (1996). *Introduction to Communication Studies*. London: Routledge.

Flint, C. (2003). Terrorism and Counterterrorism: Geographic Research Questions and Agendas. *The Professional Geographer*, 55(2), 119–302.

Flournoy, D., & Stewart, R. (1997). *CNN: Making News in the Global Market*. London: University of Luton Press.

Foer, F. (2002, 20 May). Flacks Americana: John Rendon's Shallow P.R. War on Terrorism. *The New Republic*.

Foerstel, H. N. (2006). *Killing the messenger: journalists at risk in modern warfare*. Westport, CT: Praeger Publishers.

Fox, J. G. (2000). Approaching Humanitarian Intervention Strategically: The Case of Somalia [Electronic Version]. Retrieved from http://www.ndu.edu/inss/books/books_2000/Essays2000/FOX.HTML.

Freund, C. P. (2001). 2001 Nights: the end of the Orientalist Critique. *Reason*, 33(7).

Friedman, T. L. (2005, 27 May). Just Shut It Down. *The New York Times*.

Friel, H., & Falk, R. A. (2004). *The Paper of Record: How the New York Times Misreports US Foreign Policy*. New York: Verso.

Friends-of-Al Jazeera. (2007). Silent coup at Al Jazeera? [Electronic Version]. Retrieved 12 December from www.mediachannel.org.

Fritsch-El-Alaoui, L. K. (2005). *Arab, Arab-American, American: Hegemonic and Contrapuntal Representations*. Unpublished PhD thesis, Technischen Universitat Dresden, Dresden.

Frum, D. (2003). *The Right Man. The Surprise Presidency of George W Bush. An Inside Account*. New York: Random House.

Gallup.com. (2002). Poll of Nine Islamic Countries: Generation Gap in Attitudes toward the West [Electronic Version]. Retrieved from http://www.gallup.com/poll/5482/Poll-Nine-Islamic-Countries-Generation-Gap-Attitudes-Toward-West.aspx.

Galtung, J., & Ruge, M. H. (1965). The Structure of Foreign News. *Journal of Peace Research*, 2, 64–91.

Galtung, J., & Vincent, R. (1992). *Global glasnost: toward a new world information and communication order?* Cresskill, NJ: Hampton Press.

Gamson, W. A. (1975). Frame Analysis: An Essay on the Organization of Experience by Erving Goffman. *Contemporary Sociology*, 4(6), 603–607.

Gamson, W. A. (1992). *Talking politics*. New York: Cambridge University Press.

Gamson, W. A., Croteau, D., Hoynes, W., & Sasson, T. (1992). Media Images and the Social Construction of Reality. *Annual Review of Sociology*, 18, 373–393.

Gamson, W. A., & Modigliani, A. (1987). The Changing Culture of Affirmative Action. *Research in Political Sociology*, 3, 137–177.

Gamson, W. A., & Modigliani, A. (1989). Media Discourse and Public Opinion on Nuclear Power: a Constructionist Approach. *American Journal of Sociology*, 95, 1–37.

Gamson, W. A., & Stuart, D. (1992). Media Discourse as a Symbolic Contest: The Bomb in Political Cartoons. *Sociological Forum*, 7(1), 55–69.

Gans, H. J. (1979). *Deciding What's News: A Study of CBS Evening News, NBC Nightly News, Newsweek, and Time*. New York: Pantheon Books.

Bibliography

Gardiner, S. (2003). Truth from These Podia; Summary of Study of Strategic Influence, Perception Management, Strategic Information Warfare and Strategic Psychological Operation in Gulf II [Electronic Version]. Retrieved from www.usnews.com/usnews/politics/whispers/documents/truth.pdf.

Gardner, J. (1998). *Master Plots: Race and the Founding of an American Literature, 1787–1845*. Baltimore: Johns Hopkins University Press.

Geertz, C. (2000). *Local knowledge: further essays in interpretive anthropology* (2nd Ed.). New York: Basic Books

George, J. (2005). Leo Strauss, Neoconservatism and US Foreign Policy: Esoteric Nihilism and the Bush Doctrine. *International Politics*, 42, 174–202.

Getler, M. (2003, 20 April). Reporting Private Lynch. *The Washington Post*, p. B6.

Ghadbian, N. (2000). Political Islam and Violence *New Political Science*, 22(1), 77–88.

Ghanem, S. I. (2005). *A comparison of the New York Times' and Al Ahram's coverage of the war in Iraq*. Paper presented at the International Communication Division, San Antonio.

Ghareeb, E. (2000). New Media and the Information Revolution in the Arab World: An Assessment. *The Middle East Journal*, 54(3).

Gibbs, D. N. (2004). Pretexts and US foreign policy: the War on Terrorism in historical perspective *New Political Science*, 26(3), 293–321.

Gierhart, C. (2008). Targeting Media: The Legal Restrictions on States Attacking Media in Times of War [Electronic Version]. Retrieved from http://works.bepress.com/cgi/viewcontent.cgi?article=1000&context=cindy_gierhart.

Gilboa, E. (2005). The CNN effect: The search for a communication theory of international relations. *Political Communication*, 27–44.

Gilboa, E. (2002). *The Global News Networks and US Policymaking In Defense and Foreign Affairs* The Shorenstein Center on the Press, Politics and Public Policy; Kennedy School of Government; Harvard University.

Gillespie, M. (2003). Crusade: Racial and religious exclusivism in George Bush's America [Electronic Version]. *Media Monitors Network*. Retrieved from http://www.mediamonitors.net/gillespie12.html.

Girardet, E. (Ed.). (1995). *Somalia Rwanda and Beyond*. Geneva: Crosslines Global Report.

Giroux, H. A. (2006). The Emerging Authoritarianism in the US *Symploke* 14(1–2), 98–151.

Gitlin, T. (1980). *The Whole World is Watching: Mass Media in the Making and Unmaking of the New Left*. Berkeley: University of California Press.

Glass, C. (2004, 13 September). Lewis of Arabia. *The Nation*.

Glasser, S. B., & Chandrasekaran, R. (2003). Clashes at Key River Crossing Bring Heaviest Day of American Casualties [Electronic Version]. *Washingtonpost.com*. Retrieved from http://www.washingtonpost.com/ac2/wp-dyn/A16610-2003Mar23?language=printer.

Goffman, E. (1974). *Frame analysis: An essay on the organization of experience*. London: Harper and Row.

Goldstein, F. L., and, & Findley, B. F. (Eds.). (1996). *Psychological Operations: Principles and Case Studies*. AL: Air University Press.

Bibliography

Goodwin, J. (1994). What's right (and wrong) about left media criticism? Herman and Chomsky's propaganda model. *Sociological Forum,* 9(1), 106–107.

Gordon, M. R. (2003). Goal of US: Avoid a Siege [Electronic Version]. *NYtimes.com.* Retrieved from http://nytimes.com/2003/04/03/international/worldspecial/03STRA.html.

Gough, S. L. (2003). *The Evolution of Strategic Influence.* Carlisle Barracks, Pennsylvania.

Graber, D. A. (2002). *Mass Media and American Politics* (6th Ed.). Washington, D.C: Congressional Quarterly.

Graber, D. A., McQuail, D., & Norris, P. (1998). *The Politics of News: The News of Politics.* Washington: CQ Press.

Graham, S. (2006). Cities and the 'War on Terror'. *International Journal of Urban and Regional Research,* 30(2), 255–276.

Gramsci, A. (1997). *Selections from the Prison Notebooks* (Q. Hoare & G. N. Smith, Trans.). New York: International Publishers.

Gray, M. (2008). Explaining Conspiracy Theories in Modern Arab Middle Eastern Political Discourse: Some Problems and Limitations of the Literature. *Critical Middle Eastern Studies,* 17(2), 155–174.

Greene, J. (1986). *Language Understanding: A Cognitive Approach.* Philadelphia: Open University Press.

Greenwald, G. (2016). Al Jazeera America Terminates All TV and Digital Operations. Retrieved 5 July 2016, from https://theintercept.com/2016/01/13/AlJazeera-america-terminates-all-tv-and-digital-operations/.

Greenwald, G. (2016, 17 June). Why Is the Killer of British MP Jo Cox Not Being Called a "Terrorist"? *The Intercept.* Retrieved 24 June 2016, from https://theintercept.com/2016/06/17/why-is-the-killer-of-british-mp-jo-cox-not-being-called-a-terrorist/.

Gregory, D. (2003). Defiled cities. *Singapore Journal of Tropical Geography,* 24.

Groshek, J. (2008). Homogenous agendas, disparate frames: CNN and CNN International coverage online. *Journal of broadcasting & electronic media,* 52(1), 52.

Guelke, A. (1995). *The Age of Terrorism and the International Political System.* London: I.B.Tauris.

Gunn, J. (2004). The Rhetoric of Exorcism: George W. Bush and the Return of Political Demonology. *Western Journal of Communication,* 68(1).

Gurevitch, M., Levy, M. R., & Roeh, I. (1991). The global newsroom: convergences and diversities. In P. Dahlgren & C. Sparks (Eds.), *Communication and Citizenship: Journalism and the Public Sphere.* London: Routledge.

Guzman, A. (2015). Evolution of News Frames During the 2011 Egyptian Revolution: Critical Discourse Analysis of Fox News's and CNN's Framing of Protesters, Mubarak, and the Muslim Brotherhood. *Journalism & Mass Communication Quarterly,* 1–19. Doi: 10.1177/1077699015606677.

Habermas, J. (2000). The Public Sphere. In Marris & Thornhaw (Eds.), *Media Studies: A Reader.* New York: New York University Press.

Hahn, O. (2007). Cultures of TV news journalism and prospects for a transcultural public sphere. In N. Sakr (Ed.), *Arab Media and Political Renewal.* London: I.B. Tauris.

Halbwachs, M. (1952). *The Collective Memory* (J. F. J. Ditter & V. Y. Ditter, Trans.). New York: Harper & Row.

Bibliography

Hall, C. (2004). Remembering Edward Said. *History Workshop Journal*, 57, 235–243.
Hall, L. (1997). CNN in Baghdad, Jan. 16, 1991. *Electronic Media*, 16(30), 33.
Hall, S. (1977). Culture, Media and the Ideological Effect. In J. Curran, M. Gurevitch & J. Woollacot (Eds.), *Mass Communication and Society*. London: Arnold.
Hall, S. (1980). Encoding/decoding. In Centre-for-Contemporary-Cultural-Studies (Ed.), *Culture, Media, Language: Working Papers in Cultural Studies 1972–79* (pp. 128–138). London: Hutchinson.
Hall, S. (1987). *The Politics of Representation*. Paper presented at the Silha Annual Lecture, University of Minnesota.
Hall, S. (1989). Ideology and Communication Theory. In B. Dervin, L. Grossberg, B. J. O'Keefe & E. Wartella (Eds.), *Rethinking Communication* (pp. 40–52). Newbury Park: Sage.
Hall, S. (1990). Cultural Identity and Diaspora. In J. Rutherford (Ed.), *Identity: Community, Culture, Difference* (pp. 222–237). London: Lawrence and Wishart.
Hall, S. (1992). The Question of Cultural Identity. In S. Hall & D. Held (Eds.), *Modernity and its Futures*. Cambridge: Polity Press.
Hall, S. (1996). The problem of ideology: Marxism without guarantees In S. Hall, D. Morley & K.-H. Chen (Eds.), *Stuart Hall: Critical Dialogues in Cultural Studies*. London: Routledge.
Hall, S. (1997). The Spectacle of the 'Other'. In S. Hall (Ed.), *Representation: Cultural Representations and Signifying Practices*. London: Sage.
Hallahan, K. (1999). Seven Models of Framing: Implications for Public Relations. *Journal of Public Relations Research*, 11(3), 205–242
Hallin, D. C. (1984). The Media, the War in Vietnam, and Political Support: A Critique of the Thesis of an Oppositional Media. *The Journal of Politics*, 46(1), 2–24.
Hallin, D. C. (1986). *The Uncensored War: The Media and Vietnam*. New York: Oxford University Press.
Hallin, D. C. (1986a). Network News: We Keep America on Top of the World. In T. Gitlin (Ed.), *Watching Television: A Pantheon Guide to Popular Culture*. New York: Pantheon Books.
Hallin, D. C. (1987). Review of TV News: 'Whose Bias? by Martin Harrison' and 'War and Peace News by the Glasgow University Media Group'. *American Journal of Sociology*, 92(6), 1544–1546.
Hallin, D. C., & Gitlin, T. (1993). Agon and Ritual: The Gulf War as Popular Culture and as Television Drama. *Political Communication*, 10, 411–424.
Hallin, D. C., & Mancini, P. (2004). *Comparing media systems: Three models of media and politics*. Cambridge: Cambridge University Press.
Halper, S., & Clarke, J. (2004). *America Alone: The Neo-Conservatives and the Global Order*. New York: Cambridge University Press.
Hanley, D. C. (2003). Two wars in Iraq: One for US audiences, the other for the Arab-speaking world. *The Washington Report on Middle East Affairs*, 22(4).
Hashemi, N. A. (2002). How Dangerous are the Islamists? [Electronic Version]. Retrieved from http://www.islamonline.net/servlet/Satellite?c=Article_C&cid=1159951464109&pagename=Zone-English-Living_Shariah%2FLSELayout.
Hauben, R. (2003). Massive Anti-War Protest in New York City Demonstrates [Electronic Version]. *Heise.de*. Retrieved from http://www.heise.de/tp/r4/artikel/14/14195/1.html.

Bibliography

Haulman, D. L. (2003). *USAF Psychological Operations*, 1990–2003. Retrieved Air Force Historical Research Agency.

Held, D., McGrew, A., Goldblatt, D., & Perraton, J. (1999). *Global Transformations*. Cambridge: Polity.

Henry, I. P., Amara, M., & Al-Tauqi, M. (2003). Sport, Arab Nationalism and the Pan-Arab Games. *International Review for the Sociology of Sport*, 38(3), 295–310.

Herman, E., & Chomsky, N. (1988). *Manufacturing Consent: the Political Economy of the Mass Media*. New York: Pantheon.

Herman, E. S. (1982). *The Real Terror Network: Terrorism in Fact and Propaganda*. Boston: South End Press.

Herman, E. S. (1996). The propaganda model revisited. *Monthly Review*, 48(3).

Herman, E. S. (2003). The Propaganda Model: A Retrospective [Electronic Version]. Retrieved from http://human-nature.com/reason/.

Herman, E. S., & McChesney, R. W. (1997). *The Global Media: The New Missionaries of Corporate Capitalism*. London: Cassell.

Herring, E., & Robinson, P. (2003). Too polemical or too critical? Chomsky on the study of the news media and US foreign policy. *Review of International Studies*, 29(4), 553–568.

Hersh, S. (1998, 12 October). The Missiles of August. *New Yorker*, 35.

Hersh, S. (2003). Who Lied to Whom? [Electronic Version]. *The New Yorker*. Retrieved from http://www.newyorker.com/archive/2003/03/31/030331fa_fact1.

Hickey, N. (2001). Enter CNN. *Columbia Journalism Review*, 40(4), 88.

Hiebert, R. E. (2003). Public relations and propaganda in framing the Iraq war: a preliminary review. *Public Relations Review* (29).

Hill, M. R. R. (1997). *The Future Military-Media Relationship: The Media as an Actor in War Execution*: The Research Department Air Command and Staff College.

Hillenbrand, C. (1999). *The Crusades: Islamic Perspectives*. Chicago and London: Fitzroy Dearborn.

Hippler, J., & Lueg, A. (Eds.). (1995). *The next threat: Western perceptions of Islam*. London: Pluto Press.

Hirsh, M. (2004). Bernard Lewis Revisited [Electronic Version]. *The Washington Monthly* Retrieved 16 September 2008 from http://www.washingtonmonthly.com/features/2004/0411.hirsh.html.

Hoffman, D. (2002). Beyond Public Diplomacy. *Foreign Affairs* (Mar/Apr).

Hope, W. (2004). *Global Television News and the Ideology of Real Time*. Paper presented at The International Association of Media Communication Research, Porto Alegre, Brazil.

Hope, W. (2006). Global Capitalism and the Critique of Real Time. *Time and Society*, 15.

Hoskins, A. (2004a). Television and the Collapse of Memory. *Time & Society*, 13(1), 109–127.

Hoskins, A. (2004b). *Televising war: From Vietnam to Iraq* London New York: Continuum International Publishing Group.

Hosmer, S. T. (1999). The information revolution and psychological effects. In J. P. White, Zalmay Khalilzad, Andrew W. Marshall (Ed.), *Strategic Appraisal: The Changing Role of Information in Warfare*. Santa Monica, CA: Rand Publications.

Hourani, A. (1991). *A History of the Arab Peoples*. Cambridge, Mass.: The Belknap Press/Harvard University Press.

Bibliography

Howeidy, A. (2004). Enter Heikal [Electronic Version]. *Al-Ahram weekly on-line.* Retrieved from http://weekly.ahram.org.eg/2004/698/fr3.htm.

Hoynes, W. (1992). War as Video Game: Media, Activism, and the Gulf War. In C. Peters (Ed.), *Collateral Damage: The 'New World Order' at Home and Abroad.* Boston: South End Press.

Hübinette, T. (2002). Orientalism Past and Present: An Introduction to a Postcolonial Critique. Retrieved 10 September, 2006, from http://www.tobiashubinette.se/orientalism.pdf

Hudson, M. (2000). Creative Destruction: Information Technology and the Political Culture Revolution in the Arab World [Electronic Version]. Retrieved 9 March 2007 from http://nmit.georgetown.edu/papers/.

Human Rights Watch. (2003). World Report [Electronic Version]. Retrieved 14 January from http://www.hrw.org/legacy/wr2k3/us.html#enemy.

Human Rights Watch. (2003, November). Background on Women's Status in Iraq Prior to the Fall of the Saddam Hussein Government. Retrieved from http://hrw.org/backgrounder/wrd/iraq-women.htm.

Huntington, S. P. (1997). *The Clash of Civilizations and the Remaking of World Order.* New York: Touchtone.

Hurd, E. S. (2003). Appropriating Islam: The Islamic Other in the Consolidation of Western Modernity. *Critique: Critical Middle Eastern Studies,* 12(1), 25–41.

Husting, G. (1999). When a War is not a War: Abortion, Desert Storm, and Representations of Protest in American TV News. *The Sociological Quarterly,* 40(1), 159–176.

Hutcheson, J., Domke, D., Billeaudeaux, A., & Garland, P. (2004). US National Identity, Political Elites, and a patriotic Press Following September 11. *Political Communication,* 21.

Hyun, K. (2004, August). *Framing frames: locations of frames and their connections in signifying processes.* Paper presented at the Annual Convention of the Association for Education in Journalism and Mass Communication, Toronto, Canada.

Ibroscheva, E. (2002). Is There Still an Evil Empire? *Global Media Journal,* 1(1).

Ignatieff, M. (2000). *Virtual War: Kosovo and Beyond.* New York: Metropolitan Books.

Ignatieff, M. (2001, 1 October). It's War – But It doesn't need to be Dirty. *Guardian,* p. 70.

Iskander, E. (2011) Connecting the national and the virtual: can Facebook activism remain relevant after Egypt's January 25 uprising? *International Journal of Communication,* 5. pp. 13–15

Iyengar, S. (1991). *Is Anyone Responsible? How Television Frames Political Issues.* Chicago, IL: University of Chicago Press.

Jackall, R. (1994). *Propaganda.* New York: New York University Press.

James, L. (2006a). *Nasser at War: Arab Images of the Enemy.* London: Palgrave Macmillan.

James, L. (2006b). Whose Voice? Nasser, the Arabs, and 'Sawt al-Arab' Radio. *Transnational Broadcasting Studies,* 16.

Jamieson, K. H. (2000). *Everything You Think You Know About Politics ... And Why You're Wrong.* New York: Basic.

Jankowski, J. (2002). *Nasser's Egypt, Arab Nationalism, and the United Arab Republic.* Boulder: Lynne Rienner Publishers.

Bibliography

Jankowski, J., & Gershoni, I. (1995). *Redefining the Egyptian nation, 1930-1945.* Cambridge: Cambridge University Press.

Jaramillo, D. L. (2006). Ugly war, pretty package: How the Cable News Network and the Fox News Channel made the 2003 invasion of Iraq high concept. Unpublished PhD Dissertation, University of Texas, Austin.

Jasperson, A. E., & El-Kikhia, M. (2002, 25 August). *US and Middle Eastern Media Perspectives on the Aftermath of the Sept. 11 Terrorist Attacks.* Paper presented at the Media and Terrorism Symposium, Harvard.

Jeffery, K. (1996). Reader's Companion to Military History: Psychological warfare. Retrieved from Http:/college.hmco.com/history/readerscomp/mil/html/ml_042100_psychologica.htm.

Jezierski, L. (2004). *Framing Stories About Cities: Narrative Analysis and Policy Frames.* Paper presented at the annual meeting of the American Sociological Association, Hilton San Francisco & Renaissance Parc. Retrieved on 26 May 2009 from: http://www.allacademic.com/meta/p110198_index.html

Johns, C. J., & Johnson, P. W. (1994). *State Crime, The Media, And The Invasion of Panama.* Westport, Connecticut: Praeger.

Johnson, C. (2000). *Blowback: The Costs and Consequences of American Empire.* New York: Metropolitan Books

Johnson, L. K. (1988). *A Season of Inquiry, Congress and Intelligence.* Chicago: Dorsey Press.

Jones, S. (2008). Television News: Geographic and Source Biases, 1982-2004. *International Journal of Communication*, 2, 223-252.

Jones, T., & Ereira, A. (1996). *Crusades.* London: Penguin Books.

Jowett, G. (1987). Propaganda and Communication: The Re-emergence of a Research Tradition. *Journal of Communication*, 37(1), 97–114.

Jowett, G. S., & O'Donnell, V. (1992). *Propaganda and Persuasion* (2nd Ed.). Newbury Park, CA: Sage Publications.

Judge, J. C. (2003, 1 April). P.R. lessons from the Pentagon. *The Wall Street Journal.*

Kagan, R. (2003). *Of Paradise and Power: America and Europe in the New World Order.* New York: Knopf.

Kagan, R., & Kristol, W. (2000). *Present Dangers: Crisis and Opportunity in American Foreign and Defense Policy.* San Francisco: Encounter Books.

Kahneman, D., & Tversky, A. (Eds.). (2000). *Choices, Values and Frames.* Cambridge: Cambridge University Press.

Kalb, M. (2003, 24 March). War and conflict. *Editor & Publisher*, 136, 34.

Kamalipour, Y. (Ed.). (1995). *The US Media and the Middle East: Image and Perception.* Westport, CT: Greenwood Press.

Kapitan, T., & Schulte, E. (2002). The Rhetoric on 'Terrorism' and its Consequences. *Journal of Political and Military Sociology*, 30(1).

Karic, E. (2002). Is 'Euro-Islam' a Myth, Challenge or a Real Opportunity for Muslims and Europe? *Journal of Muslim Minority Affairs*, 22(2), 435–442.

Karim, K. H. (2000). *Islamic Peril: Media and Global Violence.* Montreal: Black Rose.

Kedourie, E. (1976). *In the Anglo-Arab Labyrinth.* Cambridge: Cambridge University Press.

Bibliography

Kellner, D. (1990). *Television and the Crisis of Democracy*. Boulder, Col: Westview Press.
Kellner, D. (1992). *The Persian Gulf TV War*. Boulder, Col.: Westview Press.
Kellner, D. (1995). *Media culture: Cultural studies, identity and politics between the modern and the postmodern*. London: Routledge.
Kellner, D. (1999). Habermas, the Public Sphere, and Democracy: A Critical Intervention [Electronic Version]. Retrieved 15 March 2006 from www.gseis.ucla.edu/faculty/kellner/papers/habermas.htm.
Kellner, D. (2003). *From 9/11 to Terror War: The Dangers of the Bush Legacy*. Lanham, MD: Rowman & Littlefield.
Kellner, D. (2005). *Media Spectacle and the Crisis of Democracy*. Boulder, CO: Paradigm Publishers.
Kendrick, M. (1994). The Never Again Narratives: Political Promise and the Videos of Operation Desert Storm. *Cultural Critique*, 28, 129–147.
Kennan, G. F. (1993, 30 September). Somalia, Through a Glass Darkly. *New York Times*, p. A23.
Kepel, G. (1984). *Le Prophète et le Pharaon. Aux sources des mouvements islamistes* (1993 ed.). Paris: Le Seuil.
Khazen, J. (1999). Censorship and State Control of the Press in the Arab World. *The Harvard International Journal of Press Politics*, 4(3), 87–92
Khouri, G. (1998). *The Other Gulf War Syndrome: Flaws in US Media Coverage of the 1997/98 Iraq Crisis*. Washington DC: ADC Research Institute.
Kilani, S. (2004). *Freedom Fries: Fried Freedoms, Arab Satellite Channels Struggle between State control and Western Pressure*. Amman: Arab Archive Institute.
Kim, S. T., & Weaver, D. H. (2003). Reporting on Globalization: A Comparative Analysis of Sourcing Patterns in Five Countries' Newspapers. *Gazette*, 65(2), 121–144.
Klaehn, J. (2002). A Critical Review and Assessment of Herman and Chomsky's 'Propaganda Model'. *European Journal of Communication*, 17(2), 147–182.
Klandermans, B. (1988). The Formation and Mobilization of Consensus. *International Social Movement Research*, 1, 173–196.
Klein, N. (2003). America's enemy within [Electronic Version]. *Guardian*. Retrieved from http://www.guardian.co.uk/print/0,3858,4805314-103677,00.html.
Klusmeyer, D., & Suhrke, A. (2002). Comprehending 'Evil': Challenges for Law and Policy. *Ethics and International Affairs*, 16(1), 27–42.
Knightley, P. (2001, 4 October). The disinformation campaign. *Guardian*.
Knightley, P. (2003). *The First Casualty: The War Correspondent as Hero, Propagandist and Myth-maker from the Crimea to Iraq*. London: Andre Deutsch.
Kolluoglu-Kirli, B. (2003). From Orientalism to Area Studies. *The New Centennial Review*, 3(3), 93–111.
Korhonen, P. (1996). Kaukolännen orientalismi ja Kaukoidän oksidentalismi. *Politiikka*, 38(3), 158–170.
Kraidy, M. M., (2002). Arab satellite television between regionalism and globalization, *Global Media Journal*, 1, 1.
Kramer, M. (1993). Arab nationalism: mistaken identity. *Daedalus*, 122(3).
Kramer, M. (2000). Don't Absolve the Great Powers. *Middle East Quarterly*, 7(4).
Krichane, M. (2003, 3 September). Salam Shalom. *al-Quds al-Arabi*, p. 19.

Bibliography

Krichane, M. (2007, 3 January). Saddam was not the only one hanged. *al-Quds al-Arabi*, p. 19.

Krishna, S. (2002). An Inarticulate Imperialism: Dubya, Afghanistan and the American Century. *Alternatives*, 1(2).

Kumar, D. (2006). Media, War, and Propaganda: Strategies of Information Management During the 2003 Iraq War. *Communication and Critical/Cultural Studies*, 3(1), 48–69.

Kuypers, J. A. (2002). *Press Bias, Politics, and the Media Manipulation of Controversial Issues*.

Laffey, M. (2003). Discerning the Patterns of World Order: Noam Chomsky and International Theory after the Cold War. *Review of International Studies*, 29(4), 587–604.

Lage, O. D. (2005). The politics of Al Jazeera or the diplomacy of Doha. In M. Zayani (Ed.), *The Al Jazeera phenomenon* (pp. 49–65). Boulder, CO: Paradigm Publishers.

Lake, A. (1993, 21 September). From Containment to Enlargement. Retrieved from http://www.mtholyoke.edu/acad/intrel/lakedoc.html.

Lakoff, G. (1991). Metaphor and War: The Metaphor System Used to Justify War in the Gulf. *Viet Nam Generation Journal and Newsletter*, 3(3).

Lakoff, G. (2003a). Metaphors can kill [Electronic Version]. Retrieved from www.alternet.com.

Lakoff, G. (2003b). Metaphor and War, Again [Electronic Version]. *AlterNet*. Retrieved from http://www.alternet.org/story/15414.

Lakoff, G., & Johnson, M. (1980). *Metaphors We Live By*. Chicago: University of Chicago Press.

Lamb, D. (1987). *The Arabs: Journeys beyond the Mirage*. New York: Random House.

Lang, K., & Lang, G. E. (2004). Noam Chomsky and the Manufacture of Consent for American Foreign Policy. *Political Communication*, 21(1), 93–101.

Laqueur, W. (1977). *Terrorism*. Boston: Little, Brown.

Laqueur, W. (1996). Post-modern Terrorism. *Foreign Affairs*, 75(5).

Lasswell, H. (1948). Propaganda. In *Encyclopedia of the Social Sciences* (Vol. II, pp. 525). New York: MacMillan.

Lauderdale, P. (2003). *A Political Analysis of Deviance: A New Edition*. Canada: DeSitter Publications.

Lawrence, R. J., Benjamin, I. P., Melanie, B., Gregory, M., & Eric, O. (2003). What Presidents Talk about: The Nixon Case. *Presidential Studies Quarterly*, 33(4), 751.

Lazar, A., & Lazar, M. M. (2004). The discourse of the New World Order: "outcasting" the double face of threat. *Discourse & Society*, 15(2–3), 223–242.

Lazar, A., & Lazar, M. M. (2005). 'In the Pursuit of Justice': the Discursive Construction of America as Global Policeman in the New World Order. Paper presented at the International Conference on Critical Discourse Analysis: Theory into Research. Tasmania: University of Tasmania.

Leaper, G., Löwstedt, A., & Madhoun, H. (2003). Caught in the Crossfire: The Iraq War and the Media. Retrieved from http://ics.leeds.ac.uk/papers/vp01.cfm?outfit=pmt&folder=193&paper=247.

Bibliography

Lee, C.-C., Chan, J. M., Pan, Z., & So, C. Y. K. (2002). *Global Media Spectacle*. Albany: State University of New York Press.

Lena, J. C. (2003). Psyops, Propaganda and Gangsta Rap. *Radical Society*, 30(1).

Le-Nouvel-Observateur. (1998, 15 October 2001). Interview with Zbigniew Brzezinski. *Le Nouvel Observateur* Retrieved 3 October, 2006, from http://www.globalresearch.ca/articles/BRZ110A.html.

Lesch, A. M. (2002). Osama bin Laden's "business" in Sudan. *Current History*, 101(655).

Lester, M. (1980). Generating Newsworthiness: The Interpretive Construction of Public Events. *American Sociological Review*, 45(6), 984–994.

Levitt, T. (1986). *The Marketing Imagination*. New York: The Free Press.

Lewis, B. (1990, September). The roots of Muslim rage. *Atlantic Monthly*, 48–54.

Lewis, B. (2002). *What Went Wrong? Western Impact and Middle Eastern Response*. New York: Oxford University Press.

Lewis, C., & Reading-Smith, M. (2008). False Pretenses [Electronic Version]. Retrieved from http://projects.publicintegrity.org/WarCard/.

Lewis, J. (2004). Television, public opinion, and the war in Iraq: The case of Britain. *International Journal of Public Opinion*, 16, 297–310.

Little, D. (2004). *American Orientalism: The United States and the Middle East since 1945*. Chapel Hill: University of North Carolina Press.

Livingston, S. (1997). *Clarifying the CNN Effect* (Research paper). Cambridge, MA: The Joan Shorenstein Center, Harvard University.

Lizza, R. (2004, 21 June). Achille Heel: Reagan's Lousy Record on Terrorism. *The New Republic*.

Lockman, Z. (2004). *Contending Visions of the Middle East: The History and Politics of Orientalism*. Cambridge: Cambridge University Press.

London, H. I., & Weeks, A. L. (1982). *Myths That Rule America*. University Press of America.

Loory, S. H. (2005). CNN Today: A Young Giant Stumbles. *Critical Studies in Media Communication*, 22(4), 340–343.

Lule, J. (2004). War and its Metaphors: news language and the prelude to war in Iraq, 2003. *Journalism Studies*, 5(2), 179–190.

Lundsten, L., & Stocchetti, M. (2005). The War against Iraq in Transnational Broadcasting [Electronic Version]. Retrieved from www.siti.fi.

Lynch, M. (2003). Beyond the Arab Street: Iraq and the Arab Public Sphere. *Politics & Society*, 31(1), 55–91.

Lynch, M. (2005a). Watching Al Jazeera. *The Wilson Quarterly*, 29(3).

Lynch, M. (2005b). Bush, Hughes, and the Arab media [Electronic Version]. *Abu Aardvark*. Retrieved from http://abuaardvark.typepad.com/abuaardvark/alhurra/index.html.

Maalouf, A. (1994). *The Crusades through Arab Eyes*. New York: Schocken Books.

MacArthur, J. R. (1992). *Second Front: Censorship and Propaganda in the Gulf War*. Berkeley, CA: University of CA Press.

MacArthur, J. R. (2003). The Lies We Bought: The Unchallenged 'Evidence' for War. *Columbia Journalism Review*, 62(3).

Bibliography

Macaulay, T. B. (1835). Minute by the Honorable T. B. Macaulay. Retrieved from http://www.mssu.edu/projectsouthasia/history/primarydocs/education/Macaulay001.htm.

MacBride, S., & Roach, C. (2000). The new international information order. In F. J. Lechner & J. Boli (Eds.), *The globalization reader* (pp. 286-292). Malden: Blackwell Publishers.

Macdonald, S. (2007). *Propaganda and Information Warfare in the Twenty-First Century*: Routledge.

Macfie, A. L. (2002). *Orientalism*. London: Pearson Education.

Macleod, S. (1999, 15 March). Kicking Up a Sandstorm. *Time Magazine*.

Maguire, K., & Lines, A. (2005). Exclusive: Bush Plot to Bomb his Arab Ally [Electronic Version]. Retrieved from http://www.mirror.co.uk/news/top-stories/tm_objectid=16397937&method=full&siteid=115875-name_page.html.

Mann, M. (2003). *Incoherent Empire*. New York & London: Verso.

Manning, P. (2005). Media Representations of Arabs and Muslims in an "Age of Terror". Retrieved 1 September, 2006, from http://www.aac.org.au/media.php?ArtID=67

Marquand, R., & Andoni, L. (1996, 5 February). Separating the fact from the fiction in Islamic extremism. *Christian Science Monitor*.

Marris, P., & Thornham, S. (Eds.). (1996). *Media studies, A Reader*. Edinburgh: Edinburgh University Press.

Marshall, G. (1998). *A Dictionary of Sociology*. Oxford University Press.

Martin, P., & Phelan, S. (2002). Representing Islam in the Wake of September 11: A Comparison of US Television and CNN Online Messageboard Discourses. *Prometheus*, 20(3), 263-269.

Martin, S. T. (2002, 22 September). Scrappy Al Jazeera stands up. *St. Petersburg Times*.

Masmoudi, M. (1979). The Journal of Communication. *The new world information order*, 29(2).

Mason, J. G. (2004). Leo Strauss and the Noble Lie: The Neo-Cons at War. *Logos*, 3(2).

Massing, M. (2005). The End of News? *The New York Review of Books*, 52(19).

Mawlana, H. (1986). *Global Information and World Communication: new frontiers in international relations*. New York: Longman.

Mazel, Z. (2009, 26 June). Is Al Jazeera part of the Muslim Brothers' program? *Jerusalem Post*.

McChesney, R., & Nichols, J. (2002). *Our Media, Not Theirs: The Democratic Struggle Against Corporate Media*. NY: Seven Stories.

McChesney, R. W. (1997). The Global Media Giants. Retrieved 17 December, 2005, from http://www.fair.org/extra/9711/gmg.html

McChesney, R. W. (1999). *Rich Media, Poor Democracy: Communication Politics in Dubious Times*. Chicago: University of Illinois Press.

McChesney, R. W. (2002). September 11 and the Structural Limitations of US Journalism. In B. Zelizer & S. Allan (Eds.), *Journalism After September 11* (pp. 92-94). London and New York: Routledge.

McChesney, R. W. (2003). The Problem of Journalism: a political economic contribution to an explanation of the crisis in contemporary US journalism. *Journalism Studies*, 4(3), 299-329.

Bibliography

McChesney, R. W. (2006). Telling the truth at a moment of truth: US news media and the invasion and occupation of Iraq. *Socialist Register* 2006.

McCombs, M., & Ghanem, S. I. (2003). The convergence of agenda setting and framing. In S. D. Reese, J. O. H. Gandy & A. E. Grant (Eds.), *Framing Public Life: Perspectives on Media and our Understanding of the Social World*. pp. 67-81. Mahwah, NJ: Lawrence Erlbaum Associates.

McFarland, C., & T., M. D. (1994). The framing of relative performance feedback: seeing the glass as half empty or half full. *Journal of personality and social psychology*, 66(6), 1061-1073.

McInnes, C. (2002). *Spectator Sport War: The West and Contemporary Conflict*. Boulder: Lynne Rienner.

McLeod, D., & Detenber, B. (1999). Framing effects of television news coverage of social protest. *Journal of Communication*, 49(3), 3-23.

McManus, J. (1995). A Market-Based Model of News Production. *Communication Theory*, 5(4), 301-338.

McMillan, N. (2004). Beyond Representation: Cultural Understandings of the September 11 Attacks. *Australian and New Zealand Journal of Criminology*, 37(3), 380-400.

McNair, B. (1998). *The Sociology of Journalism*. London: Arnold Publishers.

McNamara, R. (2000). Britain, Nasser and the Outbreak of the Six Day War. *Journal of Contemporary History*, 35(4), 619-639.

Meeuf, R. (2006). Collateral Damage: Terrorism, melodrama, and the action film on the eve of 9/11. *Jump Cut*, 48.

Melosi, M. V. (1978). The Politics of Propaganda: The Office of War Information, 1942-1945 [Review of book by Allan M. Winkler]. *The Annals of the American Academy of Political and Social Science*, 439, 156-157.

Mermin, J. (1999). *Debating War and Peace: Media Coverage of US Intervention in the Post-Vietnam Era*. Princeton: Princeton University Press.

Merrin, W. (2005). *Baudrillard and the Media: A Critical Introduction*. Cambridge: Polity Press.

Michael, J. (2003). Beyond Us and Them: Identity and Terror from an Arab American's Perspective. *The South Atlantic Quarterly*, 102(4).

Miles, H. (2005). *Al Jazeera: How Arab TV News Challenged the World*. London: Abascus.

Miller, D. (Ed.). (2004a). *Tell Me Lies: Propaganda and Media Distortion in the Attack on Iraq*. London: Pluto Press.

Miller, D. (2004b). Information Dominance: The Philosophy of Total propaganda Control? In Y. R. Kamalipour, and & N. Snow (Eds.), *War, Media and Propaganda: A Global Perspective*: Rowman and Littlefield.

Miller, E. (2004). Television, International Understanding and Globalization. *Global Media Journal* (Spring).

Miller, J. (1996). *God Has Ninety-nine Names: Reporting from a Militant Middle East*. New York: Simon & Schuster.

Miller, S. (2002). Conspiracy theories: public arguments as coded social critiques: a rhetorical analysis of the TWA Flight 800 conspiracy theories. *Argumentation and Advocacy*, 39(1).

Bibliography

Mirzoeff, N. (2005). 'Watching Babylon': *The War in Iraq and Global Visual Culture.* New York: Routledge.

Moeller, S. D. (2004). *Media Coverage of Weapons of Mass Destruction.* Maryland: The Center for International and Security Studies.

Moisy, C. (1996, November). *The Foreign News Flow in the Information Age.* Paper presented at the Press, Politics and Public Policy, The Joan Shorenstein Center.

Mokhiber, R., & Weissman, R. (2001). Kill, Kill, Kill [Electronic Version]. Retrieved 26 November 2006 from http://www.counterpunch.org/mokhiber4.html.

Monten, J. (2005). The Roots of the Bush Doctrine: Power, Nationalism, and Democracy Promotion in US Strategy. *International Security,* 29(4), 112–156.

Mooney, J., & Young, J. (2004, June). Imagining Terrorism. Retrieved 20 November, 2006, from http://www.malcolmread.co.uk/JockYoung/imagining_terrorism_jun04-4.pdf.

Moore, M. (2003). *Dude, Where's My Country?* New York: Warner Books.

Moores, S. (1993). *Interpreting Audiences: The Ethnography of Media Consumption.* London: Sage.

Moran, T. E. (2005). Bayard Taylor and American Orientalism: 19th Century Representations of National Character and the Other: Fletcher School of Law and Diplomacy. Medford, MA.

Mordan, J. (1999). Press Pools, Prior Restraint and the Persian Gulf War [Electronic Version]. *Air & Space Power Chronicles.* Retrieved 25 January 2006 from http://www.airpower.maxwell.af.mil/airchronicles/cc/mordan.html.

Morgenthau, H. (1978). *Politics amongst Nations.* New York: Knopf.

Morman, T. (2003). In bed with the embed [Electronic Version]. Retrieved 11 May 2009 from http://www.indyweek.com/gyrobase/Content?oid=oid%3A19278.

Morris, R. (2003, 14 March). A Tyrant 40 Years in the Making. *New York Times,* p. A28.

Morthland, S. P. (2002). *Information Operations: The Need for a National Strategy.* Naval Postgraduate School Monterey, CA.

Mostari, H. A. (2005). The Language Question in the Arab World: Evidence from Algeria. *Journal of Language and Learning,* 3(1).

Mowlana, H., Gerbner, G., & Schiller, H. I. (Eds.). (1992). *Triumph of the Image: The Media's War in the Persian Gulf – A Global Perspective.* San Francisco: Westview Press.

Mral, B. (2006). The Rhetorical State of Alert before the Iraq War 2003. *Nordicom Review,* 27(1), 45–62.

Médecins Sans Frontières. (1993). *Life, Death and Aid: The Médecins Sans Frontières Report on World Crisis Intervention* (1 ed.). New York: Routledge.

Murphy, J. (2001, 14 October). Blair tells BBC to censor bin Laden. *Sunday Telegraph.*

Murswiek, D. (2003). The American Strategy of Preemptive War and International Law [Electronic Version]. Retrieved 11 March 2009 from www.allacademic.com/meta/p119655_index.htm.

Muscati, S. A. (2002). Arab/Muslim 'Otherness': The Role of Racial Constructions in the Gulf War and the Continuing Crisis with Iraq. *Journal of Muslim Minority Affairs,* 22(1).

Bibliography

Naber, N. (2000). Ambiguous insiders: an investigation of Arab American invisibility. *Ethnic and Racial Studies*, 23(1), 37–61.

Nacos, B. L. (1994). *Terrorism and the Media*. New York: Columbia University Press.

Nawar, I. (2000, May/June). *Freedom of expression in the Arab world*. Paper presented at the Aspen Institute Conference on Freedom of Expression, Wye River, Maryland.

Nelson, T. E., Oxley, Z. M., & Clawson, R. A. (1997). Toward a Psychology of Framing Effects. *Political Behavior*, 19(3), 221–246.

New York Times. (1989, 11 December). Upheaval in the East; Lenin Statue in Mothballs. *New York Times*, p. A8. Retrieved 3 June 2014, from http://www.nytimes.com/1989/12/11/world/upheaval-in-the-east-lenin-statue-in-mothballs.html.

New York Times. (2004, 26 May). From the Editors; the Times and Iraq. *New York Times*. Section A. Retrieved 1 July 2016, from http://www.nytimes.com/2004/05/26/world/from-the-editors-the-times-and-iraq.html.

Nichols, J., & McChesney, R. W. (2005). *Tragedy and Farce: How the Ameri-can Media Sell Wars, Spin Elections, and Destroy Democracy*. New Press: New York.

Nightingale, V. (1996). *Studying Audiences: The Shock of the Real*. London and New York: Routledge.

Nisbet, E. C., Nisbet, M. C., & Sheufele, D. A. (2004). Public Diplomacy, Television News, and Muslim Opinion. *Harvard International Journal of Press/Politics*, 9(2).

Norris, P. (2003). The bridging and bonding role of online communities. In P. N. Howard & S. Jones (Eds.), *Society Online: The Internet in Context*. Thousand Oaks: Sage.

Norton, A. (2004). *Leo Strauss and the politics of American empire*. New Haven, CT: Yale University Press.

O'Heffernan, P. (1993). Sobering Thoughts on Sound Bites Seen 'Round the World. In B. S. Greenberg & W. Gantz (Eds.), *Desert Storm and the Mass Media* (pp. 19–28). Cresskill, NJ: Hampton Press, INC.

Oliverio, A. (1997). The state of injustice: the politics of terrorism and the production of order. *International Journal of Comparative Sociology*, 38 (1–2).

Oliverio, A. (1998). *The State of Terror*. Albany: State University of New York Press.

Oliverio, A., Lauderdale, Pat. (2005). Terrorism as Deviance or Social Control: Suggestions for Future Research. *International Journal of Comparative Sociology* (Special Issue).

Opinion-Research-Business. (2007). September 2007 – More than 1,000,000 Iraqis murdered [Electronic Version]. Retrieved from http://www.opinion.co.uk/Newsroom_details.aspx?NewsId=78.

Palast, G. (2007). *Armed Madhouse: From Baghdad to New Orleans*. New York: Plume.

Paletz, D. (1994). Just Deserts? In W. L. Bennett & D. L. Paletz (Eds.), *Taken By Storm: The Media, Public Opinion, and US Foreign Policy in Gulf War* (pp. 277–292). Chicago: The University of Chicago Press.

Pan, Z., & Kosicki, G. M. (1993). Framing analysis: An approach to news discourse. *Political Communication*, 10, 55–75.

Pan, Z., & Kosicki, G. M. (1994). Voters' Reasoning Processes and Media Influences during the Persian Gulf War. *Political Behavior*, 16(1), 117–156.

Parenti, M. (1995). The Myth of the Liberal Media. *Humanist*, 55, 7–9.

Bibliography

Parenti, M. (2000). *Inventing Reality: the Politics of the Mass Media*. New York: St. Martin's Press.

Patai, R. (1973). *The Arab Mind*. New York: Scribner.

Payne, K. (2005). The Media and the Laws of War. *Parameters*, 81–93.

Perelman, & Olbrechts-Tyteca. (1969). *The New Rhetoric*. Notre Dame, Indiana: Notre Dame Press.

Perri. (2005). What's in a frame? Social organization, risk perception and the sociology of knowledge. *Journal of Risk Research*, 8(2), 91–118.

Peteet, J. M. (1994). Violence and the Construction of a Gendered Identity in the Occupied Territories. *PoLAR: Political and Legal Anthropology Review*, 17(1), 1–10.

Peters, R. (2002). *Beyond Terror: Strategy in a Changing World*. Mechanicsburg, PA: Stackpole Books.

Pew Research Center. (2006). America's Image Slips, But Allies Share US Concerns Over Iran, Hamas [Electronic Version]. Retrieved from http://pewglobal.org/reports/display.php?PageID=824.

Pfau, M., Haigh, M., Gettle, M., Donnelly, M., Scoot, G., Warr, D., et al. (2006). A Comparison of Embedded and Nonembedded Print Coverage of the US Invasion and Occupation of Iraq. *The Harvard International Journal of Press/Politics*, 11(2), 139–153.

Pfau, M., Haigh, M., Gettle, M., Donnelly, M., Scott, G., Warr, D., et al. (2004). Embedding journalists in military combat units: Impact on newspaper story frames and tone. *Journalism & Mass Communication Quarterly*, 81(1), 74–88.

Pilger, J. (1998). *Hidden Agendas* (2nd Ed.). London: Vintage.

Pilger, J. (2002, 14 December). Axis of Evil; John Pilger Exposes the Frightening Agenda in Washington that Is Behind the United States Threat to World Peace. *Morning Star*.

Pipes, D. (1983). *In the Path of God: Islam and Political Power* (2003 Ed.). New Brunswick, NJ: Transaction Publishers.

Pipes, D. (1990). The Muslims Are Coming! The Muslims Are Coming! *National Review* 42 (22).

Pipes, D. (2001). The Danger Within: Militant Islam in America. *Commentary* (November).

Pipes, D. (2002). *Militant Islam Reaches America*. New York: W.W. Norton.

Pipes, D. (2003, 3 June). Iraq's Weapons & the Road to War. New York Post. Retrieved 25 June 2016 from: http://www.danielpipes.org/1116/iraqs-weapons-the-road-to-war.

Plenzler, J. M. (2004). Conducting Expeditionary Public Affairs. *Marine Corps Gazette*, 88(2).

PNAC. (2000). Rebuilding American Defense: Strategies, Forces and Resources for a New American Century [Electronic Version]. *Project for the New American Century*. Retrieved from www.newamericancentury.org/RebuildingAmericasDefenses.pdf.

Podhoretz, N. (2002). In Praise of the Bush Doctrine. *Commentary* (September).

Pope Benedict XVI. (2006, 12 September). *Lecture of the Holy Father*. Paper presented at the Aula Magna of the University of Regensburg, Germany.

Pormann, P. E., & Savage-Smith, E. (2007). *Medieval Islamic Medicine*. Edinburgh: Edinburgh University Press.

Bibliography

Porras, I. M. (1995). On terrorism: Reflections on violence and the outlaw. In D. Danielsen & K. Engle (Eds.), *After Identity: A Reader in Law and Culture*. New York: Routledge.

Pratkanis, A., & Aronson, E. (1991). *Age of Propaganda: The Everyday Use and Abuse of Persuasion*. New York: WH Freeman & Co.

Prescod, C. (2004). Book Review: Al Jazeera Ambassador of the Arab World. *Race & Class*, 45(3), 87–98.

Pryce-Jones, D. (1989). *The Closed Circle. An Interpretation of the Arabs*. New York: Harper.

Puar, J. K., & Rai, A. S. (2002). Monster, Terrorist, Fag: The War on Terrorism and the Production of Docile Patriots. *Social Text* 20(3).

Public-Broadcasting-Service. (1992). Defense Planning Guidance. Retrieved 16 November, 2006, from http://www.pbs.org/wgbh/pages/frontline/shows/iraq/etc/wolf.html.

Rafael, V. L. (1994). The Cultures of Area Studies in the United States. *Social Text*, 41, 91–111.

Rai, M. (1995). *Chomsky's Politics*. New York: Verso.

Rampton, S., & Stauber, J. (2003). *Weapons of Mass Deception: The Uses of Propaganda in Bush's War on Iraq*. London: Robinson.

Rane, H. & Salem, S. (2012). Social media, social movements and the diffusion of ideas in the Arab uprisings. *The Journal of International Communication*, 18(1).

Ravi, N. (2005). Looking Beyond Flawed Journalism: How National Interests, Patriotism and Cultural Values Shaped the Coverage of the Iraq War. *Press/Politics*, 10(1), 45–62.

Reese, S. D. (2006). Theorizing a globalized journalism. In M. Löffelholz, D. Weaver & A. Schwarz (Eds.), *Global Journalism Research: Theories, Methods, Findings, Future*. London: Blackwell.

Reese, S. D., Gandy, O. H., & Grant, A. E. (Eds.). (2001). *Framing Public Life: Perspectives on Media and Our Understanding of the Social World*. Mahwah, NJ: Lawrence Erlbaum Associates.

Rendall, S., & Broughel, T. (2003). Amplifying Officials, Squelching Dissent: FAIR study finds democracy poorly served by war coverage. *Extra*, May/June 2003. Retrieved 10 June 2009 from www.fair.org/extra/0305/warstudy.html

Reporters without Borders. (2003). Qatar-2003 Annual Report. Retrieved from http://www.rsf.org/article.php3?id_article=5390.

Rich, F. (2006). *The Greatest Story Ever Sold: The Decline and Fall of Truth from 9/11 to Katrina*. New York: The Penguin Press.

Richardson, I. (2003, April). The Failed Dream That Led to Al Jazeera. Retrieved 12 March, 2007, from http://www.richardsonmedia.co.uk/al%20jazeera%20origins.html

Riegert, K. (2002). Know Your Enemy, Know Your Allies: Lessons Not Learned from the Kosovo Conflict. *Journal of Information Warfare*, 1(2), 79–93.

Robertson, R. (1992). *Globalization: Social Theory and Global Culture*. London: Sage.

Robinson, P. (2002). *The Myth CNN Effect: The Myth of News Media, Foreign Policy, and Intervention*. London: Routledge.

Rockower, P. (2008). Qatar's Public Diplomacy. *PubD* 599. Retrieved from http://home.comcast.net/~srockower/psr/QatarPDv4.pdf.

Bibliography

Rosenthal, P. (2003). Awe Arrives, But Not With Human Angle [Electronic Version]. *Chicago Sunday Times*. Retrieved from www.suntimes.com/output/rosenthal/cstnws-tv22.html.

Rosenwerth, K., Hahn, O., Schröder, R., & Lönnendonker, J. (2005). *The Case of Germany*: Erich-Brost-Institute; Centre of Advanced Study in International Journalism.

Rostrup, T. (1996). The Gulf War – the failure of the Fourth Estate? [Electronic Version]. Retrieved 6 November, 2007, from http://www.uib.no/People/ssptr/gulfwar.htm.

Rotberg, R., & Weiss, T. (Eds.). (1996). *From Massacres to Genocide*. Cambridge, Ma: The World Peace Foundation.

Rotter, A. J. (2000). Saidism without Said: Orientalism and US Diplomatic History. *The American Historical Review*, 105(4).

Rudgers, D. F. (2000). The Origins of Covert Action. *Journal of Contemporary History*, 35(2), 249–262.

Rugh, W. A. (2004). *Arab Mass Media: Newspapers, Radio and Television in Arab Politics*. Westport: Praeger.

Rugh, W. A. (2004). How Washington Confronts Arab Media. *Global Media Journal*, 3(5).

Rumelhart, D. E., & Ortney, A. (1977). The representation of knowledge in memory. In R. C. Anderson, R. J. Spiro & W. E. Montague (Eds.), *Schooling and the acquisition of knowledge* (pp. 99–135). Hillsdale, NJ: Lawrence Erlbaum.

Rumsfeld, D. H. (2002). News Transcript. Secretary Rumsfeld Media Availability En Route to Chile [Electronic Version]. Retrieved 15 August 2005 from http://www.defenselink.mil/transcripts/2002/t11212002_t1118sd2.html.

Ryan, M. (2004). Framing the War against Terrorism: US Newspaper Editorials and Military Action in Iraq. *Gazette*, 66(4), 363–382.

Saghieh, H. (2004, 2 June). *Al Jazeera: the world through Arab eyes*. Paper presented at the 11th World Editors' Forum, Istanbul.

Said, E. (1979). *Orientalism*. New York: Vintage Books.

Said, E. (1981). *Covering Islam: how the media and the experts determine how we see the rest of the world*. New York: Pantheon Books.

Said, E. (1988). Identity, Negation and Violence. *New Left Review* (September–October).

Said, E. (1996, May). Declaring war on Islam: The legacy of Sharmelsheikh. *The Progressive*, 60.

Said, E. (1997). Apocalypse Now [Electronic Version]. Retrieved from http://www.thirdworldtraveler.com/Middle_East/ApocalypseNow_Said.html.

Said, E. (2000). Orientalism Reconsidered. In A. L. Macfie (Ed.), *Orientalism: A Reaser* (pp. 345–359). New York: New York University Press.

Said, E. (2001, 22 October). The Clash of Ignorance. *The Nation*.

Sakr, N. (2001). Whys and Wherefores of Satellite Channel Ownership. In *Satellite Realms: Transnational Television, Globalization and the Middle East*. London: I.B.Tauris publishers.

Sakr, N. (2007). Challenger or lackey? The Politics of news on Al Jazeera. In D. Thussu (Ed.), *Media on the Move: Global Flow and Contra-Flow* (pp. 116–132). London: Routledge.

Bibliography

Sale, R. (2003). Exclusive: Saddam key in early CIA plot [Electronic Version]. *UPI.com*. Retrieved from http://www.upi.com/Business_News/Security-Industry/2003/04/10/Exclusive-Saddam-key-in-early-CIA-plot/UPI-65571050017416/.

Samman, K. (2005). Towards a Non-Essentialist Pedagogy of "Islam". *Teaching Theology and Religion*, 8(3), 129–198.

Sardar, Z. (1999). *Orientalism*. Buckingham: Open University Press.

Schechter, D. (2000). CNN at 20: From Chicken Noodle Network to Global Media Power [Electronic Version]. *MediaChannel.org*. Retrieved 1 November, 2007.

Schechter, D. (2002). Information Warriors: Pentagon's Ministry of Truth Shapes War Coverage. Retrieved 15 August, 2005, from: www.media-Alliance.org/article.php?story=20031022134313776&query=schecter.

Schechter, D. (2004). Information Dominance: The Philosophy of Total propaganda Control? In Y. R. Kamalipour, and & N. Snow (Eds.), *War, Media and Propaganda: A Global Perspective*: Rowman and Littlefield.

Schegloff, E. (1988). Goffman and the Analysis of Conversation. In P. Drew & A. Wootton (Eds.), *Erving Goffman: Exploring the Interaction Order*. Cambridge: Polity.

Scheuer, M. (2004). *Imperial Hubris: Why the West Is Losing the War on Terror*. Washington, DC: Brassey's Inc.

Scheufele, B. (2004). Framing-Effects Approach: Theory and Methods Communications. *The European Journal of Communication Research*, 29(4), 401–428.

Schleifer, S. A. (2003). Interview with Adnan Sharif. *Transnational Broadcasting Studies*, 11.

Schleifer, S. A. (2004). MMDS and the New Satellite Television Technologies: A Media Explosion in the Arab World. *Transnational Broadcasting Studies*, 13.

Schlesinger, P., Murdock, G., & Elliott, P. (1983). *Televising 'Terrorism': Political Violence in Popular Culture*. London: Comedia Publishing Group.

Schmid, A. P., & Yongman, A. J. (1984). *Political Terrorism* (2005 Ed.). London: Transaction Publishers.

Schudson, M. (2003). *The sociology of news*. New York: Norton.

Schudson, M. (2005). Autonomy from whom? In R. R. Benson & E. Neveu (Eds.), *Bourdieu and the journalistic field* (pp. 214–224). Cambridge: Polity Press.

Schwalbe, C. B., Silcock, B. W., & Keith, S. (2005). Visual Framing of the Early Weeks of the US-Led Invasion of Iraq: Applying the Master War Narrative to Electronic and Print Images. *Journal of Broadcasting & Electronic Media*, 4(1).

Sciolino, E. (1996, 21 January). Seeing Green; The Red Menace Is Gone. But Here's Islam. *New York Times*, p. 4.1.

Scraton, P. (Ed.). (2002). *Beyond September 11: An anthology of dissent*. London; Sterling, Va.: Pluto Press.

Semetko, H. A., & Valkenburg, P. M. (2000). Framing European Politics: A Content Analysis of Press and Television News. *Journal of Communication*, 50(2), 93–109.

Sha'ban, F. (1991). *Islam and Arabs in Early American Thought: The Roots of Orientalism in America*. Durham, NC: The Acorn Press.

Sha'ban, F. (2003). September 11 and the millennialist discourse: an order of words? *Arab Studies Quarterly* 25(1/2), 13–32.

Shafik, V. (1998). *Arab Cinema: History and Cultural Identity*. Cairo: American University in Cairo Press.

Bibliography

Shaheen, J. (1981). *ABSCAM: Arabiaphobia in America*, Washington DC.

Shaheen, J. (2001). *Reel Bad Arabs: How Hollywood Vilifies a People*. New York: Olive Branch Press.

Sharp, T. (1980). The Politics of Propaganda: The Office of War Information 1942–1945 [Review of book by Allan M. Winkler]. *International Affairs* (Royal Institute of International Affairs), 56(1), 151–153.

Shaw, I. S. (2007). Historical frames and the politics of humanitarian intervention: from Ethiopia, Somalia to Rwanda. *Globalisation, Societies and Education*, 5(3), 351–371.

Shoemaker, P., & Reese, S. D. (1996). *Mediating the Message*. White Plains, NY: Longman.

Shome, R., & Hegde, R. S. (2002). Culture, Communication, and the Challenge of Globalization. *Critical Studies in Media Communication*, 19(2), 172–189.

Siebert, F. S., Peterson, T., and Schramm, W. (1956). *Four Theories of the Press: The Authoritarian, Libertarian, Social Responsibility, and Soviet Communist Concepts of What the Press Should Be and Do*. Chicago: University of Illinois Press.

Sieting, L. A. (2003). Intelligence Support to Information Operations: Today and in the Objective Force. *The Military Intelligence Professional Bulletin* (July–September).

Sigal, L. (1973). *Reporters and Officials: The Organization and Politics of Newsmaking*. Lexington, MA: DC Heath.

Sigal, L. V. (1973). *Reporters and Officials*. Lexington: Heath.

Simmons, B., & Lowry, D. (1990). Terrorists in the news. *Journalism Quarterly*, 67(4), 692–696.

Simon, A. f. (2001). A unified method for analyzing media framing. In R. P. Hart & D. Shaw (Eds.), *Communication in US Elections*. Lanham, MD: Rowman & Littlefield.

Simpson, C. (1996). *The Science of Coercion: Communication Research and Psychological Warfare*. New York, NY: Oxford Press.

Simpson, C. (1996). *Science of Coercion: Communication Research and Psychological Warfare 1945–1960*. New York: Oxford University Press.

Sirriyeh, H. (2000). A New Version of Pan-Arabism. *International Relations*, XV(3).

Skalli, L. H. (2006). Communicating gender in the public sphere: women and information technologies in the Mena. *Journal of Middle East Women's Studies*, 2(2).

Smelser, N. (1963). *Theory of Collective Behavior*. New York: Free Press of Glencoe.

Smith, C. (2011, 11 February). Egypt's Facebook revolution: Wael Ghonim thanks the social network. *Huffington Post*. Retrieved from http://www.huffingtonpost.com/2011/02/11/egypt-facebookrevolution-wael-ghonim_n_822078.html.

Smith, P. M. (1991). *How CNN Fought the War: A View from the Inside*. New York: Carol Publication Group.

Smith, R. (2006, 16 June). When French Savants Were in Egypt's Land. *New York Times*.

Smith, T. J. (Ed.). (1989). *Propaganda: A Pluralistic Perspective*. New York: Praeger.

Smith, T. L. (1988). Intention and Morality. *Journal of Communication*, 38(3).

Snow, D. A., & Benford, R. D. (2000). Framing Processes and Social Movements: An Overview and Assessment. *Annual Review of Sociology*, 26.

Snow, N. (2002). Déjà vu All Over Again [Electronic Version]. *Common Dreams*. Retrieved from http://ics.leeds.ac.uk/papers/vp01.cfm?outfit=pmt&folder=10&paper=925.

Bibliography

Soderlund, W. C., Wagenberg, R. H., & Pemberton, I. C. (1994). Cheerleader or Critic? Television News Coverage in Canada and the United States of the US Invasion of Panama. *Canadian Journal of Political Science*, 27(3), 581–604.

Soley, L. C. (1992). *The News Shapers: The Sources Who Explain the News*. New York: Praeger.

Southern, R. W. (1978). *Western Views of Islam in the Middle Ages*. Cambridge: Harvard University Press.

Sperry, P. (2003). No shock, no awe, it never happened [Electronic Version]. *WorldNetDaily*.

Spigel, L. (2004). Entertainment Wars: Television Culture after 9/11. *American Quarterly*, 56(2).

Sproule, J. M. (1984). *The Propaganda Analysis Movement since World War*. Paper presented at the Speech Communication Association, Chicago, IL. 1–4 November. Retrieved from: http://www.eric.ed.gov/ERICWebPortal/custom/portlets/recordDetails/detailmini.jsp?_nfpb=true&_&ERICExtSearch_SearchValue_0=ED253902&ERICExtSearch_SearchType_0=no&accno=ED253902.

Sproule, J. M. (1989). Progressive propaganda critics and the magic bullet myth. *Critical Studies in Mass Communication* (6), 225–246.

Sproule, J. M. (1994). *Channels of Propaganda*. Bloomington, IN: Eric/Edinfo Press.

Sproule, J. M. (1997). *Propaganda and Democracy: The American Experience of Media and Mass Persuasion*. Cambridge, UK; New York: Cambridge University Press.

Sreberny, A. (2002). Seeing through the Veil: Regimes of Representation. *Feminist Media Studies*, 2(2).

Stam, R. (1983). Television News and its Spectator. In E. A. Kaplan (Ed.), *Regarding Television-Critical Approaches: An Anthology* (pp. 23–43). Frederick, MD: University Publications of America.

Stan, F. (2003). On the Future of "Global Television": An economic and historical approach to understanding the basics and trajectory of world television. *Ad Astra*, 2(1).

Stannard, D. E. (1992). *American Holocaust: The Conquest of the New World*. New York: Oxford University Press.

State-of-the-News-Media. (2005). *The state of the news media: An annual report on American journalism* [Electronic Version]. Retrieved from: http://www.stateofthemedia.org/2005/.

St-Clair, J. (2007). Marketing an Invasion: How to Sell a War [Electronic Version]. *Counterpunch.org*. Retrieved from http://www.counterpunch.org/stclair06122007.html.

Stein, G. J. (1996). *Information Attack: Information Warfare in 2025*. Montgomery, Alabama: Air War College.

Steinert, H. (2003). The indispensable metaphor of war. *Theoretical Criminology*, 7(3), 265–291.

Stevenson, N. (2002). *Understanding Media Cultures*. London: Sage Publications.

Stevenson, R., & D. Shaw (1984). *Foreign News and the New World Information Order*. Ames, Ia.: Iowa State University Press.

Stille, A. (2003, 13 September). The Latest Obscenity Has Seven Letters. *New York Times*, p. 19.

Stork, J. (1972). Understanding the Balfour Declaration. *MERIP Reports*, 13, 9–13.

Bibliography

Strobel, W. P. (1997). *Late-breaking foreign policy*. Washington DC: United States Institute of Peace Press.

Stubbs, R. (1989). *Hearts and Minds in Guerrilla Warfare: The Malayan Emergency 1948–1960*. New York: Oxford University Press.

Sukoharsono, E. G. (1998). *Accounting in A Historical Transition: A Shifting Dominant belief from Hindu to Islamic Administration in Indonesia*. Paper presented at the Asia-Pacific Interdisciplinary Research on Accounting (APIRA), Osaka, Japan.

Suleiman, M. (1988). *Arabs in the Mind of America*. Brattleboro, VT: Amana Books.

Sullivan, S. (2001). The Courting of Al Jazeera. *Transnational Broadcasting Studies*, 7(Fall/Winter).

Szafranski, R. (1995). A Theory of Information Warfare: Preparing for 2020. *Airpower Journal*, 9(1).

Tabar, M.-D. (2002). *Printing Press to Satellite: A Historical Case Study of Media and the Arab State*. Unpublished Master of Arts thesis, Georgetown University, Washington D.C.

Tan, Z. C. W. (1989). The role of media in insurgent terrorism: Issues and perspectives. *Gazette*, 44, 191–215.

Tankard, J. W. J. (2001). The empirical approach to the study of media framing. In S. D. Reese, O. H. Gandy & A. E. Grant (Eds.), *Framing Public Life*. Mahwah, NJ: Lawrence Erlbaum Associates.

Tatham, S. (2005). Al Jazeera: Get Used to It, It's Not Going Away. *Proceedings*, 131(8), 28–33.

Tayler, J. (2004, Nov). The Faisal factor: a talk-show host on Al Jazeera targets those he believes are the worst enemies the Arabs have: themselves. *The Atlantic Monthly*, 294.

Taylor, J. (1998). *Body Horror*. New York: New York University Press.

Taylor, P. M. (1992). *War and the Media Propaganda and Persuasion in the Gulf War*. Manchester: Manchester University Press.

Taylor, P. M. (2003, 24 October). From Information Warfare (IW) to Information Operations (IO) to the Global 'War' on Terrorism. Retrieved 18 October, 2007, from http://ics.leeds.ac.uk/papers/vp01.cfm?outfit=pmt&requesttimeout=500&folder=25&paper=828.

Taylor, P. M. (2007). 'Munitions of the Mind': A brief history of military psychological operations. *Place Branding and Public Diplomacy*, 3(3), 196.

Tchen, J. (1999). *New York Before Chinatown: Orientalism and the Shaping of American Culture, 1776–1882*. Baltimore: Johns Hopkins University Press.

Tehranian, M. (1997). Global Communication and International Relations: Changing Paradigms and Policies. *The International Journal of Peace Studies*, 2(1).

Telhami, S. (2007). Shibley Telhami Response [Electronic Version]. *Dissent Magazine*. Retrieved from http://www.dissentmagazine.org/article/?article=778.

Terranova, T. (2007). Futurepublic: On Information Warfare, Bio-racism and Hegemony as Noopolitics. *Theory, Culture & Society*, 24(3), 125–145.

The Economist (2013). Al Jazeera must do better. *The Economist*. Available at: http://www.economist.com/news/middle-east-and-africa/21569429-arabs-premier-television-network-bids-american-viewers-must-do-better.

Bibliography

The Project for Excellence in Journalism. (2004). *The State of the News Media report* 2004.
The White House Blog (2009). The President's Speech in Cairo: A New Beginning. Retrieved from http://www.whitehouse.gov/blog/NewBeginning/.
Thomas, T. L. (1999). Human Network Attacks. *Military Review*, 79(5).
Thompson, J. B. (1990). *Ideology and Modern Culture*. Cambridge: Polity Press.
Thompson, J. B. (1995). *The Media and Modernity: A Social Theory of the Media*. Cambridge: Polity Press.
Thussu, D. K. (2000a). *International communication: Continuity and change*. London: Arnold.
Thussu, D. K. (2000b). Legitimizing 'Humanitarian Intervention'? CNN, NATO and the Kosovo Crisis. *European Journal of Communication*, 15(3), 345–361.
Thussu, D. K. (2002). Managing the Media in an Era of Round-the-Clock News: notes from India's First tele-war. *Journalism Studies*, 3(2), 203–212.
Thussu, D. K. (2003). Live TV and Bloodless Deaths: War, Infotainment and 24/7 News. In D. K. Thussu & D. Freedman (Eds.), *War and The Media: Reporting Conflict 24/7*. Thousand Oaks: Sage.
Tibawi, A. L. (1964). English-speaking Orientalists. *Islamic Quarterly*, 8(1–4), 25–45.
Tibawi, A. L. (1979). A Second Critique of English-speaking Orientalists. *Islamic Quarterly*, 23(1).
Tibi, B. (1981). *Arab Nationalism: A Critical Enquiry*. London: Macmillan Press.
TimeWarner.com. (2000). CNN is Viewers Cable Network of Choice for Democratic and Republican National Convention Coverage [Electronic Version]. Retrieved from http://www.timewarner.com/corp/newsroom/pr/0,20812,667801,00.html.
Toffler, A., & Toffler, H. (1993). *War and Anti-War, Survival at the Dawn of the 21st Century*. Boston: Little, Brown & Company.
Toggia, E., Lauderdale, R., & Zegeye, A. (2000). *Crisis and Terror in the Horn of Africa*. Burlington, VT: Ashgate, Dartmouth.
Tomlinson, J. (2002). The discourse of cultural imperialism. In D. McQuail (Ed.), *Mcquail's reader in mass communication theory* (pp. 223–237). London: Sage Publications.
Toronto-Star. (1991, 9 April). General Advocates Cuts in US Military Budget.
Tounsy, A. E. (2002). Reflections on the Arab Satellites, the Palestinian Intifada, and the Israeli War. *Transnational Broadcasting Studies* (spring).
Trichur, G. K. (2005). The New Imperial Conjuncture and Alternative Futures for Twenty-first Century Global Political Economy. *Globalizations*, 2(1), 164–181.
Trivundza, I. T. (2004). Orientalism as news: Pictorial representations of the US attack on Iraq in Delo. *Journalism*, 5(4), 480–499.
Troyer, L. (2001). The Calling of Counterterrorism. *Theory & Event*, 5(4).
Tuastad, D. (2003). Neo-Orientalism and the New Barbarism Thesis: Aspects of Symbolic Violence in the Middle East Conflict(s). *Third World Quarterly*, 24(4), 591–599.
Tuchman, G. (1978). *Making News*. New York: Free.
Turk, A. T. (2004). Sociology of Terrorism. *Annual Review of Sociology*, 30, 271–286.
Turner, B. S. (1978). *Marx and the End of Orientalism*. London: George Allen and Unwin.
Turner, B. S. (2005). *Classical Sociology: on cosmopolitanism, critical recognition theory and Islam*. Singapore: Asia Research Institute.

Bibliography

Turner, T. (2003, 24 April). Q & A with Ted Turner. *Medallion Speaker Series*. Retrieved 24 July 2006, from http://www.commonwealthclub.org/archive/03/03-04turner-qa.html

Turner, T. (2004). My Beef with Big Media [Electronic Version]. *Washington Monthly*. Retrieved from http://www.washingtonmonthly.com/features/2004/0407.turner.html.

UNHCR. (2008). Iraq: Latest return survey shows few intending to go home soon [Electronic Version]. Retrieved from http://www.unhcr.org/cgi-bin/texis/vtx/search?page=search&docid=4816ef534&query=Iraq:%20Latest%20return%20survey%20shows%20few%20intending%20to%20go%20home.

United-Nations-Development-Programme. (2004). Arab Human Development Report 2004. Retrieved 16 June, 2008, from http://hdr.undp.org/en/reports/regional-reports/arabstates/name,3278,en.html.

United-Nations-Environment-Programme. (2003). Desk Study on the Environment in Iraq. Retrieved from http://www.unep.org/pdf/iraq_ds_lowres.pdf.

US Labor Against the War. (2007). 5 million Iraqi orphans, anti-corruption board reveals Voices of Iraq [Electronic Version]. Retrieved from http://www.uslaboragainstwar.org/article.php?id=15144.

Valley, P. E., & Aquino, M. A. (1980). *From PSYOP to Mind war: The Psychology of Victory*. Paper presented at the Presidio of San Francisco, California.

Van-Der-Veer, P. (2004). War propaganda and the liberal public sphere. In P. Van-Der-Veer & S. Munshi (Eds.), *Media, War and Terrorism*. London and New York: Routledge.

Van-Dijk, T. A. (1985). Structures of News in the Press. In T. A. Van-Dijk (Ed.), *Discourse and Communication: New Approaches to the Analysis of Mass Media Discourse and Communication* (pp. 69–93). New York: W. de Gruyter.

Van-Dijk, T. A. (1988). *News as Discourse*. Hillsdale, N.J.: Erlbaum.

Van-Ham, P. (2003). War, Lies, and Videotape: Public Diplomacy and the USA's War on Terrorism. *Security Dialogue*, 34(4).

Van-Tuyll, D. R. (2002). The press and war. In L. Parcell & W. Sloan (Eds.), *American Journalism: history, principles, practices*. Jefferson, NC: McFarland.

Virilio, P. (2002). *Desert Screen: War at the Speed of Light*. London: Continuum.

Vivian, J. (1991). *The media of mass communication*. Boston: Allyn and Bacon

Voice of America. (2003). Bush Officially Notifies Congress: Iraq Diplomacy Has Failed [Electronic Version] Retrieved from NewsVOA.com.

Volkmer, I. (1999). *News in the Global Sphere: A Study of CNN and its Impact on Global Communication*. Luton: University of Luton Press.

Yuval, K., Lavie-Dinur, A., & Azran, T. (2014). Broadcast coverage of Gaddafi's final hours in images and headlines: A brutal lynch or the desired death of a terrorist? *The International Communication Gazette*, 0(0), 1–18.

Wagner-Pacifici, R. E. (1986). *The Moro Morality Play by Robin Erica Wagner-Pacifici*. Chicago: University of Chicago.

Wallerstein, I. (1976). Semi-Peripheral Countries and the Contemporary World Crisis. *Theory and Society*, 3, 461–484.

Walton, D. (1997). What is Propaganda and What Exactly is Wrong With It. *Public Affairs Quarterly*, 11(4).

Bibliography

Waxman, S. (2001, 4 December). Arab TV's strong signal. *Washington Post.*
Weber, S. (2002). War, Terrorism, and Spectacle: On Towers and Caves. *The South Atlantic Quarterly* (summer).
Weinberger, J. (2003). Defining Terror. *Seton Hall Journal of Diplomacy and International Relations,* Winter/Spring.
Weiser, C. (2003). Report lists 'public diplomacy' failures [Electronic Version]. *USATODAY. com.* Retrieved from http://www.usatoday.com/news/world/2003-09-15-public-diplomacy-fails_x.htm.
Whitaker, B. (2003). Flags in the dust [Electronic Version]. Retrieved from http://www.guardian.co.uk/world/2003/mar/24/worlddispatch.iraq.
White, G. (1992). Politiques D'amenagement du Territoire au Maroc *International Journal of Middle East Studies,* 24(4).
Whitehead, Y. (1997). Information as a Weapon; Reality versus Promises. *Airpower Journal* (Fall).
White-House. (2004). Progress in the War on Terror [Electronic Version]. Retrieved from http://merln.ndu.edu/archivepdf/terrorism/WH/20040122-1.pdf.
Wildermuth, N. (2005). Defining the "Al Jazeera Effect" – American Public Diplomacy at a Crossroad. *in medias res,* 1(2).
Wilding, J. (2003). Too many civilian casualties [Electronic Version]. *The Guardian* from http://www.guardian.co.uk/world/2003/mar/29/iraq3.
Wilkins, K., & Downing, J. (2002). Mediating Terrorism: Text and Protest in Interpretations of The Siege. *Critical Studies in Media Communication,* 19(4).
Wilkinson, P. (1986). *Terrorism and the Liberal State.* London: MacMillan.
Williams, G. A. (1960). The Concept of 'Egemonia' in the Thought of Antonio Gramsci: Some Notes on Interpretation. *Journal of the History of Ideas,* 21(4), 586–599.
Williams, J. (2007). Al Jazeera's Booming Voice: Developing Qatar's Comparative Advantage in the Middle East. *Journal of Middle Eastern Geopolitics,* 2(4).
Windschuttle, K. (1999, January). Edward Said's "Orientalism revisited". Retrieved 20 September, 2006, from http://www.newcriterion.com/archive/17/jan99/said.htm
Windt, T. O. (1992). The presidency and speeches on international crises: Repeating the rhetorical past. In T. Windt & B. Ingold (Eds.), *Essays in presidential rhetoric* (3rd ed., pp. 91–100). Dubuque, IA: Kendall Hunt.
Wise, L. (2005). A Second Look at Alhurra: A US-Funded Channel Comes of Age on the Front Lines of the 'Battle for Hearts and Minds. *Transnational Broadcasting Studies,* 14.
Wolff, M. (2003, 14 April). I was only asking. *Media Guardian,* pp. 6–7.
Wolfsfeld, G. (1997). *Media and political conflict news from the Middle East.* Cambridge: Cambridge University Press.
Wood, M. (2003). On Edward Said. *London Review of Books,* 25(20).
Woods, L. T. (2006). Where's Noam? On the Absence of References to Noam Chomsky in Introductory International Studies Textbooks. *New Political Science,* 28(1), 65–79.
Woodward, B. (2002). *Bush at War.* New York: Simon & Schuster.
Woollacott, J. (1982). Messages and Meanings. In M. Gurevitch, T. Bennett, J. Curran & J. Woollacott (Eds.), *Culture, Society and the Media* (Vol. 1). London: Methuen.
Worth, R. F. (2008, 4 January). Al Jazeera no longer nips at Saudis. *New York Times.*

Bibliography

Worth, R. F. (2008, 4 January). A voice of moderation helps transform Arab media. *New York Times*.

Yemen-Newspaper. (2004). Interview with Ghassan Bin Jeddou. Retrieved from http://26sep.net/newsweekarticle.php?sid=8312.

Yemen-Times. (2005). Haikal: larger than a life's experience [Electronic Version], 14. Retrieved 30 January, 2007, from http://www.yementimes.com/article.shtml?i=883&p=opinion&a=4.

Yoneyama, L. (2005). Liberation under Siege: US Military Occupation and Japanese Women's Enfranchisement. *American Quarterly*, 57(3).

Zaimeche, S. (2002, March). Aspects of the Islamic Influence on Science and Learning in the Christian West (12th-13th century). Retrieved 6 March, 2007, from http://muslimheritage.com/topics/default.cfm?ArticleID=341.

Zaller, J., & Chui, D. (1996). Government's Little Helper: US Press Coverage of Foreign Policy Crises, 1945-1991. *Political Communication*, 13, 385-405.

Zayani, M. (2008). Courting and Containing the Arab Street: Arab Public Opinion, the Middle East, and US Public Diplomacy. *Arab Studies Quarterly*, 30(2).

Zayani, M., & Ayish, M. I. (2006). Arab Satellite Television and Crisis Reporting: Covering the Fall of Baghdad. *The International Communication Gazette*, 68(5-6), 473-497.

Zednik, R. (2002). Inside Al Jazeera. *Columbia Journalism Review*.

Zelizer, B. (1992). CNN, the Gulf War, and Journalistic Practice. *Journal of Communication*, 42(1), 66.

Zelizer, B. (1995). Reading the Past against the Grain: The Shape of Memory Studies. *Critical Studies in Mass Communication*, 12(3).

Zizek, S. (2002). Are We in a War? Do we have an Enemy? *London Review of Books*.

Zucchino, D. (2004, 3 July). Army Stage-Managed Fall of Hussein Statue. *Los Angeles Times*, p. A28.

Zulaika, J., & Douglass, W. A. (1996). *Terror and taboo: The follies, fables and faces of terrorism*. New York: Routledge.

Index

9/11, 3, 5, 6, 7, 8, 24, 26, 44, 62–66, 69–71, 73, 88, 89, 113–117, 122, 123, 137, 151, 177

ABC, 18, 113
Abdelhadi, Majed, 144, 150, 152, 157, 174
Abrams, Elliot, 121, 188, 249
Abu Dhabi television, 175
Adnan Charif, 158, 174, 181, 259
advertising, 25, 75, 108, 124, 125, 142, 146
Afghanistan, 26, 27, 72, 90, 91, 113, 114, 116, 117, 119, 123–125, 131, 132, 137, 138, 233, 251, 255, 257, 264
Africa, 35, 45, 46, 73, 77, 85, 86, 87, 93, 97, 98, 248
Algeria, 1, 16, 53, 55, 57, 85, 94, 105, 252, 254
Al Hurra, 125
Ali, Tariq, 10, 66
Al Jazeera
  2003 War in Iraq, 142, 144, 145, 149, 150, 152, 156–159, 161, 164, 165, 167, 170, 171, 174–176, 180–185, 211
  beginnings of, 2, 109, 118, 232
  Bin Laden interviews, 26, 113, 125
  censorship of, 106, 108, 126, 208
  discourse on terrorism, 64, 72, 115, 138, 233
  ethos, 114, 161, 242
  framing, 116, 117, 130, 138, 145, 152, 156, 157, 164, 165, 170, 171, 174, 175, 179–181, 189, 190, 193–196, 199, 200, 204, 205, 207, 226–229, 234
  independence of, 107, 113, 203–205, 236, 237, 241
  newsgathering, 134–136
  offices' destruction, 27, 125, 182, 185–191, 193–205, 236
  pan-Arabism, 101, 111, 112, 119, 232

  political economy of, 103, 105, 136, 137, 235
  Saddam statue, 212–214, 219–221, 226–229, 234
  viewership of, 11, 102, 110, 136, 138, 206
Alouni, Tayseer, 117, 195
Al Qaeda, 27, 50, 88, 113, 114, 115, 122–127, 129, 233, 254
Amanpour, Christiane, 86, 168, 178, 212–214, 258, 259
anti-war, 11, 69, 80, 89, 130, 134, 138, 190, 191, 201, 236
Al-Arabiya, 137, 138, 139, 227, 233
Arab Spring, 1, 2, 242, 243, 244
Arafat, Yasser, 60, 110, 253
Armageddon, 156, 178, 179, 257
Arnett, Peter, 18, 26, 76, 82, 113, 117, 246
Asia, 35, 36, 45, 73, 77, 93, 132, 251
Associated Press, 135
atrocities, 81, 85

Index

Atwan, Abdelbari, 112, 113, 129, 130
Ayyoub, Tareq, 186, 187, 190, 194, 195, 196, 204

Baath Party, 96, 102, 238
Baghdad
  Al Jazeera's coverage from, 136, 144, 145, 149, 150, 152, 153, 157–159, 164, 167, 174, 176, 179, 181, 189, 190, 194–198, 201, 202, 207, 219, 220, 228, 235
  CNNI coverage from, 151, 155, 156, 166, 171, 173, 175, 178, 186, 188, 212, 213, 215, 217, 236
  Gulf War 1991, 18, 82, 117
  historic legacy, 42, 44, 50, 134, 170
  infrared images of, 21
  looting of, 210, 225, 226, 229, 234
  Pact of, 52, 97
  Radio 21, 27
  'Shock and Awe', 131, 141, 142, 180–185, 191, 209, 211, 224, 227
Bahrain, 1, 100, 103, 104, 134, 242, 253
BBC, 19, 61, 78, 82, 103, 104, 105, 108, 112, 118, 131, 189, 202, 206, 232, 246, 253, 255, 259
Beers, Charlotte, 123, 124
beliefs, 4, 31, 83, 201, 230, 236

Bin Laden, Osama, 26, 113, 114, 115, 116, 117, 125, 131
Blitzer, Wolf, 147, 152, 153, 154, 155, 156, 168, 172, 173, 177, 222, 256, 258
Blitzkrieg, 151
Bosnia, 19, 257
Bouazizi, Mohamed, 1, 245
Bourini, Mohammed Kheir, 144, 149
Britain, 6, 7, 14, 35, 41, 52, 83, 95, 96, 97, 130, 131, 157, 164, 208, 219, 251, 261
Brown, Aaron, 143, 145, 147, 156, 160, 163, 168, 190, 192, 193, 258
Budeiri, Dana, 156, 157
Bush, George W., 3, 62, 71, 72, 88, 117, 120, 121, 141, 143, 159, 241, 261

capitalism, 56, 58
CBS Network, 26, 130, 131, 151, 256, 260
censorship, 26, 82, 100, 101, 104, 107, 113, 117, 118, 202, 203, 208, 232, 246
Cheney, Dick, 120, 126, 133, 213, 219, 240
Chomsky, Noam, 28, 49, 60, 63, 64, 66, 69, 77, 248, 250
CIA, 8, 15, 16, 49, 120, 128, 141, 145, 221, 256
civilian casualties, 11, 82, 91, 116, 137, 171, 180, 184, 199, 235, 260, 261
civilians, 18, 19, 58, 59, 60, 65, 71, 80, 81, 156, 157, 165, 171, 178, 181, 188, 190, 205, 207, 215, 254, 262
civilisation, 5, 6, 33, 35, 39, 50, 55, 69, 93, 170, 249, 258
Clancy, Jim, 129
Clark, Wesley, 146, 156, 163, 173, 241
CNN Effect, 76, 77, 84, 92
Cold War, 2, 15, 31, 32, 52, 55, 64, 77, 78, 85, 86, 97
collateral damage, 116, 125
collective memory, 94, 223, 224
colonialism, 35, 36, 41, 48, 51, 94, 174, 252
communication, 1, 3, 4, 21, 27, 30, 31, 59, 66, 75, 98, 99, 112, 118, 119, 123, 124, 127, 138, 169, 200, 232, 233
communism, 32, 54
conspiracy, 56, 201, 203, 227
Costello, Carol, 185, 186
counter-terrorism, 68, 70, 73
Couso, Jose, 189, 207, 208
covert actions, 8, 15, 16, 19, 25, 53, 88, 124, 126, 255
'Decapitation Strike', 6, 139, 140, 142–145, 149, 159, 164, 166–171, 179, 180, 234–236, 256

Index

demonisation, 3, 69, 83, 127, 169, 232, 234
'Desert Fox', 109, 111, 254
'Desert Storm', 18, 21, 25, 32, 79, 80, 81, 83, 92, 142, 168, 172
discourse, 2, 5, 6, 7, 28, 32–35, 37–39, 41–43, 46, 47, 50, 56, 62–73, 79, 85, 87, 89, 90, 99, 100, 102, 103, 110, 114, 117, 118, 160, 163, 178, 181, 185, 231, 235, 236, 241, 247, 248, 250, 258
dominance, 5, 6, 10, 19, 22–25, 28, 31, 48, 91, 138, 142, 231
Al-Durrah, Mohammed, 110, 112

Egypt, 1, 2, 34, 40, 45, 47, 48, 53, 55, 56, 94, 95–97, 99, 102, 103, 105, 108, 118, 132, 232, 242, 247, 248, 252, 254, 255, 256
evil, 74, 83, 128, 169

Firdos Square, 210–214, 219, 220, 226, 263
Fisk, Robert, 66, 81, 113
foreign policy, 15, 26, 55, 69, 77, 86, 92, 99, 104, 115, 119, 121, 123–125, 132, 203, 221, 233, 236, 254
Foucault, Michel, 36, 37, 247
Fox News, 65, 78, 136, 137, 139, 172, 233, 242, 243, 264
frames, 4, 6, 9, 11, 12, 62, 79, 88, 92, 130, 138, 143, 147, 148, 155, 159, 165, 172, 173, 179, 181, 200, 205, 211, 233, 234, 236, 243
framing, 3, 4, 5, 9, 12, 42, 54, 78, 80, 82, 84, 87, 88, 92, 118, 130, 138, 139, 147, 161, 174, 201, 203, 227, 228, 229, 232, 236, 243, 259
France, 41, 52, 57, 58, 83, 95, 97, 111, 118, 128, 129, 135, 164, 189, 190, 191, 192, 198, 201, 208, 245, 252
Franks, Tommy, 125, 215

Geneva Conventions, 72, 81, 199
globalisation, 38, 69, 102
Gramsci, Antonio, 37, 38, 67
Guantanamo, 71, 72, 255, 264
guerrillas, 20, 58, 66, 176, 226, 238
Gulf War (1991), 5, 19, 21, 27, 32, 78, 83, 85, 91, 92, 102, 108, 109, 111, 115, 122, 127, 149, 151, 172, 181, 215, 222, 232, 246

Habermas, Jurgen, 28, 33
Al-Haj, Sami, 126, 255
Hall, Stuart, 37, 38, 61, 76, 249
hegemony, 5, 10, 32, 35, 37, 38, 48, 52, 67, 103, 111, 232, 237, 254, 258
Hersh, Seymour, 50, 128, 129

Hollywood, 5, 172, 205, 222
Howeidy, Fahmy, 111, 132, 254
humanitarian intervention, 84, 85, 92
Huntington, Samuel, 5, 52, 54, 55, 56, 249
Hussein, Saddam,
  alleged link to terrorism, 69, 129
  CNN coverage of, 147, 148, 150, 162, 163, 173, 179, 186, 214, 216, 218, 225, 233
  framing of, 79, 83, 127, 148, 161, 162, 168, 169, 173, 179, 180, 220, 221, 225, 227, 228
Gulf War 1991, 32, 54, 78, 82, 221, 250
human rights, 84
interview of, 26, 82
propaganda war, 10, 91, 121, 122, 126, 134, 143, 146, 163, 169, 186, 191, 213, 214, 218, 224, 227–229, 234
removal from power, 238, 239
statue of, 139, 209–215, 217–229, 234
ultimatum to, 141, 144

icon, 7, 228
identity, 3, 31–34, 39, 42, 46, 47, 50, 64, 65, 73, 83, 89, 96, 101, 178, 224, 231

304

Index

ideology, 6, 32, 61, 65, 68, 89, 118, 121, 165, 172, 237, 247
imagery, 5, 6, 32, 38, 45, 70, 80, 90, 113, 144, 178, 196, 197, 236, 259
imagined community, 37, 111
imperialism, 5, 35, 41, 48, 51, 94, 226
information dominance, 5, 22, 23, 24
information warfare, 21–23, 27, 79, 115, 142, 181, 185, 203, 206, 240
info-warriors, 142, 172, 176, 183, 202, 216, 260
international law, 7, 64, 85
Intifada, 109, 110, 111
Iran, 49, 52, 53, 55, 84, 120, 132, 221, 248, 249, 250, 252, 262
Iranian Revolution, 53, 73
Iraq,
    1991 War in, 21, 27, 32, 77, 79, 81, 82, 103
    2003 War in, 11, 12, 139–142, 182, 183, 185, 209, 210, 211, 213, 233, 238, 239, 240
    Al Jazeera's coverage, 109, 119, 136, 137, 149, 150, 157–159, 164, 170, 171, 174–176, 186, 189, 195, 199, 203–205, 207, 220, 221, 226, 228, 235, 241

Arab Spring, 1
Baath Party, 102, 118
CNNI coverage, 82, 84, 129, 130, 135, 136, 143, 145–148, 152–156, 160, 163, 166–168, 172, 190, 215, 216, 218, 222, 242, 243
colonial time, during, 95,
demonisation, 83, 92
embedded journalists in, 9
framing of, 80, 148, 160–162, 164, 165, 179–181, 199, 204, 218, 220, 221, 223, 225, 226, 234, 236
human rights, 84, 100
neo-conservatives, 120–123
opposition to the war, 7, 134, 208
post-World War II era, 52, 53
propaganda war, 124, 126–129, 138, 145, 151, 161, 169, 170, 200, 202, 205, 224, 240
rhetoric about, 10, 11, 50, 65, 66, 69, 72, 84, 106, 132–134
war sanitisation, 81, 108, 178
Islam
Al Jazeera, 158, 174, 200, 204
Arab nationalism, 94, 96, 102, 103
CNNI, 163
history, 93, 170
Intifada, 109

Islamism, 32, 53, 102, 103, 111, 114, 134, 242
Orientalism, 38, 42, 45, 46, 48, 50–52, 54–56, 71, 72, 161
scholars, 36, 37
stereotyping, 3, 5, 32, 33, 49, 50, 51, 57, 69, 70, 71, 83, 89, 132, 231, 232
versus Christianity, 6, 34, 39, 40, 47, 52, 54, 73, 132
war in Iraq, 146, 239
Israel, 40, 43, 51–55, 57, 58, 96, 97, 98, 104, 106, 109, 110–112, 119, 122, 124, 133–135, 164, 165, 170, 179, 251, 254, 262
Al-Issawi, Omar, 114, 261

Jerusalem, 40, 109, 178, 247, 251
Jordan, 1, 52, 55, 103, 105, 112, 132, 135, 186, 196, 253, 262

Kabul, 27, 90, 125, 201
Al-Kasim, Faisal, 105, 125, 253
King, John, 143, 145, 160, 168
Kissinger, Henry, 63, 251
Kosovo, 19, 27, 44, 146, 163, 203, 257
Krichane, Mohammed, 112
Kristol, William, 120
Kuwait, 1, 32, 54, 78, 81, 100, 103, 132, 135, 141, 155, 166, 217, 221, 250, 253, 258, 263

Index

Lebanon, 40, 53, 55, 94, 95, 100, 112, 132, 134, 232, 248, 252, 253
legitimacy, 2, 7, 28, 61, 64, 73, 82, 106, 116, 236
Lewis, Bernard, 50, 54, 69
liberation, 16, 49, 58, 61, 66, 133, 159, 170, 179, 181, 212, 214, 216, 218, 223, 225, 226, 228, 234, 257
Libya, 1, 2, 53, 55, 95, 100, 107, 242, 243
Lieberman, Joseph, 147, 148, 149, 161, 169, 181, 258
Los Angeles Times, 19, 227
Lynch, Jessica, 183, 184, 186, 260

mainstream media, 6, 11, 26, 31, 63, 64, 73, 81, 82, 129, 130, 140, 151, 224, 243
'manifest destiny', 43, 44, 248, 257
Marines, 142, 182, 186, 210, 217, 218, 219, 220, 222, 227, 229, 262
martyrdom, 190, 194, 200, 204
Marxism, 32, 36
mediated, 3, 12, 69, 85, 177
metaphor, 9, 43, 127, 130, 161, 181, 223, 225, 229, 258
MI6, 120, 128
Middle East,
  1991 Gulf War, 92
  2003 War in Iraq, 140

Al Jazeera, 11, 108, 109, 112, 115, 137, 138, 221
audiences, 26, 125, 184, 203, 205,
CNN, 135, 160, 184,
conflicts, 12, 88, 236, 237
covert actions, 8
dynamics, 104
history, 36
neo-conservatives, 10, 68, 70, 120, 178, 179
pan-Arabism, 95, 96, 118, 165, 174, 232
pan-Arab media, 99, 101, 137
post-colonial era, 53, 73, 97, 120
public sphere, 2, 52, 65, 84, 102, 111, 131–134
stereotyping, 3, 6, 45, 49–51, 54–57, 70, 83, 89, 160, 231, 233
War on Terror, 115, 117, 123, 124
military propaganda, 14, 18, 27, 33, 220, 230, 236
Morocco, 1, 52, 99, 100, 102, 105, 107, 110, 118, 132, 248, 249, 253
Mosul, 136, 142, 149, 157, 209, 236, 239
mouthpiece, 82, 101, 105, 115, 119, 233
MSNBC, 78, 130, 242, 243, 264
Mubarak, Hosni, 2, 56, 243
Mujahedeen, 8, 53
myths, 3, 7, 31, 38, 43, 57, 83, 263

Namur, Jumana, 157, 159, 190, 261
narrative, 46, 80, 87, 142, 151, 156, 172, 185, 205, 212, 214, 217–223, 226, 227, 228, 229, 234, 250, 263
Nasser, Gamal Abdel, 6, 96–98, 99, 102, 112, 118, 252, 264
nationalism, 94, 95, 96, 112, 118, 174, 248, 250, 254, 258
NATO, 3, 19, 27, 30, 33, 108, 146, 163, 170, 203
NBC, 26, 130, 260
neo-conservatives, 3, 50, 68
New York Times, 11, 25, 49, 50, 55, 72, 77, 114, 124, 137, 224, 239, 240, 245, 246, 248, 255, 257, 260
NGOs, 77, 85, 241
Nicaragua, 60, 63, 249, 256
North Africa, 2, 46, 72, 93, 95, 99, 174, 247

Occidentalism, 164, 165, 247, 258
occupation, 47, 51, 94, 96, 124, 125, 216, 218, 226, 228, 229, 234, 249, 252, 263
Office of Strategic Influence, 25, 124, 246
oil, 5, 10, 53, 73, 79, 104, 120, 121, 123, 133, 141, 168, 216, 221, 225, 248, 262
Al-Omari, Diyar, 149, 152, 165, 194

Index

OPEC, 120
O'Reilly, Bill, 65
Orientalism, 3, 4, 5, 5, 34–39, 41–49, 51, 53, 55–57, 59, 61, 63–65, 67–73, 138, 164, 229, 231, 232, 236, 247–249, 258
Orientalist frame, 4, 5, 6, 7, 33, 82, 83, 86, 89, 148, 161, 181
otherness, 5, 32, 68, 82, 90, 161, 162, 165, 226, 231
Ould Fal, Mohamed, 219, 221, 226–228, 263

Pakistan, 52, 55, 132, 134, 252
Palestine Hotel, 6, 139, 182, 185–191, 193, 194, 198, 199, 202, 203, 205, 207, 209, 210, 219, 226, 259, 261
pan-Arab, 2, 6, 10, 95, 96, 97, 98, 100–102, 103, 110–112, 118, 119, 137, 204, 227, 229, 234, 254
Pentagon,
  1991 Gulf War, 80, 81, 82, 91
  2003 War in Iraq, 131, 142, 151, 167, 184, 222, 223
  Al Jazeera, 117, 125, 149, 157, 164, 170, 186, 189, 201, 207
  CNN, 79, 91, 143, 147, 154, 155, 156, 172, 173, 175, 176, 178, 181, 191, 203, 215, 216, 226

Information Warfare, 21, 26, 116, 124, 176, 185, 201, 202, 207, 217, 222–224, 231, 232, 235
  media management, 8, 17, 18, 28, 80, 81, 162, 206, 208, 230, 240, 241
  neo-conservatives, 120, 122
  Psyops, 25, 183
Perle, Richard, 120, 121
Pew Research Centre, 208
Pipes, Daniel, 10, 51, 69, 70
political violence, 7, 8, 53, 58, 61, 62, 64, 66, 67, 69, 73
Project of the New American Century (PNAC), 69, 120, 121, 122, 250
politics, 3, 25, 28, 30, 42, 43, 54, 59, 67, 70, 75, 94, 100, 102, 103, 105, 106, 112, 119, 137, 169, 177, 178, 235, 242, 247, 249, 253, 254
populism, 65
Powell, Colin 32, 82, 85, 126, 128–130, 133, 255
propaganda, 5, 13, 14, 15, 19, 22, 23, 27–31, 33, 45, 59, 63, 79, 91, 116, 117, 119, 124, 131, 172, 191, 192, 199, 200, 206, 208, 235, 236, 241, 243, 246
Protsyuk, Taras, 189, 207
psychological warfare, 24
Psyops, 5, 14, 15, 19, 20, 25, 30, 33, 91, 183, 234, 235, 246

public diplomacy, 23, 115, 125
public opinion, 4, 9, 15, 21, 83, 107, 112, 115, 119, 132, 134, 138, 160, 161, 196
public sphere, 2, 5, 27, 28, 29, 30, 33, 66, 75, 112, 118, 119, 161, 178, 232, 241, 254

Qatar, 2, 103, 104, 106, 107, 109, 111–116, 118, 119, 125, 130, 135–138, 165, 166, 170, 171, 181, 187, 189, 202–205, 213, 219, 228, 229, 236, 241, 253
Al-Quds (newspaper), 129, 132

racism, 54, 133
Radio Sawa, 26, 125
Reagan, Ronald, 53, 221
Rendon Group, 25, 123, 124, 233, 246
Reporters Sans Frontières, 208, 260
resistance, 20, 32, 68, 69, 125, 142, 149, 150, 164, 165, 170, 181–184, 195, 200, 204, 215, 221, 224, 228, 229, 239, 250, 263
Reuters, 135, 186, 191, 194, 199, 207, 208, 255
revolutionary, 2, 20, 58, 96, 112, 232, 248
rhetoric, 3, 5, 12, 38, 54, 56, 72, 73, 86, 89, 98, 111, 113, 114, 128, 131, 132, 138, 165, 169, 170, 176, 181, 212, 221, 231, 254, 259, 263

Index

Rice, Condoleezza, 26, 126
Robertson, Nic, 156, 257
Robinson, Simon, 213, 214, 217, 218, 226, 262
Rogers, Walter, 146, 168
Rumsfeld, Donald, 25, 120, 122, 124, 155, 171, 173, 176, 199, 221, 249, 259, 262

Said, Edward, 5, 35, 37, 38, 41, 49, 50, 55, 66, 68, 72, 247
sanitisation, 21, 81
Saudi Arabia, 1, 18, 52, 55, 84, 103, 104, 118, 120, 123, 132, 137, 250, 252, 253, 254
'Shock and Awe', 6, 9, 131, 139, 140, 142, 143, 151, 153–157, 168, 171, 172, 174–180, 182, 184, 222, 234, 235, 256
Somalia, 5, 18, 19, 76, 77, 84–87, 92, 232, 246
Soviet Union, 32, 52, 53, 56, 74, 97, 98, 167
spin doctors, 116, 173
Starr, Barbara, 155, 215, 216, 226
state terror, 60, 167
stereotypes, 2, 4, 32, 49, 83, 234, 243
Sykes–Picot, 95, 164
Syria, 1, 2, 53, 55, 56, 94, 95, 100, 102, 105, 112, 118, 125, 242, 247, 252, 253, 262

Taha, Tawfiq, 144, 149, 150, 164, 179
Taliban, 25, 26, 27, 65, 90, 114, 117, 123, 137
Telecinco, 189, 207
terrorism, 5, 6, 7, 8, 16, 56, 57–73, 88, 89, 122, 123, 127, 132, 133, 138, 231, 236, 240, 254, 255
Tikrit, 142, 239
Time Warner, 77, 78, 137
Tomahawk, 141, 155
transnational, 6, 11, 66, 99, 101, 108, 109, 118, 119, 161, 232
truth, 21, 25, 29, 30, 33, 37, 38, 81, 84, 116, 163, 172, 196, 204, 205, 247, 255
Tunisia, 1, 2, 99, 105, 107, 242, 254
Turkey, 52, 94, 103, 132, 141, 249, 251, 252, 253, 256
Turner, Ted, 74, 75, 77
Twitter, 1, 244

Ullman, Harlan 131, 142, 151
Umm Qasr, 142, 184, 262
United Arab Emirates, 104, 132
United Kingdom, 6, 52, 58, 140, 157, 211, 252, 256
US administration, 7, 11, 25, 26, 50, 62, 63, 71, 77–79, 86, 99, 113, 115, 117, 118, 122–124, 126–129, 131, 133, 138, 161, 168, 177, 179, 181, 203, 232, 233, 236, 240, 241, 243
US military, 8, 17, 18, 20, 21, 26, 53, 87, 109, 115, 142, 143, 150, 156, 164, 172, 183, 188, 189, 196, 200, 202–205, 207, 210, 215, 216, 220, 225, 231, 233–236, 243, 246, 254

Vietnam War, 8, 11, 17, 28, 58, 80, 230, 239, 259
viewership, 11, 75, 92, 110, 243

War on Terror, 5, 6, 63, 73, 88, 89, 90, 115–119, 122, 123, 125, 132, 138, 179, 233, 249
Welsh, May Ying, 156, 171, 259
Wolfowitz, Paul, 50, 120–122

Zahn, Paula, 137, 184, 212–215, 217, 218, 261, 262